Number One:
The W. L. Moody, Jr., Natural History Series

FISHES OF THE GULF OF MEXICO
Texas, Louisiana, and Adjacent Waters

Tropical reef fishes attracted to a crushed sea urchin on a reef off the Louisiana coast. Clockwise from upper left: tail of bluehead (*Thalassoma bifasciatum*), yellow phase; young bluehead (black and white); reef butterflyfish (*Chaetodon sedentarius*); French angelfish (*Pomacanthus paru*); blue angelfish (*Holacanthus bermudensis*); slippery dick (*Halichoeres bivittatus*); young cocoa damselfish (*Pomacentrus variabilis*); and young bluehead.

FISHES OF THE GULF OF MEXICO

Texas, Louisiana, and Adjacent Waters

by H. Dickson Hoese *and* Richard H. Moore

Underwater photography by Farley Sonnier
Drawings by Dinah Bowman

Texas A&M University Press

COLLEGE STATION AND LONDON

Library of Congress Cataloging in Publication Data

Hoese, H   Dickson
    Fishes of the Gulf of Mexico, Texas, Louisiana, and
adjacent waters.

    (W. L. Moody, Jr. natural history series: no. 1)
    Bibliography: p.
    Includes index.
    1. Marine fishes—Mexico, Gulf of. 2. Marine fishes—
Texas. 3. Marine fishes—Louisiana. 4. Fishes—Mexico,
Gulf of. I. Moore, Richard H., 1945–joint author. II. Title.
III. Series.
QL621.56.H63   597'.0923'4   76-51654
ISBN 0–89096–027–5
ISBN 0–89096–028–3 pbk.

Manufactured in the United States of America
FIRST EDITION

To
Geoffrey and Dickie Hoese,
who collected many
of the fish
illustrated and studied

CONTENTS

ILLUSTRATIONS

PREFACE

THIS work was originally begun by Moore in 1970 as an update and expansion of Hoese's (1958a) "A Partially Annotated Checklist of the Marine Fishes of Texas" (Moore, 1975b). Hoese, who at that time was involved in studies of large numbers of underwater photographs of fishes taken by Sonnier, was invited to participate and did so. Finally, Sonnier also joined the effort, which by this time had been expanded to cover Louisiana as well as Texas. With access to Sonnier's collection of excellent underwater photographs, we began a serious effort to fill the longstanding need for an illustrated guide to the marine fishes of Texas and Louisiana, with some thought of further expansion to cover all temperate and subtropical fishes in the Gulf of Mexico. Although two publications have appeared since we commenced work (Parker, Moore, and Galloway, 1972, 2d ed. 1975; and Walls, 1975), we have continually felt that our objective was still a valid one.

Rather than simply compiling records of fishes from existing literature, we attempted to verify every species of fish which had been reported by examining specimens and sometimes correcting previous misidentifications. Towards this ultimate goal, which was not completely possible, we traveled thousands of miles; collected thousands of fishes, mostly from the states of Texas, Louisiana, Mississippi, and Florida from the upper estuaries to the outer continental shelf; and examined hundreds of preserved museum specimens. We are indebted to many people in these states, especially those from the Louisiana Wild Life and Fisheries Commission, the Texas Parks and Wildlife Department, the Florida Department of Natural Resources, and the National Marine Fisheries Service Laboratory at Pascagoula. We journeyed and collected from the following vessels and boats: *Oregon II* (National Marine Fisheries Service); *Longhorn* and *Lorene* (University of Texas Marine Science Institute); *Penaeid, Kalypseaux, Squalid* (University of Southwestern Louisiana); *Ms. Coastal* (Coastal Carolina College); *Skimmer I* and *Skimmer II* (U.S. Fish and Wildlife Service); *Loverly* (Grady Loftin); *Capt. Anderson IV*; *Capt. Juel I* (Captain Frank Juel); and *Charlene* (Great Atlantic Shrimp Co.).

During our travels we were impressed by the access we were allowed to materials, information (some of which has not been published), and specimens which were necessary for study and for many of the illustrations. We were especially dependent on the extensive collections of Tulane University which have been built up by Royal D. Suttkus and his students, but we also could not have done without the collections from Texas A&I University at Kingsville, the Louisiana Wild Life and Fisheries Commission Laboratory at Grande Terre, and the Texas Parks and Wildlife Department Marine Laboratory at Rockport. Of paramount importance to the preparation of the book was help from the University of Texas Marine Science Institute (UTMSI) at Port Aransas and the University of Southwestern Louisiana (USL), whose collections, vessels, personnel, libraries, and other facilities were heavily relied upon throughout our work.

The illustrations by Dinah Bowman were made possible through a loan from the Texas A&M University Sea Grant Program. The University of Southwestern Louisiana Foundation and the USL Department of Biology provided some funds for the final typing, and other clerical work was performed by the staffs at Port Aransas and USL. Classes in fish ecology at UTMSI and in ichthyology and marine biology at USL assisted in providing specimens and checking out the keys. Some specimens were made available during studies for the Environmental Protection Agency, the U.S. Fish and Wildlife Service, and the Bureau of Land Management.

The photographs were taken by the authors except for the following: tarpon was taken by Joyce Teerling; Spanish flag by Steve Bortone; cottonmouth jack, yellowtail bass, spreadfin skate, and marbled puffer by Scott Holt; Atlantic bonito by Stu Strothers; bighead sea robin, wenchman, chub mackerel, and cownose ray by Mark Konikoff; tilefish by Steve Frishman; and hatchet marlin by Pete Laurie of the South Carolina Wildlife and Marine Resources Department. Mounted specimens were photographed at the Houston Museum of Natural History; the Louisiana Wild Life and Fisheries Commission Museum in New Orleans; and the taxidermy shop of A. R. Brundrett and Mrs. Pete's Restaurant in Port Aransas.

The drawing of the white marlin and the outline drawings in the family accounts were modified from Greenwood et al. (1966) and other sources by Dickie Hoese. The map of the northern Gulf of Mexico was drawn by Karen Dupont. Unpublished taxonomic information was provided by Margaret Bradbury (Ogcocephalidae), James Dooley (Branchiostegidae), Steve Bortone (*Diplectrum*), and Mark Leiby (*Bascanichthys*). The vernacular Cajun French names were provided mainly by Clovis Toups, Ted Falgout, and Hampton Hebert, and Henry Hildebrand supplied the Spanish names.

While we cannot thank everyone who helped in various important ways, we want to mention, in no particular order, Scott Williams, Joyce Teerling, Wayne Wiltz, John Voorhies, Ernest Simmons, Clark Hubbs, Johnie Tarver, Lynn and Grady Loftin, Faust Parker, Mark Konikoff, Tom Bright, Victor Springer, Rick Minckler, Elmer Gutherz, Perry Thompson, Don Gibson, Elgie Wingfield, Don Gooch, Geraldine Ard, Jo Ann Page, Al Chaney, Michael Stevenson, Gay Fay Kelly, Wayne Forman, Mikey and Teresa Thibodeaux, Ray and Waneta Torres, John Thompson, Curly Wohlschlag, Carl Oppenheimer, Pat Parker, Johnny Holland, Susan and Patty Herring, Guthrie Perry, Peter Perceval, Dwight Leach, Russ Miget, Gary Powell, John Durrell, Frank Schwartz, Wayne Trahan, and the many others whose names we either missed or forgot in our haste.

Several special acknowledgments are necessary: Ruth Hoese, who fed and tolerated us (and our ichthyological preoccupations) and who also helped in numerous ways throughout the work on the book; Rez Darnell and John McEachran, of Texas A&M University, who spent many hours reviewing the manuscript and illustrations; Nettie Voorhies, who typed the final draft and provided other invaluable and necessary help during the latter stages; and Robin Morris, who helped with the index. Sonnier particularly expresses his thanks to Tenneco Oil Company for the occasional supply of diesel fuel and the emergency evacuation of injured diving personnel.

We are also indebted to the many people cited in the bibliography who have collectively done most of the work. We have talked to many of them at one time or another in person, and their knowledge and assistance have helped with the originality of the book.

While most of the keys are originally constructed, we have relied on previous keys for help, since a good key should be perpetuated. The family keys were modifications of the well-established keys by Bigelow and Schroeder for elasmobranchs and Jordan and Evermann for bony fishes. A book is never really finished, or never should be, but we are proud of the time we have spent in this endeavor because it gave us a different perspective and showed us how much we have yet to learn about the Gulf of Mexico and its fish fauna. Little did we know, when we began, how much work would be involved, how many people would help and be affected by the work, and how much fun and frustration it would be. In closing, we know that this book will not be considered as an end, but hope that it will be an impetus for further exploration and inquiry into the fishes of the Gulf of Mexico.

FISHES OF THE GULF OF MEXICO

Texas, Louisiana, and Adjacent Waters

HOW TO USE THIS BOOK

This guide consists of three major sections to aid you in identifying fishes: (1) the section of identification plates; (2) the keys to fish families; and (3) accounts, or descriptions, of each family and species of fish.

Each identification plate is numbered. When you identify a fish by its picture, turn to the corresponding species number in the accounts for a full, detailed description of that fish.

The keys provide a step-by-step method of identifying families of fishes, giving the page numbers on which the family accounts begin. When you identify a fish's family by means of the keys, turn to the page number given for a description and a generalized line drawing of that family. Then use the species keys and descriptions which follow the family accounts to more closely identify the fish.

Further information on how to use this book is given in the chapter Identifying Fishes beginning on page 23.

INTRODUCTION

FISHES as a class represent the most numerous group of vertebrates. Presently there are about twenty thousand known species of fishes, and some ichthyologists suspect there may be as many as thirty thousand. On the Texas and Louisiana coast we have counted more than four hundred species.

Why are there more fishes than mammals, birds, reptiles, or amphibians? Part of the answer lies in the fact that fishes are the only group of vertebrates which spend their entire lives in the waters which occupy approximately 70 percent of the earth's surface. Furthermore, fishes, unlike most terrestrial vertebrates, live in a truly three-dimensional environment. They are not confined to living upon the surface or limited to brief excursions away from the surface as other vertebrates are. Because of their freedom, it has been stated that some fishes are like birds. If they are, then others are like 'possums, snakes, horned toads, turtles, lizards, or flying squirrels. The variety of forms and life-styles exhibited by fishes far exceeds the variety of terrestrial vertebrates, but we are only beginning to find out about the many ways in which fishes go about their day-to-day lives. While no single species of fish ranges from the surface of the ocean to its greatest depths, the ability of fishes in general to exploit all levels of their environment allows a much greater diversity of habitats and therefore of species occupying those habitats.

Fishes are important to our lives in many ways. They provide us with food and relaxation. Any angler knows that fishing is an educational, relaxing sport as well as one that he hopes will provide a delicious dinner. In addition, scientists gain knowledge from fishes. Besides those who study fishes and their habits in order to provide man with a greater abundance of food, more and more scientists use fishes in their experiments because of the variety of responses which the many species exhibit and the ease with which some species may be maintained in the laboratory. Because fishes represent the "simplest" vertebrates, scientists, including medical researchers, can study many of the same systems which are found in humans, but in a much less complicated organism.

Aquaria, ranging from the simplest goldfish bowls to elaborate tanks stocked with exotic, colorful tropical fishes, provide entertainment and education to thousands of people. Recently, technology has taken "fish watching" out of the living room, and with the help of scuba equipment man is now able to observe fish relatively undisturbed in their natural habitat. Popular places for this sport include the South Texas and Florida Panhandle jetties, grass beds, and offshore reefs and oil platforms.

Purpose and Scope

This book is meant for fishermen and scientists—for anyone interested in fishes, especially those fishes which live in the salt water of the northwestern Gulf of Mexico adjacent to Texas and Louisiana. It should also be only slightly less useful to people living in adjacent gulf states and Mexico, and somewhat less so to those on the southern U.S. Atlantic coast at least as far north as Cape Hatteras, North Carolina.

One of our largest problems in designing this book was defining the area of coverage. Since boundary lines in the ocean are seldom precise, it was obvious that no single book could be complete, and so in order to keep it to a manageable size, and because of our greater familiarity with the area, we decided to focus on the northwestern Gulf. We have attempted to include in this guide all temperate and subtropical fishes of the entire Gulf as well as tropical species most likely to be encountered in the northern Gulf. Because this fauna is largely continuous from Cape Hatteras to Cape Canaveral, Florida, and from northwestern Florida to southern Texas and Mexico (see the map), the coverage of the book is actually much greater. To assist users outside of the northwestern Gulf, we have included a list of fish species which we do not treat in detail and which occur in the northeastern Gulf or on the southeastern U.S. coast (Appendix 1). North of Cape Hatteras the fish fauna becomes quite different, but many of these cold temperate species move south of Cape Hatteras, especially in the winter. Hildebrand and Schroeder's *Fishes of Chesapeake Bay* (1928), which has recently been reprinted (1972), still serves as the best single authority on these cold temperate species.

The fish fauna of the deeper waters of the Gulf of Mexico is poorly known. Because this is primarily a guide for identifying marine fish found over the continental shelf, most of these deep-water inhabitants were also excluded, but we have, again, provided the reader with a list of slope and deep-sea fishes that occasionally venture onto the continental shelf (Appendix 2). Occurrences of slope species on the shelf are most common where the slope is steepest, as off the Mississippi Delta, or where submarine canyons (Mississippi Canyon, just west of the delta, and DeSoto Canyon, off the Florida panhandle) intrude into the shelf.

Freshwater fishes that are resident in low-salinity waters are included, and we mention other less common intruders from fresh water. Many freshwater species may tolerate salinities up to ten parts per thousand and thus may be found in bays, especially after floods (Renfro, 1959). Species not found in this book which are suspected of being freshwater fishes may be identified by consulting the references on freshwater fishes listed in the bibliography (Blair et al., 1968; Hubbs, 1969; Douglas, 1974). A list of freshwater fishes that commonly venture into brackish or salt water is given in Appendix 3, while a list of saltwater fishes that may be occasionally found in inland fresh waters is given in Appendix 4.

While the idea of a single book which pleases everybody may seem too ambitious an undertaking, we felt that this was a better goal than making it either too simple or too complex. By producing a book aimed more towards the technical we hope that we have provided a resource which will serve the needs of anyone seriously interested in our marine fishes and which will still be attractive to the person with less technical inclination.

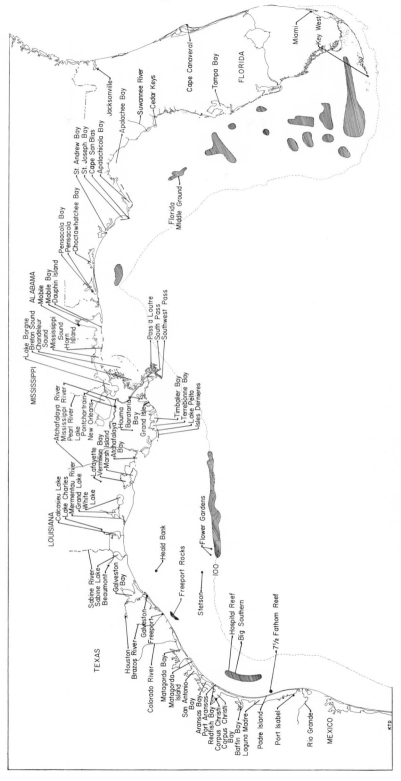

The Northern Gulf of Mexico

KTD

MEXICO

Rio Grande

Port Isabel

Padre Island

7½ Fathom Reef

Big Southern

Hospital Reef

Laguna Madre
Baffin Bay
Corpus Christi
Bay
Corpus Christi
Redfish Bay
Port Aransas
Aransas Bay
San Antonio
Bay
Matagorda
Island
Matagorda Bay
Colorado River
Freeport
Galveston
Brazos River
Houston

TEXAS

Stetson

100

Flower Gardens

Freeport Rocks

Heald Bank

Galveston
Bay
Beaumont
Sabine Lake
Sabine River

LOUISIANA

Calcasieu Lake
Lake Charles
Mermentau River
Grand Lake
White
Lake
Lafayette
Vermilion Bay
Atchafalaya
Bay
Marsh Island
Atchafalaya River
Mississippi River
Pearl River
Lake
Pontchartrain
New Orleans
Houma
Baratario
Bay
Grand Isle

Isles Dernieres
Lake Pelto
Terrebonne Bay
Timbalier Bay

Pass a Loutre
South Pass
Southwest Pass

MISSISSIPPI

Lake Borgne
Breton Sound
Chandeleur
Sound
Mississippi
Sound
Horn
Island

ALABAMA
Mobile
Mobile Bay
Dauphin Island

Pensacola Bay
Pensacola
Choctawhatchee Bay
St. Andrew Bay
St. Joseph Bay
Cape San Blas
Apalachicola Bay

Florida
Middle Ground

Apalachee Bay
Cedar Keys
Suwannee River

Jacksonville

FLORIDA

Tampa Bay

Cape Canaveral

Miami
Key West

Ecology and Life History

Many features of the marine environment affect the lives of fishes. Time and space prevent a thorough description of environmental factors, and the serious student should consult one of the more general books on ichthyology such as Marshall (1966, 1971); Lagler, Bardach, and Miller (1962); Norman and Greenwood (1975); or Nikolskii (1963), or some of the papers cited in the bibliography.

The northwestern Gulf of Mexico provides a variety of environments for fishes. Indeed, it is probably true that the Texas and Louisiana coasts contain a greater variety of marine and estuarine environments than any comparable length of coastline in the United States. Including the area across to Florida further increases the diversity. Two natural gradients contribute to this diversity of habitats. First, as one travels along the coastline from the Mississippi River to the Rio Grande, rainfall decreases and temperature slightly increases. These variations result in low salinities (less than ten parts per thousand) in the marshes and bayous of western Louisiana, the Mississippi River mouth, and East Texas; moderate salinities along much of the central Texas coast and the east central Louisiana coast; and often hypersaline conditions (over forty parts per thousand) in South Texas bays and lagoons. The seasonal extremes also vary regularly, with Port Isabel remaining subtropical for a great part of the year while salt waters on the East Texas and Louisiana coast have been known to freeze during cold winters. To the east the characteristic *Spartina* (cord grass) marshes typical of temperate estuaries are present. Extensive beds of turtle grass (*Thalassia testudinum*) occur in the Chandeleur Islands, and mixed *Spartina*-mangrove marshes extend from Barataria Bay to the Isles Dernieres. There are turtle-grass beds in the southern Laguna Madre and Redfish Bay, and a tiny one in western Galveston Bay. Grass beds without turtle grass are found in Lake Pelto and behind the Timbalier Islands. The limiting factor for turtle-grass beds is salinity below twenty-five parts per thousand, while that for mangroves is temperature. Several freezes, the last occurring in 1962, killed mangroves, so their distribution falls very neatly below about 29°20' N, except in the Chandeleurs, which are buffered by a large expanse of water.

The second important gradient is variation in depth from the shore to the edge of the continental shelf; the shelf is often divided into inner, middle, and outer zones. Other changes are correlated with depth. Temperature variation is always less extreme at the bottom than at the surface, and generally deeper waters and offshore habitats have less variable temperature and salinity than do those inshore. Surface temperature decreases offshore in the summer, but sometimes in the winter a reverse temperature gradient is found in which offshore temperatures are warmer than inshore temperatures. Temperatures at the Flower Gardens reefs and similar adjacent reefs are almost always above 68° F (20° C), at least at the bottom, allowing corals and coral reef fishes to live on these reefs, the most northerly living reefs in the Gulf of Mexico.

Bottom sediments usually become less sandy and more muddy as one progresses away from the barrier islands, but there are many exceptions. Rocky reefs occur on the forty-fathom contour off Texas as well as on most of the continental shelf off Louisiana, especially near the slope. From east of the Mississippi Delta to about off Pensacola the shelf is largely composed of coarse sand, with many areas of hard bottoms and accumulations of shells not unlike the bottom off the coast of the southeastern United States but very different from that of most of the western Gulf. The Florida west coast is largely limestone and derived detrital sediments which have favored the spread of many coral reef fishes northward. Just as some coarse sediment and rock occur on the northwestern Gulf shelf, some fine sediment and mud occur on the northeastern Gulf shelf, especially off the larger rivers. These variations contribute significantly to habitat diversity and to the accompanying diversity among the fishes and other organisms which occupy the habitats.

The four environmental variables mentioned above—temperature, salinity, depth, and sediment type—are perhaps the most important in affecting distributions of fish species. Other factors less well investigated, such as oxygen content, turbidity, and currents, seem less important only because they vary less and therefore have less effect. However, extremes of these conditions can cause death or disability among marine life. Some of these extreme conditions may cause spectacular die-offs of fishes. "Red tides," which are common off the southwest coast of Florida (Gunter et al., 1948), produce a nerve toxin that kills large numbers of fishes. Red tides are rare in the western Gulf, but one occurred in 1935 off South Texas (Gunter, 1951), and others have been reported for Offats Bayou on Galveston Island (Connell and Cross, 1950). An unusual kill in Galveston Bay was due to the formation of gas bubbles in the bloodstreams of fish (gas bubble disease) probably as a result of very high oxygen concentrations, caused by a plankton bloom, which suddenly dropped, allowing some gas to come out of solution in the blood (Renfro, 1963).

Other more significant causes of fish mortalities are the extreme freezes which occur with varying severity about every decade. Probably because northers hit the coast more abruptly, with more rapid temperature changes, around the Corpus Christi area than to the northeast, more fish are killed there, although severe freezes may kill fish across the whole southern U.S. coastline. Severe South Texas freezes have reduced populations of some species, including some game fishes, and recovery make take several years (see Brongersma-Sanders, 1957, and Gunter, 1952a, for a list of works).

Besides severe temperature changes, more subtle and long-term changes may cause population shifts from more tropical to more temperate species or vice-versa. These changes are most noticeable when tropical species, which are rare inshore, become common along the South Texas coast (Moore, 1975a). While it has been thought that temperature has been increasing up to about the middle of this century, some tropical species, such as tarpon and snook, were more common in 1900 than in 1950. Commercial fisheries for snook existed before the 1920's in Texas, and the only records of snook in Louisiana were early in the century. Tarpon, Texas, was the original name of Port Aransas; today the fish is rarely caught there. Although factors other than temperature may have caused the disappearance of these species, they serve as an example of how populations of coastal marine fishes fluctuate. Recently, both tarpon and snook have shown a minor resurgence. Many other examples of such population changes exist, and because of them we were unable to obtain photographs of some species which were common five, ten, or twenty years ago.

Floods, although spectacular in their effects on attached animals, seem mostly to run fish offshore and wash freshwater fish into the estuaries (Gunter, 1952b; Hoese, 1960). Freshwater river and marsh fishes do not seem to

Blackbar soldierfish (*Myripristis jacobus*), center; brown chromis (*Chromis multi-lineata*), lower left.

Above: Spanish hogfish (*Bodianus rufus*) in its blue-and-yellow phase; below: in its all-blue phase, with a brown chromis (*Chromis multilineata*) beneath it. (See plate 339 for the most common color variation of the Spanish hogfish.)

be adapted to open bay conditions, with few exceptions, so even during conditions of strong flooding, as occurred in Texas in 1957 and Louisiana in 1973 and 1975, the bays still contain mostly marine species such as croaker, menhaden, and saltwater killifishes. Saltwater fishes tend to predominate as long as some marine-derived salt remains in the water. Otherwise, our accounts would have to be increased by one hundred or so species. The Mississippi River and lately the Atchafalaya River release so much water that estuarine conditions may be sometimes found ten to twenty miles offshore from their mouths. At flood times freshwater fishes such as carp, pirate perch, and many others may be found in the Gulf, although in fresh water.

Hypersalinity (greater than normal oceanic salinities) has caused great mortality of fishes in the Laguna Madre because, except for a very few killifishes, all fishes are killed by increases of about twice seawater strength (seventy parts per thousand). Large mortalities occurred in the Laguna Madre in the 1930's and 1940's, but after the completion of the Intracoastal Waterway to Brownsville in 1948, sufficient water exchange has prevented the formation of excessive hypersalinity. Similar mortalities occur in the Laguna Madre de Tamaulipas just south of the Rio Grande mouth (Hildebrand, 1969). Probably more important are shifts in the amount of fresh water reaching the bays. When freshwater inflow is reduced because of drought or the use of inland water, more freshwater-intolerant (stenohaline) species such as pigfish, most sharks, and sea basses take the place of more freshwater-tolerant (euryhaline) species. Some of these effects were discussed by Copeland (1957).

The fish fauna of the northwestern Gulf of Mexico may be divided into temperate and tropical components, with a fuzzy dividing line (as discussed in the section below on zoogeography), and certain habitats, especially the offshore reefs, have a truly distinctive group of fishes. The inshore Gulf and estuarine habitats appear to share a common fauna, but there are certain species which are largely, if not entirely, restricted to certain habitats and may be regarded as "indicator species." Often assemblages of two or more species are more characteristic of a particular habitat than is any one single species. Thus, the coastal low-salinity to almost freshwater marshes of Louisiana and East Texas are characterized by such species as gar, killifish, mullet, and blue catfish. Salt marshes are characterized by several species of killifish and others. Mullet, speckled trout, redfish, and certain gobies are most commonly found on grass flats, while toadfish, clingfish, and other gobies are found on oyster beds.

Natural rocky areas are absent from the inshore area, except for one or two very small ones off Atchafalaya Bay and Port Mansfield (7½-Fathom Reef), however, piers, jetties, and bulkheads provide a suitable habitat for such species as sheepshead, crested blennies, hairy blennies, frillfin gobies, and belted sand bass.

The low-salinity (oligohaline) bay communities are dominated by sciaenids like croaker, spot, and sand trout; anchovies; mullet; and, in areas receiving enough fresh water, menhaden. The hypersaline bays of South Texas contain no distinctive species, only a greatly reduced component of the general estuarine community found in lower salinities, such as mullet, black drum, redfish, and speckled trout. In the shallow Gulf the surf zone, with its open, sandy bottom, characteristically contains fishes such as the Gulf whiting and the Atlantic threadfin. Outside this zone the bottom usually rapidly becomes more muddy, and the characteristic fish are the star drum, silver trout, and longspine porgy. Farther offshore towards the middle shelf the number of sciaenids is drastically reduced, and the fish community is dominated by small serranids, shoal flounders, and blackfin sea robins.

The middle and outer shelves have not been adequately explored, since there has been little commercial incentive to do so. The results of several exploratory fishing expeditions by the Bureau of Commercial Fisheries (now the National Marine Fisheries Service), described by Springer and Bullis (1956) and Bullis and Thompson (1965), summarize nearly all that is known of this fauna.

The offshore reefs, with their more tropical fauna, support such distinctive forms as butterflyfishes, angelfishes, damselfishes, wrasses, parrotfishes, and several species of tropical sea basses. Juveniles of some of these species may occur inshore around the jetties and pilings of South Texas and some of the inshore oil platforms. The advent of scuba diving has allowed more attention to be paid to these areas and has resulted in the addition of many tropical fish species to our fauna (Bright and Cashman, 1974; Sonnier, Teerling, and Hoese, 1976).

Life histories of many of the inshore fishes can be easily characterized because these species are estuarine dependent, which means they spend part or all of their lives in the estuaries. A typical estuarine-dependent species spawns in the Gulf of Mexico, and the larvae are presumably then carried towards shore by currents. By the time the young are big enough to swim, they are near the mouths of estuaries, which they then enter. The young fish remain in the estuaries for about one year, taking advantage of the greater availability of food and protection which estuarine habitats afford. Most estuarine-dependent species grow rapidly and reach maturity at one year of age. They may then remain in the estuary, migrate to sea to spawn (returning to the estuary between spawnings), or migrate from the shallow estuaries to spend the rest of their lives in the deeper Gulf of Mexico. Of course, some fishes may spend their entire life cycles in the estuaries, while others that typically occur farther offshore may never be found in the bays. Many species whose adults live and spawn on the outer continental shelf live on the inner or middle shelf as young.

The reader is referred to the cited references for specific life history patterns or details; however, in Appendix 5 we have included a list of spawning or birthing seasons for some of the most common inshore and estuarine species.

Zoogeography

While ecology is the study of the interrelationships between organisms and their environment (including other organisms), zoogeography studies why various species are distributed as they are, especially in reference to the distribution of other closely related species. As such, zoogeography and ecology are closely related sciences.

The evolutionary history of the geography of the northwestern Gulf is peculiarly tied to two features: the Florida peninsula and the Mississippi River. If the Florida peninsula had never existed, there would be no barrier between the Atlantic coast and the northern Gulf of Mexico, and the identification of fishes would be somewhat simpler. In addition, the Florida peninsula has not always exerted the same influence on fish distribution that it does today.

During the Pleistocene, that period of the last several million years when the climate alternately warmed and cooled, at least four major glacial periods covered North America with ice, alternating with warmer interglacial periods like the one we are presently experiencing. Of most importance to the northern Gulf of Mexico during the glacial periods was the lowering of the sea level some one hundred meters, which exposed most of the continental shelf. During that time rivers running into the Gulf cut their valleys more steeply, and increases in the amount of precipitation moved large amounts of sediment seaward. While enclosed estuaries were rare, large amounts of brackish water were found near the mouths of rivers. As the sea level rose, beginning last about fifteen thousand years ago, estuarine and near-shore sediments and fossils were left on the shelf. Old oyster reefs, often covered by more recent sediments brought in by rivers, also formed hard substrates offshore. Hard shale rock forced up by salt domes formed the basis of offshore coral reefs or "snapper banks." The presence of these areas of shale in the northwestern Gulf west of about 91° W is known, but they are not well mapped. Except where they are covered by new sediment or where erosion removed these deposits, the shelf is otherwise monotonously flat.

The glacial periods also probably saw reductions in seawater temperature and the movement of temperate species farther south than they occur today. The present temperature regime of the Northern Hemisphere is such that freezing temperatures seldom extend into the Rio Grande Valley of Texas or below middle Florida. In the waters of the Gulf of Mexico the 20° C winter isotherm falls at about those same places. Although this line may not represent the precise cause of change from temperate to tropical fauna, it closely approximates the midpoint of the area where such change occurs. Basically, to the south the tropical fauna comes closer to shore, eventually pinching the temperate fauna out of existence, while to the north it is pushed farther offshore until it disappears on the Atlantic side of Florida. On the Gulf side of that peninsula the tropical fauna pushes up to near the northern shore, where it is kept offshore by cold winters and possibly by competition with temperate fishes better adapted to cooler waters. Therefore, at Miami and at Tampico, Mexico, most fishes are similar to those to the south, but at Jacksonville, Cedar Key, and Corpus Christi most species are similar to those to the north.

In the cooler temperate area members of the croaker family (Sciaenidae) predominate, while in the tropical Gulf the grunts (Pomadasyidae) and mojarras (Gerreidae) are most abundant. Offshore, especially around reef structures, a well-developed tropical fauna exists. Young and larvae of some species, probably from adults on those reefs, make their way inshore in the warmer months and may be found around jetties, piers, and other structures where the water is relatively warm, clear, and salty.

Because the warm southern Florida coast prevents the free interchange of temperate fishes between the Atlantic and Gulf coasts, the temperate populations on either side of the peninsula have grown somewhat apart since the times when cooler temperatures extended below southern Florida. Actually, the problem is more complex, because during glacial periods oceanic conditions were continuous around the Florida peninsula, while during interglacial periods, when the sea level was close to that of today or even higher, the peninsula was often at least partially submerged and the Atlantic and Gulf were more continuous. In those warmer times the tropical fauna may have separated the temperate fauna, pushing it northward and westward around Florida (Dahlberg, 1970). At the same time, islands may have been present south of Florida where small numbers of some temperate populations may have become isolated from those near the mainland (Springer, 1959). During cooler times the tropical fauna was pushed southward into the Caribbean, and relict populations of some fishes may have been cut off by the Gulf Stream (Walters and Robins, 1961).

Inside the Gulf the tail end of the temperate fauna is nearly continuous from the Florida panhandle to Texas. However, notable exceptions exist. Fish species which are apparently limited to the northeastern Gulf are either anadromous species, such as sturgeon, which range only as far west as the vicinity of the Mississippi River, or a few subtropical species, such as the southern puffer, which may separate more temperate populations in the northwestern Gulf from those on the southeastern Atlantic coast (Springer, 1959; Shipp and Yerger, 1969). It is possible that some tropical reef species may also belong on this list, but none have been convincingly shown to occur east, but not west, of the Mississippi.

These events occurred several times during the million-year history of the Pleistocene, but the periods involved never lasted more than a few thousand years at any one time. Recent studies have tended to remove the distinction between temperate fishes on opposite sides of the Florida peninsula because the differences in populations ranging from, say, Chesapeake Bay to Texas are clinal with no clear-cut breaks. That is, the differences between a fish at Cedar Key and Jacksonville are no greater than those between Jacksonville and Savannah or Cedar Key and Panama City. Actually, judging from speciation rates (the time it takes two populations to grow far enough apart to become incapable of interbreeding), indirectly measured in freshwater fishes, the period of time that Gulf and Atlantic populations have been split by the emergence of the Florida peninsula is probably inadequate for us to expect distinct species to have occurred on either side.

This brings up the question of what a distinct species of marine fish is. Obviously, such different species as croaker and pigfish do not interbreed with each other, but a problem arises in knowing whether a group of similar fishes ranging from, say, Cape Cod to Rio de Janeiro is an interbreeding unit throughout. In the Caribbean and the Gulf of Mexico these populations are split east to west as well as north to south, further complicating the problem. Some species are continuous in the temperate-to-tropical waters of the Western Hemisphere, while some northern species are replaced in either the Caribbean or other areas to the south by a very similar species called a sibling species. Examples of sibling species also occur between the Atlantic and the Gulf for temperate species (such as *Cynoscion regalis* and *C. arenarius*) or between the Gulf and the Caribbean for tropical species (such as *Serranus subligarius* and *S. flaviventris*). Whether sibling species actually interbreed or not is difficult to prove, so taxonomists have based species on morphological differences. While these differences are significant to biologists, it remains to be proven whether the differences are of equal importance to the fish themselves.

The second major influence on the zoogeography of the northern Gulf of Mexico has been the Mississippi River. Most of the water from the river, after it leaves the delta, drifts westward carrying some of its load of silt and clay. To the west of the river's mouth the quantity of silt and clay is greater, the sand finer and darker because of the presence of heavy minerals, and the amount of fresh water greater than to the east. Except for Mobile Bay, Apalachicola Bay, and a few small estuaries east of the river, bay waters in that area are clear and salty, and much of the bay bottoms is covered by submerged plants, especially turtle grass and shoal grass, *Halodule wrighti*. As a result, the visitor to bays on each side of the Mississippi River will find them tremendously different. Offshore in the eastern Gulf, less of the coarser sand has been covered by mud. In the northwestern Gulf, attached vegetation is rare, and turtle grass is found only in the small stands in the bays. The very large stand of it behind the Chandeleur Islands, part of an old Mississippi River delta, is in clear, salty water seldom affected by the river.

The effect of bottom type on fish distribution is exemplified by the distribution of the longspine porgy, *Stenotomus caprinus* (Caldwell, 1955a). It is absent from limestone bottoms off the west coast of Florida and Yucatán, but it occurs on muddier (or mixed sand-mud) sediments from the Florida panhandle around the Gulf to Campeche. Many other distributions are similar; some species are more common on the northwest side of the Gulf because they require either mud or fine sand, and others are more common in the northeast because they need coarse sand-shell.

Conservation

Conservation of fishes in both Texas and Louisiana has generally followed the pattern set elsewhere, moving with the interests of the groups with the most political power. This is said not to denigrate the states and the many sincere people who have worked to save or better an area for all, but simply to accurately portray the use of natural resources in the area. The reasons behind this pattern are partly logical. Particular interest groups have seen benefits only in actions which might help their particular fisheries, and it has not been until the recent period of "ecological" thought that anyone has considered treating the system as a whole. It remains to be seen whether such treatment will be the trend of action in either state in the future. We see only small evidences of it at present, although implementation of the Coastal Zone Management Act should be a step in this direction, and some federal agencies are now attempting to enforce new regulations toward this goal.

Therefore, one might expect the conservation history of the area to be battles between special interest groups, and indeed, such has often been the case, especially between sports and commercial fishermen. This has been most evident in Texas, where the tourist business is relatively large, commercial and sports fishermen seek the same fishes, and sports fishermen have been well organized, politically astute, and well moneyed.

For nearly a century articles have been found in coastal Texas newspapers claiming that the commercial fishermen are ruining fishing, although there has been nearly no evidence to support this claim. This charge seems unlikely when one considers that the fishing gear allowed commercial fishermen in both states is not the most efficient. The best methods, such as pound nets, are illegal. Commercial fishermen, feeling persecuted, often rationalized themselves into turning outlaw. Allowing the removal of black drum from the Laguna Madre on the argument that they destroy shellfish and grass beds during feeding has provided some relief to commercial fishermen in that area. The seafood laws, which sometimes do things like allowing bait shrimping to supply sports fishermen while excluding commercial shrimping in the same bay (as if the shrimp could tell the difference) easily prove that the sports fisherman has had the upper hand.

Therefore, in Texas the commercial fisherman has gradually been squeezed out in all but a few areas, with the only large catches in recent decades occurring during World War II, when food was needed and recreational fishing was restricted. The fish did not seem to suffer for it. The rationalization for choosing sports fishing over commercial fishing has always been economic, but the economic theory has not taken into account all costs (to name one, increased pollution with increased tourism), and it remains to be seen if it really will win over the long term, especially since sports fishing, as great as its benefits are, is less a necessity and can only exist in an economy providing many luxuries.

In Louisiana the situation has been much less pronounced, probably because of a lack of tourism, a more depressed economy, and the difficulty of access to coastal waters. However, as sports fishing increases, so do the conflicts, and Louisiana is rapidly following in Texas' footsteps.

Commercial fishermen seeking food fishes in the area rely primarily on trotlines, beach seines, gill nets, trammel nets, and hooks and lines. Basically, the sports fishes are the same, although a few species are not common to both fisheries. The main species sought after are trout, redfish, and flounder inshore and mackerel, the billfishes, red snapper, and menhaden offshore. Probably more sports fishing is done (inadvertently) for pinfish and hardhead catfish, but these do not usually find their way onto such lists. Offshore fisheries using trawls for croaker and purse nets for menhaden are usually not in conflict with sports fishermen although a few sports fish are taken by both methods.

In Texas another problem has revolved around the so-called fish passes, or inlets to coastal lagoons. Because of well-developed barrier beaches and low river inflow, access between bay and Gulf has been difficult. During movements between these waters, fish must concentrate in the passageways, therefore packing the production of whole bay systems into small areas, an impressive sight and what was once and would still be a very efficient place to harvest fish.

It does not necessarily follow, however, that creating more inlets (passes) means more fish. Certainly fishing is convenient and often better in the passes, but there is probably an optimum distance between inlets. If the productive Laguna Madre is any example, the optimum number of passes per one hundred miles of coastline may be closer to zero than to one. Opening an inlet allows the intrusion of salt water with its fauna, and where the adjacent bay is low in salinity it changes the fish fauna considerably. Such effects can be predicted by considering the general ecology of estuaries.

Another argument for the passes into the Laguna Madre has been that the inlets improve circulation, but that effect is slight. This history of creating inlets into the laguna has been one of repetitive failure. One of the main reasons for building them has been to improve access to the Gulf by boats, since the natural unbroken stretch from Port Isabel to Port Aransas is a frustrating barrier to anyone attempting to move in a boat from the mainland to the Gulf. The history of these inlets has been given by Gunter (1945b), Price (1952), and Hoese (1958b).

In Louisiana, management of low-salinity marshes has proceeded with the intent of enhancing the habitats of furbearers and waterfowl. Mostly this plan has meant blocking tidal creeks in brackish marshes with weirs to stabilize water levels and to cut down the intrusion of salt water (actually slightly brackish in most places) in large areas of marsh. It has been difficult to demonstrate the effect this program has had on fish (Herke, 1968), but undoubtedly there has been some shift from conditions favoring some species to conditions favoring others. The probable effect has been for selection of freshwater species against the young of marine species which use the marshes for nursery grounds. Also, higher water levels may provide more area for fish. These weirs, like the Texas passes, also tend to concentrate species. These concentrations allow the fishes to be easily collected, but may change the concentrations of fishes reaching offshore areas. However, this effect would be difficult to prove, and it is probably smaller than others affecting offshore populations. These marshes are burned in winter to favor tender, fast-growing plants as food for waterfowl and furbearers. The effects of this burning on fish also seem to be poorly known.

Another predominantly Louisiana problem is potential overfishing of menhaden. These fish occur in large schools mostly on the western Louisiana and eastern Texas coasts. Used for oil and fish meal, they are caught by large vessels that send out small boats to lay purse nets around the tremendous schools that occur very close to the shore. Such a fishery can easily be overexploited because of the small area involved, the schooling habits of the fish, the ease with which schools can be observed from aircraft, and the lack of effective restraints on the fishery. As this book is being written, the northern Gulf menhaden catch has peaked, and many biologists worry that it will decline as the Atlantic one did, which forced east-coast menhaden boats to Louisiana. Despite the predictability of failure of both fisheries, the northern Gulf fishery continues to expand. A maximum sustainable yield could easily be calculated which could continue the fishery indefinitely, but such logical limitation does not seem to be the nature of ever-expansive human behavior.

One management technique used in Texas is the building of so-called artificial reefs to enhance fishing. These reefs are composed either of oyster shells placed in bays to form oyster reefs or of old car bodies, concrete blocks, pipes, or other structures, including old Liberty ships, to introduce hard substrates into an otherwise sandy or muddy environment. The theory is that these reefs somehow add to the catchable fishes. Inshore some species such as speckled trout, redfish, and drum may congregate around artificial reefs, and offshore snapper, grouper, and a few other pelagic species, especially jacks, concentrate around these structures, which are easily located by fishermen.

Some three thousand or more oil platforms built mostly off Louisiana since World War II provide a similar habitat, but one extending the whole height of the water column. Popular belief has it that some fishes were not present on the coast before these installations and that others have become much more common; however, it is certain that these species were in fact on the coast before the oil industry. While it has been shown what fishes congregate around these structures (Sonnier, Teerling, and Hoese, 1976), there has been unfortunately no published study on western Atlantic temperate fishes conclusively demonstrating the effects of oil platforms or other artificial reefs. There is some evidence that some schooling fishes may use such structures for orientation. While there are never as many kinds of fishes associated with these artificial structures as there are with natural reefs, the few species are often very abundant and thereby easy prey for fishermen.

Probably the greatest damage done to fisheries is the expansion into the coast by real estate, industrial, oil, and agricultural interests. Shallow water, often with plant cover or interspersed with marshes, serves as a nursery ground for many fishes, and when it is removed, deepened, or built into, part of the potential of the coast to produce fish is destroyed. With predicted human population pressures it seems likely that even with the best of management and protection the capacity of the coast to produce fish will be reduced. This seems to have been the trend since civilization visited the coast, although this trend is not supported by much "hard" scientific data.

Of course there are numerous other problems, such as how to place comparative values on various fisheries and on environments which are only aesthetically pleasing, and the lack of consideration of the hypothesis that due to excessive population (fishing) pressures many problems are unsolvable from a fisheries standpoint. In summary, whether one would agree completely with the foregoing, one would find it difficult to deny that the major problem is one of human behavior, and the old adage that wildlife or fisheries management is largely people management is as true as ever, with the scientific problems relatively easy to decipher, however hard to explain.

History of Ichthyological Researches

Perhaps the earliest mention of fishes of the northwestern Gulf of Mexico which has come down to us is found in Joutel's journal of La Salle's last voyage (Joutel, 1714), in which he mentions the occurrence of gar, eels, mullet, herring (menhaden), flounder, sea trout, redfish, and "dorado," or gilthead. La Salle's men caught these fish in nets, by gigging for flounder, and by picking up dead trout following a severe freeze in January, 1685, probably the first report of fish mortality due to cold on the Texas coast (see Gunter, 1952a, for a discussion of these freezes).

While there was some early scientific work concerning the marine fishes of Texas in the nineteenth century, research and exploration in Louisiana lagged far behind that in the other coastal states, even nearby Florida. The visitor to Texas might die of thirst, but in Louisiana he would more likely be nearly eaten alive by insects or lost in the maze of marshes; these difficulties might explain the history of fish collections in that state.

The United States–Mexican Boundary survey (Baird and Girard, 1854; Girard, 1858, 1859) collected forty-nine species of fishes from Brazos Santiago, the Rio Grande River mouth, Saint Joseph's Island (San Jose Island according to federal maps, but not the local residents, who often call it "Saint Jo's"), Indianola, and Galveston. No further collections were reported until Jordan and Gilbert (1883) collected fifty-one species from Galveston, including snook, which is now rarely collected that far north. Meanwhile, Goode (1879) had described the Gulf menhaden, *Brevoortia patronus*, as a species distinct from the Atlantic menhaden, *B. tyrannus*.

The first extensive coastal collecting was done in late 1891 at Galveston and Corpus Christi by Evermann and Kendall (1894). These early collections consisted almost entirely of inshore fishes, although an active red snapper fishery added at least two offshore species. An interesting sidelight that oc-

Juvenile cocoa damselfish (*Pomacentrus variabilis*) with an arrow crab and sea urchin.

Brown chromis (*Chromis multilineata*).

Bluehead (*Thalassoma bifasciatum*).

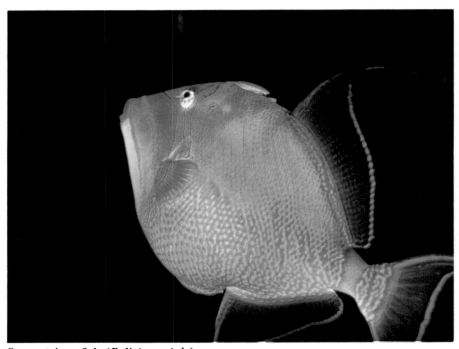

Queen triggerfish (*Balistes vetula*).

curred about that time was the introduction of salmon into Texas. As could have been, and no doubt was, predicted, those fish have not been seen since.

The twentieth century brought little in the way of new fish investigations, although attention began to be paid to oysters and shrimp. The first marine laboratory on the northwestern Gulf was established in Cameron, Louisiana, in 1902. While it did little on fish, and remained open for only ten years, it led to the establishment of the state coastal effort now in the Louisiana Wild Life and Fisheries Commission. A major contribution early in this century was a master's thesis from Tulane University (Raymond, 1905) which listed 117 species of fishes, mostly marine, from Louisiana and included most of the larger, most common inshore species as well as several offshore species and several rarely reported since. The last group included snook, *Centropomus undecimalis*; red porgy, *Pagrus pagrus* (=*sedecim*); croaker, *Micropogon furnieri* (=*undulatus?*); tilefish, *Caulolatilus microps*; and luminous hake, *Steindachneria argentea*. Raymond also apparently has the only Louisiana record of the spottail pinfish, *Diplodus holbrooki*.

In 1917 the U.S. Bureau of Fisheries Research Vessel *Grampus* made several collections off the Texas coast which provided material for descriptions of new species by Nichols and Breder (1922, 1924). Somewhat later, federally initiated studies both in Texas (Pearson, 1929) and in Louisiana (Gunter, 1938a) began emphasizing life histories and ecology instead of just the taxonomy of local fish species.

During the 1930's appeared two popular works on Texas and Louisiana fishes (Burr, 1932; Gowanloch, 1933), the latter partly based on an earlier popular account of Louisiana fishes (anonymous, 1917), as well as the first of many papers by Gordon Gunter (1935) and Isaac Ginsburg (1931) on fishes of this area. Gunter and Ginsburg had the greatest influence on the first half-century of northern Gulf ichthyology.

Just before World War II, contributions to marine biology of Texas waters were made by Cross and Parks (1937) and Reed (1941). Their papers, as well as an additional list by Woods (1942), included several species of marine fish that have only recently been rediscovered in the northwestern Gulf and others which have not been collected since or which have become scarce. It is probably worth noting that many of these earlier records that have been considered doubtful for years are now reverified. Therefore, we should not automatically disregard these earlier works simply because some species are no longer found in this area.

After World War II, expansion of marine researches was rapid. Literature references are too numerous to cite here but are given in the section of literature at the beginning of the bibliography and throughout the text. Before 1950 the Texas Game, Fish and Oyster Commission (now the Texas Parks and Wildlife Department) established a laboratory at Rockport, and the University of Texas set up one at Port Aransas. A lab at Grande Isle was maintained by Louisiana State University in the summers from the late 1920's to the early 1950's. Texas A&M conducted studies on the effect of oil on marine communities, mostly oysters, in the same area through the 1950's. In the early 1950's Tulane University completed a biological survey of Lake Pontchartrain. Since that time Tulane has built the largest collection of fishes in the South, including many marine fishes. Also in the early 1950's Texas A&M expanded its interest in the ocean, leading to an oceanographic fleet and marine laboratory at Galveston. In the late 1950's the University of Southwestern Louisiana built a fisheries field station on Vermilion Bay and began studies, and the Louisiana Wild Life and Fisheries Commission built a laboratory on Grand Terre Island.

Nicholls State University began coastal studies in the mid-1960's (mostly on pond culture), and about 1967 the National Sea Grant Program funded studies aimed toward the expansion of fisheries production. In the early 1970's Nichols State built a field station near the mouth of Bayou LaFourche, and Pan American University established a similar structure on southern Padre Island.

Today, Texas has a widespread state system oriented toward conservation, with a marine laboratory at Rockport, facilities on all major estuaries, a continental shelf research vessel, and two university-staffed marine laboratories with research vessels at Port Aransas and Galveston. Louisiana also has a conservation-oriented state system, with vessels, on all major estuarine systems, and although it has no university laboratory, at least four Louisiana universities and two vessels are pursuing research on coastal fishes.

The Gulf Coast Research Laboratory in Ocean Springs, Mississippi, has been conducting studies in Mississippi Sound and adjacent Gulf waters and maintains a large collection of marine fishes. The Alabama Marine Resources Laboratory has since the early 1960's been investigating coastal fisheries together with a later-established laboratory on Dauphin Island run by a consortium of Alabama universities. In West Florida the Florida State Board of Conservation Laboratory at Saint Petersburg operates inshore and offshore research vessels. The University of Florida operates a field station on Cedar Key, and Florida State University has a research facility and vessels at Turkey Point south of Tallahassee.

Although most of its efforts are dedicated toward shrimp research, the National Marine Fisheries Service Laboratory in Galveston has conducted some fish research. Similarly, the Environmental Protection Agency Laboratory at Gulf Breeze and the Marine Public Health Service Laboratory on Dauphin Island produce some information of value to the study of fish. The National Marine Fisheries Service Laboratory in Pascagoula serves as a base for the research vessel *Oregon II*, which has ongoing programs studying commercial fishes of the northern Gulf. Similarly, the very new Sports Fisheries Laboratories of the U.S. Fish and Wildlife Service at Panama City and Port Aransas are devoted entirely to the study of game fish.

These are the main organizations, not including research foundations and consulting firms, currently conducting marine research. Students and fishermen needing help with identification should find assistance at these places, and certainly many people at more inland and smaller coastal universities are knowledgeable about marine fishes.

IDENTIFYING FISHES

FISH come in an almost bewildering variety of shapes, forms, and sizes. The basic form of a fish requires little explanation, but for those unfamiliar with many of the terms used to describe fish, a glossary is included following page 281 along with drawings of some structures important in identification (Figs. 7–12).

Three means of identifying fishes are provided in this book: the plates, the species accounts, and the keys. The plates are the simplest of the three means to use. We have attempted to obtain photographs of all species, showing the characteristics necessary for identification. Failing that, a drawing is included for the species we were not able to photograph. While we attempted to photograph live or fresh fish, we sometimes had to settle for older preserved specimens. It should be remembered when consulting the figures that many fish are seen damaged and with faded colors and therefore may not be in the same condition as those in our photographs. Also, many fishes exhibit the ability to change their pigmentation, and natural variations in coloration may occur within a population and across a geographic area. Fish caught from clear water are usually lighter than those from more turbid areas. We have not illustrated continental slope or oceanic fishes that are less likely to occur on the shelf, although they may be included in the keys or descriptions. At this stage of exploration no book, however accurate otherwise, can be complete.

Often an unknown fish can be identified by comparing it with the illustrations of the types of fishes that are known and deciding which of the known types most closely resembles the unknown. At this point not only the plates but also the species accounts or descriptions should be consulted. In some cases when several species closely resemble one another we have included only a single plate, but the different forms will be distinguished in the text.

While we have tried to use the same general format for all species accounts, there are times when we have diverged from this format. Not all fishes have the same characteristics, so to save time and space we have chosen to abridge or alter the basic format whenever certain characteristics seemed to us inapplicable or unimportant. Full descriptions of most species are available in the literature citations.

The basic format for species accounts includes the common name of the species, its scientific name, and the name of the person or persons who first described it. Next follows a series of meristic counts (numbers of spines, rays, scales, and gill rakers) that uses standard abbreviations and terminology. Roman numerals refer to numbers of hard spines, and Arabic numerals to numbers of soft rays. The last two soft rays are often joined at their bases and are counted as one. Commas indicate connections between spinous and soft rayed parts of a fin, while a plus sign between the numbers indicates that the fins are separate. Abbreviations used are the following: D. = dorsal fin,

A. = anal fin, P. = pectoral fin, Sc. = pored lateral-line scales or the number of lateral scale rows in species which lack a complete lateral line (an obvious tube running down the side of most fishes; see the glossary), Gr. = gill rakers on the first (anteriormost) arch. Unless otherwise noted, the total number of gill rakers on the first arch is given. The phrase "on lower limb" indicates that only lower-limb gill rakers are counted. A formula like "3 + 14" indicates that upper- and lower-limb gill rakers are given separately as the two numbers in the formula. Small knoblike rudiments are not counted. Various lengths, such as head length and standard length, are often useful in identifying fishes (see the glossary). In any meristic count, a number in parentheses following a range of numbers indicates the most commonly encountered number in that range.

Following the meristic counts may be a description of the form and coloration of the fish, any other general information, and the geographic range. Regardless of what other species are discussed, the range given is only for the species first described unless otherwise specifically stated. Time and space do not permit us to include much information on food habits, life history, or ecology, for which the reader is referred to the references that may be listed with the species. Finally, in parentheses we have given the approximate maximum length the species is expected to attain in our area.

Two precautions are in order at this point. First, the maximum range says little about the density of a species within its range. Leim and Scott (1966) have listed several tropical species that occur as far north as Nova Scotia and Labrador. Because of the Gulf Stream it may be partly a matter of chance whether the northward limit for a species is North Carolina, Massachusetts, Nova Scotia, or Labrador. Where a species ranges through the Bahamian–West Indian–Caribbean tropical region we have simply added "through the Caribbean" to the range. The Caribbean islands are more or less continuous with the Bahamas and share a similar fish fauna. Where the range extends north and south of the Gulf of Mexico, the range inside the Gulf is assumed to be over the entire Gulf unless otherwise qualified. In the western Atlantic many species range repetitiously "from Massachusetts to Brazil" because the warm Gulf Stream and Brazilian currents carry most species that far towards the poles, especially during the summer. Resident populations within this range are another matter, and these must be determined from the original works cited. Even within the range of resident, reproducing populations species may be absent from long stretches of shoreline because of the lack of proper habitats.

Second, the maximum sizes given are meant as rough guides to total length. Remember that fishes mature at smaller sizes, and they may never be seen at the given sizes. These sizes should tell the reader whether a fish is a giant or a midget. For exact sizes, scientific publications or the less precise fishing records published annually by most state conservation agencies and game-fishing organizations should be consulted.

Although the metric system is now a reality in the United States, and books like this will soon use that system exclusively, we have retained the familiar English measurements, giving metric equivalents for most. Because of differences between the two systems, the equivalents are not precise, and we have rounded off the metric measurements. For reference, there are 25.4 millimeters (mm) or 2.54 centimeters (cm) to the inch and 3 feet, 3.4 inches in a meter (m); there are about 454 grams (g) in a pound and 2.2 pounds in a kilogram (kg).

Queen angelfish (*Holacanthus ciliaris*).

French angelfish (*Pomacanthus paru*).

Bonito, or little tuna (*Euthynnus alletteratus*).

Cherubfish (*Centropyge argi*) over sponges and coral.

26   *Fishes of the Gulf of Mexico*

Spotfin butterflyfish (*Chaetodon ocellatus*).

Doctorfish (*Acanthurus chirurgus*).

Creole wrasse (*Clepticus parrai*).

Graysby (*Epinephelus cruentatus*).

The third means of identification is found in the keys. A key is a concise, systematic means for identifying an organism by comparing its features with a pair of statements and by following the directions given with the choice which best describes the animal.

An example of a key which could be used to identify vehicles familiar to everyone follows:

```
1   Propelled by internal combustion engine . . . . (go to) . . . . . . . . . .  2
    Propelled by muscular effort of the rider . . . . (go to) . . . . . . . . . .  3
2   Vehicle with two wheels . . . . . . . . . . . . . . . . . . . . . . . .  motorcycle
    Vehicle with four wheels . . . . . . . . . . . . . . . . . . . . . . .  automobile
3   Vehicle with three wheels . . . . . . . . . . . . . . . . . . . . . . . .  tricycle
    Vehicle with two wheels . . . . . . . . . . . . . . . . . . . . . . . . .  bicycle
```

Rather obviously, this key is good only for identifying motorcycles, automobiles, tricycles, and bicycles. A unicycle, a steam-powered locomotive, or a military tank could not be identified or would be incorrectly identified. Common sense and experience are the most useful aids for identifying any unknown fish. The reader must provide the former, but we hope that this book can help him gain the latter through careful use of the keys, descriptions, and illustrations.

Scientific and Common Names of Fishes

We have, in this book, used both scientific (Latin) and common names following the American Fisheries Society's "List of Common and Scientific Names . . ." (Bailey et al., 1970). While standardization of common names is valuable, and although we have given the AFS common names first in the species accounts, many of the AFS names are not used commonly by the people who encounter the fish, especially in our area of coverage. Thus, when local usage has provided a fish with another more commonly used name, we give that local name after the AFS name. The names given in parentheses are interesting, but not more commonly used than the AFS name. Thus, redfish, instead of red drum or channel bass, and speckled trout, instead of spotted trout or the less-used names spotted weakfish or spotted squeteague, are used more often in the area. Many AFS common names are not realistic for this area; for example, for *Arius felis* the name "sea catfish" is rarely heard in this area outside of an ichthyology class.

Scientific names usually agree with the AFS list, or a more recent revision of the group if such exists. Scientific (or Linnaean) names are supposed to provide scientists around the world with a single name for every species of organism, while local or common names vary tremendously. (Consider again the cases of the redfish and the speckled trout, or the overly general names like "perch," "minnow," and "sand shark.") Scientific names also reflect the degrees by which different species are related. Closely related species are placed in the same genus and share a common "first name": the speckled trout is *Cynoscion nebulosus*; the sand trout is *Cynoscion arenarius*. More distantly but still closely related species are placed in the same family. Trout, redfish, croaker, drum, and whiting are all in different genera but the same family, the Sciaenidae.

The way in which a species receives its proper scientific name is governed by a complex set of rules. Sometimes scientists will decide that a certain species belongs in a different genus, that two species are really identical and should have the same name, or that one variable species is really two or more different forms which require distinct names. In any case, scientific names can and do change, often more frequently than common names do. Such changes can be very confusing to the layman, and even to the scientist if he cannot keep up with the latest reports in the literature.

Several probable unnamed species are treated in the text by listing "sp." after the proper genus. Most of these are in the process of being formally described.

In Appendix 6 we have listed some French names used in the Cajun culture in Louisiana and East Texas. It is not a complete list, but many marine fishes are called by their English names by French-speaking fishermen. Many of the names (for example, *truite, plie, requin*) are derived from European French, but others (*poisson arme, crapaud mer*) are original. Wherever we could decipher the word's meaning, we spelled the name in correct French. The list takes no account of changes in pronunciation, which varies along the coast. A few of the names had to be spelled phonetically, pending understanding of the words. A few Spanish common names in use in Mexico and rarely in Texas are listed in Appendix 7.

COLOR PLATES FOR IDENTIFYING FISHES

2. Whale shark

1. Nurse shark

3. Sand tiger; sand shark

4. Common thresher shark

5. Great white shark

6. Shortfin mako

7. Tiger shark

8. Lemon shark

9. Finetooth shark; blueback shark

10. Atlantic sharpnose shark

11. Smalltail shark

12. Silky shark

13. Sandbar shark; brown shark

14. Dusky shark; sand shark

15. Bull shark

16. Blacknose shark

17. Spinner shark

18. Blacktip shark

20. Smooth dogfish

21. Bonnethead; bonnetnose

23. Scalloped hammerhead

Fishes of the Gulf of Mexico 35

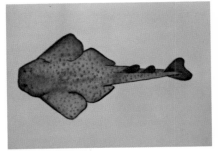

25. Atlantic angel shark

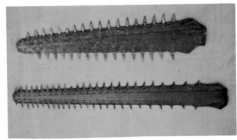

26–27. Sawfish saws: largetooth above, smalltooth below

27. Smalltooth sawfish

28. Atlantic guitarfish

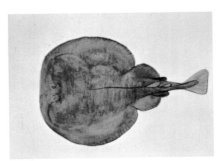

29. Atlantic torpedo

30. Lesser electric ray

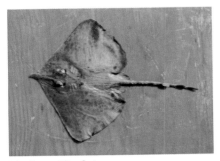

31. Spreadfin skate

32. Freckled skate

33. Clearnose skate

34. Roundel skate

35. Yellow stingray

36. Atlantic stingray; stingaree

37. Bluntnose stingray

38. Roughtail stingray

39. Southern stingray

40. Smooth butterfly ray

41. Cownose ray

42. Spotted eagle ray; duck-billed ray

43. Atlantic manta

44. Atlantic sturgeon

45. Longnose gar

46. Alligator gar

47. Spotted gar

48. Tarpon

49. Ladyfish; tenpounder; skipjack

50. Bonefish

51. American eel

52. Purplemouth moray

53. Spotted moray

54a. Ocellated moray, *G. nigromargina-tus*

54b. Ocellated moray, *G. saxicola*

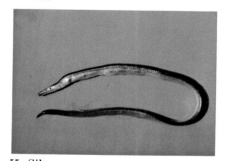

55. Silver conger

56. Yellow conger

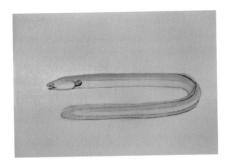

57. Slender pike eel

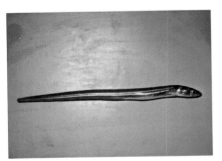

58. Margintail conger

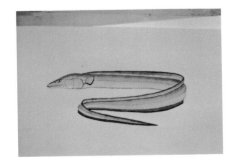

59. *Uroconger syringus*

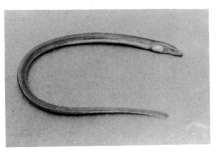

60. Speckled worm eel

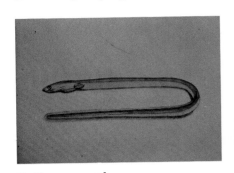

61. Key worm eel

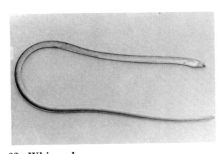

62. Whip eel

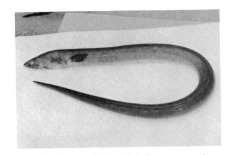

63a. Shrimp eel, *Ophichthus gomesi*

63b. Spotted snake, eel, *Ophichthus ocellatus* (see family account)

64. Banded shrimp eel

65. *Echiophis*

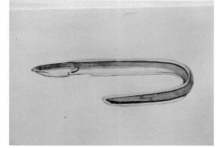

66. Shortbelly eel

67. Round herring

68. Dwarf herring

69. Atlantic thread herring; hairyback

70. Spanish sardine

71. Scaled sardine

72. Alabama shad

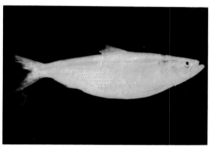

73. Skipjack herring

74. Gulf menhaden

75. Finescale menhaden

76. Threadfin shad

77. Gizzard shad

79. Bay anchovy

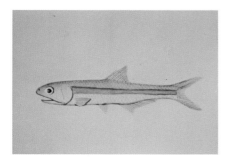

80. Cuban anchovy

81. Longnose anchovy

82. Striped anchovy

83. Snakefish

84. Inshore lizardfish

85. Red lizardfish; rockspear (below)

86. Sand diver

87. Offshore lizardfish

88. Largescale lizardfish

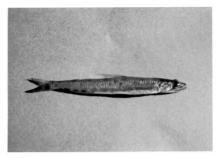

89. Smallscale lizardfish

90. Blue catfish

91. Sea catfish; hardhead

92. Gafftopsail catfish; gafftop

93. Atlantic midshipman

94. Leopard toadfish

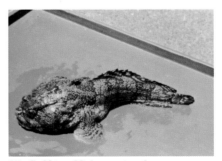

95. Gulf toadfish; oyster dog

96. Skilletfish

97. Sargassumfish

98. Singlespot frogfish

99. Splitlure frogfish

100. *Ogcocephalus* sp.

101. Polka-dot batfish

102. Pancake batfish

104. Antenna codlet

Fishes of the Gulf of Mexico 45

105. Luminous hake

106. Gulf hake

107. Spotted hake

108. Southern hake

109. Blackedge cusk-eel

110. Mottled cusk-eel

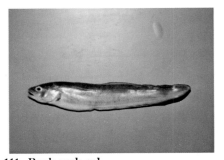

111. Bank cusk-eel

112. Crested cusk-eel

113. Blotched cusk-eel

114. Gold brotula

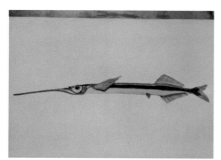

115. Bearded brotula

117. Pearlfish

118. Flying halfbeak

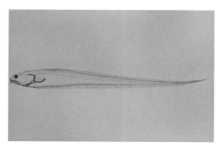

119. Halfbeak

120. Ballyhoo

121. Smallwing flyingfish

Fishes of the Gulf of Mexico 47

122. Sailfin flyingfish

123. Oceanic two-wing flyingfish

124. Blackwing flyingfish

125. Bluntnose flyingfish

126. Margined flyingfish

127. Spotfin flyingfish

128. Atlantic flyingfish, juvenile

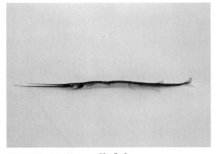

129. Keeltail needlefish

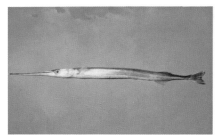

130. Atlantic needlefish; saltwater gar

131. Flat needlefish

132. Houndfish

134. Longnose killifish

135. Saltmarsh topminnow

136. Gulf killifish, ♂ above, ♀ below

137. Bayou killifish, ♂ above, ♀ below

138. Sheepshead minnow, ♂ above,
  ♀ below

139. Diamond killifish

140. Rainwater killifish

141. Sailfin molly, ♂ above, ♀ below

142. Mosquitofish, ♂ above, ♀ below

145. Longspine squirrelfish

143. Rough silverside

144. Tidewater silverside

146. Squirrelfish

147. Dusky squirrelfish

149. Blackbar soldierfish

151. Trumpetfish

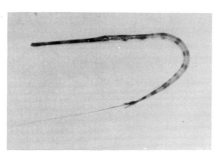

152. Bluespotted cornetfish

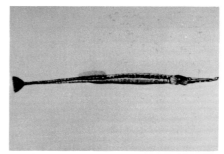

153. Opossum pipefish

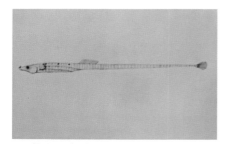

154. Fringed pipefish

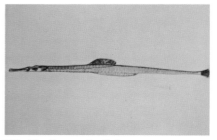

155. Northern pipefish

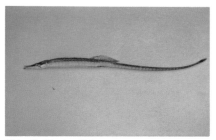

156. Gulf pipefish

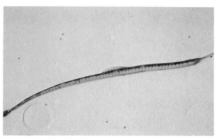

157. Chain pipefish

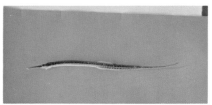

158. Dusky pipefish, ♂ with eggs in pouch

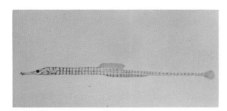

159. Sargassum pipefish

160. Dwarf seahorse

161. Lined seahorse

162. Snook; robalo; saltwater pike

163. Striped bass

164. Yellowtail bass

165. Spanish flag

166. Creole fish

168. Wrasse bass (center)

169. Longtail bass

171b. Butter hamlet, *Hypoplectrus unicolor*

172. Sand perch

173. Dwarf sand perch

171a. Yellowtail hamlet, *Hypoplectrus chlorurus*

174. Belted sand bass

175. Tattler

176. Blackear bass

177. Pygmy sea bass

178. Gulf black sea bass, dark phase

179. Rock sea bass

180. Bank sea bass

181. Graysby

182. Warsaw grouper; black jewfish

183. Yellowedge grouper

184. Snowy grouper

185. Marbled grouper

56   *Fishes of the Gulf of Mexico*

186. Jewfish; spotted jewfish

187. Speckled hind; calico grouper

188. Red grouper

190. Red hind

189. Rock hind; calico grouper

191. Nassau grouper

192. Comb grouper

193. Gag

194a. Scamp, light phase

194b. Scamp, dark phase

195. Yellowfin grouper

196. Black grouper

197. Whitespotted soapfish

58   *Fishes of the Gulf of Mexico*

199. Bigeye

200. Short bigeye

202. Freckled cardinalfish

204. Bridle cardinalfish

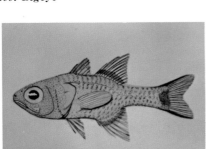

206. Flamefish

207. Twospot cardinalfish

208. Sand tilefish

209. Tilefish

211. Gulf bar-eyed tilefish

212. Bluefish

213. Cobia; ling

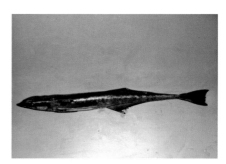

215. Sharksucker

216. Remora

217. Whalesucker

219. Spearfish remora

220. Marlinsucker

221. Leatherjacket

222. Rainbow runner

223. Florida pompano

224a. Permit, adult

224b. Permit, juvenile

225. Palometa; longfinned pompano

226. Almaco jack

227. Lesser amberjack

Fishes of the Gulf of Mexico 61

228. Greater amberjack

229. Banded rudderfish

230. African pompano

231. Atlantic moonfish

232*a.* Lookdown, adult

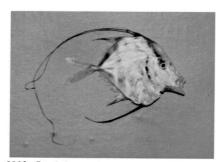

232*b.* Lookdown, juvenile

233. Rough scad

234. Round scad; cigarfish

235. Bigeye scad

236. Atlantic bumper

237a. Bluntnose jack, adult

237b. Bluntnose jack, juvenile

238. Cottonmouth jack

239. Bar jack

240. Yellow jack

241. Blue runner

242. Black jack

243. Crevalle; common jack

244. Horse-eye jack

245. Dolphin

246. Pompano dolphin

247. Vermilion snapper; bastard snapper

248. Wenchman

249. Yellowtail snapper

250. Lane snapper; candy snapper

251. Mutton snapper

252a. Red snapper, adult

252b. Red snapper, juvenile

253. Gray snapper; black snapper; mangrove snapper

254. Schoolmaster

255. Cubera snapper

256. Dog snapper

257. Tripletail

258. Yellowfin mojarra

259. Mottled mojarra

260. Irish pompano

261. Spotfin mojarra

262. Silver jenny

263. Tomtate

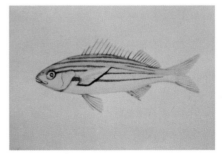

264. Striped grunt

265. Cottonwick

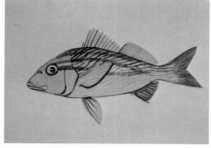
266. Sailor's choice

267. White grunt

268. Spanish grunt

269. Barred grunt

270. Pigfish

271. Burro grunt

272. Porkfish

273. Black margate

274. Longspine porgy

275. Spottail pinfish

276. Pinfish; pin perch

277. Sheepshead

278. Red porgy; silver snapper; white snapper

279a. Grass porgy

279b. Sheepshead porgy (see family account)

68   *Fishes of the Gulf of Mexico*

280. Campeche porgy

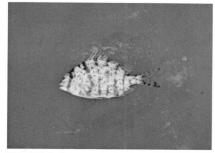

281. Whitebone porgy

282. Jolthead porgy

283. Knobbed porgy

284. Sand drum

285. King whiting

286. Southern kingfish; sea mullet

287. Gulf kingfish; Gulf whiting

288. Black drum

289. Atlantic croaker

290. Reef croaker

291. Spotted seatrout; speckled trout

292. Sand seatrout; sand trout; white trout

293. Silver seatrout

294. Red drum; redfish

295. Spot; flat croaker

296. Star drum

297. Banded croaker

298. Silver perch

299. Cubbyu

300. Jackknife fish

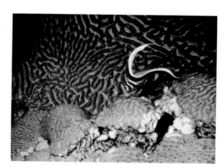

301. Spotted drum

302. Dwarf goatfish

303. Red goatfish

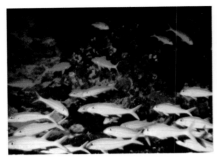

304. Yellow goatfish

305. Spotted goatfish

306. Bermuda chub

307. Yellow chub

308a. Atlantic spadefish; angelfish, adult

308b. Atlantic spadefish; angelfish, juvenile

309. Cherubfish

310. Rock beauty

312. Blue angelfish

311. Queen angelfish

314. Spotfin butterflyfish

315. Foureye butterflyfish

316. Banded butterflyfish

319*a*. French angelfish, adult

319*b*. French angelfish, transforming juvenile

74   *Fishes of the Gulf of Mexico*

320. Gray angelfish

318. Reef butterflyfish

321. Yellowtail damselfish

322. Bicolor damselfish

323*a*. Yellow damselfish, adult

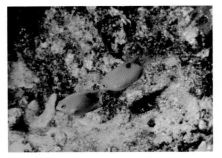

323b. Yellow damselfish, juvenile

324a. Cocoa damselfish, adult

324b. Cocoa damselfish, juvenile

326. Dusky damselfish

327. Sergeant major

328. Night sergeant

329. Blue chromis

330. Brown chromis

76 *Fishes of the Gulf of Mexico*

331. Purple reeffish

332. Yellowtail reeffish

333. Sunshinefish

334. Redspotted hawkfish

335. Hogfish, ♂

336. Creole wrasse

337. Red hogfish

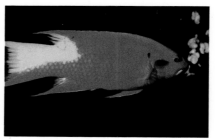

338. Spotfin hogfish

339. Spanish hogfish

340. Pearly razorfish

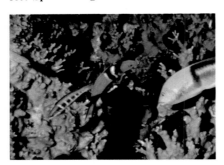

341. Bluehead, supermale center

342. Puddingwife

343. Painted wrasse

344. Slippery dick

345. Yellowhead wrasse, center

347. Princess parrotfish, ♀ above,
♂ below

348. Bucktooth parrotfish, ♂

349a. Redband parrotfish, ♂

349b. Redband parrotfish, ♀

349c. Redband parrotfish, juvenile

351. Mountain mullet; freshwater mullet

352. White mullet

353. Striped mullet

354. Northern sennet

Fishes of the Gulf of Mexico 79

355. Guaguanche

356. Great barracuda

357. Atlantic threadfin; eight-fingered threadfin

358. Swordtail jawfish

359. Southern stargazer

360a. Lancer stargazer

360b. *Gnathagnus egregius*

363. Hairy blenny

364. Molly miller

365. Seaweed blenny

367. Striped blenny

368. Florida blenny

369. Crested blenny

371. Feather blenny

372. Freckled blenny

373. Blue goby

Fishes of the Gulf of Mexico 81

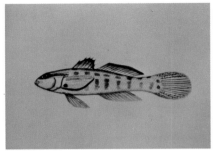

374. Spotted goby

375. Fat sleeper

376. Bigmouth sleeper

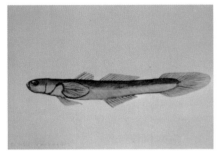

377. Emerald sleeper

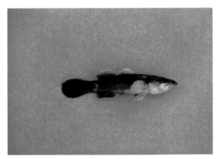

378. Spinycheek sleeper

379. Violet goby

380. Frillfin goby

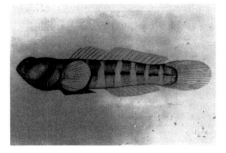

381. Twoscale goby

382. Code goby

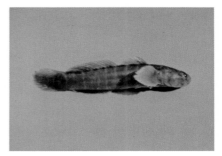

383. Naked goby

384. Clown goby, ♂

385. Green goby, ♀

386. Ragged goby

387. Lyre goby

388. Sharptail goby

389. Freshwater goby

Fishes of the Gulf of Mexico 83

390. Darter goby

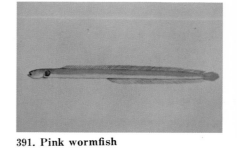

391. Pink wormfish

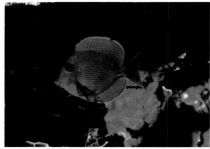

393a. Blue tang, adult

393b. Blue tang, juvenile

394. Doctorfish

395. Ocean surgeon

396. Atlantic cutlassfish; ribbonfish

397. Chub mackerel

84   *Fishes of the Gulf of Mexico*

398. Frigate mackerel

399. Wahoo

400. Skipjack tuna

401. Little tuna; false albacore; bonito

402. Bluefin tuna

403. Blackfin tuna

404. Yellowfin tuna

405. Atlantic bonito

406–407. King mackerel; kingfish (below); Spanish mackerel
(above)

408. Cero

409. Swordfish

410. Sailfish

411. Blue marlin

412. White marlin

413. Longbill spearfish

414. Hatchet marlin

415. Harvestfish

416. Gulf butterfish

423. Man-of-war fish

426. Longspine scorpionfish

427. Spinycheek scorpionfish

428. Spotted scorpionfish

429. Hunchback scorpionfish

430. Barbfish

431. Smoothhead scorpionfish

432. Slender sea robin

433. Mexican sea robin

434. Bandtail sea robin

435. Shortwing sea robin

436. Bluespotted sea robin

437. Bighead sea robin

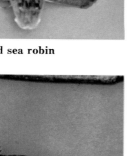

438. Blackfin sea robin

439. Blackwing sea robin

440. Leopard sea robin

441. Northern sea robin

442. Horned sea robin

443. Flying gurnard

444. Spottail flounder

446. Ocellated flounder

447. Three-eye flounder

448. Gulf flounder

449. Broad flounder

450. Southern flounder

451. Spiny flounder

452. Sash flounder

453. Spotfin flounder

454. Mexican flounder

455. Fringed flounder

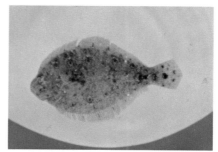

456. Shoal flounder

457. Dusky flounder

458. Horned whiff

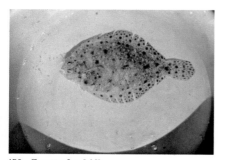

459. Spotted whiff

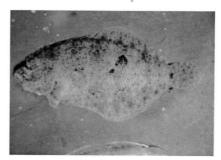

460a. Bay whiff, adult

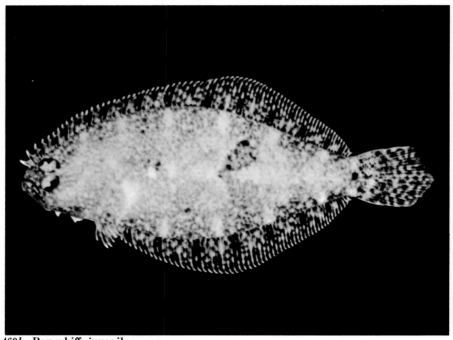

460*b*. Bay whiff, juvenile

461. Fringed sole

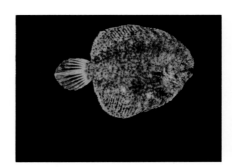

462. Lined sole

463. Hogchoker

464. Pygmy tonguefish

465. Spottedfin tonguefish

466a. Blackcheek tonguefish; patch, adult

466b. Blackcheek tonguefish; patch, juvenile

467. Offshore tonguefish; patch

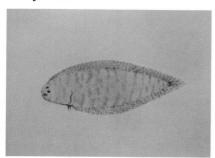

468. Deepwater tonguefish

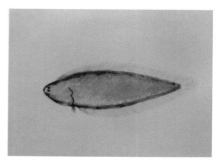

469. Longtail tonguefish

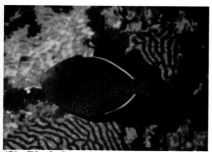

470. Black durgon; black triggerfish

471. Queen triggerfish

Fishes of the Gulf of Mexico 93

472. Gray triggerfish

474. Ocean triggerfish

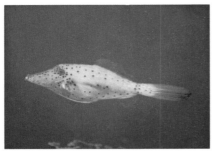
475. Scrawled filefish

476. Orange filefish

477. Dotterel filefish

478. Whitespotted filefish

479. Orangespotted filefish

480. Fringed filefish

94   *Fishes of the Gulf of Mexico*

481. Planehead filefish

482. Pygmy filefish

483. Scrawled cowfish

484. Smooth trunkfish

485. Smooth puffer

486. Sharpnose puffer

487. Marbled puffer

488. Bandtail puffer

490. Checkered puffer

491. Southern puffer

492. Least puffer

493. Striped burrfish

494. Porcupinefish

495. Balloonfish

496. Sharptail mola

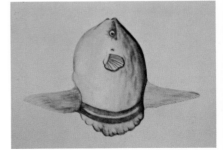

497. Ocean sunfish

KEYS TO THE FAMILIES

INCLUDED in these keys are all families of fishes which are likely to be encountered over the continental shelf of the northwestern Gulf of Mexico as well as a number of families that normally dwell in deeper water but which may at times be found over the shelf. These deeper-dwelling families, which are not further discussed, include the Hexanchidae, Chlorophthalmidae, Argentinidae, Macrorhamphosidae, Caproidae, Percophididae, Callionymidae, Lophiidae, Pleuronectidae, Macrouridae, Merlucciidae, Polymyxiidae, Zeidae, and Triacanthodidae. They are illustrated in Appendix 8. Cartilaginous fishes (sharks, skates, and rays) are easily distinguished from the bony fishes. Members of the former group have five, six, or seven gill openings, while the bony fishes possess only a single gill opening covered by a bony operculum.

Key to the Families of Shallow-water Cartilaginous Fishes

1 Gill openings partly or wholly lateral; pectoral fins not attached to head in front of gills. Order Selachii, sharks 2
  Gill openings wholly ventral; pectoral fins attached to head in front of gills. Order Batoidei, rays 12
2 Anal fin present 3
  Anal fin absent 11
3 Gill openings six or seven . . . . family HEXANCHIDAE, cow sharks
  Gill openings five 4
4 At least half of base of first dorsal fin posterior to origin of pelvic fins 5
  Base of first dorsal fin terminates over or well before origin of pelvic fins 6
5 Anterior margin of nostril with well-developed barbel . . . . family ORECTOLOBIDAE, nurse sharks (p. 107)
  Anterior margin of nostril without barbel . . . . family RHINCODONTIDAE, whale sharks (p. 108)
6 Head flattened and extended with eyes on lateral margins . . . . family SPHYRNIDAE, hammerhead sharks (p. 115)
  Head pointed, not expanded 7
7 Caudal fin lunate . . . . family LAMNIDAE, mackerel sharks (p. 109)
  Caudal fin not lunate, with upper lobe longer than lower lobe 8
8 Caudal fin length one-half total length or more . . . . family ALOPIIDAE, thresher sharks (p. 109)
  Caudal fin length much less than one-half total length 9

9 Fifth gill opening well in front of origin of pectoral; no nictitating membrane on eye .... family ODONTASPIDIDAE, sand tigers (p. 108)

Fifth gill opening over or behind origin of pectoral; eye with nictitating fold or membrane 10

10 Spiracle oval; teeth small, low, and rounded, with three cusps .... family TRIAKIDAE, smooth dogfishes (p. 114)

Spiracle, if present, a narrow slit; teeth bladelike, with one cusp .... family CARCHARHINIDAE, requiem sharks (p. 110)

11 Trunk rounded; eyes lateral; anterior margins of pectorals not overlapping gill openings .... family SQUALIDAE, spiny dogfishes (p. 116)

Trunk flattened; eyes dorsal; anterior margins of pectorals overlapping gill openings .... family SQUATINIDAE, angel sharks (p. 116)

12 Snout prolonged as a narrow blade with teethlike structures .... family PRISTIDAE, sawfishes (p. 117)

Snout pointed or rounded, not as above 13

13 Electric organs present between head and forward extension of pectorals; skin of disc naked .... family TORPEDINIDAE, electric rays (p. 118)

Electric organs not present; skin with spines, thorns, or scales (denticles) 14

14 Dorsal and caudal fins well developed, supported by horny rays; tail merges gradually with body .... family RHINOBATIDAE, guitarfishes (p. 117)

Dorsal and caudal fins, if present, not supported by horny rays; tail distinct from body 15

15 Eyes and spiracles on top of head; no subrostral lobe or fin 16

Eyes and spiracles on side of head; anterior part of pectorals forming a separate lobe or lobes 18

16 Two dorsal fins and caudal present .... family RAJIDAE, skates (p. 118)

Dorsal fins not present, caudal reduced or absent 17

17 Disc less than 1.3 times as broad as long; tail spine present .... family DASYATIDAE, stingrays (p. 120)

Disc more than 1.5 times as broad as long; tail spine usually absent .... family GYMNURIDAE, butterfly rays (p. 121)

18 Teeth tiny, in many series; anterior divisions of pectorals forming two thin, narrow, finlike projections .... family MOBULIDAE, manta rays (p. 122)

Teeth larger, in few series; anterior divisions of pectorals forming one fleshy lobe below and in front of head or two such lobes joined .... family MYLIOBATIDAE, eagle rays (p. 121)

Key to the Families of Bony Fishes

1 Ventral fins present 2

Ventral fins absent 4

2 Ventral fins below or anterior to pectorals 3

Ventral fins well behind pectorals 19

3	Ventral fins thoracic or subjugular; number of rays definitely I, 5	41
	Ventral fins thoracic or jugular; number of rays definitely not I, 5	90
4	Body elongate, flattened laterally; caudal absent	5
	Body, if elongate, not flattened laterally; caudal present or absent	6
5	Anus at throat; small transparent fishes .... family CARAPIDAE, pearlfishes (p. 148)	
	Anus near origin of anal fin; large silvery fishes .... family TRICHIURIDAE, cutlassfishes (p. 236)	
6	Body elongate (eellike fishes)	7
	Body not elongate	12
7	Posterior nostril well above level of upper lip, even with horizontal line through lower margin of eye or higher, with or without flared margin; caudal fin present, continuous with dorsal and anal	8
	Posterior nostril placed on upper lip or just above, or at position of upper lip if lip not present; caudal present or absent .... family OPHICHTHIDAE, snake and worm eels (p. 130)	
8	Gill openings well developed; pectorals present	9
	Gill openings smaller than eye; pectorals absent .... family MURAENIDAE, moray eels (p. 128)	
9	Scales present, small, and embedded; lower jaw somewhat projecting .... family ANGUILLIDAE, freshwater eels (p. 127)	
	Scales totally absent; upper jaw definitely projecting	10
10	No canine teeth on palate .... family CONGRIDAE, conger eels (p. 129)	
	Canine teeth on palate	11
11	Canine teeth on lower jaw; dorsal origin before gill openings .... family MURAENESOCIDAE, pike congers (p. 129)	
	No canine teeth on lower jaw; dorsal origin behind gill opening, slightly in front of pectoral base .... family DYSOMMIDAE, arrowtooth eels (p. 132)	
12	Gill membranes broadly joined to isthmus; gill openings restricted to sides of body	13
	Gill membranes free from isthmus; gill openings ventral as well as on sides of body	18
13	Snout tubular; body covered with bony plates .... family SYNGNATHIDAE, pipefishes and seahorses (p. 160)	
	Snout not tubular	14
14	Dorsal fins two, with the anterior of spines, posterior of soft rays .... family BALISTIDAE, triggerfishes and filefishes (p. 263)	
	Dorsal fin continuous, of soft rays only	15
15	Teeth in jaws separate; body encased in bony plates .... family OSTRACIIDAE, trunkfishes (p. 266)	
	Teeth in jaws confluent into one or two plates in each jaw	16
16	Caudal fin present	17
	Caudal fin absent .... family MOLIDAE, ocean sunfishes (p. 270)	
17	Jaws divided by median suture; body naked or covered by prickles .... family TETRAODONTIDAE, puffers (p. 267)	

Jaws not divided by median suture; body covered by thornlike spikes .... family DIODONTIDAE, porcupinefishes and burrfishes (p. 269)

18   Upper jaw prolonged into a sword .... family XIPHIIDAE, swordfish (p. 241)

Upper jaw not prolonged into sword .... family STROMATEIDAE, butterfishes (p. 244)

19   Adipose fin present 20

Adipose fin absent 24

20   Head scaled on sides 21

Head naked 22

21   Maxillary rudimentary or obsolete .... family SYNODONTIDAE, lizardfishes (p. 137)

Maxillary well developed .... family CHLOROPHTHALMIDAE, greeneyes

22   Body naked 23

Body scaled .... family ARGENTINIDAE, smelts

23   Nostrils with barbels .... family ICTALURIDAE, freshwater catfishes (p. 139)

Nostrils without barbels .... family ARIIDAE, sea catfishes (p. 140)

24   Dorsal fin followed by series of detached finlets .... family SCOMBERESOCIDAE, sauries (p. 153)

Dorsal fin not followed by detached finlets 25

25   Dorsal fin single, composed of soft rays (first ray may be modified and spinelike) 26

Dorsal fins two, the first of spines, the second chiefly of soft rays, or single dorsal preceded by free spines 36

26   Tail heterocercal 27

Tail not heterocercal 28

27   Body covered with diamond-shaped ganoid scales .... family LEPISOSTEIDAE, gars (p. 125)

Body with six series of large shields, otherwise naked .... family ACIPENSERIDAE, sturgeons (p. 124)

28   Body naked; caudal produced .... family FISTULARIIDAE, cornetfishes (p. 159)

Body scaled; caudal not produced 29

29   Pectoral fins inserted high, near axis of body; lateral line along sides of body 30

Pectoral fins inserted below axis of body 31

30   Both jaws produced; teeth tricuspid; pectorals not overly developed .... family BELONIDAE, needlefishes (p. 152)

One or both jaws not produced; teeth conical; pectorals elongate .... family EXOCOETIDAE, flyingfishes and halfbeaks (p. 149)

31   Head more or less scaly 32

Head naked 33

32   Third anal ray not branched; anal fin of male modified as an intromittent organ .... family POECILIIDAE, livebearers (p. 155)

Third anal ray branched; anal fin of male not modified but simi-

lar to that of female .... family CYPRINODONTIDAE, killifishes (p. 153)

33 Gular plate present .... family ELOPIDAE, ladyfish,
tarpon (p. 126)
Gular plate absent 34
34 Lateral line developed .... family ALBULIDAE, bonefish (p. 127)
Lateral line not developed 35
35 Mouth small to moderate .... family CLUPEIDAE,
herrings (p. 133)
Mouth large .... family ENGRAULIDAE, anchovies (p. 136)
36 Dorsal fin preceded by free spines .... family AULOSTOMIDAE,
trumpetfish (p. 159)
Dorsal fins two 37
37 Pectoral fin with lowermost rays detached and filamentous ....
family POLYNEMIDAE, threadfins (p. 225)
Pectoral fin entire 38
38 Snout tubular .... family MACRORHAMPHOSIDAE, snipefishes
Snout not tubular 39
39 Teeth strong, unequal; mouth large; lateral line present ....
family SPHYRAENIDAE, barracudas (p. 223)
Teeth small or wanting; mouth small; lateral line obsolete 40
40 Dorsal spines four; anal spines three .... family MUGILIDAE,
mullets (p. 222)
Dorsal spines four to eight; anal spine single .... family
ATHERINIDAE, silversides (p. 156)
41 Gill openings in front of pectoral fin 42
Gill openings behind pectoral fin 88
42 Body more or less scaly or armed with bony plates 43
Body scaleless, smooth or armed with tubercles, prickles, or
scattered bony plates 85
43 Ventral fins separate 44
Ventral fins united; gill membranes joined at isthmus; no lateral
line .... family GOBIIDAE, gobies (p. 230)
44 Suborbital with bony stay; cheek sometimes mailed 45
Suborbital without bony stay; cheek never mailed 46
45 Pectoral fin with detached rays .... family TRIGLIDAE,
searobins (p. 250)
Pectoral fin entire .... family SCORPAENIDAE, scorpionfishes (p. 248)
46 Spinous dorsal transformed into sucking disc .... family
ECHENEIDAE, sharksuckers (p. 180)
Spinous dorsal not sucking disc 47
47 Anal fin preceded by two free spines (obsolete in very large
fish, often connected by membrane in young fish) with no
more than one finlet; caudal peduncle not keeled 48
Anal fin not preceded by free spines 49
48 Scales small or absent; teeth, if present, not caninelike; preopercle entire .... family CARANGIDAE, jacks (p. 182)
Scales moderate; teeth caninelike; preopercle serrate .... family POMATOMIDAE, bluefish (p. 179)
49 Dorsal spines present, all or nearly all disconnected from each
other 50

Dorsal spines, if present, all or nearly all connected by membrane 52
50 Body elongate, spindle-shaped, nearly square in cross-section .... family RACHYCENTRIDAE, cobia (p. 179)
Body oblong, ovate, or compressed 51
51 Gill membranes free from isthmus .... family CENTROLOPHIDAE, ruffs (p. 246)
Gill membranes connected to isthmus .... family EPHIPPIDAE, spadefishes (p. 209)
52 Dorsal and anal each with one or more detached finlets .... family SCOMBRIDAE, mackerels and tunas (p. 236)
Dorsal and anal each without finlets 53
53 Lateral line armed posteriorly with a sharp, movable spine .... family ACANTHURIDAE, surgeonfishes (p. 235)
Lateral line not armed posteriorly 54
54 Throat with two long barbels; dorsal fins two .... family MULLIDAE, goatfishes (p. 207)
Throat without barbels 55
55 Nostril single on each side; lateral line interrupted .... family POMACENTRIDAE, damselfishes (p. 213)
Nostril double on each side 56
56 Lateral line extending to tip of middle rays of caudal 57
Lateral line not extending onto caudal fin 59
57 Anal spines one or two .... family SCIAENIDAE, croakers (p. 201)
Anal spines three 58
58 Dorsal fins two, separate .... family CENTROPOMIDAE, snook (p. 163)
Dorsal fin one, continuous .... family POMADASYIDAE, grunts (p. 196)
59 Gills three and one-half, with slit behind the last arch small or absent 60
Gills four, with long slit behind last arch 62
60 Mouth vertical; dorsal fin divided .... family URANOSCOPIDAE, stargazers (p. 226)
Mouth not vertical; dorsal continuous 61
61 Teeth in each jaw united, forming beak .... family SCARIDAE, parrotfishes (p. 220)
Teeth in jaws separate, or nearly so; anterior teeth more or less canine .... family LABRIDAE, wrasses (p. 217)
62 Teeth setiform, brushlike; soft fins scaled 63
Teeth not setiform 64
63 Dorsal continuous .... family CHAETODONTIDAE, butterflyfishes and angelfishes (p. 209)
Dorsal divided .... family EPHIPPIDAE, spadefishes (p. 209)
64 Body deeper than long, covered with rough scales; dorsal spines eight; anal spines three; soft fins very long .... family CAPROIDAE, boarfishes
Body longer than deep 65
65 Gill membranes broadly joined to isthmus; no lateral line .... family ELEOTRIDAE, sleepers (here included in GOBIIDAE) (p. 230)
Gill membranes free from isthmus, or nearly so 66

66 Premaxillaries excessively protractile .... family GERREIDAE, mojarras (p. 194)
   Premaxillaries moderately protractile or not protractile 67
67 Lateral line incomplete, running close to dorsal fin .... family OPISTOGNATHIDAE, jawfishes (p. 225)
   Lateral line, if present, not as above 68
68 Pseudobranchiae absent or covered by skin .... family CORYPHAENIDAE, dolphins (p. 189)
   Pseudobranchiae developed 69
69 Spinous dorsal with two or three short spines only; anal spines absent .... family GRAMMISTIDAE, soapfishes (p. 174)
   Spinous dorsal, if present, not as above; anal spines absent or present 70
70 Opercle ending in long scaly flap; snout depressed and spatulate; mouth large, lower jaw projecting; anal spines absent .... family PERCOPHIDIDAE, flatheads
   Opercle not ending in a scaly flap; snout not greatly depressed; anal spines present 71
71 Dorsal fin continuous, with spines few and slender; maxillary usually with enlarged tooth behind; anal fin long and even; upper and lower rays of caudal often produced 72
   Dorsal fin continuous or divided, not as above 73
72 Pectoral fin broad, with lower rays thickened and not branched .... family CIRRHITIDAE, hawkfishes (p. 217)
   Pectoral fin narrow at base, with lower rays branched like upper ones .... family BRANCHIOSTEGIDAE, tilefishes (p. 178)
73 Caudal peduncle not slender; scales well developed; dorsal fin with distinct spines; anal with at least one spine, soft rays usually few (perchlike fishes) 74
   Caudal peduncle slender; scales various, but usually not ctenoid; dorsal spines various; anal fin long (mackerellike fishes).... 82
74 Maxillary not sheathed by preorbital or only partially covered by edge of latter 75
   Maxillary slipping beneath preorbital when mouth is closed; opercle without spines 79
75 Anal spines two and rarely three; body not elongate .... family APOGONIDAE, cardinalfishes (p. 176)
   Anal spines three, never two 76
76 Vomer, and usually palatines, with teeth 77
   Vomer toothless .... family LOBOTIDAE, tripletail (p. 194)
77 Anal fin shorter than dorsal; head not covered with rough scales 78
   Anal fin scarcely shorter than dorsal, similar in appearance; head covered with rough scales .... family PRIACANTHIDAE, bigeyes (p. 175)
78 Dorsal fins separate .... family PERCICHTHYIDAE, temperate basses (p. 163)
   Dorsal fin continuous .... family SERRANIDAE, sea basses (p. 164)
79 Teeth in jaws incisorlike; intestine elongated; herbivorous fishes with moderately protractile premaxillaries .... family KYPHOSIDAE, chubs (p. 208)

Teeth in jaws not all incisorlike; intestine of moderate length; carnivorous fishes 80

80   Vomer with teeth, sometimes small; maxillary long .... family LUTJANIDAE, snappers (p. 190)

Vomer toothless; palatines and tongue also without teeth 81

81   Teeth on sides of jaws not molar; preopercle serrate .... family POMADASYIDAE, grunts (p. 196)

Teeth on sides of jaws molar; preopercle entire .... family SPARIDAE, porgies (p. 199)

82   Dorsal fin divided, spines six to eight 83

Dorsal fin not divided, spines three or four .... family BRAMIDAE, pomfrets (p. 190)

83   Jaws with canines .... family POMATOMIDAE, bluefish (p. 179)

Jaws without canines 84

84   Caudal peduncle square, with at least two lateral keels .... family ARIOMMIDAE, driftfishes (p. 245)

Caudal peduncle compressed, without lateral keels .... family NOMEIDAE, man-of-war fishes (p. 246)

85   Breast without a sucking disc 86

Breast with a sucking disc .... family GOBIESOCIDAE, clingfishes (p. 142)

86   Gill membranes broadly attached to isthmus .... family CALLIONYMIDAE, dragonets

Gill membranes free or nearly free of isthmus 87

87   Anal preceded by two free spines .... family CARANGIDAE, jacks (p. 182)

Anal without free spines .... family SCOMBRIDAE, mackerels and tunas (p. 236)

88   Gill openings behind or in upper axil of pectorals .... family OGCOCEPHALIDAE, batfishes (p. 143)

Gill openings in or behind lower axil of pectorals 89

89   Head laterally compressed; no pseudobranchiae .... family ANTENNARIIDAE, frogfishes (p. 142)

Head depressed; pseudobranchiae present .... family LOPHIIDAE, goosefishes

90   Eyes unsymmetrical, both on same side of head 91

Eyes symmetrical, one on each side of head 94

91   Margin of preopercle free, not covered with skin or scales 92

Margin of preopercle covered with skin and scales 93

92   Eyes on left side .... family BOTHIDAE, lefteyed flounders and whiffs (p. 254)

Eyes on right side .... family PLEURONECTIDAE, righteyed flounders

93   Eyes on right side .... family SOLEIDAE, soles (p. 260)

Eyes on left side .... family CYNOGLOSSIDAE, tonguefishes (p. 262)

94   Ventral fins with or without a spine, soft rays more than five 95

Ventral fins with or without spines, soft rays less than five 101

95   Caudal fin not present .... family MACROURIDAE, grenadiers

Caudal fin well developed 96

96   Tail isocercal 97

Tail not isocercal 98

97 Jaws and vomer with strong canines; no barbel .... family
     MERLUCCIIDAE, whitings
     Jaws and vomer without distinct canines; barbel on chin ....
     family GADIDAE, codfishes (p. 145)
98 Chin with two long barbels .... family POLYMYXIIDAE,
     beardfishes
     Chin without barbels 99
99 Dorsal fin divided, anterior part with single spine .... family
     BREGMACEROTIDAE, codlets (p. 145)
     Dorsal fin divided, anterior part with many spines 100
100 Body covered with firm, serrated scales; anal spines four; dorsal
     spines not greatly elongated .... family HOLOCENTRIDAE,
     squirrelfishes (p. 157)
     Body covered with small scales or naked; dorsal spines elongated
     .... family ZEIDAE, dories
101 Gill openings behind pectoral fin 102
     Gill openings before pectoral fin 103
102 Gill openings behind and above pectorals; mouth small ....
     family OGCOCEPHALIDAE, batfishes (p. 143)
     Gill openings behind and below pectoral; mouth large ....
     family ANTENNARIIDAE, frogfishes (p. 142)
103 Upper jaw prolonged into bony sword .... family
     ISTIOPHORIDAE, billfishes (p. 241)
     Upper jaw not prolonged into sword 104
104 Dorsal fin with spines or simple rays 105
     Dorsal fin of soft rays only 111
105 Pectoral fin divided into two parts, one very long .... family
     DACTYLOPTERIDAE, flying gurnards (p. 253)
     Pectoral fin not divided 106
106 Dorsal spines two to four; gills three 107
     Dorsal spines numerous; gills four 108
107 Ventral fins not reduced to single spine .... family
     BATRACHOIDIDAE, toadfishes (p. 141)
     Ventral fins reduced to single spine .... family
     TRIACANTHODIDAE, spikefishes
108 Gill membranes broadly connected, attached to isthmus or
     not 109
     Gill membranes separate, joined to isthmus .... family
     DACTYLOSCOPIDAE, sand stargazers (p. 225)
109 Gill openings moderate or large 110
     Gill openings small, reduced to oblique slits before pectorals
     .... family MICRODESMIDAE, wormfishes (p. 234)
110 Teeth separate .... family CLINIDAE, clinids (p. 226)
     Teeth comblike .... family BLENNIIDAE, combtooth
     blennies (p. 227)
111 Breast with sucking disc .... family GOBIESOCIDAE,
     clingfishes (p. 142)
     Breast without sucking disc 112
112 Tail isocercal .... family GADIDAE, codfishes (p. 145)
     Tail not isocercal .... family OPHIDIIDAE, cusk-eels (p. 146)

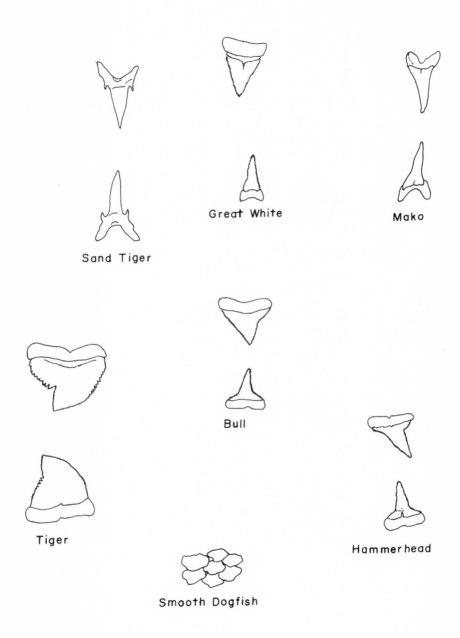

Great White

Mako

Sand Tiger

Bull

Tiger

Hammerhead

Smooth Dogfish

Fig. 1. Distinctive shark teeth

SHARKS, SKATES AND RAYS
(CHONDRICHTHYES: ELASMOBRANCHII)

ALTHOUGH not the most primitive of fishes (lampreys and hagfishes, not present in this area, are the most ancient) the elasmobranchs are very old and probably have changed little in millions of years. They are characterized by having a cartilaginous skeleton and five to seven pairs of gill slits not covered by an opercle. Their skin is composed of tiny placoid scales (dermal denticles), which give it a sandpaper consistency. These scales can be used to identify species. The number and shape of teeth may also be used to distinguish species. Some of the more distinctive teeth are illustrated in Fig. 1.

Although sharks and rays have been considered as separate groups, recent studies indicate that the distinction is artificial, with some intermediate forms such as angel sharks. Because of their size and deadliness, sharks have always attracted interest, but the reproductive methods of the elasmobranchs may be their most interesting facet. All species have internal fertilization; the males have a pair of claspers on their pelvic fins that transfer sperm. Most species are viviparous or ovoviviparous, giving birth to few young, but a few species, such as the whale shark and the skates, deposit eggs in capsules. Perhaps the species with the most spectacular reproduction method is the sand tiger, which has a single young developing in a uterus and feeding on eggs produced by the mother which pass from the ovary into the mouth of the fetus (oviphagy). Many species of sharks and rays possess a placenta, and all enter the world as well-developed juveniles.

One shark not included here may be rarely encountered. The seven-gilled shark, *Heptranchias perlo*, is known from an inshore specimen off Texas. Although it may be a stray from deeper water, the ocean contains other sharks with seven gill slits and even some with six (all the sharks included here have five).

Sharks are edible and quite good eating when properly prepared, and although the skin and liver have also been used, shark fisheries have generally been marginal. A small new fishery in Louisiana sells local species for food, mostly in New Orleans. (Baughman and Springer, 1950; Bigelow and Schroeder, 1948, 1953*b*; Springer, 1950*a*; Clark and von Schmidt, 1965; Heemstra, 1965; Wahlquist, 1966)

Orectolobidae

Nurse sharks are peculiar tropical sharks with two high dorsals, but with the first behind the origin of the pelvics. The nostril, with a fleshy barbel, is connected with the subterminal mouth by a groove. Only one species occurs in the Atlantic. Sharks with poorly developed mouths, such as young dogfish, are often called nurses.

1. Nurse shark   *Ginglymostoma cirratum* (Bonnaterre)

Brownish, the young speckled, with small eye. The nurse shark is a rarely seen tropical species, easily recognized by its mouth and barbels. It occurs commonly around offshore reefs, sporadically straying inshore. Tropical Atlantic, in the west from North Carolina (straying northward) through the Caribbean to Brazil. (14 feet; 4¼ m)

Rhincodontidae

Whale sharks are large, epipelagic fish that are occasionally struck by vessels. There is only one species in the family.

2. Whale shark   *Rhincodon typus* Smith

Head flat, square in front; gill openings very high; seven longitudinal ridges on back; brownish on back and sides with many white spots. Whale sharks are rarely sighted in the area basking or slowly swimming at the surface. This animal, the largest living fish, is a plankton feeder; its gill apparatus is modified as a sieve, but it occasionally feeds on fishes as big as small tuna. It is often called *Rhineodon* or *Rhiniodon*. The only embryo (14½ inches long in an egg case) known was taken in the Gulf off northern Mexico and is on display at the Texas Parks and Wildlife Department Marine Laboratory in Rockport. Circumtropical; in the western Atlantic from New York through the Caribbean to Brazil. Breuer, 1954; Baughman, 1955; Garrick, 1964. (45 feet; 13¾ m)

Odontaspididae

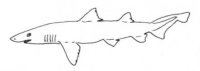

Sand tiger sharks are fairly large sharks with the second dorsal as large as the first, a pointed snout, and distinctive teeth. Other species of this family are often implicated in shark attacks, but only a single species occurs in the western Atlantic. The family was formerly known as Carchariidae.

3. Sand tiger; sand shark   *Odontaspis taurus* (Rafinesque)

Teeth long and slender with sharply pointed cusps; gray brown with darker spots on body and fins behind pectorals. This is a recently discovered shark in the Gulf, but it does not seem to be uncommon. It is more common north of Cape Hatteras. Of the larger sharks, only the sand tiger, the nurse shark, and the lemon shark have equal-sized dorsals, and in the nurse shark the first dorsal is very close to the tail. When the sand tiger is seen swimming, both dorsals may break water simultaneously. These are unusual sharks which have an oviphagous fetus, as described in the introduction to the elasmobranchs. North Atlantic, in the west from Maine to the northern Bahamas and Florida, and in the Gulf to Texas. (10 feet; 3 m)

Alopiidae

Thresher sharks are easily recognized by their long, scythelike caudal fin, which is used to herd and stun schools of fish. In addition, threshers have a very small second dorsal set ahead of the small anal fin.

4. Common thresher shark   *Alopias vulpinus* (Bonnaterre)

Rear tip of first dorsal terminating far forward of pelvic fins; bluish, undersides sometimes mottled; first dorsal low, rounded. A cold temperate species most common off New England, the thresher is rare in the Gulf. It is a big shark, maturing at about fourteen feet (4⅓ m), giving birth to young four to five feet long. The bigeye thresher, *A. superciliosis* (Lowe), may also occur at the shelf edge; it differs by having a very large eye and only ten or eleven teeth on each side of the jaw versus the twenty of the common thresher. Worldwide, in the western Atlantic from Nova Scotia to Argentina. Gunter, 1941. (20 feet; 6 m)

Lamnidae

Mackerel sharks are large, voracious fishes with a tail of almost equal lobes. Most species are known to attack humans, and although this unpleasant habit is not restricted to this family, the Lamnidae are among the worst offenders. The great white shark often eats human-sized prey, such as seals and porpoises, whole. Two and possibly three species are found in our area. These are sometimes put in the family Isuridae.

1 Upper teeth broadly triangular, with serrated cusps .... Great
   white shark, *Carcharodon carcharias.*
   Upper teeth slender, with smooth-edged cusps 2
2 Pectoral fins short, about 17 percent of total length; underside of
   snout white .... Shortfin mako, *Isurus oxyrinchus.*
   Pectoral fins long, more than 18 percent of total length; underside
   of snout dusky .... Longfin mako, *Isurus paucus.*

5. Great white shark   *Carcharodon carcharias* (Linnaeus)

Very large girth, making it heavy for its length; much white on lower
side; short caudal peduncle. Rare in the Gulf, the great white shark is usually
encountered far offshore in cooler water. The largest of predaceous sharks,
maturing at fifteen feet (4½ m), it is a cold temperate species more abundant
north of Cape Hatteras. Worldwide except near the poles. Baughman, 1950*a*;
Gunter and Knapp, 1951. (at least 25 feet; 8 m)

6. Shortfin mako   *Isurus oxyrinchus* (Rafinesque)

Slender; often bluish dorsally. This distinctive and beautiful shark is a
highly prized game fish. Another mako, *I. paucus*, might be found in the
deeper water of the Gulf during the summer but has not been confirmed.
Atlantic Ocean, in the west from Massachusetts and Bermuda to Brazil. Garrick, 1967*a*. (12 feet; 3⅔ m)

Carcharhinidae

Requiem sharks are the most abundant of sharks, being named for the
tendency of some species to occur in large "masses" near the surface. Often
called sand sharks, for want of a better name, the species are difficult to identify. The ridgeback sharks (with a ridge between the dorsals) are common
pelagic species, whereas most of the others occur near the bottom. The
oceanic whitetip, *Carcharhinus longimanus*, is common at the surface just
outside the one-hundred-fathom line but rarely, if ever, strays inshore. There
are at least twenty species in the western Atlantic, thirteen of which we have
confirmed from the northwestern Gulf. (Bigelow and Schroeder, 1948; Springer, 1950*a*; Garrick, 1967*b*)

1 Spiracles present as narrow slit; sides marked with stripes and
   blotches .... Tiger shark, *Galeocerdo cuvieri.*
   Spiracles absent; various markings possibly on sides, but never
   stripes 2
2 Cusps of upper teeth as well as lower teeth smooth-edged 3
   Cusps of upper teeth serrate; those of lower teeth serrate or
   smooth 5
3 Second dorsal at least three-fourths as long as first, with posterior
   margin deeply concave; snout rounded .... Lemon shark,
   Negaprion brevirostris.
   Second dorsal less than one-half as long as first and much smaller

in area, with posterior margin weakly concave or straight; snout
    pointed 4

4   Teeth slender, symmetrical, erect in both jaws; longest gill open-
    ing about one-half as long as dorsal base .... Finetooth shark,
    Aprionodon isodon.

    Teeth in sides of jaw oblique, with outer edges notched; longest
    gill opening only one-fourth as long as base of first dorsal ....
    Atlantic sharpnose shark, *Rhizoprionodon terraenovae.*

5   Origin of second dorsal over or behind midpoint of base of anal
    .... Smalltail shark, *Carcharhinus porosus.*

    Origin of second dorsal over origin of anal or anterior to it 6

6   Midline of back between first and second dorsals with low but
    distinct ridge* 7

    Midline of back between dorsals smooth 10

7   Apex of first dorsal broadly rounded; tip of anal reaching nearly
    to origin of caudal .... Oceanic whitetip shark, *Carcharhinus
    longimanus.*†

    Apex of first dorsal subangular; tip of anal separated from origin
    of caudal by distance at least as great as diameter of eye 8

8   Lower free edge of second dorsal more than twice as long as
    height of fin .... Silky shark, *Carcharhinus falciformis.*

    Lower free edge of second dorsal much less than twice as long as
    height of fin 9

9   Origin of first dorsal over pectoral axil; height of first dorsal equal
    to distance from eye to third gill opening .... Sandbar shark,
    Carcharhinus milberti.

    Origin of first dorsal about over posterior, inner corner of pecto-
    ral; height of first dorsal less than distance from eye to first gill
    opening .... Dusky shark, *Carcharhinus obscurus.*

10 Snout in front of line connecting outer ends of nostril less than
    one-half of distance between inner ends of nostrils .... Bull
    shark, *Carcharhinus leucas.*

    Snout in front of line connecting outer ends of nostrils two-thirds
    or more of distance between inner ends of nostrils 11

11 Upper teeth asymmetrical, directed backwards, with outer mar-
    gins notched (deeply concave) .... Blacknose shark, *Carcha-
    rhinus acronotus.*

    Upper teeth symmetrical 12

12 Origin of first dorsal over inner corner of pectoral; horizontal
    diameter of eye less than 15 percent of snout length; edges of
    lower teeth smooth .... Spinner shark, *Carcharhinus maculi-
    pinnis.*

    Origin of first dorsal over midpoint of inner margin of pectoral;
    horizontal diameter of eye about 20 percent of snout length;

* Sharks with the mid-dorsal ridge are sometimes placed in the genus *Eulamia*, but they differ by few other characters from the other *Carcharhinus* species.
They do, however, distinctly have much less affinity for the bottom.

† The oceanic whitetip shark does not occur over the continental shelf. We
have included it in the key because it might be caught by fishermen at the edge of
the shelf. It is very distinctive with white-tipped fins (Backus, Springer, and Arnold, 1956).

edges of lower teeth finely serrate . . . . Blacktip shark, *Carcharhinus limbatus.*

7. Tiger shark *Galeocerdo cuvieri* (Peron and Lesueur)

Snout bluntly rounded; teeth strongly asymmetrical and serrated; sides spotted in young, becoming striped, eventually fading; tail with long upper lobe; grayish brown. Easily recognized by its markings, teeth, and tail, the tiger shark is often taken from Gulf jetties and piers and follows boats feeding on any trash thrown overboard. A frequent food item is seabirds. Worldwide in temperate and tropical waters; in the western Atlantic from Cape Cod to Uruguay. (18 feet; 5½ m)

8. Lemon shark *Negaprion brevirostris* (Poey)

Snout bluntly rounded; central teeth symmetrical and unserrated; second dorsal nearly as high as first. This shark is a distinctive species with a slender body. The young are born in the summer, when they are often caught in marsh channels. Temperate and tropical Atlantic, in the west from New Jersey through the Caribbean to Brazil. Springer, 1950*b*. (11 feet; 3⅓ m)

9. Finetooth shark; blueback shark *Aprionodon isodon* (Valenciennes)

Head triangular in front of nostrils; teeth slender, unserrated, and symmetrical; gill openings long; second dorsal much smaller than first. A slender shark with a cobalt blue back, its young are common in the surf zone, except in the winter, and the adults seem to stay on the inshore shelf. Atlantic Ocean, in the west from New York to at least southern Texas and Cuba. (5 feet; 1½ m)

10. Atlantic sharpnose shark *Rhizoprionodon terraenovae* (Richardson)

Snout more or less pointed; teeth asymmetrical in both jaws, unserrated; origin of second dorsal over midpoint of anal base; gray with dark-edged dorsals and caudal; sides with a few small, white spots. This is one of the most common inshore species, with young appearing in the surf zone and saltier estuaries in summer. Adults are often caught far offshore at the snapper banks. It is easy to confuse with the smalltail shark, from which it is distinguished by the presence of a low interdorsal ridge, long labial furrows, and smooth teeth which are asymmetrical in the lower jaw. Bay of Fundy to Yucatán. Springer, 1964. (3 feet; 1 m)

11. Smalltail shark *Carcharhinus porosus* (Ranzani)

Snout moderately pointed; teeth asymmetrical in upper jaw, straight in most of lower, slightly serrated; origin of second dorsal over midpoint of anal base; gray with reddish tinge. The status of this small shark is uncertain because it is easily confused with the sharpnose shark, since these are the only two carcharhinid sharks with the second dorsal origin behind the anal origin. Eastern tropical Pacific; western Atlantic from the northern Gulf to Brazil. (4 feet; 1¼ m)

12. Silky shark *Carcharhinus falciformis* (Bibron)

Snout moderately pointed; interdorsal ridge present; free tips of second dorsal and anal very long; teeth nearly symmetrical, uppers broad. This is the common shark seen at the surface over the continental shelf. *C. floridanus* is a synonym. Tropical Atlantic, in the west from Massachusetts to Brazil. Garrick, Backus, and Gibbs, 1964. (10 feet; 3 m)

13. Sandbar shark; brown shark *Carcharhinus milberti* (Valenciennes)

Snout broadly rounded; first dorsal large for a requiem shark, with origin over axil of pectoral; teeth in upper jaw broad, somewhat asymmetrical, in lower jaw thin and symmetrical; gray to brown. This is a cold temperate species more common north of Cape Hatteras. It is uncommon in the Gulf. Atlantic Ocean, in the west from Massachusetts to Brazil. Springer, 1960. (8 feet; 2½ m)

14. Dusky shark; sand shark *Carcharhinus obscurus* (Lesueur)

Snout moderately rounded; first dorsal relatively low, with origin at corner of pectoral; upper teeth slightly asymmetrical, broad; interdorsal ridge present; bluish gray, sometimes pale, with pectorals sooty at tips. The habits of the dusky shark are not well known, although a number have been taken over the middle shelf. Atlantic Ocean, in the west from Massachusetts and Bermuda to Brazil. (11 feet; 3⅓ m)

15. Bull shark *Carcharhinus leucas* (Valenciennes)

Snout bluntly rounded; first dorsal origin over pectoral axil; no interdorsal ridge; upper teeth broad, slightly asymmetrical, lowers thin, symmetrical; gray. A common species inshore, this is the only shark in low-salinity estuaries, and it even penetrates fresh water. It is known from Simmesport and Saline Lake off the Red River in Louisiana, over one hundred miles from the Gulf up the Atchafalaya, although it may have come up the Mississippi, which, during very dry spells, will have salt wedges flowing along the bottom past Baton Rouge. New York and Bermuda through the Caribbean to Brazil. Gunter, 1938c; Caillouet, Perret, and Fontenot, 1969. (10 feet; 3 m)

16. Blacknose shark *Carcharhinus acronotus* (Poey)

Snout moderately pointed, with black smudge on tip lost with growth; no interdorsal ridge; upper teeth broad, asymmetrical; lower teeth thin, nearly symmetrical; second dorsal origin over anal; usually cream or yellow, with second dorsal black-tipped. A poorly known species, this shark prefers coarse shell-sand habitats; therefore, it is more common in the northeastern and southern Gulf. North Carolina through the Caribbean to Brazil. (6 feet; 1⅔ m)

17. Spinner shark *Carcharhinus maculipinnis* (Poey)

Snout very slender and pointed; upper and lower teeth slender, nearly symmetrical; gray, with dorsals, pectorals, and caudal black-tipped. This is apparently a common inshore species, named for its habit of leaving the water vertically in a spiral. Gulf of Mexico barely into the Caribbean. (8 feet; 2½ m)

18. Blacktip shark *Carcharhinus limbatus* (Valenciennes)

Snout slender, pointed; upper and lower teeth slender, nearly symmetrical; gray, with dorsals, pectorals, and caudals black-tipped, but obscured with age. Worldwide in temperate and tropical waters; in the western Atlantic from Massachusetts to Brazil. (8 feet; 2½ m)

Triakidae

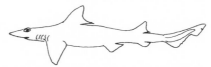

Smooth dogfishes or smoothhounds are small sharks with the second dorsal almost as large as the first; narrow, catlike eyes; and a spiracle behind each eye. Commonly called nurses because of their small teeth and rounded mouth, they are sometimes put in the Carcharhinidae, from which they differ in dentition and in lacking a well-developed nictitating membrane. The taxonomy of Gulf species is not clear, but two species are recorded. See Fig. 2. (Springer and Lowe, 1963)

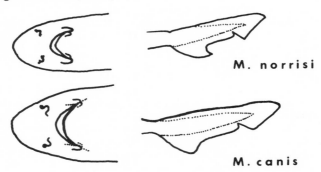

Fig. 2. Features of smooth dogfishes, genus *Mustelus*

1 Lower, anterior corner of caudal fin sharp-pointed, directed rearward . . . . Florida smoothhound, *Mustelus norrisi*.
Lower, anterior corner of caudal fin broadly rounded . . . . Smooth
dogfish, *Mustelus canis*.

19. Florida smoothhound *Mustelus norrisi* Springer

Dorsal origin behind pectoral so that midpoint is nearer to pelvic origin than to pectoral axil by one eye diameter; trunk slender; tail with lower corner sharp-pointed; probably grayish. This is a poorly known species. Florida to Texas. Briggs et al., 1964. (3 feet; 91 cm)

20. Smooth dogfish *Mustelus canis* (Mitchill)

Dorsal origin near rear corner of pectoral so that midpoint is as close to pectoral axil as to pelvic origin; trunk slender but fatter than that of Florida smoothhound; tail sometimes with lobe, but never sharp-pointed; grayish above, lighter below; dorsals with black trim; caudal with sooty spot near tip. Dogfish are commonly taken on hook and line at the snapper banks, but they also appear in trawls on the middle to outer shelf. We have not verified in-shore captures, although they have been reported. This is a cold temperate species common inshore from Cape Hatteras to Cape Cod. Bermuda; Bay of Fundy to Uruguay, including Cuba and Jamaica. (5 feet; 1½ m)

Sphyrnidae

The hammerhead sharks are among the most common sharks found in warm waters. The family possesses an exceptionally tall first dorsal fin which allows sharks cruising at the surface to be recognized.

The wide snout is thought to be an aid in locating prey by smell; it may also aid in disturbing food on the bottom and in increasing maneuverability. The shape of the head can be used to distinguish most species at a glance (Fig. 3). (Gilbert, 1967)

MOKARRAN   ZYGAENA   LEWINI   TUDES   TIBURO

Fig. 3. Hammerhead shark head shapes

1 Head spade-shaped; anterior margin of head not lobed . . . . Bonnethead, *Sphyrna tiburo.*
   Head hammer-shaped, anterior margin lobed 2
2 Anterior margin of head without a median notch . . . . Smooth hammerhead, *Sphyrna zygaena.*
   Anterior margin of head with distinct median notch 3
3 Free tip of second dorsal fin as long as height of second dorsal; cusps of teeth serrated . . . . Great hammerhead, *Sphyrna mokarran.*
   Free tip of second dorsal fin much longer than height of second dorsal; teeth not serrated on cusps 4
4 Center of eye well in front of mouth; posterior margin of anal weakly concave; posterior corner of head in front of corner of mouth; posterior margin of head straight . . . . Smalleye hammerhead, *Sphyrna tudes.*
   Center of eye about opposite front of mouth; posterior margin of anal deeply concave; posterior corner of head behind corner of mouth; posterior margin of head curved . . . . Scalloped hammerhead, *Sphyrna lewini.*

21. Bonnethead; bonnetnose   *Sphyrna tiburo* (Linnaeus)

Head rounded; dark spots on body; teeth smooth. Certainly one of the most common sharks, often occurring in schools, the bonnethead usually stays close inshore and in the saltier bays, feeding mostly on crabs. Eastern Pacific, and western Atlantic from Massachusetts through the Caribbean to Brazil. Hoese and Moore, 1958. (4 feet; 1¼ m)

22. Great hammerhead   *Sphyrna mokarran* (Rüppell)

Deep median indentation on head; deeply falcate pelvic fin; teeth serrate. This, the largest species of hammerhead, is sometimes known to attack humans. It is the common large hammerhead often reported as *S. tudes.* Circumtropical; in the western Atlantic from North Carolina through the Caribbean to Brazil. (15 feet; 4½ m)

23. Scalloped hammerhead   *Sphyrna lewini* (Griffith and Smith)
Median indentation on head; pelvic not falcate; second dorsal and anal with long extensions. This is the common hammerhead shark of our coast. Atlantic populations have been reported as *S. diplana* Springer. Another species of hammerhead with a small eye, *S. tudes* (=*S. bigelowi*), has been taken from off the mouth of the Mississippi River in the east central Gulf. It might be expected elsewhere in the Gulf. It is distinguished from *S. lewini* by having a more rounded head, smaller eyes, an inner narial groove, and a proportionally larger anal fin. The smooth hammerhead, *Sphyrna zygaena* (Linnaeus), is a cold temperate species which, although often reported, has not been verified for the Gulf of Mexico. Circumtropical; in the western Atlantic from New Jersey through the Caribbean to Brazil. (10 feet; 3 m)

Squalidae

The spiny dogfishes are distinctive sharks possessing spines before their dorsal fins and lacking anal fins. Like the smooth dogfishes, they have an oval eye. On the Atlantic coast, the common spiny dogfish, *Squalus acanthias* Linnaeus, ranges from Nova Scotia to Florida but is found south of Cape Hatteras only in winter. It is the common shark used in college biology laboratories.

24. Cuban dogfish   *Squalus cubensis* Howell Rivero
This is an upper slope species which might rarely venture onto the outer edge of the shelf. Northern Gulf to Brazil. (2 feet; 61 cm)

Squatinidae

Angel sharks are flattened, raylike fishes which have some characteristics linking them to rays but which seem to be as different from rays as from most sharks. Unlike rays, their pectoral fins are not attached in front. The gill openings are ventrolateral.

25. Atlantic angel shark   *Squatina dumerili* Lesueur
Broadly rounded, flattened head, with fairly well developed teeth; ta-

pered nasal barbel; brown to dark. This peculiar shark is another cold temperate species which resides in the Gulf on the outer shelf, rarely straying inshore. It has the habit of burying itself like many of the rays do. There is some question whether one or two species occur in the western Atlantic. The southern form, with a spatulate nasal barbel, is often called *S. argentina* Marini. Massachusetts to the West Indies and the Gulf; exact range uncertain. (5 feet; 1½ m)

Pristidae

The sawfishes are sharklike rays named for their long, toothed rostral process (saw), which they use to disturb bottom animals and to slash through schools of fish. There are two species in the Gulf, both entering low-salinity water and rarely fresh water. There are also similar true sharks called saw sharks (Pristiophoridae), but these occur in very deep water.

1 Caudal fin with a lower lobe; 16–20 rostral teeth . . . . Largetooth sawfish, *Pristis perotteti.*
  Caudal fin without a lower lobe; 25–32 rostral teeth . . . . Smalltooth sawfish, *Pristis pectinata.*

26. Largetooth sawfish *Pristis perotteti* Müller and Henle
Saw tapering, with relatively few large teeth. A tropical species not uncommon on the Texas coast during the summer, this sawfish is not verified from Louisiana but is to be expected there. Tropical Atlantic, in the west from southern Florida and eastern Texas to Brazil. (18 feet; 5½ m)

27. Smalltooth sawfish *Pristis pectinata* Latham
Saw tapering only slightly, with relatively many small teeth. Similar to the common sawfish, this species occurs close inshore. This is the common sawfish in the northern Gulf. Tropical Atlantic, in the west from New York and Bermuda to Brazil. (18 feet; 5½ m)

Rhinobatidae

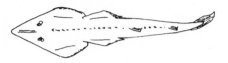

Guitarfishes are slender rays with pointed snouts and a few thorns on the median line of the back. They have small, rounded teeth used to crush small mollusks, crustaceans, and other animals they find on the bottom.

28. Atlantic guitarfish   *Rhinobatos lentiginosus* (Garman)

Rostrum translucent; gray to brown, with many small light spots on back, except in northwestern Gulf, where spots are often partly or wholly lacking. This fish, apparently an inshore shelf species, is often taken by trawlers. North Carolina to Florida and throughout the Gulf. (30 inches; 76 cm)

Torpedinidae

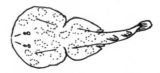

Electric rays or torpedos are flattened with a fairly large tail (for rays) extending from a more or less circular disc. They are unique among elasmobranchs in possessing electric organs—large, specialized muscles from each side of the anterior part of the disc rearward to nearly the end of the pectoral. These organs can be used to repel predators and perhaps to stun prey, or, as recent evidence in other electric fishes suggests, to receive information on the surrounding environment by perceiving changes in the electric current.

1   Disc wider than long; anterior margin nearly straight . . . . Atlantic torpedo, *Torpedo nobiliana.*
    Disc narrower than long; anterior margin rounded . . . . Lesser electric ray, *Narcine brasiliensis.*

29. Atlantic torpedo   *Torpedo nobiliana* Bonaparte

This dark-colored, large ray is a cold temperate species known from the northern Gulf only at the shelf edge off the Mississippi Delta. It has been reported more widely, but it may have been confused with the lesser electric ray. Atlantic Ocean, in the west from Nova Scotia to Trinidad. Bigelow and Schroeder, 1965. (6 feet; 1⅔ m)

30. Lesser electric ray   *Narcine brasiliensis* (Olfers)

Large kidney-shaped electric organs on pectorals; both dorsals similar in size; varying from gray, blue, or brown to very dark, with or without dark areas outlined by spots. This is the common electric ray in the Gulf, being limited to the inshore shelf, often in the surf zone. It can deliver a sizable shock of over thirty-five volts, which could disable a sensitive person. North Carolina to Brazil. (18 inches; 46 cm)

Rajidae

Skates are small rays with slender tails and varying degrees of armament, mostly in the form of small thorns and prickles. They resemble stingrays somewhat, but they have no tail spines, and they do have well-developed dorsal and caudal fins. Characteristic of the shelf bottom, their egg cases, called "mermaids' purses," are commonly washed ashore. (Bigelow and Schroeder, 1958, 1965; McEachran and Musick, 1975)

1 No large thorns on disc posterior to spiracles . . . . Spreadfin skate, *Raja olseni*.
   Disc with spines posterior to spiracles 2
2 Distance from origin of first dorsal to axils of pelvics as long as distance from axils of pelvics to front of orbits, or longer . . . . Freckled skate, *Raja lentiginosa*.
   Distance from origin of first dorsal fin to axils of pelvics shorter than or hardly longer than distance from axils of pelvics to rear of orbits 3
3 No ocellated spots on upper surface of pectorals . . . . Clearnose skate, *Raja eglanteria*.
   Ocellated spots on upper surface of pectorals . . . . Roundel skate, *Raja texana*.

31. Spreadfin skate *Raja olseni* Bigelow and Schroeder

Thorns lacking on middle of disc; pectoral fins broadly rounded but somewhat subanugular. This is an outer shelf–upper continental slope species (30–130 fathoms) closely related to the barndoor skate, *Raja laevis* Mitchill, of the Atlantic coast. Northern Gulf from the Florida panhandle to northern Mexico. (20 inches; 51 cm)

32. Freckled skate *Raja lentiginosa* Bigelow and Schroeder

Pectorals broadly rounded; disc midline with thorns; back speckled. This continental slope species occurs rarely on the lower shelf. Throughout the Gulf south to Nicaragua. (17 inches; 43 cm)

33. Clearnose skate *Raja eglanteria* Bosc

Rostrum translucent; no spots on back; central row of median spines on back with a few scattered to the side. This is the common skate of the eastern seaboard; it is also common in the northeastern Gulf, but was only recently reconfirmed for Texas. Massachusetts to at least eastern Texas. (3 feet; 91 cm)

34. Roundel skate *Raja texana* Chandler

Rostrum translucent; two ocellated spots on back; median row of spines on back. The common inshore and middle shelf skate of the northwestern Gulf, it was named by a parasitologist who, while studying its parasites, realized that it was unknown to science. This skate feeds mostly on mollusks and benthic polychaetes. Throughout the Gulf. (2 feet; 61 cm)

Dasyatidae

Stingrays possess one to many serrated spines on the tail which are covered with a toxin and can inflict painful wounds that often become infected. They are usually shy creatures and avoid humans if given the chance. Although stingrays are plentiful in the bay and gulf surfs, a swimmer or wader generally makes sufficient noise to scare away any that might be in his path. Stingrays may be safely handled by picking them up by the tip of the tail or by grasping them from the front with the thumb and forefinger in the spiracles.

Most stingrays are bottom animals, burying with only their eyes and spiracles showing, but the pelagic stingray, *Dasyatis violacea* (Bonaparte), which has a very blunt snout, occurs in the open ocean.

1   Caudal fin moderately developed; entire disc rounded . . . . Yellow
     stingray, *Urolophus jamaicensis*.
    Caudal fin tapering to a whiplike filament; portions of disc variously angled or rounded   2
2   Outer edges of disc broadly rounded   3
    Outer edges of disc subangular, not rounded   4
3   Snout anterior to eyes longer than distance between spiracles; no
     back fins on tail, only low cutaneous folds . . . . Atlantic stingray, *Dasyatis sabina*.
    Snout anterior to eyes shorter than distance between spiracles;
     black fins on tail . . . . Bluntnose stingray, *Dasyatis sayi*.
4   No cutaneous fold on upper surface of tail; sides of body and tail
     covered with tubercles or thorns . . . . Roughtail stingray, *Dasyatis centroura*.
    Upper surface of tail with low cutaneous fold; sides of body and
     tail without tubercles and thorns . . . . Southern stingray, *Dasyatis americana*.

35. Yellow stingray   *Urolophus jamaicensis* (Cuvier)

Body rounded, almost circular; tail with caudal fin; color a reticulum of darker lines on light background. Only recently confirmed for Texas, this fish is a rare tropical stray. North Carolina and through the Caribbean to Trinidad. (width 1 foot; 30 cm)

36. Atlantic stingray; stingaree   *Dasyatis sabina* (Lesueur)

Disc broadly rounded; snout pointed; tail very slender with low brownish fold dorsally and ventrally; brown, often tan. The common inshore stingray, this species is found from nearly fresh to marine salinities. It leaves the bay during the colder months, but stays on the inshore shelf. Known occasionally to enter Louisiana rivers, it is perhaps more common in Texas. Chesapeake Bay to at least northern Mexico. Sage et al., 1972. (width 2 feet; 61 cm)

37. Bluntnose stingray *Dasyatis sayi* (Lesueur)

Disc broadly rounded; snout rounded; tail slender with well-developed dusky to black fold on both sides of tail; dark, often nearly black. Large rays, often bearing young, are common inshore during the summer, but are rarely found in the bays. Massachusetts to Brazil. (width 3 feet; 91 cm)

38. Roughtail stingray *Dasyatis centroura* (Mitchill)

Disc subangular; snout somewhat pointed; tail relatively thick with many thorns and prickles and only lower tail fold; dark, with tail black. This ray is found in deeper water than most stingrays. Not much is known about it in the Gulf, but it is a cold temperate species common on the North Atlantic coast. North Atlantic, in the west from Massachusetts to South Carolina, and in the Gulf at least off Louisiana. (width at least 7 feet; 2 m)

39. Southern stingray *Dasyatis americana* Hildebrand and Schroeder

Disc subangular; snout somewhat pointed; tail slender, no thorns, with large lower fold but tiny upper fold, both black; disc gray or dark brown. An inshore ray over much of its range, it occurs in the northern Gulf from the saltier bays to the edges of offshore reefs. New Jersey through the Caribbean to Brazil. (width 5 feet; 1½ m)

Gymnuridae

Butterfly rays are similar to stingrays but have a very short tail and a disc about twice as broad as long. Their habits are poorly known but are thought to be similar to those of stingrays. The spiny butterfly ray, *Gymnura altavela* (Linnaeus), possibly occurs in the area as well. It can be recognized by the presence of a tail spine and a tentacle on the spiracle.

40. Smooth butterfly ray *Gymnura micrura* (Bloch and Schneider)

Disc broad, subangular; tail without spine; spiracle without tentacle; brown with dark blotches. This is a small ray that frequents the inshore shelf and saltier bays, where it prefers sandy bottoms. This habit may account for its apparent scarcity in Louisiana. Atlantic Ocean, in the west from Massachusetts to Brazil. (width 4 feet; 1¼ m)

Myliobatidae

Eagle rays are large, free-swimming rays with wide, pointed pectorals. The mouth is ventral and supplied with teeth modified as crushing plates for breaking shells of mollusks and crustaceans. Eagle rays have blunt snouts, no cephalic lobes, and a spine near the base of the tail. The genus *Myliobatis*, represented by at least one species in the Gulf, may also occur in the area. It is easily recognized, since it has seven series of teeth instead of the single series in *Aetobatus*, and it lacks the spotted back.

1   One subrostral lobe   2
     Two subrostral lobes . . . . Cownose ray, *Rhinoptera bonasus*.
2   Single series of teeth in each jaw; back spotted . . . . Spotted eagle ray, *Aetobatus narinari*.
     Seven series of teeth in each jaw; back unspotted . . . . *Myliobatis* sp. (probably southern eagle ray, *M. goodei*).

41. Cownose ray   *Rhinoptera bonasus* (Mitchill)

Disc broad; pectorals angular; slender tail with spine at base; brown; usually seven series of teeth. Large schools of these rays are found in the saltier bays and on the inshore shelf in summer, with masses often seen leaving at the onset of cold weather. Sometimes this species is put into a separate family Rhinopteridae, but it is very similar to the eagle rays. Massachusetts to Brazil. (width 3 feet; 91 cm)

42. Spotted eagle ray; duck-billed ray   *Aetobatus narinari* (Euphrasen)

Disc wide; pectorals angular; snout elongated somewhat like bill of a duck; brown to black with light spots on back; tail slender. Individuals occur sporadically on the shelf during the warmer months. Worldwide in temperate and tropical waters. (width 7 feet; 2 m)

Mobulidae

Manta rays are giant, free-swimming rays with large fins on their heads which, when unrolled, are used to channel larger plankton such as schools of small fishes and crustaceans into their mouth. The devil ray, *Mobula hypostoma* (Bancroft), occurs sporadically in the eastern Gulf and may be more widespread. It differs from the manta in having teeth in both jaws and a more terminal mouth.

43. Atlantic manta   *Manta birostris* (Walbaum)

Disc wide with pointed pectorals; tail long and slender; mouth terminal; teeth in lower jaw only. Large rays often in schools may be seen almost anywhere and have been captured in Corpus Christi Bay. They often frequent the surface and sometimes jump high out of the water, smacking the water flat to produce much noise and spray. At the surface they can be seen at a distance because of their habit of curling the pectoral tip up out of the water.

Young are born at a size of four or five feet (1–1½ m), and maturity is reached at about twelve feet (3½ m). Because of their large size (up to one and one-half tons) they are poorly represented in collections. Circumtropical, unless Pacific populations are distinct, in the western Atlantic from Massachusetts and Bermuda through the Caribbean to Brazil. (width 22 feet; 6⅔ m)

BONY FISHES
(OSTEICHTHYES)

THE so-called bony fishes have at least some bone in their skeletons, but they are more readily identified by having only one gill slit covered by an operculum. Actually there are usually three or four pairs of gill arches under the operculum. The sturgeons and the gars are considered the most primitive of the bony fishes, and the remainder are divided into a large number of orders. We have bypassed the orders for the families. Details of orders are available in many of the references.

Most bony fishes are egg layers (oviparous) of floating eggs, but in a few families (Gobiidae, Blenniidae, Clinidae, Batrachoididae, Gobiesocidae, and a few others) the females attach their eggs to hard objects such as shells. The marine catfishes (Ariidae) are mouth breeders, the male pipefishes (Syngnathidae) incubate the eggs in a pouch, and the live-bearers (Poeciliidae) give birth to living young. Most families have a pelagic, almost transparent larval stage, but in the toadfishes (Batrachoididae) the juveniles hatch directly from the egg. (Bigelow, 1963; Greenwood et al., 1966; Nelson, 1976)

Acipenseridae

Sturgeons are primitive fishes with naked skin embedded with bony plates (scutes). They have small, ventral mouths, preceded by barbels, for feeding on small bottom animals, but they may feed elsewhere, and they have been caught on hook and line. Most species are freshwater fishes, and those occurring in salt water are anadromous. Sturgeons are not common in the Gulf of Mexico, although specimens over 6 feet (1⅔ m) long are still caught.

44. Atlantic sturgeon *Acipenser oxyrhynchus* Mitchill

Scutes in dorsal rows 7–13, in lateral rows 24–35; other small ossifications in skin common. Gulf populations are considered a subspecies, *A. o. desotoi* Vladykov. A freshwater sturgeon, the shovelnose, *Scaphirhynchus platorhynchus* (Rafinesque), occurs in all the larger rivers of the area, but it is not believed to enter salt water. The pallid sturgeon, *S. albus* (Forbes and Richardson), may rarely enter low-salinity waters in Louisiana. Species of *Scaphirhynchus* are distinguished from *Acipenser* by their lack of a spiracle. Labrador and Bermuda to French Guiana; in the Gulf from the Florida west coast to Lake Pontchartrain and the vicinity of the Mississippi River mouth. Gowanloch, 1933; Vladykov, 1955. (14 feet; 4¼ m—but in the Gulf may be only 6 feet; 1⅔ m)

Lepisosteidae

Gars are freshwater fishes with great tolerance for salt water. Alligator gars especially are known to enter coastal bays and the Gulf of Mexico, where they have been found with crabs, mullets, and ducks in their stomachs. Three local species may be found in salt water. A fourth species, the shortnose gar, *Lepisosteus platostomus*, is found in coastal areas of Louisiana, but only in fresh water or extremely low salinities. It is recognizable by its short snout and lack of spots. (Suttkus, 1963)

1 Snout long and slender, nearly six times interorbital width; head length 32–41 percent of total length . . . . Longnose gar, *Lepisosteus osseus.*
   Snout short and broad, not more than three times interorbital width; head length less than 36 percent of total length   2
2 Gill rakers 59–81; row of enlarged teeth on palatines inside major tooth rows; spots, if present, largely limited to fins . . . . Alligator gar, *Lepisosteus spatula.*
   Gill rakers 15–24; no inner row of teeth; many dark spots on body and fins . . . . Spotted gar, *Lepisosteus oculatus.*

45. Longnose gar *Lepisosteus osseus* (Linnaeus)
D. 6–9; A. 8–10; P. 10–13; Sc. 57–63; Gr. 14–31; body olive above, white below, with dark spots on median fins and body. The longnose gar seems most common in coastal waters of the northwestern Gulf near and in Lake Pontchartrain. It may be expected in salt water, where it occurs close to the coast, especially in marsh channels. Atlantic coast from Canada to Florida, except in the New England region, and in the Great Lakes; south along the Mississippi drainage to the Gulf of Mexico and the northern Mexican coast. (5 feet; 1½ m)

46. Alligator gar *Lepisosteus spatula* Lacépède
D. 7–10; A. 7–10; P. 11–15; Sc. 58–62; Gr. 59–81; body olivaceous above, white below, with a few dark spots on body and median fins becoming indistinct with age. Alligator gars are common in brackish water, especially near marshes, and they even enter the Gulf of Mexico, where they are frequently seen gulping air near the surface. They are common market fish in

Louisiana and are fierce fighters. Little is known of their habits in salt water. *L. spatula* is replaced to the south by the similar *L. tropicus* (Gill). Mississippi and Ohio river drainages and along the coast of the Gulf of Mexico from the Florida panhandle to northern Mexico. (9 feet; 2¾ m)

47. Spotted gar *Lepisosteus oculatus* (Winchell)

D. 6–9; A. 7–9; P. 9–13; Sc. 53–59; Gr. 15–24; body olivaceous, darker than in other species of gar, with profusion of dark spots on fins and sides of body and head. This species does not enter salt water as readily as the alligator gar does, and it is usually confined to low salinities. Records of *L. productus* refer to this species. A rare gold-colored variant is also known. On the Florida peninsula it is replaced by the Florida gar, *L. platyrhincus* DeKay, which also may enter salt water. Great Lakes, along the Mississippi River, and in the Gulf of Mexico from western Florida to Corpus Christi. (4 feet; 1¼ m)

Elopidae

The tarpon and ladyfish are two representatives of this primitive family of bony fishes that is characterized by a gular plate, a hard, bony plate located at the center of the lower jaw. Both of these fishes are excellent game fish, although the ladyfish or tenpounder seldom exceeds three pounds. Tarpons, which are also known as silver kings or *grande écaille*, are commonly regarded as a prime inshore game fish, although their scarcity in recent years has greatly reduced the number of fishermen who pursue them. Ladyfish, tarpons, and the related bonefish possess an elongate, transparent larva called a leptocephalus, a larval type characteristic of eels, indicating a close relationship between these otherwise dissimilar fishes. (Hildebrand, 1963)

1 Last ray of dorsal fin produced . . . . Tarpon, *Megalops atlantica*.
Last ray of dorsal fin not produced . . . . Ladyfish, *Elops saurus*.

48. Tarpon *Megalops atlantica* Valenciennes

D. 13–15; A. 22–25; Sc. 41–48. The produced last ray of the dorsal fin, the large, silver, platelike scales, and the underslung mouth make the tarpon unmistakable. Young fish frequent low-salinity waters, often in small marsh channels, and the adults are often found far upstream in the larger rivers of South Texas. Tarpon and snook (*Centropomus undecimalis*) are very similar in many of their habits and requirements and frequently occur together, except that snook are more tropical. Atlantic Ocean, in the west from Nova Scotia through the Caribbean to Brazil. (8 feet; 2½ m)

49. Ladyfish; tenpounder; skipjack *Elops saurus* Linnaeus

D. 21–25; A. 14–17; Sc. 103–120. This smaller, finer-scaled relative of the tarpon is also a noted game fish. The common name tenpounder is derived from this small fish's fighting ability, not its actual weight. Leptocephali of *E. saurus* are found during most of the year, but their greatest abundance occurs in the late spring and early summer. Massachusetts and Bermuda through the Caribbean to Brazil. Herke, 1969. (3 feet; 91 cm)

Albulidae

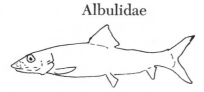

Bonefish are silvery bottom fish with a subterminal mouth and a sloping forehead. They differ from the elopids by lacking the gular plate, but they also have a leptocephalus larva. (Hildebrand, 1963)

50. Bonefish *Albula vulpes* (Linnaeus)
D. 17–18; A. 8–9; Sc. 65–71. The bonefish is a rare visitor to the coast of South Texas known from larvae and young fish up to about eighteen inches (46 cm) long. Bonefish are highly regarded sport fish in Florida and throughout the tropical Atlantic and Caribbean. Circumtropical; in the western Atlantic from Massachusetts and Bermuda through the Caribbean to Brazil. Leary, 1957; Hoese, 1965. (3 feet; 91 cm)

Anguillidae

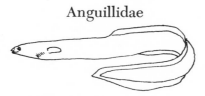

The American eel, *Anguilla rostrata*, is the only representative of this family in the western Atlantic.

51. American eel *Anguilla rostrata* (Lesueur)
This species is easily distinguished from other local eels by the presence of small, embedded scales in the skin. The edges of the tongue are free. Pectoral fins are well developed, and the dorsal, anal, and caudal fins are present and confluent. The American eel spawns in the Sargasso Sea, and the leptocephalus larvae then swim thousands of miles before they ascend freshwater streams, where they grow to maturity. Large eels are often caught in the bays during fall through spring. Greenland to the Guianas. (3 feet; 91 cm)

Muraenidae

Moray eels have the worst reputation of all the eels because of the vicious nature ascribed to the larger members of the family. The less well known smaller species are important members of the continental shelf fauna of the area. They are just as feisty as their larger relatives and should be handled with the same care. One additional species, the green moray, *Gymnothorax funebris*, which can be distinguished by its color, may also occur on offshore reefs. Also, two species of the tropical *Enchelycore* have been found at the Flower Gardens reefs. (Ginsburg, 1951a)

1   Teeth entire; two or three fangs on palate; reticulated brown on
    lighter background 2
    Teeth serrate; no fangs on palate; color solid or with white spots
    on darker background .... Ocellated moray, *Gymnothorax
    ocellatus*.
2   Inside of mouth purple; background color uniform .... Purple-
    mouth moray, *Gymnothorax vicinus*.
    Inside of mouth not purple; lower jaw pale; background color well
    marked, often separating reticulations into spots .... Spotted
    moray, *Gymnothorax moringa*.

52. Purplemouth moray   *Gymnothorax vicinus* (Castelnau)
This species is generally unpatterned, although a spotted race is known from elsewhere in its range. It is a tropical reef species as yet known in the area only from the 7½-Fathom Reef off South Texas. Atlantic Ocean, in the west from Bermuda, Florida, and the Bahamas through the Caribbean to Brazil. (2 feet; 61 cm)

53. Spotted moray   *Gymnothorax moringa* (Cuvier)
This moray is another tropical species—the common moray on the off-shore reefs. It is characterized by a brown or blackish speckled pattern on a white to yellow background. North Carolina to Brazil. (3 feet; 91 cm)

54. Ocellated moray   *Gymnothorax ocellatus* Agassiz
The ocellated moray is common over much of the middle shelf of the northern Gulf of Mexico. West of the Mississippi Delta it has been called *G. nigromarginatus* (Girard), and east of the delta, *G. saxicola* (Jordan and Davis), based on color differences illustrated in Plates 54a and b. Near the Mississippi River mouth, however, intergrades are common, and some specimens are identical in color to *G. ocellatus* originally described from Brazil. Local populations probably are part of a wide-ranging species perhaps divisible into subspecies. This is the common moray caught by shrimpers. Large individuals have dark, sometimes greenish dorsals, anals, and posterior bodies. Northern Gulf and North Carolina to Brazil. (2 feet; 61 cm)

Muraenesocidae

The pike congers are silvery eels with very slender bodies and long jaws supplied with canines above and below, the most conspicuous being the vomerine fangs in the upper jaw. (Lane and Stewart, 1968)

1 Two lateral rows of vomerine teeth 2
  No lateral rows of vomerine teeth .... Silver conger, *Hoplunnis macrurus.*
2 Lateral vomerine teeth movable and concealed by flesh of mouth; five or six branchiostegals .... *Hoplunnis diomedianus.*
  Lateral vomerine teeth fixed and not concealed; seven branchiostegals .... *Hoplunnis tenuis.*

55. Silver conger   *Hoplunnis macrurus* Ginsburg

The silver conger is distinguished by its large palatal teeth, lizardlike head, and bright, silvery sides. It is the most abundant eel in shrimp trawls in the inshore Gulf. A second species, *H. tenuis* Ginsburg, with two lateral rows of vomerine teeth, has also been described, but its status is uncertain. Another species with these teeth, *H. diomedianus*, is known from the northeastern Gulf. *H. macrurus* has no lateral vomerine teeth. Both *H. tenuis* and *H. diomediana* are deepwater species which may occur at the edge of the shelf. Northern Gulf to Surinam. (20 inches; 51 cm)

Congridae

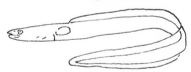

Although conger eels are among the most common of fishes, most coastal residents have never seen one. Less spectacular than the morays, these eels are most apt to be encountered at night. The life histories of all species are poorly known at best. Like the ophichthids, few are known by common names other than "conger eel." In addition to these species, one deeper-living eel, *Conger oceanicus*, has been rarely found near the Mississippi Delta. (Kanazawa, 1958)

1 Dorsal origin near anus; tail shorter than body .... Slender pike eel, *Neoconger mucronatus.*
  Dorsal origin near pectoral fin insertion; tail longer than body 2
2 Snout projecting well past lower jaw 3
  Snout projecting only slightly; jaws subequal 4
3 Body depth under 4 percent of length; tail over 70 percent of

length; palatal teeth in wedge-shaped patch, the posteriormost teeth large .... Whiptail conger, *Congrina gracilior.*

Body depth over 4.5 percent of length; tail less than 70 percent of length; palatal teeth in oblong patch; all teeth of similar size .... Yellow conger, *Congrina flava.*

4   Upper end of gill opening as high as upper end of pectoral; dorsal origin behind pectoral origin and near posterior end of pectoral fin .... Margintail conger, *Paraconger caudilimbatus.*

Upper end of gill opening only as high as center of pectoral fin base; dorsal origin over pectoral base .... *Uroconger syringus.*

56. Whiptail conger   *Congrina gracilior* Ginsburg
Yellow conger   *Congrina flava* (Goode and Bean)

A greenish eel with a long snout, *Congrina* is a very abundant eel on the middle shelf, but the species is uncertain. Tail lengths (see species key) vary from very short and blunt to extremely long and tapering; it appears that the tails are subject to damage and heal well enough to disguise the damage. Also, the shape of the tooth patch is variable. Further study is necessary, but probably only one species is present, in which case *C. flava* would be the correct name. *Congrina macrosoma* (Ginsburg, 1951a) from off the Isles Dernieres is definitely a stubby version of *C. flava*. Northern Gulf of Mexico to Trinidad. (3 feet; 91 cm)

57. Slender pike eel   *Neoconger mucronatus* Girard

Gill opening low on side; dorsal origin over or behind anus. This eel is seldom seen because of its nocturnal habits. It is apparently common on the middle and inner shelf, with small specimens seen inshore. Off the Mississippi Delta to southern Texas, Cuba, and Colombia. Smith and Castle, 1972. (2 feet; 61 cm)

58. Margintail conger   *Paraconger caudilimbatus* (Poey)

Gill opening extending to upper pectoral base; dorsal origin after pectoral base. Another poorly known but distinctive eel with golden hues on its body, this conger is widespread on at least the middle shelf of the Gulf of Mexico and Cuba. Kanazawa, 1961. (1 foot; 30 cm)

59. ———   *Uroconger syringus* Ginsburg

Gill opening extending to lower pectoral base; dorsal origin reaches pectoral base. A rare eel known only from off South Texas. (1 foot; 30 cm)

Ophichthidae

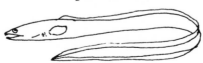

The snake and worm eels are common in many habitats, where they burrow tail-first into the sediments. The snake eels are characterized by a hard, pointed, finless tail; the worm eels, on the other hand, possess a tail fin. The worm eels were formerly considered to be in a separate family (Echelidae); however, they have recently been included in the Ophichthidae. The Ophichthidae have recently been reviewed and revised to the generic level by McCosker (1973), and the genus *Bascanichthys* has been revised by Leiby (unpublished), but much work still needs to be done, particularly on the genus *Echiophis* and its three uncertain, hard-to-separate species. The spotted snake eel, *Ophichthus ocellatus* (Lesueur), illustrated in the color plates as no. 63*b*, is common from off Mississippi to North Carolina but is not known to the west. (Ginsburg, 1951*a*; McCosker, 1973)

1   Caudal fin rays conspicuous and continuous with dorsal and anal fins; gill opening constricted   2
    Caudal fin rays lacking, with tip of tail a hard or fleshy finless point; gill opening not constricted   3
2   Origin of dorsal fin in front of anus; palatine (vomerine) teeth numerous . . . . Speckled worm eel, *Myrophis punctatus.*
    Origin of dorsal fin above or behind anus; at most, only one or two palatine teeth . . . . Key worm eel, *Ahlia egmontis.*
3   Dorsal origin behind gill opening; tail longer than body; pectoral fin well developed   4
    Dorsal origin ahead of gill opening; tail shorter than body; pectoral fins not well developed . . . . Whip eel, *Bascanichthys* sp.
4   Jaws subequal; eye over middle of upper jaw; teeth not fanglike . . .   5
    Jaws about equal; eye anterior to middle of upper jaw; some teeth long and fanglike   6
5   Tail longer than body (about 55 percent of total length); dorsal origin over or before end of pectoral . . . . Shrimp eel, *Ophichthus gomesi.*
    Tail equal to or shorter than body; origin of dorsal behind end of pectoral; dark bands on body . . . . Banded shrimp eel, *Ophichthus* sp.
6   Largest spots same size as or larger than snout   7
    Largest spots smaller than snout length, in six rows . . . . Stippled spoon-nose eel, *Echiophis punctifer.*
7   Largest spots same size as snout length . . . . Snapper eel, *Echiophis mordax.*
    Largest spots as big as snout plus eye length . . . . Spotted spoon-nose eel, *Echiophis intertinctus.*

60. Speckled worm eel   *Myrophis punctatus* Lütken
This is one of the more common eels found on mud bottoms inshore and in the bays, even occasionally coming into fresh water. Only the juveniles are found inshore, with the strange leptocephalus larvae that probably come from offshore spawning areas appearing on the coast from December through May. North Carolina to Brazil. (2 feet; 61 cm)

61. Key worm eel   *Ahlia egmontis* (Jordan)
This tropical worm eel is so far known in this area only from 7½-Fathom Reef. Florida through the Caribbean to Brazil. (16 inches; 41 cm)

62. Whip eel *Bascanichthys* sp.

This very slender eel is common in the bays and shallow Gulf where hard-packed fine sand occurs. The nominal species *B. teres* (Goode and Bean) is now considered as a synonym of *B. scuticaris* (Goode and Bean), which occurs in the eastern Gulf. Alabama to Texas. Leiby, pers. comm. (2 feet; 61 cm)

63. Shrimp eel *Ophichthus gomesi* (Castelnau)

The shrimp eel is a very common inshore eel usually found in muddy habitats in the shallow Gulf of Mexico and the high-salinity bays. Massachusetts to Brazil. (2 feet; 61 cm)

64. Banded shrimp eel *Ophichthus* sp.

This unusually large eel has its dark bands more prominent anteriorly. It is known so far only from the northwestern Gulf off Louisiana and from Port Aransas. (6 feet; 1⅔ m)

65. Stippled spoon-nose eel *Echiophis punctifer* (Kaup)
Snapper eel *Echiophis mordax* (Poey)
Spotted spoon-nose eel *Echiophis intertinctus* (Richardson)

These three species of spotted snake eels are closely related or else may represent differently spotted variants of just one or two species. Their habits are not well known, but all occur on the inshore to middle shelf and may occasionally be found in the saltier bays. Large individuals are caught from the Galveston and Port Aransas jetties during the fall months. The appellation "spoon-nose" comes from the unusually flattened skull found in large individuals. All three species were formerly placed in the genus *Mystriophis*. Total range from North Carolina through the Caribbean to Brazil, but details uncertain. (4 feet; 1¼ m)

Dysommidae

The so-called arrowtooth eels are poorly known fishes which differ from the conger eels by having a row of canines on the upper jaw. Similar also to the pike congers, they differ from them by having jaws more typical of an eel and no canines in the lower jaw. (Ginsburg, 1951a; Robins and Robins, 1970)

66. Shortbelly eel *Dysomma aphododera* Ginsburg

Tail much longer than body; jaws long, with lower jaw about 40 percent of head length; tongue adnate; three median canines on palate. This is a poorly known eel, known only from the middle to outer shelf in the western Gulf, unless, as Robins and Robins (1970) suggest, it is a synonym with the probably worldwide *D. anguillare* Barnard. Southern Texas to Campeche. (1 foot; 30 cm)

Clupeidae

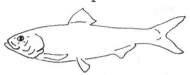

The herrings are schooling fishes occurring in masses of seemingly innumerable individuals that move together as if coordinated by some unseen force. They are important as food for many of the larger species of fish, including important sports and commercial species. In the Gulf of Mexico the menhaden support a sizable commercial fishery. The North Atlantic herring fishery is also well known, and other species of clupeids are exploited in other parts of the world.

Some tropical species not included in this discussion may occur far offshore in the summer. A good introduction to these may be found in Hildebrand, Rivas, and Miller (1963) and Berry (1964). *Harengula* was revised by Rivas (1950), *Dorosoma* by Miller (1960), *Opisthonema* by Berry and Barrett (1963), *Etrumeus* by Whitehead (1963), and *Brevoortia* by Dahlberg (1970).

1   Body rounded; abdomen with ordinary scales   2
    Body compressed; abdomen with keel of modified scales   3
2   Pelvic fins much smaller than pectorals, inserted behind base of
       dorsal . . . . Round herring, *Etrumeus teres*.
    Pelvic fins only slightly smaller than pectoral fins, inserted under
       base of dorsal . . . . Dwarf herring, *Jenkinsia lamprotaenia*.
3   Back in front of dorsal fin scaled; fewer than 150 gill rakers   4
    Back in front of dorsal fin with unscaled median strip; more than
       150 gill rakers   10
4   Vertical edge of shoulder girdle under opercle with two lobes
       (Fig. 4)   5
    Vertical edge of shoulder girdle under opercle smooth, not lobed . .   7

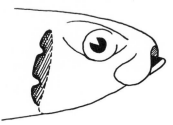

Fig. 4. Shoulder girdle of *Opisthonema*, *Sardinella*, and *Harengula*, showing projecting lobes

5   Last ray of dorsal fin extended, with length about twice dorsal
       height; 20–25 anal rays . . . . Atlantic thread herring, *Opis-
       thonema oglinum*.
    Last ray of dorsal same length as rest; 15–20 anal rays   6
6   Last two anal rays enlarged, almost finletlike; 41–47 scale rows
       . . . . Spanish sardine, *Sardinella anchovia*.

Last two anal rays normal; 34–41 scale rows . . . . Scaled sardine, *Harengula pensacolae.*

7 Median scales in front of dorsal normal; eight or nine pelvic rays . .   8
Median scales in front of dorsal enlarged; seven pelvic rays   9

8 Teeth usually lacking in adults; body deep, 25–36 percent of standard length; lower margin of upper jaw at a 45-degree angle; gill rakers on lower limb more than 40 . . . . Alabama shad, *Alosa alabamae.*

Teeth always present in lower jaw; body slender, 24–28 percent of standard length; lower margin of upper jaw nearly vertical except at tip; gill rakers on lower limb fewer than 30 . . . . Skipjack herring, *Alosa chrysochloris.*

9 Scale rows 36–50; preopercle striated; shoulder spot in adults usually followed by smaller spots . . . . Gulf menhaden, *Brevoortia patronus.*

Scale rows 60–75; preopercle smooth; shoulder spot single . . . . Finescale menhaden, *Brevoortia gunteri.*

10 Mouth terminal; fewer than 50 scale rows; last dorsal ray twice height of dorsal fin; anal rays 27 or fewer . . . . Threadfin shad, *Dorosoma petenense.*

Mouth subterminal or inferior; more than 50 scale rows; last dorsal ray less than 1.5 times height of dorsal fin; more than 25 anal rays . . . . Gizzard shad, *Dorosoma cepedianum.*

67. Round herring   *Etrumeus teres* (DeKay)

D. 16–20; A. 10–12; P. 14–16; Sc. 48–55; Gr. 14 + 32–38. The round herring is a poorly known species occurring over much of the shelf. It is often considered to be in a separate family, the Dussumieridae. The name *E. sadina* Mitchill is often used for Atlantic populations. Bay of Fundy to northern Florida and in the northern Gulf of Mexico; also in the North Pacific. Fore, 1971. (6 inches; 15 cm)

68. Dwarf herring   *Jenkinsia lamprotaenia* (Gosse)

D. 9–13; A. 12–15; P. 10–13; Sc. 33–37; Gr. 19–24 on lower limb; scales usually lost in preservation; greenish above with distinct silver lateral band. Dwarf herring occur in large schools, probably numbering in the millions, chiefly inshore throughout the tropical western Atlantic, but they apparently are rare in the northwestern Gulf. Bermuda, Florida, and the Bahamas through the Caribbean to Venezuela. Bullis and Thompson, 1965. (2 inches; 5 cm)

69. Atlantic thread herring; hairyback   *Opisthonema oglinum* (Lesueur)

D. 17–21; A. 21–25; P. 15–17; Gr. 40–100 + ; body silvery, greenish on back, with dark humeral spot; some Gulf specimens showing additional spots, usually with row of less distinct spots behind humeral spot but sometimes with short row of spots along base of dorsal fin and mid-dorsal row after dorsal fin; dorsal and caudal fins yellow. The fish is fairly common in saltier waters and possibly represents an unexploited fishery. Large schools occur, although the fish is often taken singly inshore. Cape Cod and Bermuda to Brazil. (10 inches; 25 cm)

70. Spanish sardine *Sardinella anchovia* Valenciennes

D. 17–19; A. 16–18; P. 15–16; Sc. 41–46; Gr. 55–125; body fairly elongate, with no shoulder spot. The Spanish sardine is reported from Galveston Bay and Caminada Pass and is not rare in the northeastern Gulf; however, it is primarily a tropical species. It may be confused with the deeper-bodied scaled sardine. The name *S. aurita* refers to this species. Massachusetts and Bermuda through the Caribbean to Brazil. (6 inches; 15 cm)

71. Scaled sardine *Harengula pensacolae* Goode and Bean*

D. 17–20; A. 16–18; P. 13–17; Sc. 39–43; Gr. 34–40; relatively deep-bodied, with silvery sides, greenish above; often with a dark humeral spot. This is the most common inshore clupeid on the continental shelf, except where it is replaced inshore off Louisiana by the menhaden. It sometimes enters high-salinity estuarine areas. East coast of Florida (rarely Georgia) throughout the Gulf of Mexico and Caribbean to Brazil. (6 inches; 15 cm)

72. Alabama shad *Alosa alabamae* Jordan and Evermann

D. 16–20; A. 19–22; P. 16–17; Sc. 55–60; Gr. 42–48. Alabama shad is an anadromous species, rare west of the Mississippi River and not known west of Grand Isle or east of the Florida panhandle. (20 inches; 51 cm)

73. Skipjack herring *Alosa chrysochloris* (Rafinesque)

D. 16–21; A. 18–21; P. 16–17; Sc. 51–60; Gr. 20–24 on lower limb. This is an anadromous fish rare west of the Mississippi River, where it probably occurs only as a stray. It has been caught in salt water from Pensacola to Corpus Christi. Single adults appear in low salinities in Louisiana during the fall and winter. It is sometimes placed in the genus *Pomolobus*. (18 inches; 46 cm)

74. Gulf menhaden *Brevoortia patronus* Goode

D. 17–21; A. 20–23; P. 14–17; Sc. 36–50; Gr. 40–150; body silvery, greenish on back, with dark humeral spot and usually with series of smaller spots behind humeral one. This is the commercial "pogy," with the center of its abundance off western Louisiana. Juveniles are found in very low salinity marshes, and the adults are only rarely taken far offshore. Throughout the Gulf of Mexico. (10 inches; 25 cm)

75. Finescale menhaden *Brevoortia gunteri* Hildebrand

D. 17–20; A. 20–25; P. 15–16; Sc. 60–75; Gr. 97–150. In general appearance *B. gunteri* is like *B. patronus*, except that it is much more silvery and it never has more than one spot on its sides. Although it is known from the entire area, this fish is more common off southern Texas. The very closely related *B. smithi* Hildebrand may rarely occur in the Chandeleurs and replaces *B. gunteri* in the eastern Gulf. It differs by a number of overlapping characteristics, making identification difficult. Chandeleur Islands to Yucatán. (10 inches; 25 cm)

---

* Whitehead (1973) presents evidence that the correct name for this species is *H. jaguana* Poey.

76. Threadfin shad *Dorosoma petenense* (Günther)

D. 11–14; A. 17–27; P. 12–17; Sc. 41–48; Gr. 300+. The threadfin shad is a freshwater fish known to enter the bays, especially in the summer and fall. Throughout the central United States and Gulf, south to Belize. (7 inches; 18 cm)

77. Gizzard shad *Dorosoma cepedianum* (Lesueur)

D. 10–13; A. 25–36; P. 14–17; Sc. 52–70; Gr. 300+. This is another freshwater fish, but one common in low-salinity bays. Atlantic drainages of North America and Mexico. (12 inches; 30 cm)

Engraulidae

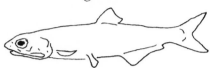

The anchovies are the most abundant of the schooling, pelagic fishes. Although most of the local species are not large enough to be of commercial importance, they serve as food for many of the larger commercial and sports fishes. Only four species of anchovies have been confirmed from the northwestern Gulf of Mexico, but other tropical species should be expected offshore during the summer. Although individuals of the four species of *Anchoa* are occasionally found together, the schools are usually limited to distinct areas. (Hildebrand, 1964; Daly, 1970)

1   Posterior part of maxilla square or rounded, not reaching mandible . . . . Flat anchovy, *Anchoviella perfasciata*.
    Posterior part of maxilla pointed, reaching mandible 2
2   Anal fin origin under origin of dorsal fin . . . . Bay anchovy, *Anchoa mitchilli*.
    Anal fin origin under or behind midpoint of dorsal fin 3
3   Gill rakers thin and usually more than 45; upper jaw hardly projecting . . . . Cuban anchovy, *Anchoa cubana*.
    Gill rakers usually fewer than 45; upper jaw clearly projecting 4
4   Snout projecting beyond lower jaw more than 6.5 percent of standard length; gill rakers on lower limb of first arch 24–28; anal fin origin behind end of dorsal fin . . . . Longnose anchovy, *Anchoa nasuta*.
    Snout projecting beyond lower jaw less than 6.5 percent of standard length; gill rakers on lower limb of first arch 18–24; anal fin origin at midpoint of first dorsal . . . . Striped anchovy, *Anchoa hepsetus*.

78. Flat anchovy *Anchoviella perfasciata* (Poey)

D. 12–15; A. 15–18; P. 14–16; Sc. about 40–44; Gr. 19–23 + 24–28; sides with distinct silvery lateral band, nearly as broad as eye. The status of this species in the western Gulf is not known, but it is occasionally taken in the northeastern Gulf. As indicated by its occurrence elsewhere, it should be expected over much of the continental shelf. Tropically distributed, it is known from the West Indies, the northeastern and southern Gulf of Mexico, and the Atlantic coast from Florida to North Carolina. It is generally found inshore but is not known to enter brackish water. (4 inches; 10 cm)

79. Bay anchovy   *Anchoa mitchilli* (Valenciennes)
D. 14–16; A. 24–30; P. 11–12; Sc. 38–40; Gr. 15–19 + 21–23; sides with silvery lateral band scarcely as wide as pupil of eye. This is an extremely common fish, restricted to the bays and close inshore areas. The local subspecies is *A. m. diaphana*. The species ranges from Maine to Florida and also occurs throughout the Gulf of Mexico, but it is rarely taken from the Florida Keys or from Yucatán. (4 inches; 10 cm)

80. Cuban anchovy   *Anchoa cubana* (Poey)
D. 14–16; A. 20–24; Sc. 40–43; Gr. 17–23 + 23–33. This is a slender anchovy poorly known from scattered specimens from Louisiana. Throughout the Caribbean to the northern Gulf. (2½ inches; 6 cm)

81. Longnose anchovy   *Anchoa nasuta* Hildebrand and Carvalho
D. 14–16; A. 21–24; P. 12–15; Gr. 19–23 + 24–28; Scales usually lost in preservative. A poorly known species, this anchovy occurs in schools over the continental shelf, with occasional individuals straying inshore. Its distribution may at times overlap that of other anchovies, but it is usually found in deeper water. Large schools appear reddish on the surface when seen from a distance; the explanation for this phenomenon is not clear. The taxonomy of this species is also confused, as it has been reported under the name *A. lyolepis* (Evermann and Marsh), a species which does not occur in the Gulf and from which *A. nasuta* can be distinguished by the higher number of gill rakers. North Carolina to Brazil. (2½ inches; 6 cm)

82. Striped anchovy   *Anchoa hepsetus* (Linnaeus)
D. 13–17; A. 18–24; P. 13–17; Sc. 37–43; Gr. 15–20 + 18–24; sides with silvery stripe about 75 percent as wide as eye. This common species is usually found farther offshore than the bay anchovy. These are fish of saltier, clearer waters and may be found from the beach to the middle shelf. Nova Scotia through the Caribbean to Uruguay. (5½ inches; 14 cm)

Synodontidae

The lizardfishes (also known as cigarfishes) are a family of mostly small, benthonic, carnivorous fishes. All are elongate and possess a fleshy, adipose fin. They are occasionally caught on hook and line, and they show up regularly in shrimp trawls; however, they are of no commercial value. In some parts of the southern United States they are mistakenly believed to be poisonous. A large lizardfish might inflict a painful bite, but none of them are known to possess any toxin or venom. One species, *Saurida normani*, is known from the northeastern but not the northwestern Gulf. (Anderson, Gehringer, and Berry, 1966*a, b*)

1   Ventral rays eight, with inner rays much longer than outer rays; single band of teeth on each side of palate 2
     Ventral rays nine, with inner rays about as long as outer ones; double row of teeth on each side of palate 6
2   Anterior profile rounded; anal fin origin about midway between base of caudal fin and insertion of pectoral fin; anal fin closer to origin of ventral fins than to base of caudal; anal fin base more than 23 percent of standard length; anal rays 14–16 ....
     Snakefish, *Trachinocephalus myops*.
     Anterior profile pointed; anal fin origin much nearer to base of caudal fin than to insertion of pectoral fins; anal fin origin closer to caudal base than to origin of ventrals; anal fin base only 18 percent of standard length; anal rays 8–13, rarely 14 ... 3
3   Scales in lateral line more than 52 (usually 54–65) 4
     Scales in lateral line fewer than 52 (usually 43–50) 5
4   Anal rays usually 10–13; anterior rays of dorsal fin reaching past tips of posterior rays when fin is depressed .... Inshore lizard-fish, *Synodus foetens*.
     Anal rays usually 8–10; anterior rays of depressed dorsal fin not reaching past posterior rays .... Red lizardfish, *Synodus synodus*.
5   Dorsal fin with anterior rays not extending beyond tips of posterior rays when fin is depressed; lower jaw rounded and without fleshy knob at tip; black patch on shoulder girdle under gill cover .... Sand diver, *Synodus intermedius*.
     Dorsal fin with anterior rays extending to and usually beyond tips of posterior rays when fin is depressed; lower jaw ending in fleshy knob; no black patch on shoulder girdle under gill cover .... Offshore lizardfish, *Synodus poeyi*.
6   Scales in lateral line 40–50 .... Largescale lizardfish, *Saurida brasiliensis*.
     Scales in lateral line 51–60 .... Smallscale lizardfish, *Saurida caribbaea*.

83. Snakefish   *Trachinocephalus myops* (Forster)

D. 11–13; A. 14–16; P. 11–13; Sc. 53–59; anterior profile rounded; dark spot at the upper corner of gill opening. The snakefish is a tropical species, usually found on coarse bottoms from twenty to over two hundred fathoms. Circumtropical; in the western Atlantic from Massachusetts and Bermuda through the Caribbean to Brazil. (7 inches; 18 cm)

84. Inshore lizardfish   *Synodus foetens* (Linnaeus)

D. 10–13; A. 10–14; P. 12–15; Sc. 56–65; adults brownish with greenish tint on back; small fish with distinctive spots along back (generally true for all lizardfishes; for key to juveniles of this family, see Gibbs, 1959). Regularly occurring inshore and in the bays, this is the only lizardfish which commonly enters brackish water; however, the larger individuals occur farther offshore in depths out to one hundred fathoms. The scientific name *foetens* refers to the fetid smell which the fish rapidly develops when left out in the sun. Massachusetts and Bermuda through the Caribbean to Brazil. (16 inches; 41 cm)

85. Red lizardfish; rockspear   *Synodus synodus* (Linnaeus)

D. 12–14; A. 8–10; P. 11–12; Sc. 54–59. This bright red tropical species is known here only from an offshore reef, and it is probably limited to such habitats. Tropical Atlantic, in the west from the northern Gulf, the Bahamas, through the Caribbean to Brazil. (6 inches; 15 cm)

86. Sand diver   *Synodus intermedius* (Spix)

D. 11–13; A. 10–12; P. 11–13; Sc. 42–52. The large dark spot on the shoulder, partly covered by the opercle, makes this species the synodontid with the most distinctive color pattern. This species is most common in 20 to 60 fathoms; however, it has been collected in depths between 8 and 175 fathoms. North Carolina and Bermuda through the Caribbean to Brazil. (18 inches; 46 cm)

87. Offshore lizardfish   *Synodus poeyi* Jordan

D. 11–12; A. 9–12; P. 10–12; Sc. 43–48. A dark fleshy knob at the tip of the lower jaw sets this species apart. It is an offshore species usually found between 15 and 175 fathoms; its distribution is much the same as that of *S. intermedius*. (6 inches; 15 cm)

88. Largescale lizardfish   *Saurida brasiliensis* Norman

D. 9–12; A. 10–13; P. 11–13; Sc. 43–49; usually three and sometimes four complete rows of scales between dorsal fin and lateral line. Generally found between 10 and 125 fathoms, this species is not rare in the middle shelf region. North Carolina to Brazil and Africa. (4 inches; 10 cm)

89. Smallscale lizardfish   *Saurida caribbaea* Breder

D. 10–12; A. 11–12; P. 12–13; Sc. 54–60; always four complete rows of scales between dorsal fin and lateral line. Generally found in 3 to 250 fathoms, this species has been reported only once from the western Gulf of Mexico. North Carolina to Brazil. Bullis and Thompson, 1965. (3 inches; 8 cm)

Ictaluridae

Although several freshwater catfishes occur in the coastal plain, only a single species regularly enters salt water. Channel catfish, *Ictalurus punctatus*, is an important commercial fish, but it only rarely ventures into very low salinities. (Perry, 1969)

90. Blue catfish   *Ictalurus furcatus* (Lesueur)

D. I, 5–6; A. 32–35. Eight barbels easily separate the blue catfish from the saltwater catfishes. The long anal fin, with usually three to eight more rays, and the absence of spots on the body distinguish the blue catfish from the channel catfish. Its color is variable, but often light blue to slate blue. A very common fish in low salinities, normally entering open bay waters in winter, it is caught commercially on trotlines and set lines over much of the Louisiana coast and in some areas of Texas. Mississippi Valley west to Mexico; Gulf coast from at least Mobile Bay to the central Mexican coast. (18 inches; 46 cm—larger in fresh water)

Ariidae

The sea catfishes have two representatives in the northwestern Gulf of Mexico. Both species resemble "typical" catfishes, with naked skin and large serrated spines on the dorsal and pectoral fins. Both species also have the oral incubation habit in which the males carry the fertilized eggs in their mouths.

Catfishes may be safely handled by firmly grasping the body from the front with the whole hand so that the fingers push against the backsides of the erect pectoral spines and the front of the erect dorsal spine.

1   Barbels on lower chin rounded, six in number; dorsal and pectoral
        fins without elongated first rays . . . . Sea catfish, *Arius felis.*
     Barbels on lower chin flattened, four in number; dorsal and pecto-
        ral fins with elongated first rays . . . . Gafftopsail catfish, *Bagre
        marinus.*

91. Sea catfish; hardhead (tourist trout; TR)   *Arius felis* (Linnaeus)

D. I, 7; A. 16; sides blue or gray; venter white; barbels relatively short. The hardhead is quite abundant in the bays and the shallow Gulf. The species is generally considered to be a pest by most fishermen and is rarely eaten by man. Hardheads are known for their diverse food habits, and their young have been observed scraping the sides of other fish, presumably feeding on the mucus, scales, and ectoparasites. There is evidence that these fish possess "sonar." For many years this species was placed in the genus *Galeichthys,* which is now considered to be a synonym of *Arius.* Massachusetts to Mexico. Ward, 1957; Hoese, 1966a; Tavolga, 1971. (2 feet; 61 cm)

92. Gafftopsail catfish; gafftop   *Bagre marinus* (Mitchill)

D. I, 7; A. 23; sides light blue; venter white; barbels and first rays of pectoral and dorsal fins elongate. Common in the bays and shallow Gulf, the larger individuals of the species are good food fish, unlike the hardheads, which may or may not taste good. Massachusetts to Panama. (2 feet; 61 cm)

Batrachoididae

The toadfishes are primarily benthonic fishes, spending most of their time near or even buried in the bottom. They attach their eggs to hard substrates and have no free-swimming larval stages. Some members of the family are highly venomous; however, of the local species only the midshipman has venom, and even it has no serious effects on large organisms like humans. On the other hand, large toadfishes can inflict painful bites with their powerful jaws, but their blunt teeth usually do not break the skin.

1   Dorsal spines three; opercle with two strong, diverging spines   2
    Dorsal spines two; opercle very small but with single spine; sides
        of body and venter lined with buttonlike photophores . . . .
        Atlantic midshipman, *Porichthys porosissimus.*
2   Background color light, overlaid with brown spots as large as pupil
        of eye covering head, body, and fins; pectoral fins with brown
        spots on light background . . . . Leopard toadfish, *Opsanus
        pardus.*
    Background color dark, overlaid with lighter crossbars or by a
        mottled pattern, but not as above; pectoral fin with light cross-
        bars, each composed of row of definite light spots . . . . Gulf
        toadfish, *Opsanus beta.*

93. Atlantic midshipman   *Porichthys porosissimus* (Valenciennes)
    D. II + 34–36; A. III, 30–37; P. 15–20; sides and ventral surface of body covered with regularly arranged rows of photopores; body light tan to golden on sides, often with large or small brown blotches. Fishes living in areas with predominantly light sediments show a lighter pattern than most midshipmen from the northwestern Gulf of Mexico. The opercle is small but ends in a sharp spine, by which the fish's venom may be injected. Members of the genus *Porichthys* are the only North American shore fishes which possess photopores, and the common name and a former generic name, *Nautopaedium,* refer to the rows of photopores, which resemble the buttons on a nineteenth-century naval midshipman's uniform. Virginia to Argentina. Lane, 1967. (8 inches; 20 cm)

94. Leopard toadfish   *Opsanus pardus* (Goode and Bean)
    D. III + 25–26; A. III, 20–23; P. 20–21; body with light background covered by darker spots. This species is found offshore on reefs and other rocky areas. From the southern U.S. Atlantic coast throughout the tropical Gulf and Caribbean. Moseley, 1966a; Causey, 1969. (1 foot; 30 cm)

95. Gulf toadfish; oyster dog (dogfish; mudfish)   *Opsanus beta* (Goode and Bean)
    D. III + 23–26; A. III, 19–23; P. 19–20; body dark, with irregular light

blotches or crossbars. Gulf toadfish are common in the bays, on oyster reefs, and around jetties. Small individuals sometimes enter sunken cans or jars and subsequently grow to fill them and become trapped while feeding on other animals which also seek shelter in the containers. Found from Cape Sable, Florida, through the Gulf of Mexico to Yucatán, and in the West Indies. This species is replaced on the Atlantic coast north of Cape Sable by the closely related species, *O. tau*. (15 inches; 38 cm)

Gobiesocidae

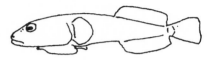

Clingfishes are a group of small, bottom-dwelling fishes often called skilletfishes because of their large flat heads and slender bodies. They have a complicated sucker composed jointly of the underside of their body, their pectoral fins, and their ventral fins. Only one species is known from the in-shore area, but other species may be expected to occur offshore on reefs. A specimen of a second species of *Gobiesox*, *G. punctulatus*, in the U.S. National Museum is supposed to have been collected near Corpus Christi, Texas (Schultz, 1944). This species differs from *G. strumosus* in lacking the papillae on the head and the upper lip and in the various fin ray counts, most notably the pectoral with 19–22 rays and the caudal with 7–9 rays.

96. Skilletfish *Gobiesox strumosus* Cope
    D. 10–13; A. 9–11; P. 22–26; C. 11–13; body usually plain, sometimes with longitudinal streaks; vertical fins dark, often black; pectoral fins lighter than vertical fins; upper lip and head with well-developed papillae. A wide-ranging species reported from New Jersey to Brazil. Older records of this species refer to it as *Cotylis nigripinnis*. Briggs, 1955. (3 inches; 8 cm)

Antennariidae

The frogfishes are rather grotesque creatures characterized by having the first two dorsal spines detached and modified into a movable "fishing rod," the illicium, which is complete with "lure." The batfishes (Ogcocephalidae) also share this trait, but their illicium is more concealed. In both families the shape of the "lure" differs in the different species and is used as an important taxonomic distinction. Frogfishes have distensible stomachs which allow them to eat fish longer than themselves. (Schultz, 1957)

1   Two fleshy cirri on dorsal midline before first modified dorsal spine
        . . . . Sargassumfish, *Histrio histrio*.

No cirri on snout in front of first modified dorsal spine 2
2   End of illicium bulbous; dorsal rays 13; anal rays 8 . . . . Single-
    spot frogfish, *Antennarius radiosus.*
    End of illicium forked (bifid); dorsal rays 11–12; anal rays 6–7
    . . . . Splitlure frogfish, *Phrynelox scaber.*

97. Sargassumfish   *Histrio histrio* (Linnaeus)

D. I + I + 12 (incl. illicium); A. 6; numerous cirri about mouth and
head, with two on the dorsal midline before illicium being characteristic of
the species. The coloration of this fish closely resembles that of the *Sargassum*
weed in which the fish usually lives, but is quite variable when the fish is
found elsewhere. In general the body is tan, variously mottled, streaked, and
spotted with cream, yellow, and darker brown. The fish is found in all warm
seas, wherever *Sargassum* is found. *H. gibba* is a synonym. (6 inches; 15 cm)

98. Singlespot frogfish   *Antennarius radiosus* Garman

D. I + I + I + 13; A. 8; illicium bulbous; body dark brown or gray
with single large, ocellated spot at base of soft dorsal fin. This species is common on the middle shelf off most of the coastline. It has been included in
Phrynelox. Bermuda; Georgia south through the Gulf. (3 inches; 8 cm)

99. Splitlure frogfish   *Phrynelox scaber* (Cuvier)

D. I + I + I + 11–12; A. 6–7; illicium bifid, Y-shaped; body either
plain or pale purple with dark brown stripes and spots and with spots on fins.
The plain color phase has been described as a separate species, *P. nuttingi*
(Garman). This species is not as common here as the preceding is, and it
occurs farther offshore. New Jersey to Brazil, including the West Indies. (5
inches; 13 cm)

Ogcocephalidae

The grotesque family of flattened batfishes causes a great amount of
wonder the first time a representative is seen. They are fairly common inhabitants of the shelf and deeper areas and occur regularly in shrimp trawls.
They frequent the bottom, using a downward projecting "bait" (known as the
esca), located between the mouth and the tip of the rostrum, to attract food
out of the bottom. As in the related frogfishes, the shape of the "bait" can be
used to separate genera and species. The generic limits of the batfishes have
been revised, but as yet a much-needed work on the taxonomy of the different species has not appeared. Batfishes, together with practically all other
ugly fishes, are colloquially called "dogfish."

Due to the confusion in application of names, the species occurring in
the Gulf and their ranges are uncertain. Besides the species below, all of
which occur off Louisiana, Texas, and at least part of Mexico, three additional
species are known in the Gulf: (1) the tricorn batfish, *Zalieutes mcgintyi,* with

two longitudinal rows of bucklers on the underside and a three-pointed rostrum, primarily a slope species; (2) the roughback batfish, *Ogcocephalus parvus*, with 10–11 pectoral rays, wide bands on the outer part of the pectorals, a short rostrum, and a triangular body, known from the shelf of the northeastern but not the northwestern Gulf; and (3) *Ogcocephalus* sp., with a long rostrum, a triangular body, and pectorals with an outer band, known from the shelf of the northeastern but not the northwestern Gulf. (Bradbury, 1967 and personal communication)

1   Dorsal fin usually with four rays; dorsal body outline triangular;
       eyes lateral   2
     Dorsal fin with five to seven rays; dorsal body outline rounded;
       eyes partly dorsal   3
2   Pectoral rays 10–11; pectoral fin with a few small spots not in
       reticulated pattern; tips without fleshy pads on ventral side . . . .
       Ogcocephalus sp.
     Pectoral with 12–13 rays; pectoral fin and shoulder with numerous
       brown spots forming reticulated pattern; tips with fleshy pads
       on ventral surface . . . . Polka-dot batfish, *Ogcocephalus radiatus.*
3   Vomer and palatines with teeth; two and one-half gill arches; disc
       circular; esca not lobed . . . . Pancake batfish, *Halieutichthys aculeatus.*
     Vomer and palatines toothless; two gill arches; disc oval to subtriangular; esca lobed . . . . Offshore batfish, *Dibranchus atlanticus.*

100. ——— *Ogcocephalus* sp.
     D. 4; A. 4; P. 10–11; head narrowly triangular, but body behind pectorals relatively thick; pectorals and body not spotted; back very rough; rostrum short and not upturned. This is perhaps the most common middle shelf batfish from Louisiana to northern Mexico. In the past it has been confused with *O. parvus* Longley and Hildebrand because of its pectoral ray counts. (6 inches; 15 cm)

101. Polka-dot batfish   *Ogcocephalus radiatus* (Mitchill)
     D. 4; A. 4; P. 12–13; head broadly triangular, with body behind pectorals relatively thin; body and pectorals spotted, often with reticulations on fin; rostrum short and upturned. This seems to be the common inshore species from Louisiana to Mexico. It has been reported as *O. vespertilio* and *O. cubifrons.* (1 foot; 30 cm)

102. Pancake batfish   *Halieutichthys aculeatus* (Mitchill)
     D. I, 4–5; A. 4; P. 16–18; head rounded; no rostrum; pectorals and caudal banded; body very flat; brown. This is a common species on the middle shelf, but its young may be taken inshore. North Carolina at least to the Lesser Antilles and throughout the Gulf. (4 inches; 10 cm)

103. Offshore batfish   *Dibranchus atlanticus* Peters
     D. 6–7; A. 4; P. 13–15; head oval to subtriangular; tail long. This continental slope species rarely occurs on the shelf. Atlantic ocean, in the west

from Rhode Island to at least the Lesser Antilles and the northern Gulf of Mexico.

Bregmacerotidae

The codlets are small midwater fishes related to the cod family. A single species occurs in the northwestern Gulf of Mexico.

104. Antenna codlet   *Bregmaceros atlanticus* Goode and Bean

D. I + 15, X, 16; A. 15–16, X, 21–22; Sc. 65; dorsal and anal fins with centermost rays depressed. The greatly elongate ventral fins and single free dorsal ray give this fish its common name and make it rather distinctive. Common on the middle shelf in the northwestern Gulf, it is seldom caught except in plankton nets because of its small size and habit of migrating off the bottom at night. It is widespread in the Gulf, and it or a similar species is widespread in the western Atlantic. Dawson, 1966. (2 inches; 61 cm)

Gadidae

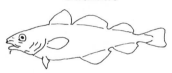

The codfishes are mostly fishes of the deeper, colder waters; however, a few regularly occur inshore, and one species even regularly enters the bays. Despite their importance as food fishes elsewhere, none are fished in the Gulf. Only juvenile cod usually occur on the shelf. The Merlucciidae and Macrouridae, two families of codlike fish sometimes included in the Gadidae, occur even farther offshore. *Physiculus fulvus* Bean, with six or seven ventral rays, a well-developed chin barbel, and villiform teeth, has been reported once from inside one hundred fathoms, although it usually occurs well outside this depth. (Svetovidov, 1948)

1 Dorsal and anal rays more than 100; tail tapering . . . . Luminous
    hake, *Steindachneria argentea.*
    Dorsal and anal rays fewer than 75; tail with distinct caudal fin   2
2 Dorsal rays 62–68; anal rays 55–59 . . . . Gulf hake, *Urophycis*
    cirratus.
    Dorsal rays 40–59; anal rays 42–53   3
3 Dorsal rays usually 48; anal rays usually 45; length of mandibular
    barbel less than one-half eye diameter . . . . Spotted hake,
    Urophycis regius.
    Dorsal rays normally 57; anal rays normally 50; mandibular barbel

more than one-half eye .... Southern hake, *Urophycis florida-nus.*

105. Luminous hake *Steindachneria argentea* Goode and Bean

D. VIII + 123+; A. 10 + 113; Sc. very small and numerous; head large, with gradually tapering body and tail (often damaged) ending in filament; body silvery, not luminous; eye large. A continental slope species, it is common on the steep outer and middle shelf off the Mississippi River mouth, where it was first discovered nearly a century ago. Sometimes put in the Macrouridae or Steindachneriidae. Its range is uncertain. Marshall and Cohen, 1973. (1 foot; 30 cm)

106. Gulf hake *Urophycis cirratus* (Goode and Bean)

D. 10 + 66; A. 57; Sc. 93; Gr. 2 + 12; first dorsal fin without elongate rays; ventral fins very long, reaching beyond origin of anal fin; body light, silvery, tan on back, spotted below. The Gulf hake occurs in the northern Gulf of Mexico often deeper than one hundred fathoms, but young are found inshore to the middle shelf. At least southern Texas to southern Florida. (1 foot; 30 cm)

107. Spotted hake *Urophycis regius* (Walbaum)

D. 8–9 + 46–51; A. 43–49; P. 16; Sc. 89–97; Gr. 3 + 12; brown, darker above; first dorsal fin black with white border; lateral line darker than rest of body, with row of pale spots along it; face with two rows of dark spots but without facial bars. Because of confusion with the southern hake, the spotted hake's range is uncertain, but it is at least in the northeastern Gulf and in the Atlantic up to Massachusetts. (16 inches; 41 cm)

108. Southern hake *Urophycis floridanus* (Bean and Dresel)

D. 12–13 + 54–59; A. 40–49; Sc. 110–112; Gr. 2 + 11; back brown, belly silvery; lateral line dark with row of pale spots; first dorsal black, without white margin; other vertical fins brown with darker margins. Normally an offshore species, the young move into shallow water and saltier bays during the winter months. North Carolina to Mexico. (9 inches; 23 cm)

Ophidiidae

The cusk-eels and closely allied brotulids are now generally considered to be one family instead of two. These are curious, elongate fishes possessing filamentous ventral fins. Most are highly nocturnal, remaining hidden in crevices or in burrows in the mud during the daylight hours. Primarily deep-water fishes, two brotulids are found in the shallow northwestern Gulf. Five cusk-eels have also been found. The specific names and generic affinities of the commoner species of cusk-eels are still in a state of flux pending a major revision of the group.

1	Ventral fins inserted well forward near anterior tip of lower jaws (Ophidiidae of authors)	2
	Ventral fins inserted below shoulder gridle (Brotulidae of authors) ..	6
2	Snout with a decurved spine (hook) at tip; head scaly on top	3
	Snout without a decurved spine; head scaleless; scales of body rudimentary	4
3	Dorsal and anal fins blackedged .... Blackedge cusk-eel, *Lepophidium graellsi*.	
	Dorsal and anal fins with large dark spots along margin .... Mottled cusk-eel, *Lepophidium jeannae*.	
4	Sides of body variously mottled, striped, or blotched	5
	Sides of body plain .... Bank cusk-eel, *Ophidion holbrooki*.	
5	Sides of body with three or four longitudinal stripes .... Crested cusk-eel, *Ophidion welshi*.	
	Sides of body spotted .... Blotched cusk-eel, *Ophidion grayi*.	
6	Caudal fin distinct, separated from dorsal and anal fins .... Gold brotula, *Gunterichthys longipenis*.	
	Caudal fin continuous with dorsal and anal fins	7
7	Lower jaw and snout with barbels .... Bearded brotula, *Brotula barbata*.	
	Lower jaw and snout without barbels .... *Neobythites gillii*.	

109. Blackedge cusk-eel *Lepophidium graellsi* (Poey)

This fish is the most common cusk-eel in the northwestern Gulf. When brought up in a shrimpers net, the pale silver blue color of the body takes on an irridescent sheen which lasts only as long as the fish remains alive. Earlier literature refers to this species as *L. brevibarbe* (Cuvier), the short-bearded cusk-eel. Northern Gulf of Mexico and perhaps to Brazil. (8 inches; 20 cm)

110. Mottled cusk-eel *Lepophidium jeannae* Fowler

Common in the eastern Gulf, it occurs as far west as eastern Mississippi. Also Georgia to Florida and off Yucatán. (8 inches; 20 cm)

111. Bank cusk-eel *Ophidion holbrooki* (Putnam)

This plain-sided cusk-eel with dark-edged fins is uncommon in the northwestern Gulf of Mexico, although there have been several reports from Texas in the bays and on 7½-Fathom Reef and from off eastern Louisiana. It is more common in the northeastern Gulf of Mexico and occurs as far north as Georgia and the Carolinas. Several undescribed species similar to *O. holbrooki* are probably present in the northwestern Gulf as well. Nichols and Breder, 1922; Causey, 1969. (8 inches; 20 cm)

112. Crested cusk-eel *Ophidion welshi* (Nichols and Breder)

The second most abundant cusk-eel from the shrimp grounds, this species is distinguished from the related *O. grayi* by its possessing complete stripes instead of blotches on its sides. Large males (over six inches) are distinguished by a swollen nape or crest. Originally described as *Otophidium welshi*. A similar cusk-eel, *Ophidion* (*Rissola*) *marginatum* (DeKay), has also been reported from the northwestern Gulf of Mexico. We have been unable to verify its presence, and, pending completion of a revision of the genus, we are referring all western Gulf records of striped cusk-eels to *O. welshi*. Throughout the Gulf of Mexico, especially common in the northwestern Gulf. Recorded on the Atlantic coast from Georgia and possibly New Jersey. (8 inches; 20 cm)

113. Blotched cusk-eel   *Ophidion grayi* (Fowler)

This rare fish is only recorded twice from Texas waters but is more common off eastern Louisiana. It is the only spotted cusk-eel in the northwestern Gulf. *Otophidium omostigmum*, the other spotted cusk-eel (found in the eastern Gulf) has a prominent humeral spot. Georgia to Yucatán and Florida to at least Texas. (8 inches; 20 cm)

114. Gold brotula   *Gunterichthys longipenis* Dawson

D. 64–68; A. 45–50; P. 18–21; caudal fin distinct; no scales on top of the head; maxillary with horizontal expansion; males with single pair of genital claspers. This distinctive pink or gold little fish has been reported before under a variety of names. It was described as a species only in 1966. It has been reported from 7½-Fathom Reef as *Ogilbia* sp. and from areas near Port Aransas either as that or as *Dinematichthys* sp. Southern Texas to Mississippi. Dawson, 1966c, 1971a; Moore, 1975b. (2 inches; 5 cm)

115. Bearded brotula   *Brotula barbata* (Bloch and Schneider)

The body of the bearded brotula is brownish red, and the small fish are covered with many dark spots and distinctive stripes on the cheeks which are lost with growth. This is a fairly common fish on the rocky areas of our coast. Small fish are found over muddy bottoms in the shallow Gulf, while slightly larger fish are found near the jetties, where they perplex anglers when caught. Large fish, which are good eating, have been caught on the offshore banks. Bermuda and Florida to Jamaica and throughout Gulf. (3 feet; 91 cm)

116. ——   *Neobythites gillii* Goode and Bean

Body compressed, its depth about 21.5 percent of total length; head longer than body depth and 22 percent of total length; interorbital space convex, equal to diameter of eye, 27.3 percent of head length; scales on body in 88 vertical, 7 horizontal rows above and 16–17 rows below lateral line (on diagonal from origin of dorsal fin to vent); yellow or tan with irregular dark blotches on dorsum, with two largest blotches extending onto dorsal fin (these may be the only apparent marks). Recorded from fifty-three fathoms to eighty-five fathoms off Port Aransas and seventy-five fathoms off Grand Isle, this species is not usually considered a part of the shelf fauna. Gulf of Mexico to Brazil. (6 inches; 15 cm)

Carapidae

Pearlfishes are long, slender animals with no ventral fins. They are designed to live inside other animals such as mollusks and sea cucumbers in a close symbiotic relationship. Some are parasites for at least part of their life.

117. Pearlfish   *Carapus bermudensis* (Jones)

A very elongate, tapering, transparent fish that lives inside tropical sea cucumbers. The relationship is thought to be commensalism, but study is needed. This species is found elsewhere throughout the tropical western Atlantic, but it is not known in the western Gulf. Bermuda; Bahamas; southern Florida through the Caribbean to Venezuela; in the Gulf from Florida to Mississippi. Dawson, 1971*b*; Haburay et al., 1974. (7 inches; 18 cm)

Exocoetidae

The exocoetids include the flyingfishes and the halfbeaks. The latter have often been placed in a separate family, Hemiramphidae, but Greenwood et al. (1966) consider the two groups too closely related to warrant separation. The flyingfishes are best characterized by their elongate pectoral fins by which they are able to glide for considerable distances. The nonflying halfbeaks frequently jump from the water or skip over the surface, and some halfbeaks possess relatively long pectorals which aid them in their extended leaps. There are flyingfishes with shorter pectorals (approaching the condition usually seen in halfbeaks) and halfbeaks which lack the elongate lower jaw which is generally characteristic of the group. The presence of such intermediate types makes the separation into two families difficult. Ecologically, however, there are two groups: those which are basically offshore species living more than two hundred miles from land, and those which are inshore species living closer than two hundred miles from land and entering the bays. Here, too, the division is not absolute, since several offshore species occasionally venture into inshore waters. Generally, few flyingfishes come very close to shore. (Bruun, 1935; Breder, 1938; Miller, 1945; Staiger, 1965)

1   Lower jaw elongate, much longer than upper jaw   2
    Lower jaw not elongate, scarcely if at all longer than upper jaw . .   4
2   Pectoral fins very short, less than one-half length of lower jaw . . .   3
    Pectoral fins long, more than one-half length of lower jaw . . . .
      Flying halfbeak, *Euleptorhamphus velox*.
3   Dorsal fin inserted above anal fin origin; upper lobe of caudal about as long as lower lobe; snout with scales . . . . Halfbeak, *Hyporhamphus unifasciatus*.
    Dorsal inserted well before anal fin origin; lower lobe of caudal much longer than upper lobe; snout without scales . . . . Ballyhoo, *Hemiramphus brasiliensis*.
4   Pectorals short, scarcely reaching insertion of ventral fins . . . .
    Smallwing flyingfish, *Oxyporhamphus micropterus*.
    Pectorals long, reaching well beyond origin of dorsal fin   5
5   Pectorals reaching well beyond end of dorsal fin; ventral fins long, reaching past anal origin, or else very short, reaching no more than halfway to anal origin   6

Pectorals reaching only to middle of dorsal base; ventral fins moderate, reaching no farther than anal origin . . . . Sailfin flyingfish, *Parexocoetus brachypterus.*

6　Ventral fins short, inserted nearer to snout than to caudal base and failing to reach anal origin by their own length . . . . Oceanic two-wing flyingfish, *Exocoetus obtusirostris.*

　　Ventral fins long, inserted nearer to caudal base than to snout and reaching well beyond anal origin 7

7　Origin of dorsal fin over origin of anal fin; anal rays equal to or greater than dorsal rays in number . . . . Blackwing flyingfish, *Hirundichthys rondeleti.*

　　Origin of dorsal fin anterior to origin of anal fin; anal rays fewer than number of dorsal rays 8

8　First and second rays of pectoral fin simple, unbranched; third pectoral ray bifurcate . . . . Bluntnose flyingfish, *Prognichthys gibbifrons.*

　　First ray of pectoral simple, second bifurcate 9

9　Dorsal with prominent dark spot covering all, most of, or just upper area of fin . . . . Margined flyingfish, *Cypselurus cyanopterus.*

　　Dorsal without spot 10

10　Pectorals grayish, with light outer margin narrower than diameter of pupil and with inconspicuous light cross-band . . . . Atlantic flyingfish, *Cypselurus heterurus.*

　　Pectorals nearly black, with broad, light outer margin wider than diameter of eye and with prominent light crossband . . . . Spotfin flyingfish, *Cypselurus furcatus.*

118. Flying halfbeak　*Euleptorhamphus velox* Poey

D. 22; A. 21; pectorals long, greater than one-half length of lower jaw. This halfbeak is an offshore species capable of short flights. Massachusetts and Bermuda to Hispaniola. (2 feet; 61 cm)

119. Halfbeak　*Hyporhamphus unifasciatus* (Ranzani)

D. 14–16; A. 15–17; body silvery, greenish above; tip of jaw red. This is the most common inshore halfbeak in the northwestern Gulf of Mexico, and it commonly enters the bays. Maine through the Caribbean to Argentina. (8 inches; 20 cm)

120. Ballyhoo　*Hemiramphus brasiliensis* (Linnaeus)

D. 12–15; A. 11–15; body silvery, greenish on back; upper lobe of caudal fin and dorsal fin orange; tip of lower jaw orange. The similar balao, *H. balao*, with a red-tipped lower jaw, may also occur here. Atlantic Ocean, in the west from New England through the Caribbean to Brazil. (15 inches; 38 cm)

121. Smallwing flyingfish　*Oxyporhamphus micropterus* (Valenciennes)

D. 13–15; A. 14–15; Sc. 51–53; mandible produced as in halfbeaks in small individuals up to two inches (50 mm) standard length. The similarity of this fish to the halfbeaks has, in the past, led to its inclusion in a third, separate family, the Oxyporhamphidae. Circumtropical; in the western Atlantic in offshore waters from North Carolina to Brazil.

122. Sailfin flyingfish   *Parexocoetus brachypterus* (Richardson)

D. 11–12; A. 12–13; Sc. 39–42; pectoral fin intermediate in length, only reaching middle of dorsal base. Breder (1938) differentiates two subspecies on the basis of the relative length of the ventral fins and jaw proportions. Both forms occur from Cape Cod to Brazil in offshore waters, usually more than four hundred miles from land. (6 inches; 15 cm)

123. Oceanic two-wing flyingfish   *Exocoetus obtusirostris* Günther

D. 12–14; A. 12–14; Sc. 38–42; juveniles of this species, less than 1⅝ inches (40 mm) in standard length, are quite high-bodied, with depth about 25–30 percent of standard length, decreasing to 20–23 percent in adults. As the common name implies, this species is usually found farther offshore than most of the other species. In offshore waters from about 40° N (New Jersey) to Brazil. (6 inches; 15 cm)

124. Blackwing flyingfish   *Hirundichthys rondeleti* (Valenciennes)

D. 11–12; A. 12–13; Sc. 42–49. The blackwing is the common inshore flyingfish of the northwestern Gulf of Mexico, its young occurring even in the bays. The most noteworthy characteristic of the species is the black coloration of the pectorals and ventrals. Atlantic Ocean, in the west from Massachusetts and Bermuda to Columbia. (10 inches; 25 cm)

125. Bluntnose flyingfish   *Prognichthys gibbifrons* (Valenciennes)

D. 12; A. 9–10; Sc. 33; ventrals very long, reaching past caudal origin. This is another offshore species in Atlantic oceanic waters. In the west from Massachusetts to Brazil. (8 inches; 20 cm)

126. Margined flyingfish   *Cypselurus cyanopterus* (Valenciennes)

D. 11–14; A. 8–11; Sc. 50–53; prominent dark spot on upper part of dorsal fin, most apparent in specimens over 4¾ inches (120 mm) in standard length (below this size spot may cover entire dorsal fin); pectoral fins evenly pigmented, not banded; body silvery, darker on back, with no banding apparent even in juveniles. This is essentially a coastal species, rarely occurring more than four hundred miles offshore, but not venturing into the nearshore areas, either. Tropical Atlantic, in the west from New Jersey to Brazil. (1 foot; 30 cm)

127. Spotfin flyingfish   *Cypselurus furcatus* (Mitchill)

D. 11–15; A. 8–12; Sc. 47–50; adults pale silvery on venter, darker dorsally, with dorsal fin only sparsely pigmented; juveniles with six dark bands on body which disappear with age; pectoral fins with clear V-shaped area between dark blotches. Atlantic Ocean, in the west from New Jersey and Bermuda to Brazil. (1 foot; 30 cm)

128. Atlantic flyingfish   *Cypselurus heterurus* (Rafinesque)

D. 10–15; A. 8–12; Sc. 46–52; adults darker dorsally, silver ventrally and pectorals with a pale, narrow band along posterior border; juveniles with body banded as in *C. furcatus*, and pectorals with two large pigment spots along first ray and third spot at base of fin. Atlantic Ocean, in the west from Nova Scotia to Brazil. (16 inches; 41 cm)

Belonidae

The needlefishes are elongate fishes with both jaws prolonged into a beak. The jaws are well supplied with teeth, indicating the carnivorous habits of all the species. (Berry and Rivas, 1963; Collette and Berry, 1965)

1 Dorsal rays 12–17 2
   Dorsal rays 21–26 3
2 Gill rakers present; caudal peduncle compressed dorsoventrally
   . . . . keeltail needlefish, *Platybelone argalus.*
   Gill rakers absent; caudal peduncle not compressed . . . . Atlantic needlefish, *Strongylura marina.*
3 Anal rays 25–28; head and body compressed laterally . . . . Flat needlefish, *Ablennes hians.*
   Anal rays 18–22; body not strongly compressed laterally . . . .
   Houndfish, *Tylosurus crocodilus.*

129. Keeltail needlefish   *Platybelone argalus* (Lesueur)

D. 12–15; A. 17–19; P. 11; Gr. (only in this species among the belonids) 1–5 + 4–9; lower jaw projecting beyond upper jaw by about one-fourth of its length (when both jaws unbroken). This is primarily an offshore, tropical species. The name *Strongylura* (or *Belone*) *longleyi* refers to this species (Berry and Rivas, 1962). Circumtropical; in the western Atlantic from the Carolinas through the Gulf of Mexico and West Indies and in the Bahamas. (15 inches; 38 cm)

130. Atlantic needlefish (needlegar); saltwater gar   *Strongylura marina* (Walbaum)

D. 14–17; A. 16–20; P. usually 11 in both, but sometimes 10 or 12 in one or both; both jaws approximately equal in length; no gill rakers. This species is quite common in the inshore Gulf and bays during the spring and summer, and it even ascends far up rivers. *S. timucu* is generally regarded as a synonym, and reports of *S. notata* from Texas are probably based on *S. marina. S. notata* differs from *S. marina* in possessing 13–15 dorsal rays and 13–16 anal rays. Massachusetts to Brazil, including Cuba and Jamaica. (2 feet; 61 cm)

131. Flat needlefish   *Ablennes hians* (Valenciennes)

D. 23–26; A. 25–28; P. usually 14 in both, rarely 15 in both; no gill rakers; jaws about equal; body strongly compressed, not rounded or square in cross-section; sides silvery; back green. Usually found offshore, this species is apparently quite rare. Probably circumtropical; in the western Atlantic from Massachusetts and Bermuda through the Caribbean to Brazil. (3 feet; 91 cm)

132. Houndfish *Tylosurus crocodilus* (Peron and Lesueur)
D. 22–24; A. 18–22; P. 14 in both; no gill rakers; jaws approximately equal; body somewhat compressed laterally, but not as noticeably as in flat needlefish; sides silvery; back green. This fish is primarily found in off-shore waters, but it ventures inshore occasionally. *Tylosurus* (or *Strongylura*) *raphidoma* (Ranzani) refers to this species. Atlantic Ocean, in the west from Massachusetts through the Caribbean to Brazil. (2 feet; 61 cm)

Scomberesocidae

A single representative of the sauries probably occurs here.

133. Atlantic saury *Scomberesox saurus* (Walbaum)
D. 10–11 + V; A. 12–13 + VI; Sc. 115. The saury is an epipelagic fish to be expected in the open waters of the Gulf far from land. Although not reported from the northwestern Gulf of Mexico, this fish may certainly be found when collections can be made in the proper offshore habitat. It resembles a large needlefish, but differs by possessing a series of five dorsal and six ventral finlets behind the dorsal and anal fins, respectively. A temperate fish, it is found around the world. (18 inches; 46 cm)

Cyprinodontidae

The killifishes are shore fishes which venture or are driven into the open bay waters only under extreme conditions such as low temperatures. All tolerate a wide range of salinities, so the same species can be found inhabiting freshwater marshes in Louisiana as well as the hypersaline Laguna Madre of Texas. Most of the species also invade coastal fresh water. They normally lack brillant colors; however, the males develop irridescent blues during the breeding season. In coastal fresh water about four additional species may be expected, but these are absent from marine or brackish waters. Keys including these forms are given by Eddy (1969), Blair et al. (1968), Rosen (1973), and Douglas (1974). The goldspotted topminnow,

Floridichthys carpio, is common on the Florida peninsula and is sometimes confused with *Cyprinodon*. (Kilby, 1955; Simpson and Gunter, 1956; Forman, 1968a, b; Rosen, 1973)

1   Dorsal fin origin closer to caudal base than to preopercle   2
    Dorsal fin origin closer to preopercle than to caudal base   5
2   Snout length more than two times eye diameter; body with about
      15 dark vertical bars, the last with dark spot dorsally . . . .
      Longnose killifish, *Fundulus similis*.
    Snout length less than two times eye diameter; body sometimes
      with bars but never with dark spot on last   3
3   Dorsal fin origin posterior to anal fin origin; fewer than 15 scales
      rows in front of ventral fin origin; large black spots on body in
      two irregular rows . . . . Saltmarsh topminnow, *Fundulus jen-
      kinsi*.
    Dorsal fin origin anterior to or over anal fin origin; more than 15
      scale rows in front of ventral fins   4
4   Males with only faint vertical stripes at best; females without
      markings; distance between eyes one-third of head length . . . .
      Gulf killifish, *Fundulus grandis*.
    Males with 12–14 distinct vertical bars; females with spots; dis-
      tance between eyes about one-half of head length; upper jaw
      length less than one-third of head length . . . . Bayou killifish,
      Fundulus pulvereus.
5   Teeth compressed, with three cusps; more than 15 scale rows
      in front of ventral fins   6
    Teeth conical, without cusps; 8–13 scale rows before ventrals;
      sides of body mottled . . . . Sheepshead minnow, *Cyprinodon
      variegatus*.
6   Body with vertical bars; 9–10 dorsal rays . . . . Diamond killifish,
      Adinia xenica.
    Body with no large markings; 10–12 dorsal rays . . . . Rainwater
      killifish, *Lucania parva*.

134. Longnose killifish   *Fundulus similis* (Baird and Girard)

D. 11–13; A. 10; Sc. 33. This is a fairly large killifish not usually found in very low salinities. The long snout and the spot on the caudal peduncle distinctively mark the species. There is evidence that this species is identical to the striped killifish, *F. majalis* (Walbaum), in which case the latter name is correct. Northeastern Florida, northern Gulf to Central Mexico. (6 inches; 15 cm)

135. Saltmarsh topminnow   *Fundulus jenkinsi* (Evermann)

D. 8–9; A. 11–13; Sc. 33. This rare species is restricted to coastal streams and adjacent bay shores from the western shore of Galveston Bay eastward through Louisiana to the Florida panhandle. (2 inches; 5 cm)

136. Gulf killifish   *Fundulus grandis* Baird and Girard

D. 11; A. 10–11; Sc. 35–38. The Gulf killifish is a large, widespread shore fish occasionally used as bait. In low salinities in East Texas and Louisiana, where *F. similis* is absent, a form of *F. grandis* with dark stripes similar to those of *F. similis* is found. This form, originally described as the nominal species *F. pallidus* Evermann, is readily separable from *F. similis* by its short snout and lack of a spot on the caudal peduncle. *F. similis* from areas where *F. grandis* is absent may also lack the spots. *F. grandis* frequently has stripes when young, but except in the above case these stripes usually fade with growth, unlike the stripes in *F. similis* and *F. pulvereus*. This species goes under a variety of common names. Bait dealers refer to most cyprinodontid fishes as "chubs" or just "minnows," and *F. grandis* is sometimes mistakenly sold as "finger mullet." There is evidence that this species is identical to the Atlantic mummichog, *F. heteroclitus*. Cuba, eastern Mexico to Florida. (6 inches; 15 cm)

137. Bayou killifish *Fundulus pulvereus* (Evermann)
D. 9; A. 11; Sc. 33. This is a small, usually uncommon, but beautiful fish with great color differences between the sexes. Males in breeding colors are the most attractive members of the family. As the name implies, this species commonly inhabits marshes and inlets at least from the upper Laguna Madre to Alabama, where it integrades with the marsh killifish, *Fundulus confluentus*, which some biologists think is the same species. (3 inches; 8 cm)

138. Sheepshead minnow *Cyprinodon variegatus* Lacépède
D. 11; A. 10; Sc. 26. Perhaps the most common member of the family and certainly the most pugnacious, the sheepshead minnow is found along shores, in marsh ponds, and in a variety of extreme habitats in which no other fish are found. This species has the greatest tolerance of salinity of any known fish. Maine to Venezuela and throughout the West Indies. (3 inches; 8 cm)

139. Diamond killifish *Adinia xenica* (Jordan and Gilbert)
D. 9–10; A. 11–12; Sc. 25. This poorly known fish, often found singly with other killifish, seems to prefer bay margins and marshes. Previously known as *A. multifasciata*. Florida panhandle to southern Texas. (2 inches; 5 cm)

140. Rainwater killifish *Lucania parva* (Baird)
D. 10–12; A. 10–11; Sc. 26. This killifish is generally limited to vegetated areas such as turtle-grass flats and algal communities. It also occurs in vegetated areas in coastal fresh water. The breeding males of this species possess a reddish orange anal fin tinged with black and a bright yellow caudal fin. Massachusetts to Tampico. (2 inches; 5 cm)

Poeciliidae

The livebearers are a freshwater family with only two species which enter salt water in our area. Both are quite tolerant of salt and are common in coastal marshes. All species of this family bear live young. The males are easily recognized since they are much smaller than the females and possess an elongated anal fin which is specialized as an intromittent organ for sperm. The common guppy of home aquaria belongs to this family. (Rosen, 1973)

1   Dorsal fin originating anterior to anal fin; more than ten dorsal
       rays . . . . Sailfin molly, *Poecilia latipinna.*
     Dorsal fin originating posterior to anal fin; fewer than ten dorsal
       rays . . . . Mosquitofish, *Gambusia affinis.*

141. Sailfin molly   *Poecilia latipinna* (Lesueur)

D. 13–16; A. 8; Sc. 26. A common resident of Texas and Louisiana coastal marshes, the occasionally black wild individuals of this and closely related species are the same as the black molly of tropical fish aquaria. Another molly, the Amazon molly, *P. formosa,* occurs in southern Texas and has been introduced into the Nueces River but is not yet known from salt water. The latter species has fewer than 13 dorsal rays and a definite diamond-shaped pattern on the sides, while the sailfin molly has 13–16 dorsal rays and a spotted pattern. South Carolina to Campeche. Hubbs, 1964; Darnell and Abramoff, 1968. (2 inches; 5 cm)

142. Mosquitofish   *Gambusia affinis* (Baird and Girard)

D. 7–9; A. 8–10; Sc. 29–32; females look a little like the rainwater killifish, *Lucania parva.* Like the sailfin molly, this fish is common in low-salinity marshes; however, it is generally found in fresher water than the molly. This small species has been widely introduced as a mosquito control agent. New Jersey to Central Mexico. (3 inches; 8 cm)

Atherinidae

Silversides are small fishes found in relatively shallow water along bay margins. There are two estuarine and marine species in our area and two freshwater species which occasionally might be found in very low salinities. Members of this family are famous for their interest in surface objects, butting into and jumping over twigs, string, and other floating things. (Gunter, 1953)

1   Scales rough to the touch, with serrated edges; bases of dorsal
       and anal fins covered with deciduous scales; two rows of spots
       along dorsum . . . . Rough silverside, *Membras martinica.*
     Scales smooth; bases of dorsal and anal fins scaleless; no definite
       rows of spots along dorsum, but dorsal scales outlined in black
       . . . . Tidewater silverside, *Menidia beryllina.*

143. Rough silverside *Membras martinica* (Valenciennes)

D. V + I, 7; A. I, 14–21; Sc. 43–48; scales rough to the touch; caudal fin with dusky posterior margin; lateral silver stripe wider than eye. Reports of *Membras vagrans* refer to this species, which is generally found in the deeper, more saline portions of the bays and out into the Gulf as far as fifteen miles offshore. New York to Mexico. (3½ inches; 9 cm)

144. Tidewater silverside *Menidia beryllina* (Cope)

D. V + I, 10 (rarely 9 or 11); A. I, 15–18; Sc. 38–40; scales quite smooth, offering no resistance to the thumb when it is run along the sides of the body; caudal fin usually plain and without dusky margin; silvery lateral stripe narrower than pupil of eye. This species is generally limited to the shorelines. In very low salinities in the lower Atchafalaya River it seems to intergrade with the freshwater silverside, *Menidia audens*. Recently it has been again suggested that two species occur in Florida and Texas— this one and *M. peninsulae*, which generally occurs in saltier water (more than 15 parts per thousand compared to less than 19 parts per thousand for *M. beryllina*). These two forms are statistically separable by a combination of biochemical and morphological characters. Massachusetts to southern Mexico. Johnson, 1975. (3 inches; 8 cm)

Holocentridae

Squirrelfishes are a tropical family represented by several species found, so far, only on the offshore reefs. In all local species except *Myripristis jacobus*, the swimbladder is connected to the skull so that it serves as a sound amplifier. Many species of squirrelfishes use sound as part of their courtship behavior. Squirrelfishes are all good to eat, although they may be rather small. In the United States they are occasionally marketed as "red snapper." Additional tropical species might occur rarely on some offshore reefs. (Woods, 1955; Bright and Cashman, 1974; Woods and Sonoda, 1973)

1	Strong preopercular spine present	2
	No preopercular spine present	5
2	Gill rakers on lower limb of first arch 14–17; upper lobe of caudal fin noticeably longer than lower	3
	Gill rakers of lower limb of first arch 11–13; upper and lower lobes of caudal fin about equal in length	4
3	Length of upper jaw 12 percent to 14 percent of standard length; pored lateral-line scales 50–55 to base of caudal fin; interspinous membrane of dorsal fin white-edged .... Longspine squirrelfish, *Holocentrus rufus*.	
	Length of upper jaw 14 percent to 16 percent of standard length; pored lateral-line scales 45–50; interspinous membrane of dorsal fin orange .... Squirrelfish, *Holocentrus ascensionis*.	

4   Axil of pectoral black; anal rays nine .... Dusky squirrelfish, *Holocentrus vexillarius.*
    Axil of pectoral pale; anal rays eight .... Saddle squirrelfish, *Holocentrus poco.*
5   Prominent bar crossing body just behind head .... Blackbar soldierfish, *Myripristis jacobus.*
    No such bar; body uniformly colored .... Cardinal soldierfish, *Plectrypops retrospinus.*

145. Longspine squirrelfish   *Holocentrus rufus* (Walbaum)

D. XI, 14–16; A. IV, 9–11; P. 15–17; Sc. 50–57; maxillary not reaching to center of eye; body reddish with longitudinal yellow or white stripes; interspinous membranes of dorsal fin with white spot at upper margin and with long second dorsal. This squirrelfish is known in the area only from offshore reefs. Florida and the northern Gulf through the Caribbean. (12 inches; 30 cm)

146. Squirrelfish   *Holocentrus ascensionis* (Osbeck)

D. XI, 14–16; A. IV, 10; P. 15–17; Sc. 46–51; maxillary reaching to or beyond midpoint of eye; coloration like that of *H. rufus* except dorsal fin membranes without white spots and uninterrupted orange or with orange spots near edge. This is the most common local squirrelfish. New York through the Caribbean to Brazil. (2 feet; 61 cm)

147. Dusky squirrelfish   *Holocentrus vexillarius* (Poey)

D. XI, 13; A. IV, 9; P. 15; Sc. 40–44; body reddish with lighter longitudinal stripes; dorsal fin red with white along membranes next to spines; other fins reddish. This small squirrelfish is sometimes put in the genus *Adioryx.* It is found off Florida and rarely on reefs in the northwestern Gulf. Florida and the northern Gulf through the Caribbean. (6 inches; 15 cm)

148. Saddle squirrelfish   *Holocentrus poco* (Woods)

D. XI, 13; A. IV, 8; P. 14; Sc. 37–40; sides red, often with dark blotch or saddle at base of soft dorsal and another on caudal peduncle. This rare squirrelfish is known only from the Bahamas, Grand Cayman Island, and the West Flower Garden Reef, but obviously it must occur elsewhere. Woods, 1965; Bright and Cashman, 1974. (5 inches; 13 cm)

149. Blackbar soldierfish   *Myripristis jacobus* Cuvier

D. X + I, 14; A. IV, 13; P. 15; Sc. 34–36; no large spines on head; reddish brown on back; body silvery with distinct dark (reddish brown to black) bar behind opercular opening; spinous dorsal with blue blotches; soft dorsal red anteriorly and blue posteriorly; ventral and anal fins blue; caudal red with blue margin. This fish is not rare on offshore reefs. Tropical Atlantic, in the west from the Bahamas, Florida, and the northern Gulf through the Caribbean to Brazil. (8 inches; 20 cm)

150. Cardinal soldierfish   *Plectrypops retrospinus* (Guichenot)

D. XII, 14; A. IV, 11; P. 16–17; Sc. 32–35; body uniformly red; lobes of caudal rounded; strong forward-pointing spines beneath eye. The cardinal soldierfish is an elusive and deeper-dwelling squirrelfish known in our area only from the West Flower Gardens Reef. Elsewhere, from Bermuda, the Bahamas, Florida, Gulf of Campeche, and throughout the Caribbean. Bright and Cashman, 1974. (5 inches; 13 cm)

Aulostomidae

The trumpetfishes are an oddly shaped family of tropical reef fishes related to the pipefishes, seahorses, and cornetfishes. The common name is derived from the trumpetlike shape the fish acquire when they open their mouths.

151. Trumpetfish *Aulostomus maculatus* Valenciennes
D. IX–XII + 24–28; A. 25–28; dorsal spines supporting separate fins or finlets; brownish, with scattered spots and streaks. This fish often aligns itself with gorgonians (whip corals) or other vertical features in the water and is consequently hard to detect. Throughout the tropical Atlantic; in the northwestern Gulf of Mexico it has so far been reported only from off-shore reefs. (30 inches; 76 cm)

Fistulariidae

The bluespotted cornetfish is the only representative of this small family which occurs in our area.

152. Bluespotted cornetfish *Fistularia tabacaria* Linnaeus
D. and A. 13–15; body very long and slender with produced median section of caudal fin and elongate snout. The cornetfish lacks the separate dorsal spines found in the similar trumpetfish (*Aulostomus maculatus*). This species occurs in the tropics, where it is commonly found in vegetated areas while *Aulostomus* is more of a reef dweller. There have been several reports of this species from offshore, although it probably is not common anywhere in the area. West Indies to Brazil, occasionally following the Gulf Stream as far north as Nova Scotia. (6 feet; 1⅔ m)

Syngnathidae

The pipefishes and seahorses are among the most curious and interesting of marine fishes. Their armored bodies and odd shapes make them attractive aquarium fish. One interesting biological characteristic of the family is that the males carry the fertilized eggs in a special brood pouch. The location and size of this pouch is important in determining species. Syngnathids are commonly found in vegetated areas, and they closely resemble the vegetation in which they live. One peculiar and distinctive member of this family, the pipehorse, *Amphelikturus dendriticus*, has been taken off the Mississippi coast. It looks like a pipefish but has a prehensile tail like a seahorse. Two additional pipefishes, *Syngnathus springeri* and *S. elucens*, have been taken from the northeastern Gulf and may be expected west of the Mississippi River. (Ginsburg, 1937; Herald, 1942, 1965; Dawson, 1972)

1   Head and body continuous, in straight line; tail not prehensile; caudal fin present 2

     Head and body at about right angle; tail prehensile; caudal fin absent 8

2   Median trunk ridge deflected ventrally at anus and continuous with inferior trunk ridge (Fig. 5A) 3

     Median trunk ridge terminated at anus; lateral tail ridge beginning just posterior to it, with lateral swinging upward (Fig. 5B) 4

          A   B

Fig. 5. Lateral ridges in syngnathid fishes

3   Snout long, more than half head length .... Opossum pipefish, *Oostethus lineatus*.

     Snout short, less than half head length .... Fringed pipefish, *Micrognathus crinigerus*.

4   Trunk rings 23, rarely 24 .... Bull pipefish, *Syngnathus springeri*.

     Trunk rings 15–21 5

5   Dorsal fin short, with 21–25 rays, beginning approximately over anal fin .... Shortfin pipefish, *Syngnathus elucens*.

     Dorsal fin long, with 27 or more rays, usually beginning in advance of anal fin 6

6   Snout short, 40–50 percent of head length; dorsal fin 88–116 percent of head length 7

     Snout long, 49–66 percent of head length; dorsal fin 53–100 percent of head length 8

7 Dorsal rays 33 or more; tail rings 34–40; dorsal fin covering 4–6 trunk rings and 4–5 tail rings .... Northern pipefish, *Syngnathus fuscus.*

Dorsal rays fewer than 35; tail rings 30–34; dorsal fin covering 2–4 trunk rings and 4–6 tail rings .... Gulf pipefish, *Syngnathus scovelli.*

8 Trunk rings 19–21, usually 20; dorsal rays 32–40 .... Chain pipefish, *Syngnathus louisianae.*

Trunk rings 16–18, rarely 19; dorsal rays 27–33 9

9 Tail rings 35–40 .... Dusky pipefish, *Syngnathus floridae.*

Tail rings 33–34 .... Sargassum pipefish, *Syngnathus pelagicus.*

10 Dorsal rays 16–21; pectoral rays 13 or more .... Lined seahorse, *Hippocampus erectus.*

Dorsal rays 10–14; pectoral rays 10–12 .... Dwarf seahorse, *Hippocampus zosterae.*

153. Opossum pipefish   *Oostethus lineatus* (Kaup)

D. 40–47; trunk rings 21; tail rings 20–26. The spiny projections on the rings and the location of the brood pouch (on males) under the belly make this species distinctive. This species has not been reported from the northwestern Gulf of Mexico, but it may be found in many habitats, including *Spartina* marshes or in *Sargassum*. Dawson, 1970. (3½ inches; 9 cm)

154. Fringed pipefish   *Micrognathus crinigerus* (Bean and Dresel)

D. 16–18; trunk rings 14–16; tail rings 37–39. The pattern of body ridges and the lack of an anal fin are the best traits for distinguishing this species. An early report from Cameron, Louisiana, is probably erroneous, because this is another grassflat species not otherwise known west of the Mississippi River. It occurs in grass beds in the Chandeleur Islands. Florida through the Caribbean to Brazil, but not Texas, Louisiana, and northern Mexico. Powell and Strawn, 1963. (3 inches; 8 cm)

155. Northern pipefish   *Syngnathus fuscus* Storer

D. 36–39; trunk rings 18–19; tail rings 33–36. The best characteristics for distinguishing this species are the number of trunk rings (usually 19), the position of the dorsal fin (covering 4–6 trunk rings and 4–6 tail rings), and the moderate snout length (44–59 percent of head length). There is often a banded pattern on the sides, but never a reticulated pattern. This species is normally distributed along the Atlantic coast of the United States (southwards to northern Florida); however, a population regarded as a distinct subspecies, *S. f. affinis*, is known from Corpus Christi Bay. There are only four known specimens. (6 inches; 15 cm)

156. Gulf pipefish   *Syngnathus scovelli* (Evermann and Kendall)

D. 27–36; trunk rings 15–17; tail rings 30–34. This pipefish is also distinguished by its short snout (40–45 percent of head length) and its dorsal fin covering 2–4 trunk rings and 3–5 tail rings (usually 3 and 5 respectively). The dorsal fin is usually banded in females of this species. In males the brood pouch covers 10–13 tail rings. This is a common pipefish in many areas, and a breeding population has been reported in Louisiana fresh water at Lake Saint John about 150 miles inland. It is also found in fresh water in much of peninsular Florida. Florida to Mexico. Whatley, 1962, 1969. (6 inches; 15 cm)

157. Chain pipefish *Syngnathus louisianae* Günther

D. 33–36; trunk rings 19–21; tail rings 34–37. The very long snout (53–63 percent of head length), the position of the dorsal fin (covering 2½ to 3¼ trunk rings and 4–6 tail rings, usually 3 and 4, respectively), and a chainlike pattern of bands and reticulations on the sides identify this species. Females are always flat-bellied (in the other species of *Syngnathus* they are V-bellied). This is the most common pipefish in the area, especially in the bays. Rare individuals occasionally turn up offshore. Maryland south to Jamaica and the whole Gulf. (10 inches; 25 cm)

158. Dusky pipefish *Syngnathus floridae* (Jordan and Gilbert)

D. 29–33; trunk rings 17–18; tail rings 35–40. This dusky-sided fish is best distinguished by its moderate snout (48–66 percent of head length) and high number of tail rings. Although the snout length commonly overlaps that found in *S. louisianae*, *S. floridae* is usually a stouter-bodied fish. The subspecies in our area is *S. f. floridae*. Generally not as common as the chain and Gulf pipefishes, it is seasonally abundant (during the summer) in high-salinity grassflats. Bermuda, the Bahamas, and Chesapeake Bay to Texas. (8 inches; 20 cm)

159. Sargassum pipefish *Syngnathus pelagicus* Linnaeus

D. 28–31; trunk rings 16–18; tail rings 30–34. Böhlke and Chaplin (1968) remark that this species is usually distinctively marked with narrow vertical white lines margined with black which occasionally take the form of ocellated spots common to most other animals that live in or around *Sargassum*. The specimens we have examined lacked this coloration. Very similar to *S. floridae*, this species is known only from far offshore, where it inhabits the floating *Sargassum*. Since other species of pipefish, notably *S. louisianae* juveniles, also occur in the *Sargassum* community, any identifications of *S. pelagicus* from inshore waters should be carefully checked. Worldwide in *Sargassum*. (6 inches; 15 cm)

160. Dwarf seahorse *Hippocampus zosterae* Jordan and Gilbert

D. 10–14; trunk rings 10; tail rings 31–33. This is the common small seahorse limited to high-salinity grassflats. Western Gulf populations have been reported as *H. regulus*. It ranges from green to nearly black in color. The Caribbean to Florida and the whole Gulf. Strawn, 1958. (1½ inches; 3 cm)

161. Lined seahorse *Hippocampus erectus* Perry

D. 16–21; trunk rings 12; tail rings 32–35; usually dark, but gold individuals are known. Some lined seahorses have filaments spread over their bodies, giving them the appearance of plants. This species is the common larger seahorse of the bays and shallow Gulf of Mexico. It was previously reported as *H. hudsonius*. A doubtful species, *H. obtusus*, with more tubercles on the back, has been reported, but these specimens may only be variants of *H. erectus*. Nova Scotia through the Caribbean to Argentina. (5 inches; 13 cm)

Centropomidae

One species of the genus *Centropomus*, the snook, *C. undecimalis*, is found in the northwestern Gulf of Mexico. There are other tropical species in the southern Gulf. (Rivas, 1962; Greenfield, 1975)

162. Snook; robalo; saltwater pike   *Centropomus undecimalis* (Bloch)
D. VIII + I, 10; A. III, 6; Sc. 69–80; Gr. 7–10 on lower limb; body silvery, countershaded tan to olive brown above; lateral line black. The distinct lateral line, together with the high, divided dorsal fin, the sloping forehead, and the large mouth, make the snook unmistakable. Snooks commonly frequent freshwater or brackish areas near the mouths of rivers or mangrove or salt marshes. These habitats are not extensive on the northwestern Gulf coast, which probably accounts for the relative scarceness of the species. Young snooks are usually caught in the bays, and the adults in the Gulf. This species is known to be extremely sensitive to cold (Böhlke and Chaplin, 1968), not tolerating temperature below 60° F (15° C). The similarity of the favorite habitats of snook and tarpon supports hypotheses of habitat destruction or environmental change as a common cause for the disappearance of both species in recent years. Baughman's report (1943a) on this species indicates that its distribution has moved southward since the first of the century.

This fish reaches a weight of fifty pounds (23 kg), ten pounds (4.5 kg) being the usual limit. In areas where it is more abundant, it is a highly prized game and food fish. North Carolina to Brazil, including the Gulf of Mexico and the Caribbean coast of Central America. In the Gulf from about Galveston and Tampa south but rarely in between. Baughman, 1943a; Marshall, 1958. (3 feet; 91 cm)

Percichthyidae

A few genera of freshwater, anadromous, and marine fishes called the temperate basses are now considered separate from the Serranidae. Of those on our coast, only one species is normally in salt water, but the yellow bass (*Morone mississippiensis*), with its interrupted horizontal stripes, occasionally enters very low salinities in Louisiana and east Texas.

163. Striped bass   *Morone saxatilis* (Walbaum)
D. IX + I, 12; A. III, 11; Sc. 57–67. A slender species with about

seven uninterrupted horizontal dark stripes on a silver background, striped bass (often put in the genus *Roccus*) are an anadromous fish with landlocked populations, native from the streams entering Lake Pontchartrain east to the Florida panhandle. Widespread introductions into most southern and some western states have increased its range and abundance, and individuals have been caught in salt water in Louisiana and Texas. The future of this western range extension is uncertain, but currently the fish can be expected almost anywhere. New Brunswick to northeast Florida and across the Gulf to (at least temporarily) somewhere along the Texas coast. (1 foot; 30 cm—but on the Atlantic coast up to 4 feet; 1¼ m)

Serranidae

The serranids or sea basses comprise a family of generally unspecialized, advanced teleosts. The limits of the family are not well understood, many genera are often separated into distinct families such as the Percichthyidae and the Grammistidae, and the status of certain species which appear to bridge the serranid-lutjanid-pomadasyid division is, at best, confusing. Fortunately, these transitory forms are not present in the shallow northwestern Gulf of Mexico.

Serranids are typically bottom-dwelling fish, although a few, such as the creole fish, are pelagic. Most live near rocky areas, reefs, or manmade habitats such as oil platforms, jetties, and pilings. A few are found over open bottoms.

Eleven genera and thirty-four species of serranids have been reported from this general area, but only a dozen species are commonly encountered in trawls or by hook-and-line anglers. The common species range in size from the tiny *Serraniculus pumilio*, which rarely attains a length of one and one-half inches (40 mm), to the giant groupers, which may weigh over half a ton. These larger fishes are among the most important sports and commercial fishes.

One interesting aspect of the biology of serranids is that many species are hermaphroditic; that is, the same individual may be both male and female. Most groupers, as well as the species of *Centropristis*, begin life as females and transform into males as they reach a certain age. Other species, such as *Serranus subligarius*, possess functional testes and ovaries at the same time and are capable of self-fertilization. (Baughman, 1943*a*; Robins and Starck, 1961; Smith, 1964, 1965, 1971)

1	Dorsal spines 8 or 9	2
	Dorsal spines 10 or 11	7
2	Spinous dorsal continuous	3
	Spinous dorsal interrupted by scaled-over area, with one or two free spines usually protruding	6
3	Dorsal spines eight	4

Dorsal spines nine 5
4   Opercle without prominent, knifelike spine; pectoral fin sym-
    metrical .... Yellowtail bass, *Pikea mexicana.*
    Opercle with a prominent, knifelike spine; pectoral fin with up-
    per rays longest .... Spanish flag, *Gonioplectrus hispanus.*
5   Caudal fin forked; head short, less than 35 percent of standard
    length; body red without obvious markings except series of
    white spots beneath dorsal fin base .... Creole fish, *Paran-
    thias furcifer.*
    Caudal fin truncate; head more than 35 percent of standard
    length; body variously colored with obvious spots and always
    with series of three white or black spots at base of dorsal fin
    .... Graysby, *Epinephelus cruentatus.*
6   Dorsal spines eight (VI + I + I); sides with five dark bands
    and alternating red and orange bands .... Peppermint bass,
    Liopropoma rubre.
    Dorsal spines nine (VI + I + I + I); sides with single wide,
    dark band .... Wrasse bass, *Liopropoma eukrines.*
7   Dorsal spines 10; inner teeth of jaws not depressible or hinged 8
    Dorsal spines 10 or 11; inner teeth of jaws depressible or hinged .. 19
8   Gill rakers long and slender 9
    Gill rakers short 10
9   Gill rakers about 30 on lower limb of first arch .. Red barbier,
    Hemanthias vivanus.
    Gill rakers about 26 on lower limb of first arch .... Longtail
    bass, *Hemanthias leptus.*
10 Body long and slender; no serrations on horizontal margin of
    preopercle 11
    Body short and deep (depth greater than 40 percent of standard
    length); several forward-pointing serrations on free portion of
    horizontal margin of preopercle .... Yellowtail hamlet,
    Hypoplectrus chlorurus.
11 Caudal fin truncate or lunate 12
    Caudal fin rounded or with three distinct lobes 16
12 Preopercle with numerous strong, diverging spines at its angle 13
    Preopercle simply and finely serrated 14
13 Preopercle with two clusters of spines at its angle .... Sand
    perch, *Diplectrum formosum.*
    Preopercle with single cluster of divergent spines .... Dwarf
    sand perch, *Diplectrum bivittatum.*
14 Dorsal soft rays 13; caudal, soft dorsal, pectoral, and anal fins
    spotted; belly white or silver, sharply defined against adjacent
    pattern .... Belted sand bass, *Serranus subligarius.*
    Dorsal soft rays 12 or fewer 15
15 Top of head naked; opercular spines well developed; scales
    ctenoid, not deciduous; pectoral rays 16 .... Tattler, *Ser-
    ranus phoebe.*
    Top of head scaled forward to posterior edge of interorbital
    region; opercular spines poorly developed; scales often decidu-
    ous .... Blackear bass, *Serranus atrobranchus.*
16 Branchiostegal rays six; caudal rounded in fish of all sizes ....
    Pygmy sea bass, *Serraniculus pumilio.*

| | Branchiostegal rays seven; caudal fin rounded in young, but with elongated tips and central rays in adults .... | 17 |

17 Median fins dark; gill rakers on first arch usually more than 21 .... Gulf black sea bass, *Centropristis striata*.

Median fins light, may have dark markings; gill rakers on first arch usually 21 or fewer, most commonly 19 or 20 18

18 Dorsal spines with dermal flaps which often project well beyond ends of spines; about seven broad, diffuse brown bars on sides of body; dark spot at base of last three dorsal spines .... Rock sea bass, *Centropristis philadelphica*.

Dorsal spines with dermal flaps scarcely reaching end of spine; sides with three horizontal rows of seven quadrate black blotches; middle caudal ray and dorsal spines with jet black spots .... Bank sea bass, *Centropristis ocyura*.

19 Anal rays 8–10, usually 9; at least a few canines present, most noticeable on anterior jaw; lateral crests of skull diverging 20

Anal rays 10–12; no canines present; lateral crests parallel 29

20 Dorsal soft rays 13–15; pelvic inserted under or in advance of upper end of pectoral base; pelvic fin longer than pectoral 21

Dorsal soft rays 15–20, usually 16 or 17 (19 in *E. inermis*); pelvic fins inserted under or behind lower end of pectoral fin base; pelvic fins shorter than pectorals 23

21 Dorsal spines 10 .... Warsaw grouper, *Epinephelus nigritus*.

Dorsal spines 11 22

22 Posterior nostril as large as anterior nostril; margin of spinous dorsal yellow in life, lighter in preserved specimens; saddle-shaped dorsal blotch on caudal peduncle of young not extending ventrally to lateral line or anteriorly to end of dorsal fin .... Yellowedge grouper, *Epinephelus flavolimbatus*.

Posterior nostril three to five times larger than anterior nostril; margin of spinous dorsal dusky in living and preserved specimens; saddle-shaped dorsal blotch on caudal peduncle of small fish extending ventrally to lateral line and anteriorly to end of dorsal fin .... Snowy grouper, *Epinephelus niveatus*.

23 Dorsal soft rays usually 16 or 17 (15–18) 24

Dorsal soft rays usually 19, rarely 20 .... Marbled grouper, *Epinephelus inermis*.

24 Gill rakers 13–15, usually 14, on lower limb of first arch .... Jewfish, *Epinephelus itajara*.

Gill rakers 15–19, usually 16–18, on lower limb of first arch 25

25 Anal rays nine or ten; posterior margin of caudal fin straight or concave 26

Anal rays seven to nine, usually eight; posterior margin of caudal fin convex 27

26 Pectoral rays 18; gill rakers 17–18 on lower limb of first arch; no black specks about eye; head, fins, and sides of body with many white speckles; dark, saddle-shaped blotch on caudal peduncle .... Speckled hind, *Epinephelus drummondhayi*.

Pectoral rays 16–18, usually 17; gill rakers 15–16 on lower limb of first arch; black spots about eye; white spots, if any, only on sides of body; no saddle-shaped blotch on caudal peduncle .... Red grouper, *Epinephelus morio*.

27 Gill rakers 16–19, usually 17, on lower limb of first arch; head
    and body with numerous dark spots on lighter background 28
    Gill rakers 15–17, usually 16, on lower limb of first arch; head
    and body without numerous spots (a few scattered spots),
    but dark barring on sides always present; dorsal rays 16–18,
    usually 17; saddle-shaped blotch on dorsal surface of caudal
    peduncle .... Nassau grouper, *Epinephelus striatus.*
28 Dorsal rays 16–18, usually 17; dark, saddleshaped blotch on
    dorsal surface of caudal peduncle and three dark blotches
    along base of dorsal fin .... Rock hind, *Epinephelus adscen-
    sionis.*
    Dorsal rays 15 or 16; no dark, saddle-shaped blotch on caudal
    peduncle; no dark blotches along base of dorsal fin .... Red
    hind, *Epinephelus guttatus.*
29 Preopercle angulate; upper and lower limbs meeting an at angle
    slightly greater than 90 degrees 30
    Preopercle gently rounded; upper and lower limbs meeting at
    a broadly obtuse angle 32
30 Total gill rakers on first arch 45 to 54 .... Comb grouper,
    Mycteroperca rubra.
    Total gill rakers on first arch fewer than 40 31
31 Dorsal, anal, and caudal fins without produced rays; predomi-
    nantly gray with vermiculations .... Gag, *Mycteroperca mi-
    crolepis.*
    Dorsal, anal, and caudal fins with some produced rays; brown or
    gray with large blotches or spots .... Scamp, *Mycteroperca
    phenax.*
32 Distal one-third of pectoral bright yellow in life, sharply de-
    lineated from rest of fin and lighter in preserved specimens;
    large individuals with light spots on lower part of body and
    head; gill rakers short, about eight on lower limb of first arch;
    caudal lunate .... Yellowfin grouper, *Mycteroperca venenosa.*
    Pectoral with very narrow orange margin about one-fifth length
    of fin, gradually shading into basal color, which is dark and
    lacks distinct spots; sides of head and lower part of body with
    brassy yellow spots; gill rakers slender, about ten on lower
    limb of first arch .... Black grouper, *Mycteroperca bonaci.*

164. Yellowtail bass *Pikea mexicana* Schultz
    D. VIII, 14; A. III, 8; Gr. 21–23; in life, reddish with more or less
regular rows of yellow spots on sides (about one spot on each scale) and
yellow margins to dorsal and anal interspinous membranes; caudal fin yellow.
Altogether, this fish bears an amazing resemblance to the wrasse *Decodon
puellaris.* Preserved specimens are straw-colored without markings except
for traces of dark on the outer margins of the pectoral fins. This species was
only described in 1958 from specimens taken off the Texas coast, where
it apparently is not uncommon. Recent collections indicate that it does not
usually occur inside fifty fathoms. Distribution outside the northern Gulf
is not well established. Schultz, 1958. (6 inches; 15 cm)

165. Spanish flag *Gonioplectrus hispanus* (Cuvier)
    D. VIII, 13; A. III, 7; background rose with yellow orange spots;

striped on head, resembling Spanish flag; dark spot at base of anal fin, extending onto fin; large, knifelike opercular spine. This species, recorded only once from the snapper banks off Port Aransas, Texas, occurs elsewhere throughout the tropical western Atlantic, including off the Florida panhandle. Briggs et al., 1964. (1 foot; 30 cm)

166. Creole fish *Paranthias furcifer* (Valenciennes)

D. IX, 18–19; A. III, 9–10; Gr. 35–40; caudal fin deeply forked; general color of head and body red with darker countershading above, pale red to pink on lower sides and belly; lower parts of head yellow with grooves around mouth lined with red; dorsal fin dark red with orange or red spot behind each spine; anal and caudal fins also red. The creole fish differs from most other serranids in being essentially a midwater fish. This species has only recently been reported from Texas and Louisiana. North Carolina to Brazil and in the Pacific from Baja California to Peru; also reported off West Africa. (14 inches; 36 cm)

167. Peppermint bass (Swissguard basslet) *Liopropoma rubre* Poey

D. VI + I + I, 12; A. III, 8; Sc. 48–49; Gr. 16–18 (17); sides of head, body, and caudal fin with alternating pink, orange, and reddish brown or black stripes (five or six each); soft dorsal and anal each with dark spot; caudal fin with two spots, sometimes coalesced, near posterior border. This secretive little basslet is known from fairly deep waters off Texas and Louisiana. Known elsewhere from Florida, Yucatán, the West Indies, and Venezuela in 10 to 140 feet. Bright and Cashman, 1974. (3½ inches; 9 cm)

168. Wrasse bass *Liopropoma eukrines* (Starck and Courtenay)

D. VI + I + I + I, 12; A. III, 8; Sc. 44; Gr. 14–17; body with dark brown band from snout through eye, expanding rearward to cover most of caudal; this band with yellow on either side bordered by red; tip of lower jaw also brown. In our area this species is known from the West Flower Gardens Reef and from offshore reefs of Louisiana. Also known from North Carolina and Florida. Starck and Courtenay, 1962; Bright and Cashman, 1974. (2 inches; 5 cm)

169. Longtail bass *Hemanthias leptus* (Ginsburg)

D. X, 14; A. III, 8; Sc. 78; Gr. 10 + 26; eye large, subequal to snout length; caudal fin deeply lunate, with filamentous lobes; third dorsal spine not elongated in young, becoming so in adults; golden above, silvery below; fins yellow; adults with ocellated spot near ventral base of caudal fin. Originally described as *Anthiasicus leptus*, this species occurs near the edge of the continental shelf, where it has been caught by anglers and in trawls. Known only from the northwestern Gulf of Mexico. Ginsburg, 1952a, 1954; Briggs et al., 1964. (12 inches; 30 cm)

170. Red barbier *Hemanthias vivanus* (Jordan and Swain)

D. X, 14–15; A. III, 7–8; Sc. 53; Gr. 14 + 30; eye larger than snout; third dorsal spine elongated in moderate to large-sized specimens; general body color carmine, deepest on back and shading into violet on sides, freckled with olive; bright gold stripe from eye to upper base of pectoral fin; another gold stripe from tip of snout running under eye to middle of pectoral fin base.

Like *H. leptus* (which may be the same species), this attractive fish is another rare offshore form. Known also from the eastern coast of the United States as far north as North Carolina. Walls, 1973. (12 inches; 30 cm)

171. Yellowtail hamlet   *Hypoplectrus chlorurus* (Valenciennes)

D. X, 14–16; A. III, 7; body dark brown with bright yellow tail. *Hypoplectrus unicolor* (Plate 171*b*) has also been reported from southern Texas. Members of this genus are poorly known and distinguishable only on the basis of coloration. They may all belong to a single polymorphic species. It is also possible that records of *H. chlorurus* may refer to juveniles of *Epinephelus* species. A tropical species reported only three times from southern Texas. West Indies, Venezuela, and Texas. Woods, 1942; Gunter and Knapp, 1951; Randall, 1968. (5 inches; 13 cm)

172. Sand perch   *Diplectrum formosum* (Linnaeus)

D. X, 12; A. III, 7; two prominent groups of spines on margin of preopercle, one at the angle and one above; body with blackish bands alternating with blue and orange stripes. A small fish common over coarse sand bottoms, it is more common off the eastern coast of the United States, off the northeastern Gulf, and in the Caribbean than in the northwestern Gulf of Mexico. North Carolina to Uruguay. (1 foot; 30 cm)

173. Dwarf sand perch   *Diplectrum bivittatum* (Valenciennes)

D. X, 12; A. III, 7; like *D. formosum* but with only a single prominent group of spines at angle of preopercle; caudal fin slightly forked; upper half of body greenish with two lateral stripes on irregular series of double bars; cheek with oblique blue lines; two blue-edged spots at upper edge of caudal base. A smaller species than *D. formosum*, the dwarf sand perch frequents muddy areas where it is often caught by shrimpers. The local subspecies has sometimes been considered as a separate species (*D. arcuarium*). It is replaced to the south by *D. radiale* (Quoy and Gaimard). North Carolina to northern Caribbean and throughout the Gulf. Ginsburg, 1948. (6 inches; 15 cm)

174. Belted sand bass   *Serranus subligarius* (Cope)

D. X, 12–13; A., III, 7; P. 16; body brown; caudal and pectoral fins with alternating dark and light bands; belly white to silver, sharply delineated from background color; soft dorsal with large black spot anteriorly. This small serranid is one of the commonest fishes near the southern Texas and northern Florida jetties. It has previously been placed in the genera *Serranellus* and (incorrectly) *Dules*. North Carolina, around southern Florida to somewhere off Mexico. (4 inches; 10 cm)

175. Tattler   *Serranus phoebe* Poey

D. X, 12; A. III, 7; P. 16; color distinctive, but varying with age; juveniles characterized by dark diagonal band from second to sixth dorsal spines continuing across body to belly; in adults, diagonal band obscure and silvery bar present extending upwards from anus just anterior to where dark bar was; intermediate forms exhibiting both dark bar and silvery bar. Scattered specimens of the tattler have been taken off most Gulf states; however, it is probably more common than these collections indicate. Bermuda, South Carolina, and Florida through the Caribbean to Brazil. Moseley, 1966a; Moore, 1975b. (8 inches; 20 cm)

176. Blackear bass   *Serranus atrobranchus* (Cuvier)

D. X, 12; A. III, 7; P. 15; black lanceolate to ovate mark on inner surface of operculum, commonly visible through operculum. This species was reported in earlier literature as *Paracentropristes pomospilus* Ginsburg, but Robins and Starck (1961) recognized that the Gulf of Mexico fish represented a northern, disjunct population of *Prionodes atrobranchus* and subsequently included *Prionodes* in the genus *Serranus*. This small bass occurs between six and fifty fathoms in the northern Gulf of Mexico. Northern Gulf through the Caribbean to Brazil. Hildebrand, 1954. (6 inches; 15 cm)

177. Pygmy sea bass   *Serraniculus pumilio* Ginsburg

D. X, 10–11; A. III, 7; P. 14–15; Gr. 8–11, of which 3–5 occur on lower limb; four diffuse and irregular major crossbands on sides of body, sometimes barely distinguishable from background; yellowish spot behind last band on caudal peduncle, sometimes with second spot above first; ventral and anal fins black; other fins clear. This fish is the smallest American serranid, quite abundant around rough bottoms in eight to thirty-five fathoms. Its small size and secretive nature make it difficult to collect or observe. North Carolina to Guyana; absent from the West Indies. Hastings, 1973. (2 inches; 5 cm)

178. Gulf black sea bass   *Centropristis striata* (Linnaeus)

D. X, 11; A. III, 7; P. 16–18 (17–18); Gr. 21–26 (23); preserved specimens generally dark, including median fins and belly; in small fish, series of longitudinal lines possibly apparent as well as dark spot at bases of last dorsal spines; others possibly showing pattern of seven vertical bands similar to *C. philadelphica*, which has light-colored belly and fins. The subspecies *C. striata melana* Ginsburg occurs commonly in the eastern Gulf of Mexico and may stray into our area, but we have not been able to verify its presence in the western Gulf of Mexico. Another subspecies, *C. striata striata*, occurs on the Atlantic coast from Maine to Florida. These subspecies are listed as distinct species by Bailey et al. (1970). Miller, 1959. (in Gulf of Mexico, 11 inches; 28 cm—in Atlantic, 18 inches; 46 cm)

179. Rock sea bass   *Centropristis philadelphica* (Linnaeus)

D. X, 11; A. III, 7; P. 15–20 (18); Gr. 17–22 (19–21); preserved specimens with several distinct vertical bars and large dark spot at base of last three dorsal spines; in life, fins olivaceous above, whitish below, with bright blue and orange stripes and markings on head and fins; anal fin of males nearly twice as long, in proportion to body size, as that of females. In this as well as other species of *Centropristis* the younger adults are predominantly female and transform into males as they get older and grow larger. The rock sea bass is very common in the shallow northwestern Gulf of Mexico, especially between ten and fifty fathoms. Despite its common name, it is an unusual sea bass in that it occurs more frequently over sandy or muddy bottoms. It rarely has been taken in the bays. Elsewhere, it is found from the Carolinas around Florida and throughout the Gulf of Mexico. Hildebrand, 1954; Miller, 1959. (8 inches; 20 cm)

180. Bank sea bass (rock squirrel) *Centropristis ocyura* (Jordan and Evermann)

D. X, 11; A. III, 7; P. 16–18 (17); Gr. 19–21; preserved specimens with three longitudinal rows of rectangular black blotches, with blotches in center being most distinct; in small fish, these blotches possibly fused into seven black bars; dorsal spines with three or four inky black spots, evenly spaced, with similar inky spots at pectoral fin base and on opercle; outer rays of caudal fin pale; in life, head and fins and forward portion of body with numerous blue and yellow stripes and spots. This fish generally occurs in deeper water than *C. philadelphica* and shows a more pronounced preference for hard (rocky) bottoms. It appears to be most common in the northern and eastern parts of its range, where it is more abundant than *C. philadelphica*. *C. springeri* is regarded as a synonym. North Carolina to Florida and throughout the Gulf of Mexico. Miller, 1959. (12 inches; 30 cm)

181. Graysby *Epinephelus cruentatus* (Lacépède)

D. IX, 14; A. III, 8; P. 16; light gray or brown with numerous dark orange brown spots over head, body, and all fins; three or four dark spots below dorsal fin (becoming white if fish exhibits dark color pattern). This is one of the most common serranids around Caribbean reefs, and it is also common on the offshore reefs in the northwestern Gulf of Mexico. This species was formerly assigned to the genus *Petrometopon*. Bermuda, Florida, and the northern Gulf through the Caribbean to Brazil. Briggs, 1964; Smith, 1971. (1 foot; 30 cm)

182. Warsaw grouper; black jewfish *Epinephelus nigritus* (Holbrook)

D. X, 13–15 (14); A. III, 9; P. 18–19 (18). This species differs from most others of *Epinephelus* in possessing ten instead of eleven dorsal spines. This character, as well as differences in skull morphology, has sometimes led to the placing of this species in the separate genus *Garrupa*. Small Warsaw groupers are common about the jetties and offshore oil platforms, and fish up to forty pounds (18 kg) are not unusual in these waters. Elsewhere the species is found throughout the tropical and subtropical western Atlantic from Massachusetts to Brazil and in the Caribbean. (5 feet; 1½ m)

183. Yellowedge grouper *Epinephelus flavolimbatus* Poey

D. XI, 13–15 (13–14); A. III, 9; P. 18; round white spots on body; dark, saddlelike blotch on dorsal surface of caudal peduncle (becoming obscure with age). This species has only recently been discovered in the northwestern Gulf of Mexico, where it occurs on the middle shelf. Gulf of Mexico, West Indies, and northern coast of South America. (1 foot; 30 cm)

184. Snowy grouper *Epinephelus niveatus* (Valenciennes)

D. XI, 13–14; A. III, 9; P. 18; small individuals with pearly white spots on brown background; distinguished from yellowedge grouper by larger size of saddlelike blotch on caudal peduncle, posterior nostril much larger than anterior nostril, and margin of spinous dorsal not edged with yellow in live fish and remaining dusky to its margin in preserved fish. This is one of the rarer small groupers around the offshore oil rigs. Massachusetts to Brazil and in the Pacific from Baja California to Panama. (6 inches; 15 cm)

185. Marbled grouper *Epinephelus inermis* (Valenciennes)

D. XI, 19; A. III, 9; P. 18–19; pectoral fin elongate (29–35 percent of standard length); usually dark brown to black with large white blotches and white line through eye; particularly conspicuous white spot at base of maxilla. This is the deepest-bodied grouper; the marbled color pattern of this species is unmistakable and is responsible for the common name. Common throughout most of the West Indies, this species has only recently been reported from the northwestern Gulf of Mexico, where it occurs on offshore reefs and near oil platforms. It was formerly placed in the genus *Dermatolepis*. Gulf of Mexico, southern Florida, and the West Indies. (2 feet; 61 cm)

186. Jewfish; spotted jewfish *Epinephelus itajara* (Lichtenstein)

D. XI, 15–16; A. III, 8; P. 19; dorsal spines relatively short, third through eleventh being about the same size and not much longer than soft rays; mouth large, extending behind eye; eye small, being one-sixth to one-twelfth of head length; body brownish green or yellow with small irregular brown spots on head, body, and fins and five oblique, irregular dark bars (becoming obscure in large adults) on sides. This fish reaches a size of about seven hundred pounds (320 kg), however, most in the northwestern Gulf are much smaller. This is the most common large inshore grouper off Texas from April through October. It was formerly placed in the genus *Promicrops*. In the Atlantic from Florida to Brazil and in the Pacific from Costa Rica to Peru. (6 feet; 1⅔ m)

187. Speckled hind; calico grouper *Epinephelus drummondhayi* Goode and Bean

D. XI, 15–16 (16); A. III, 9; P. 18; head, body, and fins profusely covered with light speckles on reddish brown background; caudal fin truncate to emarginate. According to some, this is the most beautiful of our groupers, but unfortunately it is rare in the northwestern Gulf of Mexico. North Carolina to Florida and Bermuda as well as the northern Gulf of Mexico. (18 inches; 46 cm—rarely up to 40 inches; 1 m)

188. Red grouper *Epinephelus morio* (Valenciennes)

D. XI, 16–17 (16); A. III, 9 (rarely 10); P. 16–18 (17); second dorsal spine longest, with interspinous membranes of dorsal not deeply incised; reddish brown with scattered pale blotches; no saddle-shaped blotch on caudal peduncle; median fins blackish with white margins; caudal truncate to emarginate. This species occurs offshore on the snapper banks but is more common in the northeastern Gulf. It reaches a size of about fifty pounds (23 kg). Massachusetts to Brazil, Bermuda, and West Africa. Moe, 1969. (4 feet; 1¼ m)

189. Rock hind; calico grouper *Epinephelus adscensionis* (Osbeck)

D. XI, 16–17; A. III, 8; P. 18–19 (19); head, body, and fins spotted orange brown; brown spots on upper part of caudal peduncle; series of five dark blotches along base of dorsal fin; margin of caudal fin convex; posterior nostril larger or about same size as anterior nostril. This species is common about jetties and offshore oil rigs and on the snapper banks. It reaches a size of five to eight pounds (2.3–3.6 kg). Massachusetts to Brazil, the West Indies, and western South Africa. (2 feet; 61 cm)

190. Red hind   *Epinephelus guttatus* (Linnaeus)

D. XI, 15–16 (16); A. III, 9; P. 17; body with pale greenish yellow or light red ground color covered with large red spots; no saddle-shaped blotch on caudal peduncle; outer third of soft dorsal, anal, and caudal fins darkened. The coloration of this species is similar to that seen in *E. adscensionis*; however, it lacks the large dark blotches or bars along the sides and on the caudal peduncle and has small dark flecks inside the red spots. This is a common species in the Caribbean as well as off Yucatán, but in the northwestern Gulf of Mexico it appears to be restricted to the offshore reefs. Bermuda and South Carolina to Venezuela. (2½ feet; 76 cm)

191. Nassau grouper   *Epinephelus striatus* (Bloch)

D. XI, 16–18; A. III, 8; P. 17–19 (18); third dorsal spine longest, with interspinous membranes of dorsal deeply notched; posterior nostril about twice size of anterior nostril; background light olive brown with dark stripe running from base of dorsal fin to snout and through eye; sides of body with irregular dark bars and saddlelike blotch on caudal peduncle. This is a rare species in the northwestern Gulf, where it is known to reach fifty-five pounds (25 kg). It exhibits a remarkable ability to change colors, and consequently the numerous color descriptions may be confusing. Bermuda, Florida, and the Caribbean. Gunter and Knapp, 1951. (4 feet; 1¼ m)

192. Comb grouper   *Mycteroperca rubra* (Bloch)

D. XI, 15–17; A. III, 10–12; Gr. 18–21 + 29–36 (with no obvious rudiments); caudal fin truncate in young, becoming emarginate in adults; sides of body brown with indistinct but characteristic horizontal stripes; head with 3–5 dark bars radiating from mouth and eyes, also characteristic. This is a rather attractive fish which may be more common than reports have indicated. Small specimens have been taken from the jetties at Port Aransas, and it is common on 7½-Fathom Reef. It also occurs on other offshore reefs in Texas and Louisiana waters, where it may also be common. Earlier literature calls this fish *Parepinephelus acutirostris*. Scattered localities on both sides of the Atlantic; Bermuda to Brazil; the Mediterranean and West Africa. Smith, 1971. (1 foot; 30 cm)

193. Gag   *Mycteroperca microlepis* (Goode and Bean)

D. XI, 16–19; A. III, 11; Gr. 21–29; nostrils subequal; color variable, with fish from shallow water showing greater variation than those from deeper water; generally brownish gray with or without faint spots or "kiss-shaped" markings on sides and usually with black bar or "moustache" above mouth; fins generally dark, with edges of caudal, dorsal, and anal fins and first ray of ventral fins whitish. This is a small species (usually under five pounds) which seems to be fairly common on the offshore banks. It is often confused with the black grouper, *M. bonaci*, which may not occur in the northwestern Gulf. Massachusetts to Brazil; not found in the West Indies. Smith et al., 1975. (3 feet; 91 cm)

194. Scamp   *Mycteroperca phenax* Jordan and Swain

D. XI, 15–18; A. III, 10–12 (11); Gr. 3–7 + 14–18 (excluding rudiments); background light tan, with numerous small brown spots on body and fins occurring on ventral as well as dorsal sides. Scamp is a common species occurring year-round on the snapper banks. It is sometimes referred to as *M. falcata phenax* in the older literature. There is a closely related grouper, the yellowmouth, *M. interstitialis* (Poey), which is sometimes reported from here but is definitely more common in the Caribbean and on the U.S. east coast. Its status is uncertain, but we have only found one such fish from here, and it seems to be *M. phenax*. Although color is said to differ, the main characteristic is that in *M. interstitialis* the nostrils are the same size, while *M. phenax* has a larger posterior nostril. The two forms may represent a single, variable species, in which case *M. interstitialis* would be the correct name. Along the Atlantic and Gulf coasts of the United States and Mexico from Massachusetts to Yucatán. Smith, 1971; Bright and Cashman, 1974; Smith et al., 1975. (3 feet; 91 cm)

195. Yellowfin grouper *Mycteroperca venenosa* (Linnaeus)

D. XI, 15–16; A. III, 11; Gr. 4–5 + 10–13 (excluding rudiments); caudal fin slightly emarginate; background gray or olivaceous with dark brown blotches arranged in lengthwise rows and numerous small, dark reddish orange spots; outer edges of pectorals sharply defined with broad orange zone. This is a medium-sized offshore grouper. Bermuda, southern Florida, and the West Indies. (3 feet; 91 cm)

196. Black grouper *Mycteroperca bonaci* (Poey)

D. XI, 16–17; A. III, 11–13; Gr. 2–5 + 8–11 (excluding rudiments); caudal fin usually truncate. This species closely resembles *M. venenosa* but has additional fin rays in the dorsal and anal fins. The soft dorsal, anal, and caudal fins have a broad, dark outer zone set off by a white margin. The general body coloration is dark. The pectorals are brownish orange at the tips, but not as abruptly so as in *M. venenosa*. These commonly possess "kiss marks" similar to those of *M. microlepis*, with which it has been often confused; however, the black grouper lacks the white first ventral rays found in the gag. The species has been reported as common near the Texas jetties and offshore reefs and from Louisiana; however, most of these records seem to be assignable to *M. microlepis*, and we have not been able to verify the presence of *M. bonaci* here. Florida to Brazil, including the eastern Gulf of Mexico, Yucatán, and the Bahamas. Pew, 1955; Smith, 1971; Smith, 1974. (3½ feet; 1 m)

Grammistidae

The soapfishes are closely related to the sea basses and are sometimes included in the Serranidae. The common name is derived from the soapy mucus produced by the skin of these fishes. (Courtenay, 1967)

1   Color pattern consisting of scattered pale spots on somewhat dark-

er background . . . . Whitespotted soapfish, *Rypticus maculatus.*
Color pattern consisting of dark, sometimes ocellated spots on pale
background . . . . Spotted soapfish, *Rypticus subbifrenatus.*

197. Whitespotted soapfish   *Rypticus maculatus* Holbrook
D. II, 24–26; A. 25–26; pale tan, sometimes gray or black with a few
scattered pearly spots on sides; sides often mottled in addition. Reports of
R. saponaceus (with three dorsal spines and diffuse pale blotches on the sides)
from the western Gulf appear to be all referrable to this species. This species
is not uncommon at times in the inshore Gulf, occurring over hard bottoms
and reefs and near oil platforms and jetties. North Carolina to Florida and
the northern Gulf of Mexico. Moore, 1975*b*. (1 foot; 30 cm)

198. Spotted soapfish   *Rypticus subbifrenatus* (Gill)
D. III, 23; A. 15; body pale with widely spread round, dark spots, ocellated in young and in preserved specimens. Known from the West Flower
Gardens Reef in our area and from Florida, the Bahamas, and Yucatán south
to the northern coast of South America. Courtenay, 1967; Bright and Cashman, 1974. (5 inches; 13 cm)

Priacanthidae

The bigeyes are best noted for their distinctively large eyes. As a group,
the family is found over hard bottoms in relatively deep water. Two species
occur in the northwestern Gulf, both on the middle to outer shelf. The glass-
eye snapper, *Priacanthus cruentatus*, with a strong preopercular spine, has
been taken once from the Flower Gardens Reef and should be looked for at
the shelf edge. (D. K. Caldwell, 1962*a*)

1   Scales small, more than 60 in lateral line; body oblong, with depth
        not one-half standard length; dorsal and anal with 12–15 rays
        each . . . . Bigeye, *Priacanthus arenatus.*
    Scales large and rough, fewer than 40 in lateral line; depth of
        body more than one-half standard length; dorsal and anal each
        with 9–11 rays . . . . Short bigeye, *Pseudopriacanthus altus.*

199. Bigeye   *Priacanthus arenatus* Cuvier
D. X, 13–15; A. III, 14–16; Sc. 61–73; Gr. 6–8 + 21–26; depth of body
33–40 percent of standard length; bright red or red stripes or mottling on
lighter red background; median fins with dark edges. This fish is not uncommon on the deeper parts of snapper banks and over the twenty- to twenty-six-
fathom shrimp grounds. Both sides of the Atlantic, in the west from Bermuda
and Massachusetts to Argentina, including the Caribbean. Gunter and
Knapp, 1951. (1 foot; 30 cm)

200. Short bigeye   *Pseudopriacanthus altus* (Gill)

D. X, 10–12; A. III, 9–11; Sc. usually 37; Gr. 6–9 + 17–21; depth of body one-half or more of standard length; red, median fins edged with black. The short bigeye is frequently put in the genus *Pristigenys*. It is generally found in deeper water out to about sixty fathoms. Gulf of Maine to Florida, with scattered localities about the Gulf of Mexico and the West Indies. D. K. Caldwell, 1962*b*. (10 inches; 25 cm)

Apogonidae

The cardinalfishes are small reef fishes. They are usually red with black spots or bars on the body, but exceptions to this coloration are found in the genera *Synagrops*, which is uniformly dark, and *Phaeoptyx*, which is silvery with dark spots on each scale. More species will probably be found on off-shore reefs as divers continue their explorations. Many cardinalfishes live in close association with reef invertebrates, and most are nocturnal. (Böhlke and Randall, 1968; Fraser and Robins, 1970; Livingston, 1971; Colin and Heiser, 1973)

1   Canine teeth present in jaws . . . . Blackmouth cardinalfish, *Synagrops bella.*
Canine teeth not present in jaws, although some species may have enlarged teeth   2
2   Angle of free preopercular margin with fleshy tab extending posteriorly   3
Angle of free preopercular margin smoothly rounded, without fleshy tab   4
3   Gill rakers on lower limb of first arch 14–16; teeth in jaws small, comblike . . . . Freckled cardinalfish, *Phaeoptyx conklini.*
Gill rakers on lower limb of first arch 11–12, rarely 13; anterior teeth in upper jaw and lateral teeth in lower jaw enlarged . . . . Dusky cardinalfish, *Phaeoptyx pigmentaria.*
4   Sides of body without definite dark pigmentation; gill rakers on lower limb of first arch 10–11 . . . . Bridle cardinalfish, *Apogon aurolineatus.*
Sides of body with definite dark spots or vertical bars beneath second dorsal fin; gill rakers on lower limb of first arch 12–18   5
5   Sides of body with dark spot beneath second dorsal fin   6
Sides of body with dark bar beneath second dorsal fin . . . . Belted cardinalfish, *Apogon townsendi.*
6   Caudal peduncle with broad, blackish saddle extending below lateral line on each side . . . . Flamefish, *Apogon maculatus.*
Caudal peduncle with small, sharply defined black spot on each side, not extending below lateral line . . . . Twospot cardinalfish, *Apogon pseudomaculatus.*

201. Blackmouth cardinalfish   *Synagrops bella* (Goode and Bean)

D. IX + I, 9; A. IV, 7; Gr. on lower limb 14. An indescript, dark-bodied fish, this is a deeper-water species more typically found in seventy-five to over one hundred fathoms. A second species of this genus, *S. spinosa* Schultz, which possesses serrations on the second spines of the first dorsal and the anal fins, is known in the northern Gulf from one hundred to two hundred fathoms, but it may also occur on the shelf. Known from both sides of the Atlantic, in the west from North Carolina to Florida and throughout the Gulf of Mexico. Hoese, 1958. (3 inches; 8 cm)

202. Freckled cardinalfish   *Phaeoptyx conklini* (Silvester)

D. VI + I, 9; A. II, 8; P. 11–13; Gr. on lower limb 14–16; silvery-bodied, with dark stripes on soft dorsal fin and anal fin and numerous dark spots on scales, producing freckled appearance. Bermuda, Bahamas, and Florida to Curaçao. Causey, 1969; Bright and Cashman, 1974. (2 inches; 5 cm)

203. Dusky cardinalfish   *Phaeoptyx pigmentaria* (Poey)

D. VI + I, 9; A. II, 8; P. 11–13; Gr. on lower limb 11–13; body pale with dark spots on head and on each scale; large dark blotch at base of caudal fin. Bahamas to Curaçao; in the northwestern Gulf known only from the West Flower Gardens Reef. Bright and Cashman, 1974. (1½ inches; 4 cm)

204. Bridle cardinalfish   *Apogon aurolineatus* (Mowbray)

D. VI + I, 9; A. II, 8; Gr. on lower limb 10–11; body not conspicuously marked; two dusky streaks on head radiating from eye. A few specimens of this fish are known from deep water off Texas. Bahamas and Florida through the Caribbean to Curaçao. Hoese, 1958. (2 inches; 5 cm)

205. Belted cardinalfish   *Apogon townsendi* (Breder)

D. VI + I, 9; A. II, 8; Gr. on lower limb 16–18; body red with wide black band across caudal peduncle and second, narrower black bar beneath posteriormost rays of soft dorsal. Bahamas and Florida to Curaçao; in the northwestern Gulf known only from the West Flower Gardens Reef. Bright and Cashman, 1974. (2 inches; 5 cm)

206. Flamefish   *Apogon maculatus* (Poey)

D. VI + I, 9; A. II, 8; Gr. on lower limb 13–14; body red with dark spot beneath base of soft dorsal and dusky saddle across caudal peduncle. This is the commonest cardinalfish off both Texas and Louisiana, occurring on reefs and around oil platforms. New England and Bermuda to Brazil; Gulf of Mexico and Caribbean. Briggs et al., 1964; Bright and Cashman, 1974; Sonnier, Teerling, and Hoese, 1976 (3 inches; 8 cm)

207. Twospot cardinalfish   *Apogon pseudomaculatus* Longley

D. VI + I, 9; A. II, 8; Gr. on lower limb 12–14; body red with dark spot beneath base of soft dorsal fin and sharply defined spot on caudal peduncle, not extending below lateral line. New England and Bermuda to Brazil, including the Gulf of Mexico and Caribbean. Sonnier, Teerling, and Hoese, 1976. (3 inches; 8 cm)

Branchiostegidae

Tilefishes are rather elongate fishes with long dorsal and anal fins. Most species are usually found over hard, sandy bottoms; however, the tilefish usually occurs in very deep water at the edge of the shelf and deeper. Much of the information on this family was provided by Dr. James K. Dooley (1974 and personal communication).

1 Preopercle entire . . . . Sand tilefish, *Malacanthus plumieri.*
   Preopercle serrate 2
2 Nape with fleshy process . . . . Tilefish, *Lopholatilus chamaeleon-
   ticeps.*
   Nape without fleshy process 3
3 Eye small, about one-fifth of head length; gill rakers 21–26 . . . .
   Gray tilefish, *Caulolatilus microps.*
   Eye larger, about 25–28 percent of head length; gill rakers 18–22
   . . . . Gulf bar-eyed tilefish, *Caulolatilus intermedius.*

208. Sand tilefish   *Malacanthus plumieri* (Bloch)

D. IV–V, 53–57; A. I, 50–56; Sc. 140–144. This tropical species is usually found on sandy bottoms surrounding coral reefs. Bermuda, Bahamas, and South Carolina through the Caribbean to Brazil and Ascension. Baughman, 1947, 1950b; Bright and Cashman, 1974. (2 feet; 61 cm)

209. Tilefish   *Lopholatilus chamaeleonticeps* Goode and Bean

D. VII, 14–15; A. II, 14–15; Sc. about 93; fleshy appendage on nape before dorsal fin. This deep-water species is known from the edge of the continental shelf off both Texas and Louisiana, where a small commercial and wintertime sports fishery has developed. Otherwise, the species occurs off the entire eastern coast of the United States and north to Labrador. (3½ feet; 1 m)

210. Gray tilefish   *Caulolatilus microps* Goode and Bean

D. VII, 25; A. I, 23; Sc. 80–91; Gr. 21–26; plain-sided, without definite blotch in axil of pectoral fin; some yellow pigment on caudal and dorsal fins under eye; eye quite small, about one-fifth of head length; tail truncate, with extended uppermost and lowermost rays. This species has commonly been confused in the past with *C. cyanops*, for which there are no verified records from the Gulf of Mexico. An additional species, *C. chrysops*, is, however, known from Yucatán and the Gulf of Campeche. See Randall, 1968, for a photograph and description of *C. chrysops*. (1 foot; 30 cm)

211. Gulf bar-eyed tilefish   *Caulolatilus intermedius* Howell-Rivero

D. VII, 24–25; A. I, 22–23; Sc. 73–81; Gr. 18–22; upper body uniformly brownish gray without yellow on fins or head; small dark blotch in axil of pectoral fin and dark bar beneath eye; eye about 25–28 percent of head length. The tail in small specimens, including the type specimen, which may be damaged, is rounded; however, larger specimens may have caudal fins with produced upper, middle, and lower rays, resulting in a trilobed tail. This species also has not been generally recognized in the northwestern Gulf of Mexico. (1 foot; 30 cm)

Pomatomidae

The bluefish is the only member of this family.

212. Bluefish *Pomatomus saltatrix* (Linnaeus)
D. VII–VIII + I, 23–26; A. II + I, 25–27; Sc. about 95; no keels on lateral line; color bluish or greenish on back, lighter below. Bluefish, which are not especially common on the Texas coast but are more so off Louisiana, resemble jacks, basses, or croakers, and many anglers mistakenly associate the bluefish with these other families. Bluefish are common along the Atlantic coast of the United States, where they reach considerable size. Known for their voracity, bluefish make an exciting game fish, and in addition one which is well worth eating. They have been known to bite chunks out of other fish and people. In the northwestern Gulf the bluefish reflects its generally northern distribution by appearing inshore only in the cooler months of the year. Worldwide, in the western Atlantic from Nova Scotia to Argentina, but rare or absent in the tropics. (3½ feet; 1m)

Rachycentridae

The cobia, also known as the ling, cabio, lemonfish, or sergeantfish, is the only member of this family. Cobia and sharksuckers (family Echeneidae) resemble one another, especially as juveniles, and many ichthyologists believe them to have more than a superficial resemblance—that is, that the resemblances indicate a close relationship between the two types of fish. Aside from these similarities, the cobia shows little relationship to any other living fish.

213. Cobia; ling *Rachycentron canadum* (Linnaeus)
D. VIII–IX + I, 27–33; A. II, 23–27; adults brownish, stocky-bodied, almost square in cross-section, lighter on the belly, sometimes with trace of broad lateral stripe found in juveniles; juveniles darker, often almost black,

with dark lateral stripe set off by light bands above and below; caudal fin of juveniles rounded to lanceolate and margined with white almost exactly like that of sharksucker, *Echeneis naucrates*; dorsal spines low, separate, and in adults often embedded. Small ling are found in the saltier bays during the summer. Larger fish, which may weigh fifty to one hundred pounds (23–45 kg), congregate about drifting or stationary objects in the Gulf of Mexico, where they are a favorite game and food fish for most saltwater anglers. Worldwide; in the western Atlantic from New Jersey to Brazil. Dawson, 1971*c*. (5 feet; 1½ m)

Echeneidae

The sharksuckers are distinguished by the presence of a laminated adhesive disc on top of the head. The disc is actually a highly modified spinous dorsal fin. These fish attach themselves, by means of this disc, to various species of sharks, rays, bony fishes, turtles, cetaceans, and even ships and other floating inanimate objects.

There are only eight described species of echeneids in the world, five or six of which occur in our waters. Most are rather specific about the animal they will attach themselves to; however, the less particular species are the most commonly encountered. *Echeneis naucrates* and *Remora remora* have a variety of hosts, including sharks, snapper, and dolphins. *Remora brachyptera* and *R. osteochir* are found almost always on billfish (sailfish, marlin, spearfish, or swordfish); *Remora australis* only occurs on whales. *Remorina albescens*, though not reported from the northwestern Gulf, should be expected here, as should *Phtheirichthys lineatus*. The family is believed to be related to the Rachycentridae (cobia or ling). (Schultz, Woods, and Lachner, 1966)

1   Disc lamellae 9 to 11 .... Slender suckerfish, *Phtheirichthys lineatus*.
      Disc lamellae 13 or more 2
2   Caudal fin of young lanceolate, with middle rays produced; lower jaw with fleshy flap; body elongate, usually with dark stripe down side; pelvic fins narrowly adnate to ventral surface .... Sharksucker, *Echeneis naucrates*.
      Caudal fin forked in young, becoming more or less emarginate in adults; lower jaw without flap; no lateral stripe; pelvic fins usually broadly emarginate to ventral surface (except in *Remorina albescens*) 3
3   Gill rakers numerous, more than 27 .... Remora, *Remora remora*.
      Gill rakers fewer than 21 4
4   Disc lamellae numerous, more than 24 .... Whalesucker, *Remora australis*.
      Disc lamellae fewer than 20 5

5   Pelvic fins narrowly adnate to ventral surface; disc lamellae
    13–14 . . . . White suckerfish, *Remorina albescens.*
    Pelvic fins broadly adnate to ventral surface; disc lamellae 15–19
      6
6   Dorsal fin rays 27–34; disc 28–40 percent of standard length;
    pectoral fins flexible . . . . Spearfish remora, *Remora brachyp-
    tera.*
    Dorsal rays 20–26; disc 27–49 percent of standard length, ex-
    tending well beyond ends of depressed pectoral fins; pectoral
    fins stiff to their tips . . . . Marlinsucker, *Remora osteochir.*

214. Slender suckerfish   *Phtheirichthys lineatus* (Menzies)

D. 33; A. 33; disc lamellae 9–11 (usually 10); disc less than 22 percent of body length. This fish is an elongate species resembling *Echeneis
naucrates* found on sharks, billfishes, and barracuda. It is not reported from
the northwestern Gulf, but it occurs in all tropical seas. (28 inches; 71 cm)

215. Sharksucker   *Echeneis naucrates* Linnaeus

D. 33–34; A. 31–41; disc lamellae 21–27 (usually 23–24); length of
disc 26–29 percent of body length; brown or dark gray above, lighter below,
with distinct light stripe down middle of side running from snout through
eye, generally diminishing in intensity; young with lanceolate tail with
white or yellow tips on dorsal, anal, and caudal fins. The sharksucker,
which generally attaches to larger fish, sometimes hitching rides on boats
(while scuba divers watch), seems to be the least particular about its hosts.
The very similar *E. neucratoides* Zuieuw (whitefin sucker) may occur in our
area. It looks like *E. naucrates* but is generally stouter, has fewer disc
lamellae (modally 21), and has dorsal and anal fin rays modally 36 (32–41)
and 33 (30–38). It is known from all temperate and tropical waters. (32
inches; 81 cm)

216. Remora   *Remora remora* (Linnaeus)

D. 21–27; A. 20–24; disc lamellae 16–20; ventral fins connected to
body for more than one-half their length; uniformly black or gray. The
remora attaches to large sharks, turtles, or boats and is found worldwide in
temperate and tropical waters. (3 feet; 91 cm)

217. Whalesucker   *Remora australis* (Bennett)

D. 22; A. 21–23; disc lamellae 24–27; brown. The whalesucker is
found on dolphins and whales. It is sometimes put in the genus *Remilegia,*
and it is believed to inhabit all tropical seas. (30 inches; 76 cm)

218. White suckerfish   *Remorina albescens* (Temminck and Schlegel)

D. 22; A. 22; disc lamellae 13–14. This small remora is found in the gill
cavities of manta rays and sharks. It is not reported from the northwestern
Gulf but is to be expected here. Circumtropical. Schmidt, 1969. (1 foot;
30 cm)

219. Spearfish remora   *Remora brachyptera* (Lowe)

D. 27–34; A. 25–30; disc lamellae 15–19. The spearfish has only been reported once from our area, so it is not surprising that this sucker is equally rare. Worldwide; tropical. (1 foot; 30 cm)

220. Marlinsucker *Remora osteochir* (Cuvier)
D. 21–23; A. 20–21; disc lamellae 28; body light brown; underside of head, parts of ventral fins, and ventral line light; pale spots on pectoral fins. This sucker usually attaches to species of billfish. It is often placed in the genus *Rhombochirus*. Both sides of the Atlantic; Massachusetts to Cuba. (1 foot; 30 cm)

Carangidae

Jacks are large, fast-swimming fishes often found schooling. All are predaceous, and several are prized game and food fishes. Identification of some species accurately requires more precision than is needed in some other groups, but most of the common species can readily be learned. The name "crevalle" is sometimes applied to the entire family, sometimes to any member of the genux *Caranx*, and sometimes only to the common jack.

Pompano (*Trachinotus carolinus*) are the most sought after members of the family, with a few thousand pounds harvested annually, mostly from Louisiana. There is presently considerable interest in the pond culture of pompano, but there are many associated problems.

Many juvenile carangids associate with floating objects, flotsam, jellyfish, and the like in the open waters. Many of these small fish make interesting aquarium fishes.

The most distinctive features of the family are the rather narrow caudal peduncle and the two free spines found before the anal fin. In young fish these two spines may be connected together by a membrane. However, in very large fish these spines, and frequently the anteriormost spines of the dorsal, become overgrown with skin, making their detection difficult. In the African pompano all spines in the first dorsal and anal fins may be so obscured.

The pilot fish, *Naucrates ductor* (Linnaeus), has not been reported from the northern Gulf. It is a pelagic fish known from all warm seas and so should be expected here. The common name is derived from its habit of accompanying sharks and other large carnivorous fish. It is similar to *Seriola* except that it has fewer dorsal spines (IV), which are not connected by membranes except in very young fish. (Ginsburg, 1952a; Berry, 1959; Fields, 1962)

1   Maxillary not protractile; soft dorsal and anal fins followed by
        more than one finlet .... Leatherjacket, *Oligoplites saurus*.
    Maxillary protractile; dorsal and anal fins with no more than one
        finlet apiece   2

2   Lateral line without well-developed scutes (large modified scales)
    3
    Lateral line with well-developed scutes 12
3   Dorsal contour elevated, with forehead oblique or almost verti-
    cal; lower-limb gill rakers fewer than 30 4
    Dorsal contour rounded, tapering forward to snout; lower-limb
    gill rakers 31 or more .... Atlantic bumper, *Chloroscombrus
    chrysurus.*
4   Anterior profile nearly vertical; lobes of dorsal and anal fins not
    greatly elongate .... Atlantic moonfish, *Vomer setapinnis.*
    Anterior profile oblique; lobes of dorsal and anal fins elongated
    .... Lookdown, *Selene vomer.*
5   One finlet behind dorsal and anal fins .... Rainbow runner,
    Elagatis bipinnulata.
    No finlets 6
6   Snout blunt; second dorsal with four or fewer more rays than
    anal 7
    Snout tapering; second dorsal with seven or more rays than anal .. 9
7   Dorsal rays 18–21; anal rays 16–18 8
    Dorsal rays 23–27; anal rays 20–23 .... Florida pompano,
    Trachinotus carolinus.
8   Body deep, 53–72 percent of standard length; dorsal and anal
    lobes reaching base of caudal fin; sides of body without verti-
    cal lines .... Permit, *Trachinotus falcatus.*
    Body more slender, 37–54 percent of standard length; dorsal and
    anal lobes reaching beyond base of caudal fin in adults; sides
    of body usually with vertical stripes .... Palometa, *Trachi-
    notus goodei.*
9   Gill rakers 25–28; lateral-line scales 121–137; dorsal rays 28–32 .. 10
    Gill rakers 21–25 (number reduced with growth); lateral-line
    scales 141–187; dorsal rays 30–40 11
10 Dorsal spines seven; dark band from eye reaches base of first
    dorsal; body with five or six bands .... Almaco jack, *Seriola
    rivoliana.*
    Dorsal spines eight; band from eye not reaching dorsal fin; body
    with seven bands .... Lesser amberjack, *Seriola fasciata.*
11 Lateral-line scales 141–163; dorsal rays 30–35; body depth 32–
    35 percent of standard length .... Greater amberjack, *Seriola
    dumerili.*
    Lateral-line scales 160–187; dorsal rays 33–40; body depth 25–
    30 percent of standard length .... Banded rudderfish, *Seriola
    zonata.*
12 First dorsal reduced, with at least last four spines very small;
    body thin laterally, almost a knife edge .... African pom-
    pano, *Alectis crinitus.*
    First dorsal not reduced; body relatively thick 13
13 Pectoral never reaching beyond vertical through origin of soft
    anal; interorbital and interopercle scaled 14
    Pectoral reaches beyond origin of soft anal; interorbital and in-
    teropercle scaleless 16
14 Anterior lateral-line scales scutelike; shoulder girdle (under

operculum) without papillae .... Rough scad, *Trachurus lathami.*

Anterior lateral-line scales not scutelike; shoulder girdle with two papillae (Fig. 6) 15

Fig. 6. Shoulder girdle of *Decapterus* and *Selar*, showing projecting lobes

15   Finlet behind dorsal and anal fins; body depth 19–23 percent of standard length .... Round scad, *Decapterus punctatus.*

No finlets behind dorsal or anal fins; body deeper, 25–30 percent of standard length .... Bigeye scad, *Selar crumenophthalmus.*

16   Vomer without teeth; teeth in jaw not enlarged; no keels on caudal peduncle 17

Vomer with teeth; teeth in outer jaw enlarged; two keels on caudal peduncle 18

17   Spines of scutes directed rearward; chest scaled .... Bluntnose jack, *Hemicaranx amblyrhynchus.*

Spines of scutes directed forward; chest scaleless .... Cotton-mouth jack, *Uraspis secunda.*

18   Anal rays 22 or more 19

Anal rays 21 or fewer 20

19   Lateral-line scutes 27–35; black band from below soft dorsal to lower lobe of caudal .... Bar jack, *Caranx ruber.*

Lateral-line scutes 20–31; no blackish band on body .... Yellow jack, *Caranx bartholomaei.*

20   Scutes 45–54; anal rays 19–21 .... Blue runner, *Caranx fusus.*

Scutes 42 or fewer; anal rays 15–19 21

21   Body silvery, usually with black spot on opercle; anal rays 15–17 22

Body brown to black; anal rays 17–19 .... Black jack, *Caranx lugubris.*

22   Chest mostly scaleless .... Crevalle (common) jack, *Caranx hippos.*

Chest completely scaled .... Horse-eye jack, *Caranx latus.*

221. Leatherjacket   *Oligoplites saurus* (Bloch and Schneider)

D. V + I, 19–21; A. II + I, 18–21; P. 15–17; Gr. 6–9 + 13–15; sides silvery, greenish in young fish; vertical fins of young yellow; most rays of dorsal and anal fins fan-shaped, forming finlets attached together at bases. The spines of this fish contain a small amount of poison, so it should be handled with care. Gulf of Maine through the Caribbean to Uruguay. (10 inches; 25 cm)

222. Rainbow runner   *Elagatis bipinnulata* (Quoy and Gaimard)

D. VI + I, 25–26; A. II + I, 16–17; P. 20–21; Gr. 10–11 + 25–26; sides with blue, green, and reddish tones (hence the common name); light underneath; fins yellowish. This is a beautiful but uncommon species known in our area only from a few specimens. It is a good game fish and an excellent food fish as well. New England through the Caribbean to Venezuela. Gunter and Knapp, 1951. (1 foot; 30 cm)

223. Florida pompano   *Trachinotus carolinus* (Linnaeus)

D. V–VI + I, 23–27; A. II + I, 20–23; P. 17–19; Gr. 5–9 + 7–11; sides silvery. Small pompano abound in the surf in the summertime. The pompano is the most popular jack, sought after by both sports and commercial fishermen. Massachusetts to Brazil. Fields, 1962; Bellinger and Avault, 1970, 1971. (17 inches; 43 cm)

224. Permit   *Trachinotus falcatus* (Linnaeus)

D. VI + I, 18–20; A. II + I, 17–18; P. 16–19; Gr. 5–9 + 9–13. Although the permit's sides are usually silvery, this species experiences considerable color changes, sometimes becoming almost black. Its body depth is greater than that of other pompano. The young, which like the young of all pompano species occur in the surf, frequently have reddish fins. Permit are relatively uncommon, and relatively little is known about their life history. New England to Brazil and also near most Caribbean islands. (31 inches; 79 cm)

225. Palometa; longfinned pompano   *Trachinotus goodei* Jordan and Evermann

D. VI + I, 19–20; A. II + I, 16–18; P. 16–19; Gr. 5–9 + 8–12; sides silvery; adults with about five thin vertical bars on sides and very long dorsal and anal fins. An uncommon species, usually regarded as a stray from more tropical waters, in older literature this fish goes by the names *T. glaucus* or *T. palometa*. Massachusetts through the Caribbean to Brazil. Gunter and Knapp, 1951; Moore, 1975*b*. (12 inches; 30 cm)

226. Almaco jack   *Seriola rivoliana* Valenciennes

D. VII + I, 28–32; A. II + I, 19–22; P. 19–22; Sc. 122–137; Gr. 7–8 + 16–18; depth of body (at point just behind end of head) 34.5–40 percent of standard length. This species is a wide-ranging but little-reported amberjack. Because of their high dorsal and anal lobes, western Atlantic populations are sometimes reported as *S. falcata*. Both sides of the Atlantic and in the Mediterranean; in the western Atlantic from New Jersey through the Caribbean to Argentina. (36 inches; 91 cm)

227. Lesser amberjack   *Seriola fasciata* (Bloch)

D. VIII + I, 30–32; A. II + I, 19–20; P. 19–20; Sc. 129–134; Gr. 7–8 + 18–20; depth of body 37–42 percent of standard length. Another widespread but little-known jack, this species has not been confirmed from the northwestern Gulf. However, it is included here since as a group the amberjacks are difficult to identify, and small specimens may turn out to be *S. fasciata*, which does not grow as large as the other species. Apparently it is most common in the open waters of the Caribbean and tropical Atlantic. (1 foot; 30 cm)

228. Greater amberjack *Seriola dumerili* (Risso)

D. VIII + I, 30–35; A. II + I, 19–22; P. 19–22; Sc. 141–163; Gr. 2–3 + 11–17; depth of body 29–31 percent of standard length. The largest and most common amberjack in our area, this fish is rather easily confused with the eastern Atlantic species, S. *lalandi*, reports of which in this area probably refer to S. *dumerili*. In very large fish both the dorsal spines and the gill rakers are reduced in number. This phenomenon also occurs in the almaco jack (S. *rivoliana*); however, the greater amberjack always has lower counts as well as a thinner body. It occurs widely throughout the tropical and temperate Atlantic ocean; Bermuda and Massachusetts to the Caribbean. (3 feet; 91 cm)

229. Banded rudderfish *Seriola zonata* (Mitchill)

D. VII–VIII + I, 33–40; A. II + I, 19–21; P. 18–21; Sc. 160–180; Gr. 2–3 + 11–13; body depth 25–30 percent of standard length. This small jack usually retains its bands, characteristic of the younger fish, longer than do the other species of *Seriola*. Young fish are sometimes found inshore, around pilings and wharves, but more commonly this fish is seen offshore, where it associates with floating objects. Nova Scotia to Brazil and throughout the Gulf of Mexico. (2 feet; 61 cm)

230. African pompano *Alectis crinitus* (Mitchill)

D. VII + I, 18–19; A. II + I, 15–16; P. 18–20; Gr. 5–6 + 14–16. The young of this species are characterized by extremely long, filamentous dorsal and anal fins and the presence of well-developed scutes along the posterior lateral line. In adults the spinous portions of both the dorsal and anal fins becomes overgrown and obscured, and the filamentous fins are usually lost through abrasion, although it is usually apparent that these fin rays are (were) exceptionally longer than normal. Like all jacks, the young are banded, and traces of bands remain on the sides of the silvery adults. This is a tropical species with only scattered reports of young or adults inshore off southern Texas, but adults are fairly common offshore of Louisiana. Both coasts of the Atlantic and in the eastern Pacific as well. Massachusetts through the Caribbean to Brazil. (2 feet; 61 cm)

231. Atlantic moonfish *Vomer setapinnis* (Mitchill)

D. VIII + I, 20–23; A. II + I, 17–19; P. 17–19; Gr. 5–8 + 25–29. The young of this species are rather square fish similar to *Alectis* or *Selene* except that they lack the filamentous fins. The silvery adults are more elongate and lack the produced fin rays; the young are silvery but with a black spot on the sides. The moonfish is a common small fish inshore, occurring in large schools in the bays during the summer. Eastern Pacific and both sides of the Atlantic; in the west from Nova Scotia to Uruguay. (15 inches; 38 cm)

232. Lookdown *Selene vomer* (Linnaeus)

D. VIII + I, 21–23; A. II + I, 18–20; P. 20–21; Gr. 6–8 + 23–27. Lookdown young look rather like the young of *Alectis* but lack developed scutes, and they differ from *Vomer* in having filamentous dorsal, anal, and ventral fins. The young are basically silvery but with dark bands sometimes apparent; adults are silvery with moderately produced dorsal and anal lobes. Nova Scotia to Argentina, including the Gulf and Caribbean, and in the eastern Atlantic and Pacific. (1 foot; 30 cm)

233. Rough scad *Trachurus lathami* Nichols
D. VIII + I, 28–32; A. II + I, 25–27; P. 21–22; Gr. 12–14 + 34–37; body elongate, spindle-shaped, with well-developed scutes posteriorly and scutelike scale anteriorly on lateral line. This little-known schooling fish occurs commonly on the inshore continental shelf of the eastern and Gulf coasts of the United States from Maine to Mexico. (8 inches; 20 cm)

234. Round scad; cigarfish *Decapterus punctatus* (Agassiz)
D. VIII + I, 28–32; A. II + I, 25–27; P. 19–21; scutes 36–44; Gr. 12–15 + 34–40; two papillae on shoulder girdle under opercular flap (Fig. 6). This poorly known but widespread jack is not uncommon on the outer shelf and occurs inshore east of the Mississippi. Another species, *D. tabl*, occurs in the eastern Gulf, and a third species, *D. macarellus*, in the Atlantic. Bermuda and Nova Scotia through the Caribbean to Brazil and in the eastern Atlantic. Berry, 1968. (7 inches; 18 cm)

235. Bigeye scad *Selar crumenophthalmus* (Bloch)
D. VIII + I, 24–26; A. II + I, 21–23; P. 20–22; scutes 30–40; Gr. 9–11 + 27–30; two papillae on shoulder girdle under opercular flap (Fig. 6). This little-known fish, not commonly taken on the inshore shelf at least west of the Mississippi, is normally found closer inshore in the northeastern Gulf. Circumtropical. (12 inches; 30 cm)

236. Atlantic bumper *Chloroscombrus chrysurus* (Linnaeus)
D. VIII + I, 26–28; A. II + I, 25–27; P. 19–20; Gr. 9–11 + 31–35. This small species is common in the shallow Gulf and high-salinity bays. Aside from its slender caudal peduncle and free anal spines, this fish is easily identified by its yellow tail and dark spot atop the caudal peduncle. Atlantic Ocean, in the west from Massachusetts to Uruguay. (1 foot; 30 cm)

237. Bluntnose jack *Hemicaranx amblyrhynchus* (Cuvier)
D. VII + I, 27–29; A. II + I, 23–25; P. 19–22; scutes 45–54; Gr. 8–10 + 19–23. This is a small jack seldom exceeding about ten inches (25 cm). Its young hide in the bell and among the tentacles of several common jellyfishes. This species is distinguished from *Caranx* by the lack of keels on the caudal peduncle, generally darker coloration, a more strongly arched lateral line, and the absence of vomerine and enlarged jaw teeth. The bases of the soft dorsal and anal fins are sheathed. Young fish between one inch and six inches (22–150 mm) have vertical bars, the last one more forward than in *Caranx* young. North Carolina to Brazil. (11 inches; 28 cm)

238. Cottonmouth jack *Uraspis secunda* (Poey)
D. VIII + I, 29; A. I, 21; P. 23; scutes about 38; Gr. 6 + 14; tongue milky white; soft dorsal and anal fins with almost vertical margin over middle of caudal peduncle. This is the only carangid in which the scute spines point

forward. Although a distinctive species, it may have been confused with *Hemicaranx*, from which it differs by the above traits. Older reports of *U. heidi* refer to this species. New Jersey to southern Texas. (8 inches; 20 cm)

239. Bar jack   *Caranx ruber* (Bloch)

D. VIII + I, 27–28; A. II + I, 24; P. 19–21; scutes 20–27; Gr. 12–15 + 29–34; general body form that of elongate *Caranx*, but distinguished by dark bar running along base of dorsal fin onto lower lobe of caudal. A rare species in the northwestern Gulf, this fish is generally confined to the more offshore waters. It is more common in more tropical waters. New Jersey through the Caribbean to Brazil. Baughman, 1947; Berry, 1959. (22 inches; 56 cm)

240. Yellow jack   *Caranx bartholomaei* Cuvier

D. VIII + I, 25–27; A. II + I, 22–24; P. 20–21; scutes 20–31; Gr. 7–9 + 19–21. This fish is similar to *C. ruber*, but without the dark band. All its fins, especially the caudal, are yellow, but this is not uncommon in most species of *Caranx*. The young, however, are known to have yellow blotches on their sides. It is another uncommon, tropical species. Adults are known only from offshore; however, young fish occur inshore. Massachusetts through the Caribbean to Brazil. (36 inches; 91 cm)

241. Blue runner (hardtail)   *Caranx fusus* Geoffroy Saint-Hilaire

D. VIII + I, 23–24; A. II + I, 19–20; P. 21–23; scutes 45–54; Gr. 12–14 + 23–28. Another elongate *Caranx*, *fusus* is distinguished from *ruber* and *bartholomaei* by its more numerous scutes, lack of coloration as described for these other species, and generally black lobes on the caudal fin as well as a black opercular spot. This jack is occasionally caught inshore. Western Atlantic populations are sometimes separated as *C. crysos*. Nova Scotia through the Caribbean to Brazil and in the eastern Atlantic. (26 inches; 66 cm)

242. Black jack   *Caranx lugubris* Poey

D. VIII + I, 21–22; A. II + I, 17–19; P. 20–22; scutes 26–33; Gr. 6–8 + 18–20. A distinctively shaped and colored jack, this fish is rarely encountered far offshore. Circumtropical. Sonnier, Teerling, and Hoese, 1976. (36 inches; 91 cm)

243. Crevalle; common jack   *Caranx hippos* (Linnaeus)

D. VIII + I, 15–21; A. II + I, 15–17; P. 20–21; scutes 24–39; Gr. 6–8 + 14–16. The common jackfish of inshore waters, crevalle juveniles and adults are often found inshore. The young have dark bars similar to those of *Hemicaranx*, with which it can be confused, but young *Caranx* are more silvery, have a low arch in the anterior lateral line, and usually have the anterior soft dorsal and anal fins lobed. This is a very large species, reaching over forty pounds (18 kg). Although it is not generally considered a food fish (jacks are edible), it is most prized as a hard-fighting game fish. Crevalle are voracious scavengers that may follow boats dumping trash. They are found in tropical and temperate waters around the world. (40 inches; 1 m)

244. Horse-eye jack   *Caranx latus* Agassiz

D. VIII + I, 20–22; A. II + I, 16–17; P. 19–21; scutes 30–42; Gr. 6–8 + 14–18. Less common than *C. hippos*, the young of these two species often occur together and are easily confused. *C. latus* possesses a fully scaled chest, a less distinct dark spot on the opercle, and usually a black spot on the lobe of the dorsal fin. It occasionally enters the bays. New Jersey and Bermuda through the Caribbean to Brazil. (22 inches; 56 cm)

Coryphaenidae

The dolphins or dorados are a small family of epipelagic fishes. Both species occur in our range as well as in all warm seas around the world. Dolphins are colorful fish, capable of rapid changes in their coloration. Although nothing is known of dolphin behavior, it is likely that color changes play an important role in communication between these fish. Most fishermen are familiar with the change in appearance of freshly caught dolphin after they are removed from the water.

Generally speaking, the pompano dolphin does not grow as large as the common dolphin. Any dolphin over 30 inches (76 cm) and most over two feet (61 cm) belong to the latter species. In the western Gulf most moderately small dolphin 8–18 inches (20–46 cm) are *Coryphaena equisetis*. Very small fish 1–8 inches (25–200 mm) long are easily distinguished by color differences. For larger fish, coloration, meristic counts, and body proportions must be used. Above 38 inches (95 cm) *C. hippurus* shows distinct sexual dimorphism, the males possessing a characteristic high, nearly vertical forehead. (Gibbs and Collette, 1959)

1   Small fish, less than 8 inches (200 mm)   2
    Large fish, more than 8 inches (200 mm)   3
2   Sides with alternating light (orange) and black bars, continuing
       onto dorsal, anal, and caudal fins (caudal dark except for tips of
       lobes) . . . . Dolphin, *Coryphaena hippurus*.
    Sides uniformly colored; dorsal and anal fins weakly barred; pos-
       terior margin of caudal and sometimes entire fin unpigmented
       . . . . Pompano dolphin, *Coryphaena equisetis*.
3   Depth of body less than one-fourth of standard length; lateral-line
       scales 240–280; total dorsal rays (including buried anteriormost
       rays) more than 55 . . . . Dolphin, *C. hippurus*.
    Depth of body more than one-fourth of standard length; lateral-
       line scales fewer than 200; total dorsal rays 55 or fewer . . . .
       Pompano dolphin, *C. equisetis*.

245. Dolphin   *Coryphaena hippurus* Linnaeus
    D. 50–65 (usually 59–65); A. 25–30 (27); P. 17–20 (20); Sc. 240–280; large males over 38 inches (95 cm) with high, crested forehead; body in life colorful, in various shades of blue, violet, yellow, orange, and white, with many small blue spots. Dark vertical bands, present in small fish, are sometimes seen also in adults. This species occurs more inshore than *C. equisetis* and also ranges into cooler waters. Young fish have been reported from saltier

bays. Dolphin, like sailfish, are apparently a rapidly growing fish with short lives of two or three years. A highly prized sports fish (up to forty pounds— 18 kg), generally regarded as one of the best tasting fishes in the Gulf. Circumtropical, in the western Atlantic from Nova Scotia and Bermuda through the Caribbean to Brazil. Pew, 1957. (5 feet; 1½ m)

246. Pompano dolphin *Coryphaena equisetis* Linnaeus

D. 47–58 (usually 53); A. 23–29 (26); P. 18–21 (20); Sc. 170–200; coloration much like *C. hippurus*, except that dark banding is never apparent and dark spots are more obvious. Does not grow as large as *C. hippurus*; in the Gulf most fish are under 18–24 inches (45–60 cm) long. Fish over 9 inches (230 mm) long are sexually mature throughout the late spring and summer (April to August). Most small dolphins caught in the Gulf belong to this species. Circumtropical, in the western Atlantic from New Jersey and Bermuda through the Caribbean to Brazil. (30 inches; 76 cm)

Bramidae

The pomfrets are a poorly known family remarkable for undergoing great changes in body shape with growth. They are probably closely related to the dolphins (Coryphaenidae), but their general body form is more like that of the butterfishes. They have long, lunate dorsals and anals and very small ventral fins. Juveniles of several species of the genera *Taractes*, *Collybus*, and *Brama* may rarely occur on the shelf, but generally they occur in deeper waters. (Mead, 1957; Mead and Maul, 1958)

Lutjanidae

The snappers are large, carnivorous fishes which are native to the offshore reefs or snapper banks that are scattered from forty to one hundred fathoms in the northwestern Gulf of Mexico. Snappers are generally bottom-dwelling fishes, but they often feed well away from the bottom or over more open bottoms and occasionally are found far from reefs. The young of most species occur in shallower water than do the adults, and one species, the gray snapper, occurs commonly inshore as an adult. *Lutjanus* and *Rhomboplites* occur in the shallowest water, and other genera not included here are found in water one hundred to three hundred fathoms deep. Also, additional tropical species may occur on the offshore reefs.

The Gulf red snapper supports a considerable commercial fishery and is highly regarded as a sports fish as well, especially where it is caught around oil platforms and wrecks. A sizable fishery is landed in Florida and Texas, but the largest catches are probably made off Louisiana and the Campeche Bank. Other snappers are frequently caught together with the red snapper; however, none except the vermilion snapper are as common. (Baughman, 1943b; Randall, 1966; Anderson, 1967; Rivas, 1966, 1970)

1 Dorsal spines X; lateral line scales fewer than 60 2
   Dorsal spines XII; lateral line scales more than 60 . . . . Vermilion snapper, *Rhomboplites aurorubens.*
2 Scales on soft dorsal and anal fins, with last rays of these fins not produced; dorsal rays 12–14; gill rakers on lower limb of first arch few (7–10) or numerous (19–21) 3
   No scales on soft dorsal and anal fins, with last rays produced as filaments (which may be broken off); dorsal rays 10–11; gill rakers on lower limb of first arch 16–17 . . . . Wenchman, *Pristipomoides aquilonaris.*
3 Gill rakers on lower limb of first arch few (7–10); caudal lobes not produced in adults; no pterygoid teeth 4
   Gill rakers on lower limb of first arch numerous, 19–21; caudal lobes produced in adults; pterygoid teeth present . . . . Yellowtail snapper, *Ocyurus chrysurus.*
4 Dorsal rays usually 14, rarely 13 5
   Dorsal rays normally 12 . . . . Lane snapper, *Lutjanus synagris.*
5 Vomerine tooth patch with posterior extension 6
   Vomerine tooth patch without posterior extension 8
6 Gill rakers on lower limb of first arch 7–8; anal rays usually 8 7
   Gill rakers on lower limb of first arch 9–10; anal rays usually 9 (8 in 11 percent of Gulf specimens) . . . . Red snapper, *Lutjanus campechanus.*
7 Body comparatively stout, with greatest depth 36–43 percent (usually 37–42 percent) of standard length; pectoral fin in adults longer than distance from tip of snout to posteriormost edge of preopercle (in juveniles pectoral fin as in *Lutjanus griseus*) 9
   Body comparatively slender, with greatest depth 31–38 percent (usually 32–37 percent) of standard length; pectoral fin in adults as long as distance from tip of snout to posteriormost edge of preopercle . . . . Gray snapper, *Lutjanus griseus.*
8 Lateral-line scales 45–47; body depth 29–32 percent of standard length; caudal without pointed lobes . . . . Cubera snapper, *Lutjanus cyanopterus.*
   Lateral-line scales 47–51; body depth 31–40 percent of standard length; caudal with pointed lobes . . . . Mutton snapper, *Lutjanus analis.*
9 Scales large, with 39–44 (usually 40–43) transverse rows between "scale bone"* and base of caudal fin; 40–45 pored scales in lateral line; 5–7 rows between base of dorsal and lateral line . . . . Schoolmaster, *Lutjanus apodus.*

* Snappers possess an enlarged scale known as the scale bone above and behind the gill slit.

Scales small, with 45–49 transverse rows between "scale bone" and base of caudal; 46–48 pored scales in lateral line . . . . Dog snapper, *Lutjanus jocu.*

247. Vermilion snapper; bastard snapper *Rhomboplites aurorubens* (Cuvier)

D. XII, 11; A. III, 8; Sc. about 72; Gr. 6 + 21; vomer with diamond-shaped (rhomboid) patch of teeth; vermilion red to pink, paler below with series of yellow lines along sides; yellow orange edges on dorsal and anal fins. As common as or more common than the red snapper, the vermilion snapper is found year-round on the snapper banks. Apparently this species occurs most commonly on the level areas on the reefs or about their bases instead of on the steep slopes. North Carolina and Bermuda through the Caribbean to Brazil. (20 inches; 51 cm)

248. Wenchman *Pristipomoides aquilonaris* (Goode and Bean)

D. X, 10–11; A. III, 8; Sc. 48–52; Gr. 7–9 + 17–19. The wenchman is one of the most common fish over the hard-bottomed regions on the middle to outer shelf. References to *P. macrophthalamus* and *P. andersoni* from this area refer to this species. North Carolina to French Guiana and at least part of the West Indies. Anderson, 1966. (9 inches; 23 cm)

249. Yellowtail snapper *Ocyurus chrysurus* (Bloch)

D. X, 12–14; A. III, 8–9; Sc. 48–49; Gr. 21–22; vomerine teeth in arrow-shaped patch. Caudal fin deeply forked; prominent mid-lateral yellow stripe beginning on snout, broadening as it passes along body, and continuing onto tail; yellow spots on blue background above this line, with narrow yellow stripes on lighter background below. More pelagic than the other snappers, it is seldom seen here in abundance. Massachusetts through the Caribbean to Brazil. (2 feet; 61 cm)

250. Lane snapper; candy snapper *Lutjanus synagris* (Linnaeus)

D. X, 12–13; A. III, 8; Sc. 47–52; Gr. 8–11 on lower limb, excluding rudiments, which may be fused in adults; vomerine teeth in arrow-shaped patch; diffuse black spot, as large as eye, below soft dorsal, with lateral line passing through bottom of this spot or running just beneath it; body pink to red with seven or eight yellow longitudinal stripes; caudal fin light red; soft dorsal, anal, and ventrals yellow. This fish is frequently encountered on the snapper banks, the young occurring regularly inshore, where they are caught in shrimp trawls. North Carolina to Brazil, including the Gulf of Mexico and western Caribbean. (18 inches; 46 cm)

251. Mutton snapper *Lutjanus analis* (Cuvier)

D. X (rarely IX or XI), 13–14; A. III, 8 (rarely 7); Sc. 47–51; Gr. 7–9 on lower limb, excluding rudiments; vomerine teeth in crescent-shaped patch; black spot, smaller than eye, present above lateral line and below soft dorsal; often with wavy blue line beneath eye and another from snout to middle of anterior edge of orbit and continuing behind eye for a short distance; fins reddish, especially ventrals, anal, and lower portion of caudal; posterior edge of caudal dusky. This is a moderate-sized snapper (up to thirty pounds—14 kg) whose status here is uncertain. From Massachusetts (rare north of the Carolinas) through the Caribbean to Brazil. (2½ feet; 76 cm)

252. Red snapper   *Lutjanus campechanus* (Poey)

D. X, 14; A. III, 9; Sc. 46–50; Gr. 8–11; vomerine teeth broadly arrow-shaped; various intensities of red, often composed of alternating dark and lighter vertical red bands; diffuse black spot above lateral line and below soft dorsal, disappearing in larger specimens. This is the commercial red snapper of the Gulf of Mexico. It is replaced to the south by the similar or identical species *L. purpureus.* Literature before 1966 referred to this species as either *L. blackfordi* (Goode and Bean) 1878 or *L. aya* (Bloch) 1790. Massachusetts (rare north of Cape Hatteras) to Yucatán, including the Gulf but not the Caribbean. Camber, 1955; Carpenter, 1965; Moseley, 1966*b.* (30 inches; 76 cm)

253. Gray snapper; black snapper; mangrove snapper   *Lutjanus griseus* (Linnaeus)

D. X, 14; A. III, 7–8; Sc. 43–47; Gr. 7–9 on lower limb, excluding rudiments; vomerine teeth in arrow-shaped patch; dark gray green to brown on body and fins; no black spot on side of body; median fins dark brown to black, often edged with white or yellow; young with black bar from tip of snout through eye and often with blue streak beneath eye and generally lighter color; large adults on offshore banks more reddish in color. This is a common snapper inshore; young and adults regularly occur in saltier bays. In the southern Gulf this species frequents mangrove swamps. North Carolina to Florida, through the Caribbean to Brazil. (3 feet; 91 cm)

254. Schoolmaster   *Lutjanus apodus* (Walbaum)

D. X, 14; A. III, 8; Sc. 40–45; Gr. 7–9 on lower limb, excluding rudiments; vomerine tooth patch arrow-shaped; body brown with series of pale vertical bars but sometimes partly blotches; median and ventral fins yellow; young with blue stripe below eye, often broken into series of blue spots. This is the most common snapper of Caribbean reefs, but it is fairly rare in the northwestern Gulf. Massachusetts through the Caribbean to Brazil. (2 feet; 61 cm)

255. Cubera snapper   *Lutjanus cyanopterus* (Cuvier)

D. X, 14; A. III, 7–8; P. 16–18; Sc. 45–57; Gr. 6–8 on lower limb, excluding rudiments; vomerine teeth without median extension; upper and lower canines equally developed, very strong; body depth less than 32 percent of standard length for a 10-inch or larger fish. The largest species of *Lutjanus,* known to exceed one hundred pounds (45 kg), the cubera snapper is rarely reported from scattered Gulf locations. Its status is uncertain because of confusion with large dog and gray snapper. Bahamas and Gulf of Mexico to Brazil. Moe, 1968. (3 feet; 91 cm)

256. Dog snapper   *Lutjanus jocu* (Bloch and Schneider)

D. X, 13–14; A. III, 8; P. 16–17; Sc. 45–49; Gr. 8–11 on lower limb, excluding rudiments; body deep, 36–43 percent of standard length; arrow-shaped vomerine tooth patch; canines in upper jaw enlarged. The most characteristic coloration of this species is a pale bar running from beneath the eye to the posterior corner of the maxillary, broadening ventrally, but unfortunately this trait is sometimes not apparent. A row of blue spots or a blue bar appears in small fish, beneath the eye, but it is not common. This is a rare but continually occurring snapper. Massachusetts through the Caribbean to Brazil. (2 feet; 61 cm)

Lobotidae

The tripletail, *Lobotes surinamensis*, is the single representative of this family.

257. Tripletail *Lobotes surinamensis* (Bloch)
D. XII, 15; A. III, 11; Sc. 47; body deep brown to olivaceous above, grayish yellow below, often blotched; color changeable from yellow to brown and often variously mottled. A fish of sluggish habits, the tripletail often floats horizontally on the surface like the ocean sunfish, *Mola mola*, with which it is commonly confused. Small fish associate with flotsam in open waters and occur around pilings and bulkheads in enclosed areas. Uncommon in the bays and shallow Gulf during the warmer months. An excellent eating fish, although bony; it reaches twenty pounds. Circumtropical; in the western Atlantic, Cape Cod to Argentina, including the Caribbean. Baughman, 1941*a*, 1943*c*. (3 feet; 91 cm)

Gerreidae

The mojarras, family Gerreidae (often misspelled Gerridae), are silvery, high-bodied fishes with deeply forked tails and greatly protrusible jaws. As in many other groups, the taxonomy of the mojarras has only been incompletely settled for this area, and in addition the family is poorly known ecologically. The family has sometimes been combined with the Indo-Pacific Leiognathidae. (Curran, 1942)*

1 Body with narrow, dark bars, more obvious in life than in preserved specimens . . . . Yellowfin mojarra, *Gerres cinereus*.
  Body without narrow, dark vertical bars; young of some species mottled, blotched, or with diagonal bars, but none with vertical bars 2
2 Anal spines three 3
  Anal spines two . . . . Mottled mojarra, *Ulaema lefroyi*.

* Dockart (1973) has revised the genus *Diapterus*, but since we have not seen his thesis we did not include his name changes.

3   Preopercle entire; second interhaemal bone enlarged, hollowed, and surrounding posterior extension of swim bladder 4
Preopercle serrate; second interhaemal bone normally developed, not hollow and not surrounding part of swim bladder .... Irish pompano, *Diapterus olisthostomus.*
4   Premaxillary groove continuous, naked, uninterrupted by a transverse row of scales; spinous dorsal sometimes with black spot; depth about one-third of standard length .... Spotfin mojarra, *Eucinostomus argenteus.*
Premaxillary groove interrupted by transverse row of scales across anterior end; spinous dorsal usually without black spot; depth 40 percent or less of standard length .... Silver jenny, *Eucinostomus gula.*

258. Yellowfin mojarra   *Gerres cinereus* (Walbaum)

D. IX, 10; A. III, 7; Sc. 39–44; body depth 37–43 percent of standard length; sides silvery with seven darker, vertical bars; ventral and anal fins yellow. This species is found mostly in the fall in the bays and shallow Gulf. Eastern Pacific and western Atlantic from Florida and Bermuda through the Gulf of Mexico. 4 inches; (10 cm)

259. Mottled mojarra   *Ulaema lefroyi* (Goode)

D. IX, 10; A. II, 8; Sc. 44–47; body depth 28–32 percent of standard length; sides silvery; dark, irregular markings about base of dorsal fin rays. This mojarra is a rarely reported form not known from Louisiana. North Carolina to Brazil. (1 inch; 2½ cm)

260. Irish pompano   *Diapterus olisthostomus* (Goode and Bean)

D. IX, 10; A. III, 8; Sc. 37–40; body rhomboid, with depth one-half standard length; anterior profile steep, with prominent notch above eye; dorsal fin margin concave; second dorsal spine well developed, about as long as head; second anal spine strong, about three-fourths head length; third anal spine thinner but slightly longer than second. The similar species *D. rhombeus,* which possesses only two anal spines, was incorrectly reported from Texas; however, that species, as well as *D. plumieri* and *D. olisthostomus,* are known from the Laguna Madre de Tamaulipas. Northeastern Florida to Brazil, including the Gulf of Mexico and the West Indies. (8 inches; 20 cm)

261. Spotfin mojarra   *Eucinostomus argenteus* Baird and Girard

D. IX, 10; A. III, 7; Sc. 44–48; depth 30–36 percent of standard length; premaxillary groove not interrupted by transverse scale row; body silvery with irregular blotches or diagonal bars on upper half. Both coasts of Central America; in the western Atlantic from New Jersey and Bermuda through the Caribbean to Brazil. (4 inches; 10 cm)

262. Silver jenny   *Eucinostomus gula* (Quoy and Gaimard)

D. IX, 10; A. III, 8; Sc. 42; depth 42 percent of standard length; premaxillary groove crossed by scale row. *E. gula* tends to be found more in the Gulf and *E. argenteus* more in inland waters. New England through the Caribbean to Argentina. (8 inches; 20 cm)

Pomadasyidae

The grunts are a family of fishes allied to the snappers, but lacking the canines and vomerine teeth found in all lutjanids. The common name of the group is derived from the noise they make when they rub their pharyngeal teeth together. Only the pigfish is common inshore, but others are important predators on offshore reefs. The adults and young of each species are quite distinct. For identification of the young of *Haemulon*, the reader should refer to other works. Older literature may refer to this family as Haemulidae. (Courtenay, 1961; Böhlke and Chaplin, 1968)

1 Soft dorsal and anal fins densely scaled to their margins 2
  Soft dorsal and anal fins not scaled except at bases 7
2 Dorsal spines XIII (XII + I) 3
  Dorsal spines XII (XI + I), rarely XI 4
3 Scales around caudal peduncle 22; gill rakers 24–28; dorsal rays
    14–15; anal rays usually 9 . . . . Tomtate, *Haemulon aurolineatum*.
  Scales around caudal peduncle 24 or more, usually 26; gill rakers
    27–36; dorsal rays 13–14; anal rays 7–8 . . . . Striped grunt,
    Haemulon striatum.
4 Scales around caudal peduncle 23 or more; scales below lateral
    line 13–14; dark stripe along base of soft dorsal fin extending
    onto upper lobe of caudal . . . . Cottonwick, *Haemulon melanurum*.
  Scales around caudal peduncle 22 or fewer; scales below lateral
    line 12 or 13; color not as above 5
5 Pectoral fins scaled for more than one-third of their length; dor-
    sal fin rays 16–18, usually 17–18 . . . . Sailor's choice, *Haemulon parrai*.
  Pectoral fins not scaled 6
6 Scales above lateral line larger than those below; pectoral rays
    17, rarely 16 . . . . White grunt, *Haemulon plumieri*.
  Scales above lateral line not larger than those below; pectoral
    rays 17–18, usually 18 . . . . Spanish grunt, *Haemulon macrostomum*.
7 Preopercle strongly serrate, with serration on lower margin di-
    rected anteriorly; two enlarged spines at angle . . . . Barred
    grunt, *Conodon nobilis*.
  Preopercle moderately, or not at all, serrate, with none of serra-
    tions directed anteriorly 8
8 Body elongate, 33–36 percent of standard length 9
  Body deep, 43–48 percent of standard length 10
9 Anal rays 12–13; gill rakers on lower limb of first arch 12 . . . .
    Pigfish, *Orthopristis chrysoptera*.

Anal rays 6–7; gill rakers on lower limb of first arch 7–9 ....
Burro grunt, *Pomadasys crocro*.
10   Body marked with alternating blue and yellow stripes; scales
small, 10–11 in vertical row between base of spinous dorsal
and lateral line .... Porkfish, *Anisotremus virginicus*.
Body without alternating blue and yellow stripes; scales larger,
6–7 in oblique row between base of spinous dorsal and lateral
line .... Black margate, *Anisotremus surinamensis*.

263. Tomtate   *Haemulon aurolineatum* Cuvier

D. XII–XIV, 14–15 (usually XIII, 15); A. III, 9; P. 17–18; Sc. 49–52;
Gr. 24–28; depth of body 27–37 percent of standard length; body silvery
with golden stripe running from eye to round black spot located at base of
caudal; second narrow stripe on sides above lateral line; inside of mouth red.
Only this species and *H. striatum* have thirteen dorsal spines. Because of this
difference, these two species have often been placed in the genus *Bathystoma*.
Northwestern Gulf members of this species are sometimes separated into the
subspecies (or species) *rimator*. This is a common fish around offshore reefs,
and it is occasionally found near platforms. Massachusetts and Bermuda
through the Caribbean to Brazil. (9 inches; 23 cm)

264. Striped grunt   *Haemulon striatum* (Linnaeus)

D. XIII, 13–14; A. III, 7–8 (usually 8); P. 17–19; Sc. 51–53; Gr. 28–34;
body more elongate than those of other grunts, depth 26–32 percent of
standard length; body silvery gray with five dusky yellow stripes. The striped
grunt is known here only from a specimen collected offshore of central Texas.
Southern Texas and the Bahamas through the Caribbean. Courtenay, 1961.
(9 inches; 23 cm)

265. Cottonwick   *Haemulon melanurum* (Linnaeus)

D. XII, 15–17; A. III, 8–9 (usually 8): P. 16–18; Sc. 49–52; Gr. 20–23;
body silvery white with five or six yellow stripes on sides and strong black
stripe running from dorsal fin origin to caudal peduncle, then separating into
two stripes running to each lobe of caudal fin; sometimes with additional
longitudinal black stripes on body. In the northern Gulf, this grunt is not uncommon around offshore reefs. Bermuda, Bahamas, and the northern Gulf
through the Caribbean to Brazil. Bright and Cashman, 1974; Sonnier, Teerling, and Hoese, 1976. (1 foot; 30 cm)

266. Sailor's choice   *Haemulon parrai* (Desmarest)

D. XII, 16–18; A. III, 8; P. 17; Sc. 51–52; Gr. 21–26; body silvery, with
each scale edged with brown; scales on upper half of body with brownish
spots which form oblique rows; black blotch usually present under opercular
edge; inside of mouth red. There is one report of this fish from Texas, but its
status in the northern and western Gulf is not known. Bahamas and Florida
through the Caribbean to Brazil. Reed, 1941. (16 inches; 41 cm)

267. White grunt   *Haemulon plumieri* (Lacépède)

D. XII, 15–17; A. III, 8–9 (usually 9); P. 16–17; Sc. 48–52; Gr. 21–27;
scales above lateral line larger than those below; usually yellowish; head with

narrow blue stripes; scales on upper part of body with blue or white spots; inside of mouth red; black blotch possibly present beneath free edge of opercle. This grunt is known only from a few specimens taken far offshore. Bermuda and Virginia through the Caribbean to Brazil. (18 inches; 46 cm)

268. Spanish grunt *Haemulon macrostomum* Günther

D. XII, 15–17; A. III, 9; P. 17–18 (usually 18); Sc. 50–52; Gr. 26–28; body silvery gray with faint dark stripes on upper portion; caudal peduncle yellow. There is one report of this species from Texas. Bermuda, Florida, and Texas through the Caribbean to Columbia. (14 inches; 36 cm)

269. Barred grunt *Conodon nobilis* (Linnaeus)

D. XI + I, 13; A. III, 7; Sc. 55; dorsal fin divided; preopercle strongly serrated; silver with eight broad vertical bars; sides with yellowish stripes underlying bars; ventral, anal, and caudal fins yellow; belly and lower sides with yellow during breeding season. The barred grunt is common during the late spring and summer on the southern Texas coast, but less common on the northern Gulf coast. Mississippi Delta to Yucatán; through the West Indies to Brazil; not in northeastern Gulf or Florida. Dawson, 1962a. (1 foot; 30 cm)

270. Pigfish *Orthopristis chrysoptera* (Linnaeus)

D. XII–XIII, 16; A. III, 12–13; Sc. 60; body blue above, silvery below, each scale with blue center and bronze edge, forming series of yellow brown stripes on sides; snout and head with orange bands not always evident in life. This is a very common fish in the saltier bays and shallow Gulf; its young live in grass beds. Bermuda and Massachusetts to Florida and throughout the Gulf. (1 foot; 30 cm)

271. Burro grunt *Pomadasys crocro* (Cuvier)

D. XIII, 11–12; A. III, 6–7; Sc. 54; brown with 3–4 ill-defined dark stripes on sides, one from point of snout to base of caudal fin. There have been several reports of this species from Texas, including the young from the Port Aransas jetties. Southern Florida and southern Texas through the Caribbean to Brazil. Hoese, 1965. (1 foot; 30 cm)

272. Porkfish *Anisotremus virginicus* (Linnaeus)

D. XII, 16–17; A. III, 9–11; P. 17–18; Sc. 51–53; Gr. 27–29; diagonal black band from mouth through eye, another running from opercular opening to origin of dorsal fin; behind this bar, body with alternating blue and yellow stripes. Bermuda, Bahamas, southern Florida, and southern Texas through the Caribbean to Brazil. Briggs et al., 1964. (1 foot; 30 cm)

273. Black margate *Anisotremus surinamensis* (Bloch)

D. XII, 16–18; A. III, 8–10 (usually 9); P. 18–19; Sc. 50–53; Gr. 30–36; body silvery, each scale with dark center, tending to form dark diagonal lines on sides; large irregular dark area on lower body behind opercular opening; soft dorsal and anal fins dusky. Rare reports exist from southern Texas. The Bahamas, southern Florida, and southern Texas through the Caribbean to Brazil. (2 feet; 61 cm)

Sparidae

The porgies are a family of moderately sized fish, some of which resemble the grunts. They are best characterized by their anteriormost teeth, which are either flattened incisors or peglike canines. Most species are omnivorous, browsing on attached vegetation or invertebrates. The genus *Calamus* has recently been revised by Randall and Caldwell (1966), who state that the sheepshead porgy, *C. penna* (Plate 279*b*), reported by Baughman (1950*b*) from off Galveston, does not occur in the northwestern Gulf.

1 Teeth in front of jaws flattened, incisorlike, not molar 2
   Teeth in front of jaws conical or caninelike 5
2 First and second dorsal spines short, about one-third of eye diameter in length; third dorsal spine greatly elongate, often longer than head . . . . Longspine porgy, *Stenotomus caprinus*.
   First and second dorsal spines as long as or longer than diameter of eye 3
3 Broad dark bar across top of caudal peduncle . . . . Spottail pinfish, *Diplodus holbrooki*.
   Color variable, but not as above 4
4 Incisors deeply notched; dark shoulder spot; lateral-line scales 65–70 . . . . Pinfish, *Lagodon rhomboides*.
   Incisors not notched; no shoulder spot; lateral-line scales 45–50; five or six (rarely four) broad, black, vertical bands on sides . . . . Sheepshead, *Archosargus probatocephalus*.
5 Anal rays 8 . . . . Red porgy, *Pagrus sedecim*.
   Anal rays 10 or 11 6
6 Pectoral rays usually 15–16 (rarely 14); no enlarged canines in front of jaws; lateral-line scales 43–49 7
   Pectoral rays usually 14–15 (rarely 13 or 16); one or two enlarged canines on each side of jaw; lateral-line scales 50–57 9
7 Pectoral fins short, 28–33 percent of standard length; eyes small; black spot along anterior portion of lateral line 8
   Pectoral fins longer, 29–42 percent of standard length; no black spot on anterior lateral line, or if present not notably darker than surrounding spots . . . . Whitebone porgy, *Calamus leucosteus*.
8 Pectoral rays usually 16; total gill rakers on first arch 10 . . . . Grass porgy, *Calamus arctifrons*.
   Pectoral rays usually 14–15; total gill rakers on first arch 12 . . . . Campeche porgy, *Calamus campechanus*.
9 Pectoral rays usually 14 (rarely 13 or 15); forehead steep, at an angle of 57–65 degrees; large knob above posterior nostril; anal rays usually 11 . . . . Knobbed porgy, *Calamus nodosus*.
   Pectoral rays usually 15 (rarely 14 or 16); forehead not steep, but at an angle of 43–55 degrees; anal rays usually 10 . . . . Jolthead porgy, *Calamus bajonado*.

274. Longspine porgy *Stenotomus caprinus* Bean

D. XII, 12; A. III, 12; Sc. 50; 5 scales above and 15 below lateral line; deep-bodied; silvery-sided, with third, fourth, and fifth dorsal spines greatly elongated. This species, which is found throughout the Gulf of Mexico except the Florida west coast, is commonest on the middle shelf off Louisiana and East Texas. A close relative, *S. chrysops*, which occurs off the Atlantic coast, has also been reported from Texas waters, but it probably does not occur here. In addition, Atlantic populations may be divisible into two species, the northern porgy, *S. chrysops*, and the southern porgy, *S. aculeatus*. The latter form is more similar to *S. caprinus* than is *S. chrysops*; that fact may be responsible for a lot of the apparent confusion in the common and scientific names of these fishes. Caldwell, 1955*a*. (6 inches; 15 cm)

275. Spottail pinfish *Diplodus holbrooki* (Bean)

D. XII, 14–15; A. III, 13; Sc. 55–57; 7 scales above and 14 below lateral line; silvery-sided, with dark saddle or spot on dorsal surface of caudal peduncle. The species occurs along the Atlantic and Gulf coasts of the United States from North Carolina to Florida and from the northern Gulf to southern Texas, where juveniles are sometimes found schooling with the common pinfish. A similar fish occurs in the Caribbean. Caldwell, 1955*b*. (7 inches; 18 cm)

276. Pinfish; pin perch *Lagodon rhomboides* (Linnaeus)

D. XII, 11; A. III, 11; Sc. 65–70; 10 scales above and 17 below lateral line; body olivaceous above, lighter below, with numerous blue and yellow stripes and spots; adults with traces of six vertical bars on sides (becoming more prominent after death) and prominent humeral spot. One of the most common inshore fishes except in the highly turbid brackish waters of western Louisiana, the pinfish is usually found around wharves and pilings and over grassflats. A voracious feeder, well noted for its bait-stealing activities, it is edible, but it rarely reaches sufficient size to warrant keeping unless it is cooked whole. Massachusetts and Bermuda to Florida and throughout the Gulf, rarely crossing the Gulf Stream. Caldwell, 1957. (10 inches; 25 cm)

277. Sheepshead *Archosargus probatocephalus* (Walbaum)

D. XII, 10–12; A. III, 10–11; Sc. 48; 8 scales above and 15 below lateral line; 6–7 vertical black bands on sides and no distinct humeral spot. Western Gulf populations of the sheepshead were considered to be a separate species, *A. oviceps*, because of the number of stripes; however, the differences between eastern and western Gulf populations are probably not at the species level. A common inshore sports fish, it is often caught using fiddler crabs or barnacles for bait. Massachusetts to Yucatán; through the West Indies to Brazil. Ginsburg, 1954; Hildebrand, 1955; Caldwell, 1965. (2 feet; 61 cm)

278. Red porgy; silver snapper; white snapper *Pagrus sedecim* Ginsburg

D. XII, 9–11; A. III, 8; Sc. 56–59. A common fish on the Atlantic coast of the United States, the species has been reported only once from the western Gulf but is common off the Florida panhandle. The western Atlantic form may be the same as the eastern Atlantic *Pagrus pagrus*. (18 inches; 46 cm)

279. Grass porgy *Calamus arctifrons* Goode and Bean

D. XII, 12; A. III, 10; P. 16; Sc. 48; 6 scales above and 13 below lateral line; Gr. 10; body olivaceous with dark bars on sides, sometimes confined to six spots along lateral line. This species is smaller than most other porgies. It is found over shallow grassflats on the Florida Gulf coast and rarely strays to Louisiana and Texas. Bullis and Thompson, 1965; Randall and Caldwell, 1966. (8 inches; 20 cm)

280. Campeche porgy *Calamus campechanus* Randall and Caldwell

D. XII, 12; A. III, 10; P. 14–15; Sc. 48; 6 scales above and 13–14 below lateral line; Gr. 12; body with five indistinct blotches on sides and pattern of wavy horizontal lines on cheek and snout. Presently known only from the Campeche Bank, this porgy may range north along the Mexican coast to southern Texas. (8 inches; 20 cm)

281. Whitebone porgy *Calamus leucosteus* Jordan and Gilbert

D. XII, 12; A. III, 10; P. 16; Sc. 51; 7–8 scales above and 14 below lateral line; body silvery with faint crossbars; dorsal and anal fins with dark blotches; ventrals dusky; axil of pectoral not distinctly colored. Southern Atlantic and northern Gulf coasts of the United States, mainly in deeper water. (14 inches; 36 cm)

282. Jolthead porgy *Calamus bajonado* (Bloch and Schneider)

D. XII, 12; A. III, 10; Sc. 54; 7 scales above and 17 below lateral line; eye diameter about 40 percent of head length of adults; body silvery with faint blue or violet iridescence; blue line under eye; axil of pectoral with blue spot; two horizontal white bands on cheek, most obvious in live specimens. Records of *C. macrops* refer to this species according to Randall and Caldwell (1966), who have synonymized the two forms. From Rhode Island to Belize (British Honduras); also Bermuda and throughout the West Indies in water to 150 feet deep. (20 inches; 51 cm)

283. Knobbed porgy *Calamus nodosus* Randall and Caldwell

D. XII, 12; A. III, 11; P. 14 (13–15); Sc. 56; 7–8 scales above and 17–20 below lateral line; body silver, no obvious bars on sides; snout, unscaled part of cheek, and preopercle dark purple with irregular yellowish spots and darker stripes; often with large, diffuse dark spot in axil of pectoral. The knoblike tubercle found above the posterior nostril identifies this species. Reports of *C. calamus* from Texas probably refer to this species. From North Carolina to Yucatán, usually in six to forty-three fathoms. (2 feet; 61 cm)

Sciaenidae

The croakers are perhaps the most characteristic group of northern Gulf inshore fishes. In numbers of species they exceed all other families, and in numbers of individuals, or biomass, they are among the top three (the others being the mullets and the much smaller anchovies). Many species grow to a large size and are important commercial and sports fish. Most spawn in the shallow Gulf, with the larvae entering the bays, where they spend their first summer in brackish water. Most are fast-growing and short-lived. Although most species are adapted to living on muddy bottoms, a few are found in more sandy habitats, and a few are adapted to rocky habitats. Some species move from soft, muddy substrates to harder ones as the fish grow older. (Pearson, 1929; Welsh and Breder, 1923; Hildebrand and Cable, 1934)

1   Second dorsal rays fewer than 32 2
    Second dorsal rays more than 36 16
2   Lower jaw with one or more barbels 3
    Lower jaw without barbels 8
3   One thick barbel on front underside of lower jaw 4
    Many barbels, minute to large, sometimes wearing off 7
4   Preopercle serrate; thin vertical bars on sides of body .... Sand
        drum, *Umbrina coroides.*
    Preopercle not serrate; sides may be blotched, but without defi-
        nite thin vertical bars 5
5   Second dorsal spine elongate, extending to twice height of rest of
        fin; body with V-shaped blotch on each side .... King whit-
        ing, *Menticirrhus saxatilis.*
    Second dorsal spine only slightly elongate, barely extending be-
        yond others; body silvery, blotched or with oblique bars 6
6   Inside of operculum dusky; body with irregular dark stripes or
        blotches .... Southern kingfish, *Menticirrhus americanus.*
    Inside of operculum silvery; body plain, silvery .... Gulf king-
        fish, *Menticirrhus littoralis.*
7   Many large barbels on lower jaw; body with about five dark
        vertical bars .... Black drum, *Pogonias cromis.*
    Row of minute barbels on each side of lower jaw (often worn off
        in larger fish, with series of small pits along edge of jaw to
        show their former location); body not barred .... Atlantic
        croaker, *Micropogon undulatus.*
8   Black spot at base of pectoral fin .... Reef croaker, *Odontoscion
        dentex.*
    No spot at base of pectoral fin (*Cynoscion* with some black pig-
        ment on pectoral, but with large canines) 9
9   Lower jaw projecting; one pair of enlarged canine teeth in upper
        jaw 10
    Lower jaw not projecting; mouth terminal or inferior; no en-
        larged canines in upper jaw 12
10 Upper portions of sides of body with well-defined spots ....
        Spotted seatrout, *Cynoscion nebulosus.*
    Upper portion of body without definite spots 11
11 Anal rays 10–11; scales firm .... Sand seatrout, *Cynoscion
        arenarius.*
    Anal rays 8–9; scales deciduous .... Silver seatrout, *Cynoscion
        nothus.*
12 Mouth inferior, below horizontal line drawn from lower edge of
        eye 13

Mouth terminal, with at least tip of upper jaw above line drawn
through lower edge of eye 14

13 Dark spot present above lateral line in front of caudal fin (possibly several such spots); no shoulder spot .... Red drum,
Sciaenops ocellata.

No dark spot at base of caudal fin, but spot on shoulder ....
Spot, *Leiostomus xanthurus*.

14 Space between eyes (interorbital) hollow; caudal lanceolate ....
Star drum, *Stellifer lanceolatus*.

Space between eyes slightly convex; caudal truncate 15

15 Edge of preopercle serrate; mouth oblique; body with vertical
bars .... Banded croaker, *Larimus fasciatus*.

Edge of preopercle smooth; body without bars; mouth only
slightly oblique .... Silver perch, *Bairdiella chrysura*.

16 Dorsal soft rays fewer than 40; midlateral dark stripe extending
from caudal fin to eye; dorsal and caudal fins not greatly elongate in adults, and in young still less than one-half body
length .... Cubbyu, *Equetus umbrosus*.

Dorsal soft rays more than 45; midlateral dark stripe curving
upward to join dark bar on spinous dorsal fin; dorsal and
caudal fins greatly elongate, especially in young 17

17 Pectoral and anal fins pale; median fins not spotted; more than
48 dorsal rays .... Jackknife fish, *Equetus lanceolatus*.

Pectoral and anal fins dark; median fins (except anal) spotted;
fewer than 48 dorsal rays .... Spotted drum, *Equetus punctatus*.

284. Sand drum (roncador) *Umbrina coroides* Cuvier

D. X + I, 27–28; A. II, 6–7; Sc. 48; Gr. 5 + 9; body silvery with
nine dark cross-bands; undulating streaks along rows of scales; spinous
dorsal darkish. The sand drum is a tropical sand-beach species, known only
south from Port Aransas and Chesapeake Bay through the Caribbean to
Brazil but not in the northern and eastern Gulf. Gilbert, 1966. (1 foot; 30 cm)

285. King whiting *Menticirrhus saxatilis* (Bloch and Schneider)

Gulf of Mexico specimens with D. X + I, 24–25; A. I, 8; Sc. 75–86;
Gr. 5 + 7–10; dusky gray above, sometimes blackish; sides and back with
distinct dark oblique blotches forming V-shaped pattern; second ray of
spinous dorsal elongate. This is a rare but characteristic species known only
from the inshore shelf. Fish from the Gulf of Mexico were once described
as a separate species, *M. focaliger* Ginsburg, but recent work has shown
that the two forms intergrade along the Florida coast. The Atlantic populations of *M. saxatilis* are commonly known as the northern kingfish, while
the Gulf populations are called Gulf minkfish. Since neither common name
is applicable to both groups, we choose to use the older common name,
king whiting, for both. Cape Cod to Florida, throughout the Gulf of Mexico
to Campeche. Ginsburg, 1952a; Irwin, 1969. (1 foot; 30 cm)

286. Southern kingfish; sea mullet *Menticirrhus americanus* (Linnaeus)

D. X + I, 24–25; A. I, 7; Sc. 80–90; body silver gray to coppery with
irregular dark patches; gill cavity dusky. This common inshore and bay

species is found mostly in deeper water in these areas. New York to Argentina. (16 inches; 47 cm)

287. Gulf kingfish; Gulf whiting   *Menticirrhus littoralis* (Holbrook)
D. X + I, 23–25; A. I, 7; Sc. 70–74; body silvery, not blotched; gill cavity pale. The Gulf whiting is almost entirely a surf species; the young are sometimes found in the bays, especially in shallow water. Virginia to Florida and throughout the Gulf. (1 foot; 30 cm)

288. Black drum   *Pogonias cromis* (Linnaeus)
D. X + I, 21; A. II, 5–6; Sc. 41–47; Gr. 4 + 12; 4–5 broad, dark bands on sides of body, becoming obscured in large fish, which are more uniformly dark; underside of lower jaw with numerous large barbels. The largest of the family (up to 150 pounds—68 kg), it is predominately a bay species, more abundant off southern Texas. Massachusetts to Argentina. Simmons and Breuer, 1962. (3 feet; 91 cm)

289. Atlantic croaker   *Micropogon undulatus* (Linnaeus)
D. X + I, 28–29; A. II, 7; Sc. 64–72; Gr. 7 + 16; young silvery, and older fish brassy yellow; middle of body with short, irregular brown streaks formed by spots on scales. This is perhaps the commonest bottom-dwelling estuarine species, with the young occuring in the deeper parts of the bays in the summer but departing in the fall. Only a few large fish live past their first year, but very large croakers are found off the mouth of the Mississippi. South of the United States the taxonomy of the croakers becomes confused, as this species or a very similar one may occur as far south as Argentina. *M. furnieri* (Desmarest), which occurs on the Mexican coast, may venture sometimes into our area; however, records of that species often show it to be confused with *M. undulatus*. It differs from *M. undulatus* because of its larger scales (seven between the dorsal origin and the lateral line *vs.* nine in *M. undulatus*) and because its spots on the scales above the lateral line form more continuous vertical lines. Massachusetts to at least central Mexico. Suttkus, 1954; Avault, Birdsong, and Perry, 1969. (2 feet; 61 cm)

290. Reef croaker   *Odontoscion dentex* (Cuvier)
D. XI or XIII + I, 23; A. II, 8; Sc. 49–52; Gr. 5 + 14; body silvery with distinct black blotch at base and in axil of pectoral fin. This rare species, known off Texas only from 7½-Fathom Reef and the Flower Gardens Reef, is also found in all reef areas throughout the tropical western Atlantic. (7 inches; 18 cm)

291. Spotted seatrout; speckled trout (spotted weakfish; spotted squeteague)   *Cynoscion nebulosus* (Cuvier)
D. X + I, 24–26; A. II, 10–11; Sc. 66 or more; Gr. 4 + 7–9, short and thick (the longest about as long as width of pupil); mouth orange inside, body silvery, greenish above, with numerous dark spots on upper sides of body and on dorsal and caudal fins; young fish similarly spotted and with lanceolate caudal fin, which becomes truncate or slightly concave with growth. The spotted seatrout is an important inshore sports and commercial fish. It spawns in the bays, and the young often spend their first year in

or near grassflats, where those are present. The adults are commonest in deeper areas and are sometimes found over oyster reefs. Very large "specks" are believed to feed almost exclusively on fish, mostly mullet. Because of the size of their prey, they probably feed only once or twice a week, which results in disproportionately low sports catches of these large (but most under three feet) fish. They may be more common in the Laguna Madre. North Atlantic, in the west from New York to Tampico. Guest and Gunter, 1958; Sundararaj and Suttkus, 1962. (4 feet; 1¼ m)

292. Sand seatrout; sand trout; white trout   *Cynoscion arenarius* Ginsburg

D. X + I, 25–27; A. II, 11; Sc. about 60; Gr. 3–4 + 10; body silvery, greenish above, often with large, irregular dark blotches on back when viewed from above; mouth large, orange on inside. This species is a sports fish of some importance. Although it does not grow as large as *C. nebulosus*, the sand trout is a popular fish with most anglers. These fish spawn in the deeper channels of the bays or in the shallow Gulf, the young staying over muddy bottoms. They become almost entirely piscivorous (fish-eating) at a smaller size than does *C. nebulosus*. For many years this species, the common seatrout of the bays and shallow Gulf, was confused with *C. nothus*, the silver seatrout, which is usually found more offshore. The sand seatrout is confined to the Gulf of Mexico, but it may be identical to the Atlantic weakfish, *Cynoscion regalis*, which ranges to Nova Scotia. (16 inches; 41 cm)

293. Silver seatrout   *Cynoscion nothus* (Holbrook)

D. X + I, 27–29; A. II, 9; Sc. 55–58; Gr. 3 + 10, long and slender (the longest greater than diameter of eye); scales very deciduous; flesh weaker than that of other trouts; mouth orange inside. This species is usually found more offshore. During the summer it first appears at about eight fathoms; between eight and twelve fathoms it gradually replaces *C. arenarius*, and it is the only *Cynoscion* normally found outside of twelve fathoms. During the colder months it comes inshore and may even be found in the bays. New York to Florida and throughout the Gulf of Mexico. Ginsburg, 1931. (1 foot; 30 cm)

294. Red drum; redfish (channel bass)   *Sciaenops ocellata* (Linnaeus)

D. X + I, 24; A. II, 8; Sc. 45–50; Gr. 5 + 7; body in young silvery, becoming coppery brown or reddish in older fish; all sizes with one large black spot above lateral line at base of caudal, sometimes with additional spots located anteriorly. The redfish is one of the largest of the sciaenids and is probably the most important commercially; from a sports standpoint it is probably the most highly prized croaker. The young are numerous around the mouths of passes in the spring and early summer; the adults are largely solitary fish living in quite shallow water in the bays, where they may be seen swimming about with their dorsal fins protruding from the water. Large numbers of redfish migrate to the Gulf in the fall and return in the spring. These "runs" attract large numbers of anglers, and it is during those times that larger fish are caught. The largest, however, may stay offshore. Large fish (usually females) are known as bullreds. Massachusetts to northern Mexico. Simmons and Breuer, 1962; Boothby and Avault, 1971. (5 feet; 1½ m)

295. Spot; flat croaker (Lafayette)   *Leiostomus xanthurus* Lacépède

D. X + I, 31; A. II, 12; Sc. 60–70; Gr. 8 + 22; body silvery, with shades of yellow during spawning season (fall); irregularly wavy lines on sides; black humeral spot; fins olivaceous except for clear caudal. Spot is a very common bay and shallow Gulf species, the young maturing in shallow bay waters and moving to deeper water as they grow. Like the croaker, most spot probably live only one year. During the spawning season this fish is known as the golden croaker (the Atlantic croaker is also called golden croaker during this same time). Cape Cod to northern Mexico. (10 inches; 25 cm)

296. Star drum   *Stellifer lanceolatus* (Holbrook)

D. XI + I, 20–23; A. II, 7–8; Sc. 47–50; Gr. 13 + 22; body silvery, plain; caudal fin lanceolate at all sizes; body rather rounded (moreso than in other croakers); interorbital space broad, concave. This small fish is common in the shallow Gulf and deeper parts of the bays. It is predominantly a mud-bottom species. The center of its abundance in the northwestern Gulf is off Louisiana, and it becomes less common along the Texas coast. Virginia to Texas. (6 inches; 15 cm)

297. Banded croaker   *Larimus fasciatus* Holbrook

D. X + I, 24–26; A. II, 5–6; Sc. 49; Gr. 12 + 24; body long, fairly deep, with 7–9 conspicuous vertical black bands on sides; mouth very oblique (greater than 45 degrees). Found in the shallow Gulf, this small fish rarely enters the bays. It has no commercial value, and larger individuals are big enough to be a nuisance to fishermen. It is somewhat more common off Louisiana. Massachusetts to northern Mexico. (8 inches; 20 cm)

298. Silver perch   *Bairdiella chrysura* (Lacépède)

D. XI + I, 22; A. II, 10; Sc. 52; Gr. 8 + 16; sides silvery; fins yellow. This species occurs in the saltier bays, the young often in grass beds. It rarely reaches a size large enough to warrant its exploitation as either a commercial or sports fish. New York to Mexico. (9 inches; 23 cm)

299. Cubbyu   *Equetus umbrosus* Jordan and Eigenmann

D. X + I, 38–40; A. II, 7; Sc. 45–50; Gr. 6 + 9; nearly black, with long white stripes on body (or color white with long black stripes on body and fins); dorsal fin somewhat elevated. The cubbyu is a rock-dwelling species found on the offshore reefs and rarely near the jetties. In Florida the young are found inshore around wharves and the adults in shallow water around reefs. It was formerly reported as, and may be identical to, *E. acuminatus* of the Caribbean; the taxonomy of this genus requires study.

A dark-colored form of *Equetus* from Louisiana which may be a distinct species will key to *E. umbrosus* but has a distinct color pattern. Although its body is generally dark, especially in older individuals, it lacks the thin horizontal bars of typical *E. umbrosus* but instead has a thick bar extending in a curve from the first dorsal to the caudal much like other species of *Equetus*. Its first dorsal is about normal in height for *E. umbrosus*.

Considerable work is needed on this group. There is also considerable confusion about the young, but apparently only the spotted drum has a spot on its snout, and only the cubbyu has several horizontal stripes. The name "high-hat" has been used for several species, including this one, but probably best belongs to the spotted drum. (8 inches; 20 cm)

300. Jackknife fish *Equetus lanceolatus* (Linnaeus)

D. XIV–XVI + I, 53; A. II, 5; Sc. 49–55; Gr. 9 + 12; body white with three dark stripes, each bordered with silver; first stripe nearly vertical through eye; second stripe running posteriorly from top of head above eye to base of ventral fin and onto fin; third stripe V-shaped, covering forward edge of spinous dorsal and then running from base of spinous dorsal posteriorly along midline of body and onto caudal fin. This tropical reef species is known in our area only from Stetson Bank. Bermuda and South Carolina through the Caribbean to Brazil. (9 inches; 23 cm)

301. Spotted drum (high-hat) *Equetus punctatus* (Bloch and Schneider)

D. XI–XII + I, 46; A. II, 6–7; Sc. 52–56; Gr. 6 + 11; body with alternating light and dark stripes running more or less vertically on anterior body and becoming horizontal on posterior; largest stripe black, running along forward edge of spinous dorsal fin and then back along midline of side to base of caudal fin; soft dorsal, anal, and caudal fins with pale spots, with young lacking the spots; spinous dorsal greatly elongate. This is another tropical reef species rarely known from offshore reefs. It is very secretive, so it may be more abundant. Southern Florida and Bahamas through the Caribbean to Hispaniola. (10 inches; 25 cm)

Mullidae

The goatfishes are unfamiliar to most people since they only occur on reefs or in the open Gulf, but one species is frequently caught by shrimpers. They are easily recognized by the two distinct dorsal fins and the two barbels on the lower jaw. (M. Caldwell, 1962)

1   Teeth present on upper jaw and roof of mouth; opercular spine
       absent   2
       Teeth absent from roof of mouth or upper jaw; usually opercular
       spine present   3
2   Caudal, dorsal, and anal with black bands . . . . Dwarf goatfish,
       Upeneus parvus.
       Median fins without dark bands . . . . Red goatfish, *Mullus
       auratus.*
3   Lateral yellow stripe present, sometimes faint, running from eye
       to tail; lateral-line scales 34–39 . . . . Yellow goatfish, *Mul-
       loidichthys martinicus.*
       Dark blotches on sides; lateral-line scales 27–31 . . . . Spotted
       goatfish, *Pseudupeneus maculatus.*

302. Dwarf goatfish   *Upeneus parvus* Poey
D. VII + I, 8; A. II, 6; P. 14–16; Sc. 36–38; Gr. 24–27; body reddish orange with dark bars on dorsal, anal, and lobes of caudal; small teeth on roof of mouth often hard to locate in fresh specimens, but more easily found in preserved fish. This fish is commonly encountered in shrimpers' trawls over the inner continental shelf. Florida, northern Gulf of Mexico, and West Indies. (6 inches; 15 cm)

303. Red goatfish   *Mullus auratus* Jordan and Gilbert
D. VIII (first minute) + I, 8; A. II, 6; P. 15–17; Sc. 29–35; Gr. 18–21; body blotched with red, without other distinguishing markings, but often with light red bars on median fins. This is an uncommon form probably occurring mostly over the outer shelf. Bermuda and Nova Scotia, Gulf of Mexico, and West Indies. (9 inches; 23 cm)

304. Yellow goatfish   *Mulloidichthys martinicus* (Cuvier)
D. VIII (first minute) + I, 8; A. II, 6; P. 15–17; Sc. 34–39; Gr. 26–33; body and fins pale yellow with yellow stripes on sides. It is known only from areas around offshore reefs. Western Gulf of Mexico, Bermuda, and Florida; West Indies to Panama. (1 foot; 30 cm)

305. Spotted goatfish   *Pseudupeneus maculatus* (Bloch)
D. VIII (first minute) + I, 8; A. II, 6; P. 13–16; Sc. 27–31; Gr. 26–32; body pale with usually three blotches on sides. Another rare offshore reef fish. New Jersey and Bermuda to Brazil. (10 inches; 25 cm)

Kyphosidae

The chubs or rudderfishes are seldom-seen, schooling reef fishes. Juveniles are sometimes associated with *Sargassum*. Both of the closely related species are capable of extensive variation in coloration and are therefore difficult to distinguish. For example, both species may display a checkered pattern. (Moore, 1962)

1   Anal rays usually 11; dorsal rays usually 12; base of pectoral dark
     .... Bermuda chub, *Kyphosus sectatrix*.
    Anal rays always 12 or 13; dorsal rays almost always 13 or 14;
     base of pectoral pale .... Yellow chub, *Kyphosus incisor*.

306. Bermuda chub   *Kyphosus sectatrix* (Linnaeus)
D. XI, 12 (rarely 11 or 13); A. III, 11 (rarely 10 or 12); Sc. 51–58; Gr. 6–8 + 16–18. More of an inshore species, this fish is rarely found around jetties and some reefs and oil platforms. Massachusetts and Bermuda to Brazil, including the Caribbean. (18 inches; 46 cm)

307. Yellow chub *Kyphosus incisor* (Cuvier)

D. XI, 13–15; A. III, 12–13; Sc. 54–62; Gr. 6–8 + 19–22. More of an offshore species, this species tends to be more yellow in life than the Bermuda chub. It has only rarely been recorded from offshore. Its range is about the same as that of the Bermuda chub. (3 feet; 91 cm)

Ephippidae

The spadefishes are large, laterally flattened schooling fishes that are valued as food. There is not much market for them in our area, but they are often caught by anglers or speared by divers.

308. Atlantic spadefish; angelfish *Chaetodipterus faber* (Broussonet)

D. VIII + I, 20; A. III, 18; Sc. 65–75. Very small spadefish are dark and quite round and often float on the surface mimicking debris; however, they soon take on the black and white banded pattern characteristic of the species. The bars tend to be lost in old fish. Fish up to one pound are found inshore around jetties and wharves and in open water off the beaches. Larger fish occur more offshore around wrecks, reefs, and oil rigs, and sometimes schools are seen in open water. From Cape Cod to Brazil, including the Caribbean. (3 feet; 91 cm)

Chaetodontidae

The butterflyfishes and angelfishes are beautiful tropical reef fishes. All of the following species may be found offshore, but the juveniles of many species occur inshore as well. Very small juveniles differ appreciably from the adults in color and form; these differences are incorporated in the keys to the species. Recently it has been proposed to separate the angelfishes as the family Pomacanthidae (Feddern, 1972; Burgess, 1974).

1 Dorsal spines XII–XIV 2
   Dorsal spines IX–X 11
2 Preopercle with strong spine 3
   Preopercle without such spine 6
3 Two well-developed spines beneath eye (on preorbital bone)
    . . . . Cherubfish, *Centropyge argi.*
   Two knobby spines, or no spines at all, on preorbital bone be-
   neath eye 4

4   Head, caudal fin, and front of body yellow, with rest of body black; upper rays of caudal fin prolonged (juveniles yellow with black spot on side which enlarges with growth to cover entire posterior half of the body) .... Rock beauty, *Holacanthus tricolor.*

Body not tricolored; caudal completely rounded 5

5   Dark spot on nape of neck surrounded by light blue ring often with small light spots in its interior; caudal fin bright yellow; soft dorsal and anal fins tinged with blue (juveniles yellow and black with dark bar from nape through eye, narrow blue stripes on sides, and caudal fin clear yellow) .... Queen angelfish, *Holacanthus ciliaris.*

Dark spot on nape not surrounded by light blue and without small light spots in its interior; caudal fin yellow at tips; soft dorsal and anal also yellow-tipped (juveniles colored like *H. ciliaris* but with yellow on trailing edges of soft dorsal and anal fins) .... Blue angelfish, *Holacanthus bermudensis.*

6   Lateral-line scales fewer than 28, usually 25; snout greatly elongated; diffuse bar on head through eye and another diffuse bar along base of soft dorsal, but sides and head otherwise without distinct color pattern .... Longsnout butterflyfish, *Prognathodes aculeatus.*

Lateral-line scales more than 26, usually more than 29; snout only slightly, if at all, elongated; sides of body and head usually with definite bands or spots 7

7   Dorsal spines XIII or XIV (rarely XV) 8
Dorsal spines XII 10

8   Lateral-line scales 36 or more; anal rays 18 or more; soft dorsal rays 21 or more .... Reef butterflyfish, *Chaetodon sedentarius.*

Lateral-line scales 26–35, usually 29–33; anal rays 14–17; soft dorsal rays 18–20 9

9   Lateral-line scales 31–35; anal rays 16–17; dorsal rays 19–20; ocellated spot on side of adults; juveniles with two ocellated spots, one on side and one on soft dorsal above first spot .... Foureye butterflyfish, *Chaetodon capistratus.*

Lateral-line scales 26–32, usually 29; anal rays 15, rarely 14; dorsal rays 18–19; no ocellated spot on sides of adults or juveniles; snout moderately elongated .... Bank butterflyfish, *Chaetodon aya.*

10 Sides of body with four distinct stripes; juveniles also have ocellated spot at base of soft dorsal; dorsal rays usually 21 or 22 .... Banded butterflyfish, *Chaetodon striatus.*

Sides of body with one or two stripes; adults with unocellated spot at base of soft dorsal; juveniles with additional spot at edge of soft dorsal; dorsal rays usually 19 to 21 .... Spotfin butterflyfish, *Chaetodon ocellatus.*

11 Caudal fin rounded, without light margin in adults; dorsal spines X; juveniles with yellow margin surrounding dark central spot on caudal fin .... French angelfish, *Pomacanthus paru.*

Caudal fin truncate, with light margin in adults; dorsal spines IX; color gray; juveniles similar to *P. paru* except for yellow middorsal stripe extending below lower lip onto chin and caudal fin crossed entirely by central black area . . . . Gray angelfish, *Pomacanthus arcuatus.*

309. Cherubfish   *Centropyge argi* Woods and Kanazawa

D. XIV–XV, 15–16 (usually XIV, 16); A. III, 17; Sc. 32–34; lateral line ending beneath soft dorsal fin; lower part of head yellow, with light blue about eye and on opercle and yellow extending to base of pectoral fin; rest of body dark blue with light margins on soft dorsal and anal fins. The character of the lateral line, the spine on the preopercle, and the two free spines on the preorbital, as well as the coloration, make this small chaetodontid, less than 4 inches (100 mm) long, distinct. It is an uncommon, generally deep-dwelling fish in our area. It is poorly known from few tropical locations. (2½ inches; 6 cm)

310. Rock beauty   *Holacanthus tricolor* (Bloch)

D. XIV, 17–19; A. III, 18–20; Sc. 43–46; head, lower part of body, and caudal fin yellow; rest of body black; juveniles one inch (25 mm) long and smaller more or less entirely yellow except for blue-edged black spot on side, which enlarges with growth to become black area covering most of posterior body, including soft dorsal and anal fins. This species is found often on the offshore reefs in the northwestern Gulf of Mexico. Elsewhere it is found from Georgia to Brazil, throughout the tropical western Atlantic and Caribbean. (12 inches; 30 cm)

311. Queen angelfish   *Holacanthus ciliaris* (Linnaeus)

D. XIV, 19–21; A. III, 20–21; Sc. 45–49; body green with yellow on caudal peduncle and on anterior portion of caudal fin and on ventral fins; dorsal and anal fins edged with blue; opercle, base of pectoral, and underside of head blue; black spot edged with blue on nape; juveniles greenish yellow with five or six narrow, vertical blue stripes. This species is rarely encountered about rigs, reefs, and other offshore structures. It is known to hybridize with *H. bermudensis*; the hybrid has been named *H. bermudensis* or *H. townsendi.* Bahamas through the Caribbean to Brazil. Feddern, 1968. (12 inches; 30 cm)

312. Blue angelfish   *Holacanthus bermudensis* Goode

Meristics essentially same as those of *H. ciliaris*; body blue gray to purple; ventral fins and trailing edges of soft dorsal, anal, and caudal fins yellow; upper edge of soft dorsal blue; pectoral fin with blue axil, yellow and blue bands distally. The most distinctive feature of the adults is the large spot on the nape, which in this species is not surrounded by a lighter blue ocellus and which lacks light spots in its interior. The queen angelfish possesses both the ocellus and small light spots within the larger dark spot. This is among the most common of our angelfishes, especially on the deeper reefs. We follow most recent authorities in using this name instead of *H. isabelita*. Bahamas through the Caribbean to Brazil. (18 inches; 46 cm)

313. Longsnout butterflyfish   *Prognathodes aculeatus* (Poey)

D. XIII, 18–19; A. III, 14–16; Sc. 22–28; snout prolonged (43–45 percent of standard length); upper half of body yellow orange, becoming nearly black at base of dorsal fin; lower half of body white; soft dorsal, anal, and caudal fins with black margins. This is a deep-dwelling species, rare in less than one hundred feet and in our area uncommon even there. Its poorly known range is from the Bahamas to Florida and Louisiana. (3 inches; 8 cm)

314. Spotfin butterflyfish *Chaetodon ocellatus* Bloch

D. XII, 19–21; A. III, 16–18; Sc. 33–34; body silvery; median fins and caudal peduncle yellow; black spot at base of soft dorsal fin; black bar extending from origin of dorsal through eye; axil of pectoral yellow, continuing upwards along opercular flap. The spotfin is the most common butterflyfish in our area. Adults occur offshore for the most part, but the juveniles and occasional adults appear inshore near the jetties and occasionally in the saltier bays. New England through the Caribbean to Brazil. (6 inches; 15 cm)

315. Foureye butterflyfish *Chaetodon capistratus* Linnaeus

D. XIII, 19–20; A. III, 16–17; Sc. 31–35; single large ocellus in adults sometimes accompanied by two broad, dusky bars on sides, but more usually sides are white with series of chevron-shaped lines and dark bar through eye. This is one of the more wide-ranging "tropical" fishes occurring from Massachusetts to Florida, the Gulf of Mexico, and throughout the Caribbean. It is more common in the northeastern Gulf. (6 inches; 15 cm)

316. Banded butterflyfish *Chaetodon striatus* Linnaeus

D. XII, 21–22; A. III, 16–18; Sc. 33–36; background silvery with five broad, black bars on body and fins; bar crossing caudal peduncle less distinct than others and sometimes interrupted. In our area this species is known so far only from offshore reefs. Tropical Atlantic, in the west from New Jersey to Brazil. (6 inches; 15 cm)

317. Bank butterflyfish *Chaetodon aya* Jordan

D. XII, 18; A. III, 14–16; Sc. 34–36; two diverging black bands marking this species distinctively. A deep-dwelling species originally named for the red snapper (then called *Lutjanus aya*), from whose stomach the first specimen was collected, the bank butterflyfish is now known from the Flower Gardens Reef as well as from the shelf edge in the northeastern Gulf, and probably occurs on other, deeper reefs as well. Yucatán and off Louisiana around Florida to North Carolina. Hubbs, 1963; Bright et al., 1974. (5 inches; 13 cm)

318. Reef butterflyfish *Chaetodon sedentarius* Poey

D. XIII (rarely XIV), 21–23; A. III, 18–19; Sc. 36–39; body silvery, with dark band through eye similar to that of other *Chaetodon* species and diffuse black band posteriorly from dorsal to anal fin, covering caudal peduncle. This is an uncommon species in our area, with the adults occurring offshore and the young inshore. Caribbean and Gulf of Mexico. (6 inches; 15 cm)

319. French angelfish *Pomacanthus paru* (Bloch)

D. X, 29–31; A. III, 22–24; adults dark purple to black with yellow on edge of each scale; mouth and tip of snout blue; juveniles black and yellow striped, with median yellow band on forehead that stops at upper lip. A fairly common species offshore, the young occur uncommonly inshore. Some old records of *P. arcuatus* probably refer to this species. Tropical Atlantic, in the west from Florida through the Caribbean to Brazil. (14 inches; 36 cm)

320. Gray angelfish *Pomacanthus arcuatus* (Linnaeus)
D. IX, 31–33; A. III, 23–25; body grayish brown with black spots on each scale; mouth and tip of snout white in adults; juveniles colored similarly to *P. paru* except median yellow stripe on forehead extends below lower lip onto chin. The juvenile pattern of bars persists longer in this species than in the French angelfish, with pale bars still being present even after the "spotted" adult coloration has been assumed. In our area the species is rare on offshore reefs. Old records of *P. aureus* refer to this species. New England through the Caribbean to Brazil. (14 inches; 36 cm)

Pomacentridae

The damselfishes are another family of small, colorful reef fishes, with several species also appearing at saltier inshore localities. All make good aquarium fishes, although they may be somewhat pugnacious. The genus *Pomacentrus* is known as *Eupomacentrus* by some authors. The young of that genus, as well as other pomacentrids, may vary extensively from the color patterns found in adults. The adults themselves will vary in color depending on the time of day and their mood. Additional deepwater species occur at the edge of the shelf, but those species are not well known. (Rivas, 1960; Böhlke and Chaplin, 1968; Randall, 1968; Emery, 1973a; Emery and Burgess, 1974; Thresher, 1975)

1 Teeth fixed, not movable 2
   Teeth movable; distinct notch in preorbital bone bordering upper
      jaw .... Yellowtail damselfish, *Microspathodon chrysurus*.
2 Teeth incisorlike, in single row 3
   Teeth conical, in two or three rows 9
3 Preopercle serrate; body without wide vertical bars 4
   Preopercle smooth; body with wide vertical bars 8
4 Three rows of scales on cheek between suborbital and margin of
      preopercle; body distinctly bicolored, dark anteriorly, includ-
      ing belly, and light posteriorly* .... Bicolor damselfish, *Pom-
      acentrus partitus*.
   Four rows of scales on cheek (lowermost row may be reduced);
      body not colored as above 5
5 Profile of forehead straight or sharply angled at eye; juveniles
      and some adults bright yellow with black spot in dorsal fin and
      two other black spots in axil of pectoral and on caudal pedun-

* Like all damselfishes, *Pomacentrus partitus* is capable of extensive color changes. Emery (1973a) records individuals of this species from deep-reef habitats with black tails and lighter anterior portions.

cle; other adults dusky, without spot on dorsal and with vertical bars .... Yellow damselfish, *Pomacentrus planifrons*.
Profile of forehead convexly rounded; color variable, but not as above 6

6   Three rows of scales on opercle between margin of preopercle and opercular spine; spot on dorsal surface of caudal peduncle usually present; dusky bars on sides of body in adult .... Cocoa damselfish, *Pomacentrus variabilis*.
Two rows of scales on opercle between preopercle margin and spine; spot on dorsal surface of caudal peduncle may or may not be present; sides without dusky bars 7

7   Lowest row of cheek scales reduced in size, not extending to margin of preopercle; usually without a spot on caudal peduncle; most of body yellow, but upper and anterior body blue, with pearly blue spots on sides and head .... Beaugregory, *Pomacentrus leucostictus*.
Lowest row of cheek scales of normal size, extending to margin of preopercle; dark spot on caudal peduncle of juveniles; most of body blue with yellow or orange on upper and anterior parts of body and head; adults more uniformly dark .... Dusky damselfish, *Pomacentrus dorsopunicans*.

8   Anal rays 12–13 .... Sergeant major, *Abudefduf saxatilis*.
Anal rays 9–10 .... Night sergeant, *Abudefduf taurus*.

9   Caudal fin deeply cleft, the tips pointed 10
Caudal fin not deeply cleft, the tips rounded or only slightly pointed 11

10   Body blue; no light spot on top of caudal peduncle; dorsal, anal, and caudal fins with dark margins .... Blue chromis, *Chromis cyanea*.
Body pale (yellowish green) or dusky, light spot on top of caudal peduncle; dorsal margin and anal fin light; caudal margins usually dark .... Brown chromis, *Chromis multilineata*.

11   Body and fins almost entirely blue or purple (uniformly brown in preservative) .... Purple reeffish, *Chromis scotti*.
Body countershaded, not uniformly colored 12

12   Upper body blue (dark brown in preservative); caudal fin, posterior dorsal fin, and lower body yellow; light blue lines running from upper lip over top of eyes and along sides above lateral line (juveniles more uniformly colored blue, but with yellow fins and light blue lines) .... Yellowtail reeffish, *Chromis enchrysura*.
Upper body dark green or lime green; greenish gray or brown below; posteriormost half of caudal fin light; no blue lines on head and sides .... Sunshinefish, *Chromis insolata*.

321. Yellowtail damselfish   *Microspathodon chrysurus* (Cuvier)

D. XII, 14–15; A. II, 12–13; P. 20–22; Sc. 20–22; Gr. 15–20 on lower limb; adults dark green with yellow tail; young similarly colored but with more prominent metallic blue spots on sides of body. This fish is known from several offshore reefs. Bermuda, Florida, and the northern Gulf to Panama; also in the eastern Atlantic. Causey, 1969; Bright and Cashman, 1974; Sonnier, Teerling, and Hoese, 1976. (6 inches; 15 cm)

322. Bicolor damselfish *Pomacentrus partitus* Poey

D. XII, 14–17; A. II, 13–15; P. 18–20; Sc. 18–21; sharp, vertical demarcation between dark anterior parts of body and light posterior parts with dark margins on median fins. Apparently a deeper-water species than most damselfishes, the bicolor damselfish is not rare on offshore reefs. Florida, northern Gulf, and Caribbean. Emery, 1973*b*. (6 inches; 15 cm)

323. Yellow damselfish *Pomacentrus planifrons* Cuvier

D. XII, 15–17; A. II, 13–14; P. 18–20; Sc. 18–20; profile steep (45 degrees) and nearly straight; young bright yellow with dark spots on soft dorsal fin, caudal peduncle, and pectoral axil; adults plainer, brownish yellow with narrow dark bars on sides. Florida and throughout the Gulf of Mexico and Caribbean. Bright and Cashman, 1974. (5 inches; 13 cm)

324. Cocoa damselfish *Pomacentrus variabilis* (Castelnau)

D. XII, 14–17; A. II, 12–15; P. 18–21; Sc. 18–20; body yellowish with blue on upper half of head and anterior part of body and dorsal fin, reaching back to cover black spot on dorsal fin at junction of spinous and soft parts. A common fish on offshore reefs, oil platforms, and wrecks, with occasional juveniles appearing inshore, this fish is commonly misidentified as the beaugregory, which we have not been able to verify from the northern Gulf. Florida, Gulf of Mexico, and Caribbean. (4 inches; 10 cm)

325. Beaugregory *Pomacentrus leucostictus* Müller and Troschel

D. XII, 13–16; A. II, 12–14; P. 17–19; Sc. 17–20; dark blue on upper back, most of head, and dorsal fin; bright yellow elsewhere; black spot on dorsal fin covered by blue area; small black spot at base of pectorals; scattered blue dots and wavy lines on heads of large males, which are otherwise more drab in color. Despite numerous reports, we have been unable to verify this species from the northern Gulf of Mexico. East coast of Florida, the Bahamas, and throughout the Caribbean. (4 inches; 10 cm)

326. Dusky damselfish *Pomacentrus dorsopunicans* (Poey)

D. XII, 14–17; A. II, 13–15; P. 20–22; Sc. 18–21; anal fin short, longest rays not reaching base of caudal fin or just barely reaching it (*variabilis*, *leucostictus*, and other species have longer anals); adults dark gray to blackish with vertical dark lines on sides of body; young (one inch long) lighter with orange red coloration on spinous dorsal, adjacent region of back, and nape; large blue-edged black spot at base of dorsal fin near posterior spines; smaller blue-edged black spot on upper edge of caudal peduncle. This fish is the second most common *Pomacentrus* on the southern Texas jetties. Older reports list it as *P. fuscus* (Cuvier), and Rivas (1960) synonymized the two names; however, Emery and Burgess (1974) consider them distinct. Florida, Bermuda, throughout the Gulf of Mexico to Brazil; also in the eastern Atlantic. (2 inches; 5 cm)

327. Sergeant major *Abudefduf saxatilis* (Linnaeus)

D. XIII, 12–13; A. II, 10–12; P. 18–19; Sc. 21; relatively high-bodied and short-snouted; five distinct vertical bars on sides; background color between bars whitish or yellow. Young members of this species are often abundant near the southern Texas jetties. A year-round resident of 7½-Fathom Reef, this fish may be common on other shallow reefs as well. Both sides of Atlantic and possibly conspecific with Pacific Ocean forms; Bermuda and Rhode Island through the Caribbean to Uruguay. (7 inches; 18 cm)

328. Night sergeant   *Abudefduf taurus* (Müller and Troschel)

D. XIII, 11–12; A. II, 10; P. 18–19; Sc. 19–20; light brown or yellowish brown with five broad, dark brown bars on sides, with anterior bars often broader than those near tail; sixth bar on prominent black saddle on top of caudal peduncle; black spot at upper base of pectoral fin. This is a rare form so far known only from the Port Aransas jetties in our area. Elsewhere from Florida and throughout the Caribbean. (7 inches; 18 cm)

329. Blue chromis   *Chromis cyanea* (Poey)

D. XII, 12; A. II, 12; P. 16–18; body shape similar to that of *C. multilineata*, but blue all over; upper margin of spinous dorsal and outer rays of caudal fin dark. The blue chromis is a very common fish on some offshore reefs. Florida, Bahamas, and Caribbean. Bright and Cashman, 1974. (5 inches; 13 cm)

330. Brown chromis   *Chromis multilineata* (Guichenot)

D. XII, 12; A. II, 12; P. 18–20; moderately elongate, with deeply forked tail; brownish overall with light (yellow) edges of dorsal and tips of caudal fin and distinctive light spot on top of caudal peduncle. This is another species so far known only from offshore reefs. Florida, Bermuda, and through the Caribbean. Briggs et al., 1964; Bright and Cashman, 1974. (5 inches; 13 cm)

331. Purple reeffish   *Chromis scotti* Emery

D. XIII, 12; A. II, 12; P. 17–19 (usually 18); body and fins (except clear pectoral) uniformly blue, sometimes lighter on belly, with bright pearly blue spots on head. Florida and Gulf of Mexico. Bright and Cashman, 1974. (3 inches; 8 cm)

332. Yellowtail reeffish   *Chromis enchrysura* Jordan and Gilbert

D. XIII, 11–13 (usually 12); A. II, 12; body dark gray with raised light blue line from lip over upper eye and along side above lateral line; distal half of anal, soft dorsal, and caudal fins yellow. A deeper-dwelling species, this fish is so far known only from the Gulf of Mexico. Bright et al., 1974; Sonnier, Teerling, and Hoese, 1976. (4 inches; 10 cm)

333. Sunshinefish   *Chromis insolata* (Cuvier)

D. XII, 12; A. II, 12; P. 17; short-bodied, lacking deeply cleft tail and dark outer margins of caudal fin found in some other species of *Chromis* treated here; upper parts bright green; lower parts olive green; large fish olive-colored overall. This is a little-known species, known in this area only from Stetson Reef and a few deeper reefs. It is apparently a deeper-water species in most of its range. Older records of *C. insolata* may refer to the recently described *C. scotti*. Florida and the Caribbean to Brazil. Briggs et al., 1964. (5 inches; 13 cm)

Cirrhitidae

Hawkfishes are a small family of basslike fishes distinguished by their lower pectorals having thickened, separate rays somewhat like those of the scorpionfishes. Hawkfishes are colorful reef fishes, with only one species known in the western Atlantic. (Randall, 1963)

334. Redspotted hawkfish *Amblycirrhitus pinos* (Mowbray)
D. X, 11; A. III, 6; P. 14; Sc. 41–44; greenish, perchlike, with brownish vertical bands; large black bar on caudal peduncle; large spot under posterior soft dorsal fin; anterior body and dorsals covered with red spots. A poorly known fish from offshore reefs and wrecks, it is probably not rare but is hard to collect. Bahamas, southern Florida, northern Gulf, and Yucatán through the Caribbean to the Lesser Antilles and Saint Helena. Bright and Cashman, 1974; Sonnier, Teerling, and Hoese, 1976. (3½ inches; 9 cm)

Labridae

The wrasses are an abundant family of tropical and temperate fishes related to the parrotfishes, from which they differ by having individual teeth not fused into a beak. Species occurring on the North Atlantic coast, usually north of Cape Hatteras, which do not occur in our area are the tautog or blackfish, *Tautoga onitis*, and the cunner, *Tautogolabrus adspersus*. Gulf of Mexico species seem to be mostly tropical. It is far from certain how many species occur in the northwestern Gulf of Mexico, but the following have been recorded. Care should be taken, though, as sight records indicate the possibility of other species of *Halichoeres* on offshore reefs. (Hildebrand and Schroeder, 1928; Randall and Böhlke, 1965; Böhlke and Chaplin, 1968; Randall, 1968)

1 Dorsal spines XI–XIV	2
Dorsal spines VIII or IX	6
2 Dorsal spines XIV, the first three extending distally as filaments .... Hogfish, *Lachnolaimus maximus*.	
Dorsal spines XI or XII, rarely XIII; no filaments	3
3 Posterior canines present; anterior canines large	4
Posterior canines absent; anterior canines small; upper body purple; lower body pale, with small amount of yellow .... Creole wrasse, *Clepticus parrai*.	
4 Soft dorsal and anal with scaly bases	5

Soft dorsal and anal without scaly bases; body pink with red spots or blotches . . . . Red hogfish, *Decodon puellaris.*

5   Back bluish or purple; remainder of body yellow; no produced rays on fins; gill rakers 15–16 on first arch . . . . Spotfin hogfish, *Bodianus pulchellus.*

Back reddish anteriorly; rest of body yellow; soft dorsal, anal, and outer caudal rays produced; gill rakers 17–19 on first arch . . . . Spanish hogfish, *Bodianus rufus.*

6   Lateral line complete; body oval or rounded in cross-section   7

Lateral line interrupted posteriorly; body flattened laterally . . . . Pearly razorfish, *Hemipteronotus novacula.*

7   Dorsal spines VIII; no posterior canines present . . . . Bluehead, *Thalassoma bifasciatum.*

Dorsal spines IX; posterior canines present   8

8   Gill rakers 21–23; depth of body 28–37 percent of standard length; head with narrow dark (blue) bands radiating from eye; small black spot at upper pectoral fin base and four or five broad dark bands on sides; small specimens with black spot above midline at caudal peduncle . . . . Puddingwife, *Halichoeres radiatus.*

Gill rakers 15–20; depth of body 22–30 percent of standard length; color not as above   9

9   Anterior lateral-line scales with more than one pore (usually three or more) per scale; caudal fin rounded   10

Anterior lateral-line scales with single pore; caudal fin double emarginate in large adults . . . . Painted wrasse, *Halichoeres caudalis.*

10   Two lengthwise dark stripes on side of body; pale-edged dark spot near edge of opercle (within upper stripe); small black spot at rear base of dorsal fin . . . . Slippery dick, *Halichoeres bivittatus.*

Single broad black band down sides, disappearing in larger fish; two dark wavy lines radiating from eye . . . . Yellowhead wrasse, *Halichoeres garnoti.*

335. Hogfish   *Lachnolaimus maximus* (Walbaum)

D. XIV, 11; A. III, 10; first three spines of dorsal filamentous; body red with dark spot at base of soft dorsal; outer margins of soft dorsal, anal, and caudal fins with dark bars; mature males with long snout. This rare fish is known so far only from offshore reefs in deep water. Bermuda and North Carolina through the Caribbean to Columbia. Gunter, 1944; Sonnier, Teerling, and Hoese, 1976. (3 feet; 91 cm)

336. Creole wrasse   *Clepticus parrai* (Bloch and Schneider)

D. XII, 10; A. III, 12–13; body and fins mostly purple. This wrasse is apparently common on offshore reefs. Bermuda and Florida through the West Indies. Bright and Cashman, 1974; Sonnier, Teerling, and Hoese, 1976. (1 foot; 30 cm)

337. Red hogfish   *Decodon puellaris* (Poey)

D. XI, 10; A. III, 10; Sc. 30; body pink to light red, with deeper red blotches. This colorful fish is deepest-dwelling wrasse known from our area. It is apparently common outside of about fifty fathoms. North Carolina to Brazil. (15 inches; 38 cm)

338. Spotfin hogfish   *Bodianus pulchellus* (Poey)
D. XI–XII, 9–10; A. III, 11–13; Gr. 15–16; soft dorsal, anal, and outer caudal rays only slightly if at all produced; back bluish, usually purple; remainder of body yellow. This species is rarely seen on offshore reefs. Atlantic Ocean, in the west from Bermuda, Florida, and the northern Gulf throughout the Caribbean to Brazil. Bright and Cashman, 1974; Sonnier, Teerling, and Hoese, 1976. (2 feet; 61 cm)

339. Spanish hogfish   *Bodianus rufus* (Linnaeus)
D. XI–XII, 9–11 (usually XII, 10); A. III, 11–13 (12); Gr. 17–19; soft dorsal and anal fins as well as outer rays of caudal produced; body red anteriorly and dorsally, becoming yellow ventrally and posteriorly; spinous dorsal, ventral, and anal fins purple. Common on offshore reefs in fairly deep water. Bermuda, South Carolina, and the northern Gulf through the Caribbean to Ascension. Bright and Cashman, 1974; Sonnier, Teerling, and Hoese, 1976. (1 foot; 30 cm)

340. Pearly razorfish   *Hemipteronotus novacula* (Linnaeus)
D. IX, 12; A. III, 12; lateral line interrupted posteriorly; body light pink to yellow, with red and green on median fins; anterior profile nearly vertical. This laterally flattened wrasse has the remarkable ability to dive sideways into the sand. It is probably more common than records would indicate, especially where coarse sand occurs. So far it is known only in the northwestern Gulf from 7½-Fathom Reef, but it is common in the northeastern Gulf. *Xyrichthys psittacus* refers to this species. Atlantic Ocean, in the west from South Carolina through the Caribbean to Brazil. Briggs et al., 1964; Causey, 1969. (9 inches; 23 cm)

341. Bluehead   *Thalassoma bifasciatum* (Bloch)
D. VIII, 12–13; A. III, 10–11; males with blue head and green body separated by two black stripes; females, some males, and young yellow with broad longitudinal black stripe. This is a common wrasse on offshore reefs. Tropical Atlantic; Bermuda, Bahamas, Florida, and the northern Gulf of Mexico through the Caribbean to Columbia. (6 inches; 15 cm)

342. Puddingwife   *Halichoeres radiatus* (Linnaeus)
D. IX, 11; A. III, 12; Gr. 7–8 + 13–16; depth of body 28–37 percent of standard length; caudal fin truncate; anterior lateral-line scales with three or more pores per scale; background brownish with dark streaks radiating from eye and four or five dark bands on side of body, most distinct near base of dorsal fin; small dark spot at upper base of pectoral fin; young with prominent spot at base of caudal fin. This is the largest species of *Halichoeres* (the others rarely exceed eight inches, or about 200 mm). North Carolina and Bermuda, throughout the Caribbean and Gulf of Mexico to Brazil. Hildebrand, Chavez, and Compton, 1964; Bright and Cashman, 1974. (20 inches; 51 cm)

343. Painted wrasse (eared wrasse) *Halichoeres caudalis* (Poey)

D. IX, 11; A. III, 12; Gr. 6–7 + 11–13; anterior lateral-line scales with only single pore per scale; caudal fin emarginate; body without distinct dark markings except for dark spots behind each eye and rather diffuse dark area at base of caudal fin. This species is very similar to *H. poeyi*, which is found on Caribbean reefs, but it appears to be restricted to continental tropical America. North Carolina to Brazil. Briggs et al., 1964; Sonnier, Teerling, and Hoese, 1976. (7 inches; 18 cm)

344. Slippery dick *Halichoeres bivittatus* (Bloch)

D. IX, 11; A. III, 12; Gr. 5–7 + 9–14; anterior lateral-line scales with more than one, usually four or five, pores per scale; caudal fin rounded; body with two longitudinal stripes sometimes broken into spots; greenish above and below these stripes, white between. Probably the most common inshore member of the genus in the northern Gulf. Bermuda and North Carolina through the Caribbean to Brazil. Springer and Hoese, 1958; Causey, 1969. (9 inches; 23 cm)

345. Yellowhead wrasse (variegated wrasse) *Halichoeres garnoti* (Valenciennes)

D. IX, 11; A. III, 12; Gr. 4–7 + 8–14; depth of body usually less than 30 percent of standard length; caudal fin rounded; anterior lateral-line scales with more than one pore per scale; juveniles yellow with single dark blue stripe down middle of side (appearing as two closely spaced narrow stripes in preserved specimens); older fish with characteristic diagonal wavy lines running back from eye and yellowish brown dorsally and lighter ventrally; large adult males yellowish with large black blotch or bar about halfway along side and wavy lines behind eye. Bermuda, Florida, and northern Gulf of Mexico, throughout the Caribbean to Brazil. Bright and Cashman, 1974; Sonnier, Teerling, and Hoese, 1976. (6 inches; 15 cm)

Scaridae

Parrotfishes are members of the tropical reef fish community which is only beginning to be studied here, and therefore the species reported from this area are probably incomplete. One species is known from inshore waters; the others are known only from the offshore reefs such as the Flower Gardens. Parrotfishes are almost strictly coral reef fishes; their parrotlike beaks are used to break coral apart to reach attached animals. They are highly colorful, and the sexes often look quite different. For identification of small parrotfishes (less than four inches or 100 mm long) and species not included, the reader is referred to the tropical fish fauna books. (Böhlke and Chaplin, 1968; Randall, 1968)

1   Three or four rows of scales present below eye; front edge of

dental plate of lower jaw inside that of upper jaw when mouth
is closed   2

Single row of scales below eye; front edge of dental plate of lower
jaw outside that of upper jaw when mouth is closed   3

2   Four rows of scales below eye . . . . Queen parrotfish, *Scarus
vetula.*

Three rows of scales below eye . . . . Princess parrotfish, *Scarus
taeniopterus.*

3   Fleshy flap on anterior nostril ribbonlike . . . . Bucktooth parrotfish, *Sparisoma radians.*

Fleshy flap on anterior nostril incised, with several lobes   4

4   Saddle-shaped white area behind dorsal fin; horizontally elongate
white bar on operculum . . . . Redband parrotfish, *Sparisoma
aurofrenatum.*

No saddle-shaped area behind dorsal; no white bar on opercle
. . . . Stoplight parrotfish, *Sparisoma viride.*

346. Queen parrotfish   *Scarus vetula* Bloch and Schneider

D. IX, 10; A. III, 9; P. 14; males predominantly green, with yellow and
blue streaks on fins and head; females overall purplish green drab, with white
streak on side. This large parrotfish is quite common over most of the tropical
coral reef areas of the western Atlantic. Bahamas, Bermuda, and the northern
Gulf through the Caribbean to Columbia. Bright and Cashman, 1974. (2 feet;
61 cm)

347. Princess parrotfish   *Scarus taeniopterus* Desmarest

D. IX, 10; A. III, 9; P. 12; much more highly colored than *Scarus
vetula*; females tan, with three dark, longitudinal stripes; males in two color
phases, with blues and oranges predominating. This fish is easily confused
with the striped parrotfish, *Scarus croicensis* Bloch, as it was by Sonnier,
Teerling, and Hoese (1976). *S. croicensis* may occur here along with the
princess, however. Bermuda, Bahamas, and northern Gulf; southern range in
Caribbean uncertain. Bright and Cashman, 1974; Sonnier, Teerling, and
Hoese, 1976. (1 foot; 30 cm)

348. Bucktooth parrotfish   *Sparisoma radians* (Valenciennes)

D. IX, 10; A. III, 9; Gr. 10–13; light-colored, with numerous speckles
on sides but no distinct color pattern; males with black edges on caudal and
anal fins and black pectoral axil; drab olivaceous color phase is also known.
The smallest parrotfish in our area, both sexes are mature at about three
inches (75 mm). Known from inshore and bay waters of Texas and Florida.
Tropical Atlantic, in the west from Bermuda, Bahamas, and northern Gulf of
Mexico through the Caribbean to Brazil. Leary, 1956; Springer and Hoese,
1958. (8 inches; 20 cm)

349. Redband parrotfish   *Sparisoma aurofrenatum* (Valenciennes)

D. IX, 10; A. III, 9; Gr. 11–16; white spot behind dorsal fin; general
coloration mottled brown, orange, white, and greenish. Tropical Atlantic, in
the west from Bermuda, Bahamas, and the northern Gulf through the Caribbean to Brazil. Bright and Cashman, 1974; Sonnier, Teerling, and Hoese,
1976. (11 inches; 28 cm)

350. Stoplight parrotfish   *Sparisoma viride* (Bonnaterre)

D. IX, 10; A. III, 9; Gr. 17–21; females reddish drab; males with blue and yellow streaks on head and fins. This is a rare species known from off-shore reefs. Bermuda, Bahamas, southern Florida, northern Gulf through the Caribbean to Brazil. (21 inches; 53 cm)

Mugilidae

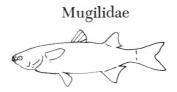

The mullets are a large family of relatively similar fishes. Most are elongate, and many have adipose eyelids. Most also show some affinity to or tolerance of fresh water. In many parts of the world mullets regularly enter fresh water and may spend considerable parts of their lifetimes in inland lakes or rivers. Some genera are found almost exclusively in fresh water. Mullets are raised for food in Africa, the Middle East, and much of the Orient and are marketed east, but not west, of the Mississippi Delta. (Moore, 1974)

1   Adipose eyelid present; scales cycloid   2
     Adipose eyelid not present; scales ctenoid . . . . Mountain mullet,
     Agonostomus monticola.
2   Anal soft rays usually 9; lateral-line scales 38; soft dorsal and anal
     fins scaled; sides without stripes at all sizes; in live specimens
     opercle with distinct bright gold spot; gold pigment in iris re-
     stricted to narrow region about vertical axis of eye . . . . White
     mullet, *Mugil curema.*
     Anal soft rays usually 8 (rarely 9 or 7); lateral-line scales usually
     41; soft dorsal and anal with few if any scales; large specimens
     with stripes on sides of body; live specimens without distinct
     bright gold spot on opercle; gold pigment in iris of eye not con-
     fined but covering most of iris . . . . Striped mullet, *Mugil
     cephalus.*

351. Mountain mullet; freshwater mullet   *Agonostomus monticola*
(Bancroft)

D. IV + I, 8; A. III, 9; Sc. 40–42. This species lacks the adipose eyelid found in other mullets in our area. Only a few scattered reports of juveniles exist from Texas and Louisiana; however, it is common in fresh water and bays of the West Indies and eastern Mexico. Mexico and Florida south to Columbia and the tropical eastern Pacific. Suttkus, 1956; Schlicht, 1959. (1 foot; 30 cm)

352. White mullet   *Mugil curema* Valenciennes

D. IV + I, 8; A. III, 9; Sc. 33–39; bases of soft dorsal and anal fins scaled; body silvery, with blue or olive on back but without distinct longitudinal stripes on sides; small dark spot at base of pectoral; opercle with gold spot; gold pigment in iris of eye confined to narrow, almost vertical region. This species is absent from the northwestern Gulf during most of the cooler months of the year. It is generally found in saltier water than *M. cephalus*, and in such habitats it may be more abundant. *M. curema* spawns offshore during the spring, reaching sexual maturity at a smaller size than *M. cephalus*. Juveniles of this species, as well as those of *M. cephalus*, were once placed as separate species in the genus *Querimanna*, because at small sizes the anal spine and ray counts differ from those of adults. The name "querimanna" has been retained for the oceanic prejuvenile stage. In both species the young possess just two anal spines but have one more "ray," making the total number of elements the same in young as in adult fish. White mullet are the preferred bait for sailfish off southern Texas but otherwise have little value. Eastern Pacific and Atlantic; in the western Atlantic from Massachusetts through the Caribbean to Brazil. (2 feet; 61 cm)

353. Striped mullet *Mugil cephalus* Linnaeus

D. IV + I, 8; A. III, 8 (rarely 7); Sc. 38–42; body silvery; back blue; sides with dark longitudinal stripes; large blue spot at base of pectoral; pigment in iris more dispersed and more brownish than that of *M. curema*. Fish below about six inches (150 mm) lack the stripes, but they are readily told from *M. curema* by the coloration of their iris and opercle, their scaleless dorsal and anal fins, and their higher lateral-line scale count. (The scales of *curema* are also different enough in appearance and texture that the species can be separated by touch.) One of our most abundant fish, large schools of striped mullet are found in practically all environments from fresh to hypersaline water. Mullet are known from many rivers in Texas and Louisiana, from as far inland as Lake Texoma and the Colorado River near Austin, Texas, two hundred miles inland, and from hypersaline Baffin Bay, where salinities often reach above 75 parts per thousand.

This species is a fall spawner. Large schools of striped mullet leave the bays during the autumn months, with smaller schools returning over about a six-month period. Striped mullet are regarded as an excellent food fish in Florida, but in the muddier western Gulf they take on an oilier taste and are not generally eaten. However, they are quite edible. One highly variable species, to which numerous names have been applied, apparently exists in all tropical and temperate waters around the world. In the western Atlantic from Nova Scotia and Bermuda to Brazil. (30 inches; 76 cm)

Sphyraenidae

The barracudas are large, predatory fishes with three species occurring here. De Sylva (1963) gives keys for identifying all juveniles and larvae as well as larger fishes and provides life history information on the species.

Barracudas are considered to be game fish, and all are edible, but in the tropics the great barracuda often causes ciguatera poisoning. No cases of this poisoning are known from our region.

1   Spinous dorsal placed well behind origin of pelvic fin; pectoral fin reaches origin of pelvic fin; tip of lower jaw without fleshy tip   2
    Spinous dorsal placed above or slightly in advance of origin of pelvic fin; pectoral fin does not reach origin of pelvic fin; tip of lower jaw with fleshy tip . . . . Northern sennet, *Sphyraena borealis*.
2   Last rays of soft dorsal and anal fins longer than anterior rays; teeth noticeably directed backwards; lateral-line scales raised, distinct, larger than surrounding scales, 108–114 in number . . . . Guaguanche, *Sphyraena guachancho*.
    Last rays of soft dorsal and anal fins equal in length to anterior rays; teeth nearly vertical in jaws; lateral-line scales not raised, no different in size from surrounding scales, 75–87 in number . . . . Great barracuda, *Sphyraena barracuda*.

354. Northern sennet   *Sphyraena borealis* DeKay

D. V + I, 9; A. II, 9; Sc. 118–135; eye diameter about 19–21 percent of head length; interorbital flattened. This species and the southern sennet, *S. picudilla*, are here regarded as conspecific, the name *S. borealis* having priority. Very small individuals (larvae to postjuveniles) of this species are apparently common in spring in the northwestern Gulf, although at this size confusion with *S. guachancho* is possible. Massachusetts to Florida, throughout the Gulf of Mexico and Caribbean, and south to Uruguay. (18 inches; 46 cm)

355. Guaguanche   *Sphyraena guachancho* Cuvier

D. V + I, 9; A. II, 7–8; Sc. 108–114; interorbital convex; three encircling bands on posterior portion of trunk, in small fish taking hourglass shape; silvery to olive, with faint golden longitudinal stripe; margin of pelvic and anal fins black; tips of middle caudal rays black. This is the most common barracuda in the Gulf. It is found in open waters and therefore often caught by shrimpers. Massachusetts to Brazil, throughout the Gulf of Mexico and Caribbean. Also in the eastern Atlantic. (2 feet; 61 cm)

356. Great barracuda   *Sphyraena barracuda* (Walbaum)

D. VIII + 123+; A. 10 + 113; Sc. very small and numerous; head small fish with longitunal series of blotches, often H-shaped, but never with encircling bands; deep green to gray on back, silver white below; upper sides with 18–22 oblique dark bands; lower sides with inky blotches; soft dorsal and caudal fins black with white tips. The great barracuda is common around oil platforms, wrecks, and reefs. Massachusetts to Brazil, throughout the Gulf and Caribbean. Also found in all other tropical seas except the eastern Pacific and the Mediterranean. (6 feet; 1⅔ m)

Polynemidae

The threadfins are a group of warm-water fishes characterized by detached rays of the pectoral fins (hence their common name) which serve as feelers or scoops as the fish feed over hard, sandy bottoms. There is one species in the northern Gulf.

357. Atlantic threadfin; eight-fingered threadfin (whiskerfish)
Polydactylus octonemus (Girard)

D. VIII + I, 12–13; A. III, 13–15; Sc. 70; pectoral filaments 8; sides silvery; snout nearly transparent. This species is abundant in the surf zone during the summer and never occurs farther out than the inner shelf. Massachusetts to Florida and the Gulf coast to Campeche, West Indies, and Caribbean Sea. (8 inches; 20 cm)

Opistognathidae

Jawfishes are moderately small, gobylike fishes with oversized jaws that live in burrows in relatively smooth bottoms adjacent to reefs. One species has been rarely caught near offshore reefs, and other species probably also occur on these reefs but have not yet been identified.

358. Swordtail jawfish   *Lonchopisthus lindneri* Ginsburg

D. XI, 19; A. III, 16; Sc. 60; caudal fin lanceolate, more than half as long as body. This fish has rarely been taken from shelly areas near offshore reefs off Texas and Louisiana. Range elsewhere unknown. Ginsburg, 1954. (7 inches; 18 cm)

Dactyloscopidae

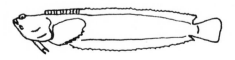

Sand stargazers resemble and are closely related to stargazers (Uranoscopidae), except they have three instead of five ventral fin rays and more rounded instead of squarish bodies. They are tropical and replace the uranoscopids in coral reef environments. They are poorly known in the Gulf, but the sand stargazer, *Dactyloscopus tridigitatus* Gill, is present in at least part of the northeastern Gulf. (Yerger, 1961; Moe and Martin, 1965)

Uranoscopidae

Stargazers are burrowing fishes with electric organs capable of delivering a mild shock and eyes set directly on top of their heads. Two species of stargazers are found inside one hundred fathoms. A third species, *Gnathagnus egregius*, with winglike projections from the lower edge of the opercular membrane, occurs near the edge of the continental shelf. Juvenile stargazers have considerably larger heads relative to body size and several projecting skull bones, unlike the adult. (Berry and Anderson, 1961)

1   Spinous dorsal fin present .... Southern stargazer, *Astroscopus y-graecum.*
     Spinous dorsal fin absent .... Lancer stargazer, *Kathetostoma albigutta.*

359. Southern stargazer   *Astroscopus y-graecum* (Cuvier)
D. IV + I, 12–13; A. 13; Sc. 80; body blue gray or brown with numerous white spots on back and upper sides; prominent dark bars on caudal, soft dorsal, and pectoral fins; bones on top of head form a Y (hence the name), and naked area on top of head is site of electric organs. North Carolina to Brazil. (17 inches; 43 cm)

360. Lancer stargazer   *Kathetostoma albigutta* (Bean)
D. 10; A. 12; upper body light brown with minute dark spots; dorsal, caudal, and anal fins with dark blotches. A deeper living species, it is caught from the middle to the outer shelf. North Carolina to Florida Keys and throughout the Gulf. (10 inches; 25 cm)

Clinidae

The clinids are tropical fishes set apart from the Blenniidae by the possession of fixed conical teeth. At present an assortment of genera formerly placed in the Blenniidae as well as other families are included here, and more work is required before the systematics of the blennylike fishes will be satisfactorily understood.

1   Body scaled 2
    Body naked .... Sailfin blenny, *Emblemaria pandionis*.
2   First two anal spines detached from fin; orbital cirrus single ....
    Checkered blenny, *Starksia ocellata*.
    First two anal spines attached to fin; orbital cirri numerous ....
    Hairy blenny, *Labrisomus nuchipinnis*.

361. Sailfin blenny   *Emblemaria pandionis* Evermann and Marsh
    D. XXI, 15–16; A. II, 22–24; anterior dorsal fin greatly elevated in males, less so in females; supraorbital cirrus trifid. In the northwestern Gulf known only from the West Flower Gardens Reef. Northern Gulf of Mexico, Florida, Bahamas, and Caribbean. Stephens, 1963, 1970; Bright and Cashman, 1974; Shipp, 1975. (2 inches; 5 cm)

362. Checkered blenny   *Starksia ocellata* (Steindachner)
    D. XX–XXII, 7–9; A. II, 16–19; sides of body mottled; ocellated brownish spots as large as eye on head; free anal spines in males serving as intromittent organ. In the northwestern Gulf this blenny is known only from West Flower Gardens Reef. North Carolina through the Caribbean to Brazil. Böhlke and Springer, 1961; Gilbert, 1971; Bright and Cashman, 1974. (2 inches; 5 cm)

363. Hairy blenny   *Labrisomus nuchipinnis* (Quoy and Gaimard)
    D. XVIII, 12–13; A. II, 17–19; body plain or banded with prominent black ocellated spot on opercle and dark spot on anterior dorsal fin. This species is abundant on the southern Texas jetties and is occasionally caught by anglers. Both sides of the Atlantic; in the west from Bermuda, Florida, and the northern Gulf of Mexico through the Caribbean to Brazil. Springer, 1958. (8 inches; 20 cm)

Blenniidae

The blennies are small, personable fishes that live in and around rocks, reefs, and other hard substrates. While the inshore species are fairly well known, the offshore species, although common, include many little-known tropical forms. The distribution and structure of hairlike cirri on the head and nape are important taxonomic features. (Böhlke and Chaplin, 1968)

1   Branchiostegal membranes not fused to body but forming well-developed fold beneath which probe may be inserted 2
    Branchiostegal membranes fused to body at sides or in ridge across breast; in any case, no distinct fold 4

2 Upper lip smooth 3
   Upper lip with lobes or papillae .... Redlip blenny, *Ophioblennius atlanticus.*
3 Median rows of cirri on raised fleshy ridge between dorsal fin and eye .... Molly miller, *Blennius cristatus.*
   No cirri on head between dorsal fin origin and posterior margin of eye .... Seaweed blenny, *Blennius marmoreus.*
4 Pectoral rays usually 12; interorbital flat; anterior lateral-line pores simple; no posterior canines in jaws 5
   Pectoral rays usually 14; interorbital concave; anterior lateral-line pores paired; canines may be present posteriorly in jaws 6
5 Snout long and relatively pointed; teeth in lower jaw slender, pointed, and usually recurved .... Striped blenny, *Chasmodes bosquianus.*
   Snout short and rounded; teeth in lower jaw short, bluntly rounded, and at most only slightly recurved .... Florida blenny, *Chasmodes saburrae.*
6 Canine teeth posterior in one or both jaws 7
   No canine teeth posterior in either jaw 8
7 Dorsal with 26 or 27 total elements, spines plus rays; anal with 20 total elements .... Crested blenny, *Hypleurochilus geminatus.*
   Dorsal with 25 total elements; anal with 16 total elements .... Barred blenny, *Hypleurochilus bermudensis.*
8 Orbital cirrus featherlike, with numerous branches between base and tip .... Feather blenny, *Hypsoblennius hentzi.*
   Orbital cirrus with only terminal branch and sometimes second branch at base .... Freckled blenny, *Hypsoblennius ionthas.*

364. Molly miller *Blennius cristatus* Linnaeus

D. XII, 14–15; A. II, 16–17; numerous cirri, often in distinct rows between orbit and base of dorsal fin; color variable, in southern Texas usually plain brownish gray to purple with reddish cirri. This fish is a common blenny on the southern Texas and western Florida jetties. It is basically herbivorous, but larger individuals may take bait. Tropical Atlantic, in the west from Florida, Bermuda, and the northern Gulf through the Caribbean to Brazil. (4 inches; 10 cm)

365. Seaweed blenny *Blennius marmoreus* Poey

D. XII, 17–18; A. II, 19–20; cirri clustered above orbit, none on nape; dark above, light below, often with dark spot between first and second dorsal spines. This blenny is rarely collected from southern Texas, but apparently a resident population exists on 7½-Fathom Reef. New York through the Caribbean to Venezuela. Briggs et al., 1964; Causey, 1969. (3 inches; 8 cm)

366. Redlip blenny *Ophioblennius atlanticus* (Valenciennes)

D. XII, 19–21; A. II, 20–21; lateral line interrupted about middle of body; single large cirrus (tentacle) above each eye, cluster of cirri above nostril (before eye), and isolated cirrus to either side of dorsal origin; body brownish; median fins dark with light borders (orange, pink, or red in life). In the western Gulf the redlip blenny is known only from offshore reefs, except for one old record from Freeport jetties. North Carolina through the Caribbean to Brazil; also in the eastern Atlantic and eastern Pacific. Baughman, 1950*b*; Bright and Cashman, 1974. (4½ inches; 11 cm)

367. Striped blenny   *Chasmodes bosquianus* (Lacépède)

D. XI, 17–19; A. II, 18–19; teeth in lower jaw slender, pointed, and recurved; snout rather long and pointed; maxillary reaching center of eye; sides of body, dorsal and anal fins striped; females variously mottled; dorsal fin of males blue anteriorly. This is a common species, especially on grassflats. New York to northeast Florida and in the Gulf of Mexico from Mobile Bay to southern Texas. Absent from most of Florida (see Florida blenny, *C. saburrae*). Springer, 1959*a*. (3 inches; 8 cm)

368. Florida blenny   *Chasmodes saburrae* Jordan and Gilbert

D. XI, 17–19; A. II, 18–19; teeth in lower jaw stout, rounded, and never recurved; snout rather blunt and rounded; maxillary reaching front of eye; coloration duller than that of *C. bosquianus*. This species is found from northeastern Florida to the Chandeleur Islands, primarily on grassflats; it occurs together with *C. bosquianus* only in the north central Gulf of Mexico from Mobile to the Chandeleurs. Springer, 1959*a*. (3 inches; 8 cm)

369. Crested blenny   *Hypleurochilus geminatus* (Wood)

D. XI, 15, to XIII, 14 (26 or 27 total rays); A. II, 18 (20 elements); body brown, usually with four quadrate blotches on sides, these often with white centers; anterior dorsal fin dark; supraorbital cirrus long in males, short in females, but usually with a cluster of four or five smaller cirri at base. This is the commonest blenny on the southern Texas jetties and oil platforms and in the shallow Gulf of Mexico and saltier bays. North Carolina to Brazil, throughout the Gulf of Mexico. (3 inches; 8 cm)

370. Barred blenny   *Hypleurochilus bermudensis* Beebe and Tee-Van

D. XII, 13 (25 total elements); A. II, 14 (16 total elements); appearance rather like that of crested blenny, except anterior dorsal fin never dark and supraorbital cirrus usually shorter. In our area this blenny is known only from the West Flower Gardens Reef, but it probably occurs on other offshore reefs as well. Otherwise known from Bermuda, Florida, and the northeastern Gulf of Mexico into the Caribbean. Bright and Cashman, 1974. (3 inches; 8 cm)

371. Feather blenny   *Hypsoblennius hentzi* (Lesueur)

D. XII, 15; A. II, 16; jaws without canines; sides of body brownish olive, with a few scattered dark spots on head; supraorbital cirrus featherlike. This species apparently prefers a softer, muddy-bottomed habitat (but may be found on oyster reefs and grassflats) with higher salinities. It is more common off southern Texas than eastern Texas or Louisiana. New Jersey to Florida and throughout the Gulf of Mexico. Hubbs, 1939. (4 inches; 10 cm)

372. Freckled blenny   *Hypsoblennius ionthas* (Jordan and Gilbert)

D. XII, 15; A. II, 16; similar in appearance to *H. hentzi* except spots on head usually more distinct and series of dark lines between eye and mouth. This species appears to prefer harder bottoms with lower salinities, although it has been taken in the Gulf. South Carolina to Florida and throughout the Gulf of Mexico. Hubbs, 1939. (4 inches; 10 cm)

Gobiidae

Gobies are usually small, secretive fishes that are very common in certain habitats, although they either hide so well or have such protective coloration that the average coastal resident rarely sees one. Gobies often enter into symbiotic relationships with other animals and are often fairly tightly restricted to certain habitats. Although most species are cryptically colored to match their backgrounds, the fins of the males are often strikingly colored during the breeding season. Reef gobies are usually more colorful than their estuarine relatives.

The sleepers are quiet, euryhaline fishes usually found in very low salinities near the coast. All are poorly known. The sleepers are often separated from the gobies proper and placed in the family Eleotridae, since the gobies have a sucking disc made from the fused pelvic fins whereas sleepers have normal, separated fins. The two groups were combined because there are intermediates with partially fused pelvics.

Several rarely seen species of tropical gobies, including the neon goby, *Gobiosoma oceanops*, occur on offshore reefs. (Ginsburg, 1932, 1933; Baird, 1965; Dawson, 1966d, 1969; Bright and Cashman, 1974)

1 Ventral fins completely separated, or joined only by small basal membrane 2
   Ventral fins completely joined 7
2 Ventral fins joined by small membrane at base; body translucent .... Spotted goby, *Coryphopterus punctipectophorus*.
   Ventral fins entirely separated; body dark (sleepers) 3
3 Fewer than 40 scale rows; maxillary reaches anterior orbit ....
   Fat sleeper, *Dormitator maculatus*.
   More than 50 scale rows; maxillary reaches back of pupil 4
4 Vomer with teeth; no spine on preopercle .... Bigmouth sleeper, *Gobiomorus dormitor*.
   Vomer without teeth; preopercle may have a ventrally directed spine 5
5 Ventral with 4 soft rays only; no spine on preopercle; more than 130 scale rows .... Blue goby, *Ioglossus calliurus*.
   Ventral with 5 soft rays; spine on preopercle; fewer than 130 scale rows 6
6 About 100 scale rows; all scales cycloid; dorsal VI + 12 ....
   Emerald sleeper, *Erotelis smaragdus*.
   About 50–70 scale rows; posterior scales ctenoid; dorsal VI + 9 .... Spinycheek sleeper, *Eleotris pisonis*.
7 Dorsal fins continuous and connected; body very long and slen-

der; standard length more than seven times as long as greatest depth .... Violet goby, *Gobioides broussonneti.*

Dorsal fins separate; body stout and robust; standard length less than seven times maximum depth 8

8   Upper pectoral rays free; tongue notched .... Frillfin goby, *Bathygobius soporator.*

Upper pectoral rays united; tongue indented but not notched 9

9   Body without scales, except possibly two small scales at base of caudal fin 10

Body mostly covered by scales 12

10   Two small ctenoid scales at base of caudal fin; seven or eight dark bars on sides .... Twoscale goby, *Gobiosoma longipala.*

No scales at base of tail; more than eight vertical bars on sides, although some may be interrupted 11

11   Body bars mostly interrupted, almost splotched; dorsal VII + 12; pelvic fin reaching to anus .... Code goby, *Gobiosoma robustum.*

Body bars not interrupted; dorsal VII + 13; pelvic fins not reaching one-half distance to anal fin origin .... Naked goby, *Gobiosoma bosci.*

12   Second dorsal rays 15–16; anal 16–17 13

Second dorsal rays 11–14; anal 12–15 14

13   Body spotted with large blotches; 22 pectoral rays; outer teeth enlarged .... Clown goby, *Microgobius gulosus.*

Body dusky, without blotches; 21 pectoral rays; outer teeth same size as inner .... Green goby, *Microgobius thalassinus.*

14   Dorsal spines VII; pectoral rays 22; scales deciduous .... Ragged goby, *Bollmannia communis.*

Dorsal spines VI; pectoral rays 16–19 15

15   Patch of scales on upper margin of opercle 16

No patch of scales on opercle 17

16   Fewer than 50 scales rows; pelvics reaching anal fin origin; eye more than one-half upper jaw length .... Lyre goby, *Evorthodus lyricus.*

More than 60 scale rows; pelvics not reaching anal fin origin; eye less than one-half upper jaw length .... Sharptail goby, *Gobionellus hastatus.*

17   Dorsal rays 12; anal rays 13; lateral-line scales 35–40; horizontal bar on cheek .... Freshwater goby, *Gobionellus shufeldti.*

Dorsal rays 11; anal rays 12; lateral-line scales 29–33; large dark spot on body above opercle .... Darter goby, *Gobionellus boleosoma.*

373. Blue goby   *Ioglossus calliurus* Bean

D. VI + 22–24; A. 22–24; body tan in preservative, bluish in life, densely spotted; fins edged with black or blue; caudal reddish. A small fish in our area presently known only from 7½-Fathom Reef, the blue goby is to be expected around all reefs, where it burrows in shell rubble. Also found on other tropical reefs in the Gulf and Caribbean. (4 inches; 10 cm)

374. Spotted goby   *Coryphopterus punctipectophorus* Springer

D. VI + 11; A. 10; P. 17–20; body plain, with dark spot on lower half of pectoral base. This is another reef form known from 7½-Fathom Reef and western Florida, but to be expected on all reefs. Springer, 1960; Causey, 1969. (2 inches; 5 cm)

375. Fat sleeper *Dormitator maculatus* (Bloch)

D. VII + 9; A. 10; P. 14; Sc. 33–36; body depth about 25 percent of standard length; brown or tan, paler ventrally, each scale with cluster of brown melanophores; younger fish with eight to ten broad bars on sides. Moderately common in marshes and ponds of upper estuaries. North Carolina to Brazil, including Gulf of Mexico, Bahamas, and West Indies. (10 inches; 25 cm)

376. Bigmouth sleeper *Gobiomorus dormitor* Lacépède

D. VI + 10; A. 10; Sc. 55–57; dark brown or olive sides interrupted by dark lateral band from under base of pectoral to base of caudal. Known only from southern Texas, where it is common in the Rio Grande, but taken as far north as the Aransas River; southern Florida and southern Texas to the Guianas. (2 feet; 61 cm)

377. Emerald sleeper *Erotelis smaragdus* (Valenciennes)

D. VI + 12; A. 10; P. 17; Sc. about 100; depth of body about 12 percent of standard length; brown above, tan below; median fins light tan with traces of brown lines. Rare in the area, this fish is known only from Grand Isle and Port Aransas. The local subspecies, *E. s. civitatum* Ginsburg, was described near Corpus Christi. Northern Gulf to Brazil. (6 inches; 15 cm)

378. Spinycheek sleeper *Eleotris pisonis* (Gmelin)

D. VI + 9; A. 9; P. 17; Sc. 56–60; depth about 22 percent of standard length; brown, frequently with darker brown lines radiating from eyes. This sleeper is restricted to low-salinity areas and is known from fresh water. Its coloration is variable depending on background and illumination. Atlantic coast from Bermuda and South Carolina to Brazil; Gulf of Mexico, Bahamas, and West Indies. (8 inches; 20 cm)

379. Violet goby *Gobioides broussonneti* Lacépède

D. VII, 15; A. 16; P. 19; depth about 9 percent of standard length; body very long and tapering; dorsal fins continuous; color purplish brown, interrupted with white; 25–30 dark, anteriorly directed chevrons along myomeres. This large, slim goby is usually taken individually over soft mud bottoms. It is found from inshore marsh channels out across the continental shelf. Atlantic coast and Gulf of Mexico from Georgia to Brazil. (18 inches; 46 cm)

380. Frillfin goby *Bathygobius soporator* (Valenciennes)

D. VI + 10; A. 9; P. 19; Sc. 42; depth about 21 percent of standard length; body brown with darker bars and blotches; fins densely spotted with brown. This tropical form is known from the Port Aransas jetties and could be expected in any rocky area, especially on the South Texas coast. North Carolina to Florida, Gulf of Mexico; other subspecies occur in the Caribbean. (5 inches; 13 cm)

381. Twoscale goby *Gobiosoma longipala* Ginsburg

D. VII + 12; A. 10; P. 17; depth about 12–18 percent of standard length; body lacking scales except for two relatively large ctenoid scales on caudal peduncle; body with 7–8 broad vertical bars, each bar with darker mid-dorsal line. This small, recently discovered goby is apparently not uncommon in the deeper bays and shallow Gulf. It may prove to be conspecific with the Atlantic coast *G. ginsburgi*, with which it is closely allied, both occurring around shells and other protected habitats. West Florida to Texas. (1½ inches; 4 cm)

382. Code goby *Gobiosoma robustum* Ginsburg

D. VII + 12; A. 10; P. 16; depth 16–23 percent of standard length; body without scales; sometimes 10–12 indistinct vertical bars on sides. This common species is usually restricted to grass beds, particularly *Thalassia*. Chesapeake Bay to Florida, through the Gulf to Yucatán. (2 inches; 5 cm)

383. Naked goby *Gobiosoma bosci* (Lacépède)

D. VII + 13; A. 11; P. 18; depth 14–20 percent of standard length; 9–10 dark vertical bars on sides, usually separated by narrow light space. This is the goby most commonly found on oyster reefs, usually hiding so well that it is not seen. Large populations sometimes develop in marsh ponds. This species closely resembles *G. robustum*, but the bars are straighter and the meristic counts are distinctive. Long Island Sound to Campeche, Mexico. Hoese, 1966b. (2½ inches; 6 cm)

384. Clown goby *Microgobius gulosus* (Girard)

D. VII + 16; A. 17; P. 22; Sc. 45–52; body spotted with dark brown; two or three dark vertical bars below second dorsal; often longitudinal bar beneath eye; outer edges of second dorsal, anal, and caudal dusky in males, spotted in females. This is a common goby on mud bottoms in bays and adjacent ponds. Chesapeake Bay to Corpus Christi. (3 inches; 8 cm)

385. Green goby *Microgobius thalassinus* (Jordan and Gilbert)

D. VII + 16; A. 16; P. 21; body more elongate and lighter in color than that of *M. gulosus*, with mouth more vertically inclined in this species. Females with prominent dark spot on first dorsal. This goby is generally considered to be very rare, probably because of its habitat. These small fish associate with and live inside sponges, particularly *Microciona*, and bryozoans. Chesapeake Bay to Corpus Christi. (2 inches; 5 cm)

386. Ragged goby *Bollmannia communis* Ginsburg

D. VII + 14; A. 14; P. 22; body bluish, irridescent in life; middle rays of dorsal fin elongate, darkened; center rays of caudal also produced. This is the common goby over muddy bottoms in the shallow Gulf. The common name refers to its usual loss of scales with handling. Known only from the western Gulf of Mexico, Mississippi to Campeche. (3 inches; 8 cm)

387. Lyre goby *Evorthodus lyricus* (Girard)

D. VI + 11; A. 12; P. 16; Sc. 30–35; depth 20 percent of standard length; brown or gray with five or six indistinct vertical bars; two dark spots on caudal fin base. An uncommon shallow-water form, usually found in salty tidal pools. Chesapeake Bay to Surinam and in the West Indies. (3 inches; 8 cm)

388. Sharptail goby *Gobionellus hastatus* Girard

D. VI + 14; A. 15; P. 19; Sc. variable, extreme range 60–93; brown, often with dark shoulder spot; another dark spot at base of lanceolate caudal fin. This large goby occurs commonly over muddy bottoms in the deeper bays and inshore Gulf. Considerable confusion has existed about this goby, with specimens also identified as *G. gracillimus* and *G. oceanicus*. Inshore and bay specimens have variable scale counts ranging from 61 to 91, with most above 73. Offshore in about twelve to twenty-two fathoms (off Port Aransas, at least) is another population with very deciduous scales numbering always below 65. These two populations are distinguishable but may not be separate species. If they are distinct, the offshore population is *G. oceanicus* and the inshore *G. hastatus*, with *G. gracillimus* a synonym of the latter. North Carolina to Campeche, Mexico. (8 inches; 20 cm)

389. Freshwater goby *Gobionellus shufeldti* (Jordan and Eigenmann)

D. VI + 12; A. 13; P. 17; Sc. 35–40; tan with four or five irregular blotches (often squares) on sides. This goby is limited to fresh water and low salinities in bays and channels. It is not known south of Galveston Bay. North Carolina to Texas. (3 inches; 8 cm)

390. Darter goby *Gobionellus boleosoma* (Jordan and Gilbert)

D. VI + 11; A. 12; P. 16; tan with four or five narrow longitudinal bars; distinct V-shaped markings on upper half of body. The darter is the most ubiquitous of gobies, being found in nearly all bay habitats and in the shallow Gulf. North Carolina to Brazil, throughout the Gulf of Mexico and Caribbean. (2½ inches; 6 cm)

Microdesmidae

The wormfishes are a peculiar group of nocturnal, burrowing, gobylike fishes with pale colors and long, slender bodies. They seem to be rare, but might be expected anywhere inshore. (Dawson, 1962*b*, 1969)

1 Fewer than 50 anal rays; caudal fin rounded . . . . Pink wormfish, *Microdesmus longipinnis*.
   More than 50 anal rays; caudal fin lanceolate . . . . Lancetail wormfish, *Microdesmus lanceolatus*.

391. Pink wormfish *Microdesmus longipinnis* (Weymouth)

D. XX–XXI, 50; A. usually about 44; caudal fin rounded. This is a rare fish found in the northern Gulf and bays, mostly in quite shallow water. Georgia to Cedar Bayou; Bermuda and Cayman Islands. (10 inches; 25 cm)

392. Lancetail wormfish *Microdesmus lanceolatus* Dawson
D. XII, 56; A. usually about 55; caudal fin lanceolate. Known only from twenty fathoms off Grand Isle, Louisiana. (2 inches; 5 cm)

Acanthuridae

The surgeonfishes or tangs are another group of laterally flattened reef fishes, but they have retractable sharp spines on each side of the caudal peduncle which serve to discourage predators and which can cut humans. All three of our species are found throughout the tropical western Atlantic, and one additional species is confined to Florida. These occur on offshore reefs, with the young sometimes occurring inshore. (Randall, 1956)

1 Body blue in life with longitudinal stripes; anal rays usually 24–25
   Blue tang, *Acanthurus coeruleus.*
   Body dark brown; anal rays usually 22–23 2
2 Brown vertical bars on body; no white on caudal peduncle . . . .
   Doctorfish, *Acanthurus chirurgus.*
   Brown vertical bars lacking; pale white area behind caudal spine
   Ocean surgeon, *Acanthurus bahianus.*

393. Blue tang *Acanthurus coeruleus* Bloch and Schneider
D. IX, 26–28; A. III, 24–26; body blue with lighter, wavy longitudinal stripes; young yellow overall; intermediate fish mixed, often blue with yellow fins; caudal spine surrounded by yellow in all sizes. A very rare fish on offshore reefs. Bermuda and New York through the Caribbean to Brazil. Bright and Cashman, 1974; Sonnier, Teerling, and Hoese, 1976. (14 inches; 36 cm)

394. Doctorfish *Acanthurus chirurgus* (Bloch)
D. IX, 24–25; A. III, 22–23; body brown with narrow, darker vertical bars; median fins sometimes bluish. Occasionally found on offshore reefs, this is probably the most common surgeonfish here. Bermuda and New York through the Caribbean to Brazil. Sonnier, Teerling, and Hoese, 1976. (13 inches; 33 cm)

395. Ocean surgeon *Acanthurus bahianus* Castelnau
D. IX, 23–26; A. III, 21–23; brown, but without dark vertical bars; usually with light area posterior to caudal spine (sometimes present in *A. chirurgus*) and broad light margin on caudal fin; short blue lines around eye. Found occasionally on offshore reefs, the ocean surgeons in the northeastern Gulf have been described as a separate species, *A. randalli* Briggs and Caldwell, these having a squarer tail and a shorter pectoral (more than 27 percent

of standard length compared to less than 26 percent in *A. bahianus*). The status of ocean surgeons in the northern Gulf requires further study to determine if this species is really different and whether populations east of the Mississippi are related or not. Briggs and Caldwell, 1957a; Sonnier, Teerling, and Hoese, 1976. (14 inches; 36 cm)

Trichiuridae

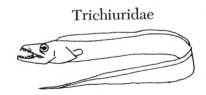

The Atlantic cutlassfish, *Trichiurus lepturus*, is the sole representative of this family occurring in our range.

396. Atlantic cutlassfish; ribbonfish   *Trichiurus lepturus* Linnaeus
D. 135; A. 100; no scales, body elongate, silvery; eye and mouth large; upper jaw with about four large barbed teeth anteriorly. Ribbonfish are common in the inshore Gulf and bays during the warmer months. Smaller individuals are used as trolling bait for kingfish (*Scomberomorus cavalla*), while larger fish are notorious bait stealers, often breaking leaders with their sharp teeth or devouring other hooked fish before the angler can land them. The flesh of the cutlassfish is edible and reportedly good eating, and the species supports a commercial fishery in other areas. It is fortunate that it dies rapidly, because its large teeth are capable of inflicting a painful bite. Virginia to Brazil; also in the Pacific from Panama to Mexico (Gulf of California). Although very common in Texas, it is more abundant in Louisiana. Dawson, 1967. (5 feet; 1½ m)

Scombridae

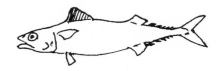

The mackerels are typified as fast-swimming, oceanic fishes. Their streamlined bodies, stiff fins, and rigid caudal peduncle enable them to swim constantly at high speeds. Indeed, in some species of scombrids the branchiostegal respiratory pump has so degenerated that the fishes must remain in motion in order to pass sufficient water over their gills to meet their respiratory needs. Some tunas, as well as other fast-swimming fish such as marlins and some sharks, can maintain body temperatures up to ten centigrade degrees above that of the surrounding water. These elevated temperatures allow for high metabolic rates, which in turn provide the large quantities of energy required for constant, high-speed swimming.

Most species travel in schools and feed on smaller fish or squid. Most are highly regarded both as game fish and as food fish, with some species supporting extensive commercial fisheries.

The mackerels superficially resemble the carangids (jacks) but lack the bony scutes on the posterior lateral line and the pair of free anal spines which are characteristic of the Carangidae. (Rivas, 1951, 1964; Klawe and Shimada, 1959; Gibbs and Collette, 1967; Collette and Chao, 1975)

1 Dorsal fins far apart, with distance between fins greater than length of snout; dorsal spines IX–X 2
Dorsal fins close together, with distance between fins less than length of snout; dorsal spines XIII–XXVI 3

2 Body entirely scaled; dorsal finlets V; anal finlets V; caudal peduncle without keel .... Chub mackerel, *Scomber japonicus.*
Body scaled only anteriorly, along lateral lines and along back to origin of second dorsal fin; dorsal finlets VIII or IX; anal finlets VII; caudal peduncle with median keels .... Frigate mackerel, *Auxis thazard.*

3 Dorsal spines XIII–XXII; gill rakers present; snout shorter than rest of head 4
Dorsal spines XXI–XXVII; gill rakers absent; snout about equal to rest of head .... Wahoo, *Acanthocybium solanderi.*

4 Gill rakers 36–40 on lower limb of first arch; distance between origin of second dorsal and last dorsal finlet less than distance between tip of snout and origin of first dorsal; three to five dark longitudinal stripes on lower sides of body, converging towards caudal peduncle .... Skipjack tuna, *Euthynnus pelamis.*
Gill rakers 7–29 on lower limb of first arch; distance between origin of second dorsal and last dorsal finlet greater than distance between tip of snout and origin of first dorsal; no longitudinal stripes 5

5 Scales present only on anterior portion of body, along anterior lateral line, and along back to origin of second dorsal fin; irregularly scattered dark blotches, as large as pupil of eye, on sides of body below pectoral fin .... Little tuna, *Euthynnus alletteratus.*
Scales covering entire body, sometimes enlarged in pectoral region; no dark blotches below pectoral fin 6

6 Dorsal spines XIII–XV; first spine as long or longer than second and third spines; pectoral fin long, reaching beyond vertical through tenth dorsal spine 7
Dorsal spines XV–XXII; first spine shorter than second; pectoral fin short, not reaching vertical through tenth dorsal spine 9

7 Pectoral fin not reaching beyond vertical through twelfth dorsal spine; gill rakers 25–28 on lower limb of first arch .... Bluefin tuna, *Thunnus thynnus.*
Pectoral fin reaching beyond vertical from twelfth dorsal spine; gill rakers 15–22 on lower limb of first arch 8

8 Gill rakers 15–19 on lower limb of first arch; dorsal finlets VII–IX, usually VIII; anal finlets VII–VIII; second dorsal and anal fins not greatly produced in older specimens .... Blackfin tuna, *Thunnus atlanticus.*

Gill rakers 20–22 on lower limb of first arch; dorsal finlets VIII–XI, usually IX–X; anal finlets VIII–X; second dorsal and anal fins produced .... Yellowfin tuna, *Thunnus albacares.*

9 Maxillary reaching beyond vertical from posterior margin of eye; dorsal spines XX–XXII; dark oblique stripes on back .... Atlantic bonito, *Sarda sarda.*

Maxillary reaching no further than vertical from posterior margin of eye; dorsal spines XV–XVIII; no dark oblique stripes on back 10

10 Gill rakers 7–9 on lower limb of first arch; dorsal spines XV–XVI; lateral line curving abruptly downward below second dorsal fin .... King mackerel, *Scomberomorus cavalla.*

Gill rakers 10–13 on lower limb of first arch; dorsal spines XVII–XVIII; lateral line not abruptly curving downward below second dorsal 11

11 Gill rakers 12–13 on lower limb of first arch; maxillary not quite reaching vertical from posterior margin of eye; pectoral fin scaled; sides of body with spots and one or two longitudinal stripes .... Cero, *Scomberomorus regalis.*

Gill rakers 10–11 on lower limb of first arch; maxillary just reaching to posterior margin of eye; pectoral fin not scaled; sides of body with spots but without longitudinal stripes .... Spanish mackerel, *Scomberomorus maculatus.*

397. Chub mackerel *Scomber japonicus* Houttuyn

D. IX + I, 12 + V–VI; A. I, 11 + V; Sc. 200; small scales covering entire body; elongate, silvery, with widely separated first and second dorsal fins; back greenish blue with wavy dark lines. The chub mackerel is sometimes separated from the Pacific mackerel and referred to as *Scomber* (or *Pneumatophorus*) *colias* Gmelin. It is a small mackerel sporadically caught in the northern Gulf. Worldwide in temperate and tropical seas; in the western Atlantic from Nova Scotia and Bermuda to Brazil. Matsui, 1967. (1 foot; 30 cm)

398. Frigate mackerel *Auxis thazard* (Lacépède)

D. X + 12 + VIII; A. VII, 13 + VII; scales covering anterior and lower posterior portions of body; unscaled portion of back with wavy, oblique dark lines; first and second dorsal fins widely separated. This is another small scombrid not commonly caught. The closely related *A. rochei*, which possesses vertical instead of wavy oblique bars, apparently occurs in the northeastern Gulf and should not be ruled out from other areas of the Gulf. Worldwide in tropical waters; in the western Atlantic from Massachusetts to Columbia. (2 feet; 61 cm)

399. Wahoo *Acanthocybium solanderi* (Cuvier)

D. XXI–XXVII + 12 + IX; A. II, 10 + IX; scales covering back of living specimens deep blue or green with prominent vertical black bars on sides; silvery blue between bars; silvery white on belly; first and second dorsal fins continuous. One of the few solitary scombrids, this fish is usually found far from shore and is a highly sought game and food fish. Individuals attain weights of over one hundred pounds (45 kg). Worldwide in tropical seas; in the western Atlantic from New Jersey to Columbia. (4 feet; 1¼ m)

400. Skipjack tuna (oceanic bonito)   *Euthynnus pelamis* (Linnaeus)

D. XV–XVI + 12 + VIII; A. II, 12 + VII; scales well developed, covering anterior body; body silvery, greenish blue above with oblique dark lines on back and dark horizontal lines on lower sides and belly; dorsal fins set close, but not continuous; first dorsal with high anterior lobe. Also known as *Katsuwonus pelamis*, this offshore species, which is not common, travels in large schools. Worldwide in tropical seas; in the western Atlantic from Maine to Brazil. (7 feet; 2 m)

401. Little tuna; false albacore; bonito   *Euthynnus alletteratus* (Rafinesque)

D. XIV–XVI + 12 + VIII; A. II, 12 + VII; scales forming corselet as in *E. pelamis*; back bluish green with oblique wavy lines; belly white with large, round black spots below pectoral fin; dorsal fins close-set; anterior dorsal lobed. This is the common bonito or "bone-eater" of Gulf sportfishermen. This species comes into shallower water than the other tunas and frequently feeds near the surface. It is a hard-hitting but small fish, generally regarded as an excellent game fish but not highly rated for its food value. Throughout the tropical Atlantic; in the west from the Gulf of Maine and Bermuda to Brazil. De Sylva and Rathjen, 1961. (2 feet; 61 cm)

402. Bluefin tuna   *Thunnus thynnus* (Linnaeus)

D. XIII–XIV + 13 + IX–X; A. II, 12 + VIII–IX; Gr. on lower limb of first arch 25–28; entire body scaly; back dark blue to black; cheeks, sides, and belly silvery white; first and second dorsal fins dark; finlets yellow with black edges; anal fin and finlets silvery gray (finlets sometimes yellowish). The giant among tunas, Atlantic Ocean specimens of bluefin attain weights of over one thousand pounds (455 kg). Rare in the northwestern Gulf, there have been several caught off the Mississippi Delta in water over one hundred fathoms deep. As yet there are no confirmed records from Texas waters. This species is one of the few marine fishes considered to be rare or endangered by the National Marine Fisheries Service, and sports fishing for bluefin tuna has recently come under federal government management. It is sometimes considered to be a single worldwide species, but the Pacific bluefin is currently placed in a separate species. The Atlantic bluefin occurs on both sides of the Atlantic Ocean, in the west from Newfoundland and Bermuda to Brazil. (14 feet; 4¼ m)

403. Blackfin tuna   *Thunnus atlanticus* (Lesson)

D. XIII–XIV + 12–15 + VII–IX; A. II, 11–15 + VII–VIII; Gr. on lower limb 15–19; pectoral fin long, ending near second dorsal (not reaching end of first dorsal in *T. thynnus*); body fully scaled; bluish black above, silvery white on belly; pectoral, dorsal, and anal fins black; finlets yellow, edged with black. The commonest true tuna (*Thunnus*) in the northwestern Gulf, this fish is exceeded in abundance only by *Euthynnus alletteratus*. It is a popular sports and food fish. Massachusetts and Bermuda to Brazil. De Sylva, 1955. (3 feet; 91 cm)

404. Yellowfin tuna   *Thunnus albacares* (Bonnaterre)

D. XIII–XV + 13–16 + VIII–XI; A. II, 12–15 + VIII–X; Gr. on lower limb 20–22; pectoral fin long, reaching second dorsal fin; body fully scaled; blue black above, silvery white below; first dorsal and pectoral fins black; second dorsal and anal fins yellow and greatly elongated in older specimens. A popular food and game fish, the yellowfin is less common than the blackfin. Circumtropical; in the western Atlantic from Massachusetts to Brazil. (6 feet; 1⅔ m)

405. Atlantic bonito   *Sarda sarda* (Bloch)

D. XXI + I, 13 + VIII; A. I, 13 + VII; body fully scaled; back blue with oblique, almost horizontal dark lines; whitish below; spinous dorsal fin long, high for most of its length. Not common in the northwestern Gulf of Mexico. Atlantic Ocean, in the west from Nova Scotia to Argentina. Collette and Chao, 1975. (2 feet; 61 cm)

406. King mackerel; kingfish   *Scomberomorus cavalla* (Cuvier)

D. XV + I, 15 + VIII–IX; A. II, 15 + VIII; mouth with large, compressed teeth, about 30 on each side of jaw; sides silvery, greenish above; young fish with dull yellow or greenish spots; very small individuals (6 inches or 150 mm) uniformly silver; dorsal fin uniformly dark; lateral line dipping suddenly below second dorsal and thereafter undulating. This is perhaps the most popular offshore gamefish in the northwestern Gulf of Mexico, where the appearance of kingfish is regarded as the marine harbinger of summer. Although some reach over one hundred pounds, those from our area average fifteen to twenty pounds. The king mackerel is generally found farther offshore than the Spanish mackerel. Gulf of Maine to Brazil. (5 feet; 1½ m)

407. Spanish mackerel   *Scomberomorus maculatus* (Mitchill)

D. XVII + I, 18 + VIII–IX; A. II, 17 + IX; mouth with 24–32 teeth in each jaw, somewhat smaller and more widely spaced than those in comparable size of S. *cavalla*; sides silvery with distinct yellow spots, brighter than those in king mackerel and retained at all sizes; lateral line gently curved beneath second dorsal; very small individuals (about 2 inches—5 cm) without spots, but spots acquired by length of 6 inches (15 cm). The young are common in the surf zone and even in low-salinity bays. This is a popular sports fish. It is fished commercially in Florida. Both sides of the Atlantic (in the eastern Pacific S. *sierra* may also represent this species); from the Gulf of Maine and Bermuda to Brazil. (2 feet; 61 cm)

408. Cero   *Scomberomorus regalis* (Bloch)

D. XVI–XVIII + I, 15–16 + VIII–IX; A. II, 14 + VIII; mouth with about 30–40 teeth in each jaw; sides silvery with well-defined yellow spots and prominent yellow streaks; first dorsal fin light, with prominent black area at front; scales present on pectoral fins (other two *Scomberomorus* species having scaleless pectoral fins); lateral line dipping gradually below second dorsal (as in Spanish mackerel). The cero is the least common of the mackerels in the northwestern Gulf of Mexico. Many anglers consider young kingfish which still have spots to be ceros. Fishermen who think they may have caught a cero should have the identity of the specimen verified by a biologist. Massachusetts to Brazil, common throughout the Caribbean. Baughman, 1941*b*; Reed, 1941. (3 feet; 91 cm)

Xiphiidae

The swordfish is the sole member of this family. While superficially it resembles the istiophorids, with which it is often classed as a billfish, *Xiphias gladius* is quite distinct and only distantly related. Swordfish possess a flattened, serrated bill and lack ventral fins. There was an attempt to develop a longline fishery for swordfish, but it was thwarted by findings that showed the amount of mercury in their flesh to exceed the amount allowed by the federal government.

409. Swordfish   *Xiphias gladius* Linnaeus

D. 41–48 + 4; A. 16–18 + 14; P. 15–18; upper jaw extended into flattened, serrated sword. The swordfish is widely distributed both north and south of the equator. In the Gulf it is not seen at the surface as it is in cooler waters. Spawning in the Gulf apparently occurs during a protracted period from late spring through late summer. The fish reaches considerable size; one from off Peru weighed 1,182 pounds (537 kg). Worldwide in cold temperate through tropical waters; in the western North Atlantic from Newfoundland south. Kramer, 1950; Arata, 1954; Eschmeyer, 1963. (16 feet; 5 m)

Istiophoridae

The Istiophoridae or billfishes constitute a family of large, pelagic fishes characterized by their elongate upper jaws or bills. They differ from the swordfish (Xiphiidae) in their possession of ventral fins and in having a rounded instead of flattened bill. All species grow to a large size, though some greatly exceed others. The Indo-Pacific black marlin, *Makaira indica*, has been known to exceed two thousand pounds (900 kg), and the blue marlin, *M. nigricans*, reaches fifteen hundred pounds (680 kg) and may even outweigh the black marlin.

Relatively little is known of the life histories and biologies of these species except for the barest of outlines. The billfishes are all "apex predators," feeding at the top of the food chain, and they maintain fairly small, widely dispersed populations. The taxonomy of the istiophorids has been fairly confused, with a great many more species described than probably exist. Recent work with specimens from the entire range of the species indicates that sailfish, at least, belong to a single species around the world. Similarly, blue marlins of the Atlantic and Pacific oceans belong to the same species. There are five species of billfishes reported from the northwestern Gulf of Mexico and four (maybe more) extralimital species found elsewhere in the world. (de Sylva, 1974)

1   Adult fish greater than 24 inches (60 cm) in standard length   2
     Postlarval or juvenile fish 4–24 inches (10–60 cm) in standard
     length   6
2   Spinous dorsal greatly elevated its entire length, with middle rays
     longest; ventral fins with two or three rays . . . . Sailfish, *Istiophorus platypterus*.
     Spinous dorsal only moderately elevated, with middle rays not
     longest; ventral fins with only one ray   3
3   Anterior lobe of spinous dorsal low, pointed, with height less than
     depth of body; flesh pale . . . . Blue marlin, *Makaira nigricans*.
     Anterior lobe of spinous dorsal pointed, rounded, or blunt and
     higher than depth of body at dorsal fin origin   4
4   Spinous dorsal fin high throughout, with posterior rays almost as
     long as anterior rays; dorsal fin unspotted   5
     Spinous dorsal low posteriorly (except in young fish); anus less
     than one-half anal fin height from base of anal fin; dorsal fin
     spotted (fading somewhat after death) . . . . White marlin,
     Tetrapturus albidus.
5   Anterior lobe of spinous dorsal pointed; anal fin pointed; anus in
     advance of anal fin base usually by more than height of first
     anal fin . . . . Longbill spearfish, *Tetrapturus pfluegeri*.
     Anterior lobe of spinous dorsal rounded or blunt; anal fin rounded;
     anus in advance of anal fin by less than one-half height of first
     anal fin . . . . Hatchet marlin, *Tetrapturus* sp.
6   Upper jaw much longer than lower; lateral line simple   7
     Upper jaw scarcely longer than lower; lateral line complex, consisting of reticulated pattern . . . . Blue marlin, *Makaira nigricans*.
7   Anus forward, about midway between bases of anal and ventral
     fins; pelvics short, not reaching base of anal fin; dorsal unspotted; dorsal spines 45–53 (49) . . . . Longbill spearfish,
     Tetrapturus pfluegeri.
     Anus close to anal fin origin; pelvics long, nearly reaching base of
     anal fin; dorsal fin spotted or unmarked; dorsal spines 38–49   8
8   Dorsal fin unmarked (?) . . . . Hatchet marlin, *Tetrapturus* sp.
     Dorsal fin mottled or spotted   9
9   Dorsal mottled, with no distinct ocelli; dorsal with 37–49 (usually
     43–45) spines . . . . Sailfish, *Istiophorus platypterus*.
     Dorsal fin with four distinct ocelli near base; dorsal with 38–46
     (usually 42) spines . . . . White marlin, *Tetrapturus albidus*.

410. Sailfish   *Istiophorus platypterus* (Shaw and Nodder)
    D. 37–49 + 6–8; A. 8–16 + 5–8; P. 17–20; adults with the most anterior rays of both the dorsal and the anal fins degenerate and covered by skin, resulting in lowered meristic counts; adults blue black above, light blue

to silver below; dorsal fin membrane dark blue with black spots; vertical rows of golden spots on sides of body; young uniformly lighter, with mottled dorsal fin membrane; lateral line simple. A recent revision of the genus has placed all sailfish in this single, cosmopolitan species. Formerly Atlantic sailfish were referred to as *I. americanus* (Cuvier) or *I. albicans* (Latreille). Off southern Texas sailfish first appear in early May in most years and usually leave by November. Fish are present on the more northern Gulf coast about one month later and leave one month earlier. The sailfish apparently avoid temperatures below 50° F, and their movements seem to be correlated with water temperatures in the 75°–80° F range. Sailfish only live four or five years, with most of their growth occurring during the first two or three years. Circumtropical; in the western Atlantic from Rhode Island to Brazil. Voss, 1953; de Sylva, 1957; Morrow and Harbo, 1969; Jolley, 1974. (6 feet; 1⅔ m)

411. Blue marlin *Makaira nigricans* Lacépède

D. 39–46 + 6–7; A. 14–17 + 6–7; P. 20–22; anteriormost rays of dorsal fin not greater than body depth at origin of dorsal fin; dorsal fin pointed; adults dark blue above, lighter below, with dark vertical stripes along sides, disappearing in larger fish; after death, more uniformly dark coloration; dorsal fin black or very dark blue; lateral line complex but often inconspicuous, forming reticulate pattern along sides of body; young with little or no noticeable bill, upper jaw being only slightly longer or no longer than lower. Blue marlin occur throughout the tropical oceans. Females attain a greater size than males, which seldom exceed three hundred pounds. The largest fish are usually caught around the middle of the season (July and August in the Gulf). Atlantic blue marlin were formerly referred to as *M. ampla* and Pacific blue marlin as *M. mazara* and *M.* (or *Istiompax*) *howardii. Makaira perezi* from the South Atlantic is also probably synonymous with *M. nigricans*. Circumtropical; in the western Atlantic from Massachusetts to Uruguay. (10 feet; 3 m)

412. White marlin *Tetrapturus albidus* Poey

D. 38–46 + 5–7; A. 12–18 + 5–7; P. 17–21; anterior rays of dorsal fin height greater than body depth at origin of dorsal fin; dorsal fin lobe rounded; anus located near the origin of the anal fin; body silvery, only slightly darker above than below; dorsal fin spotted, especially evident in dorsal groove; series of irridescent spots above lateral line (referred to as "spotlights" by Texas fishermen). White marlin seem to prefer water between 78° and 80° F. Their feeding grounds are characterized by bottom irregularities and fairly low levels of dissolved oxygen (4.8–5.5 mg/l). From this fact it would appear that marlin seek out areas of upwelling where food would be expected to be plentiful. In the Gulf there is a concentration of fish off the mouth of the Mississippi in midsummer, followed by a dispersion to other parts of the Gulf in the later summer. Spawning occurs in late spring and early summer. Though they can reach as much as one hundred pounds (45 kg), white marlin seldom exceed sixty pounds (27 kg). This fish is much longer lived than the sailfish, having a life of perhaps ten years. Nova Scotia to Brazil. Gibbs, 1957; de Sylva and Davis, 1963. (7 feet; 2 m)

413. Longbill spearfish *Tetrapturus pfluegeri* Robins and de Sylva

D. 45–53 + 6–7; A. 12–18 + 6–8; P. 18–20; posterior dorsal nearly as high as anterior; dorsal fin rounded; anus noticeably forward, about halfway between origins of anal fin and ventral fins; blue black above, silvery below; vertical bands may be present on small specimens but are absent from larger fish. This species rarely exceeds sixty pounds. It has only been reported once from Texas, but it is likely that it has been mistaken for small white marlin, which it closely resembles. Tropical western Atlantic, total range uncertain. Swann, 1957; Springer and Hoese, 1958. (6 feet; 2 m)

414. Hatchet marlin *Tetrapturus* sp.
The distinctive dorsal fin of this species, which resembles that of a small white marlin, should make its identification easier. The existence of a previously unknown species of billfish in the northern Gulf of Mexico has been shown from photographs taken by Mr. Robert Ewing of Monroe, Louisiana. A specimen of the hatchet marlin was recently taken off Charleston, South Carolina, and is being studied by scientists at Miami's Rosenthiel School of Atmospheric and Marine Sciences. Sports fishermen catching fish they feel may be hatchet marlin should report their catches to scientists and, if possible, make arrangements to preserve the fish until they can be studied. The hatchet marlin probably represents an undescribed species or a western race of the roundscale spearfish, *T. georgei*. Known from the eastern Atlantic and Mediterranean. Robins, 1974; de Sylva, 1974. (7 feet; 2 m)

Stromateidae

The butterfishes and the closely related man-of-war fish (Nomeidae) are open-water schooling fishes sometimes put in the same family. The juveniles float among the plankton and are commonly associated with jellyfish—in the case of *Nomeus*, with the Portuguese man-of-war, *Physalia*. All are small- to moderate-sized fish with small embedded scales. (Haedrich, 1967; Horn, 1970)

1   Body height more than 60 percent of standard length; no row of pores below anterior portion of dorsal fin; premaxillary teeth pointed, simple . . . . Harvestfish, *Peprilus paru*.
    Body height less than 60 percent of standard length; row of pores below anterior portion of dorsal fin; premaxillary teeth usually with three cusps . . . . Gulf butterfish, *Peprilus burti*.

415. Harvestfish *Peprilus paru* (Linnaeus)
D. 38–47; A. 35–45; P. 18–24; Gr. 20–23; body depth 60–88 percent of standard length; anterior profile moderately to strongly convex; eye diameter greater than length of snout; dorsal and anal fins falcate, with longest rays often six or more times longer than shortest; silvery. Massachusetts to Florida, throughout the Gulf of Mexico, and south to Argentina. Gulf populations

named *P. alepidotus* are considered conspecific, since the distinguishing characteristics are clinal. Mansueti, 1963; Horn, 1970. (10 inches; 25 cm)

416. Gulf butterfish   *Peprilus burti* Fowler
 D. 38–48; A. 35–43; P. 19–23; Gr. 21–26; body moderately elongate, depth 46 to 60 percent of standard length; anterior profile moderately convex; eye diameter greater than snout; dorsal and anal fins only slightly falcate. This species is somewhat more common in Louisiana. Records of *Peprilus* or *Poronotus triacanthus* in the Gulf are of this species. West coast of Florida to Yucatán. Caldwell, 1961. (1 foot; 30 cm)

Ariommidae

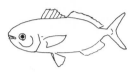

 Members of the Ariommidae, the driftfishes, were formerly assigned to other stromateoid families and are still sometimes lumped together in the Stromateidae. *Ariomma*, the only genus, superficially resembles the nomeids but also bears many characteristics which ally the genus to the centrolophids. In any case, the various species more closely resemble one another than any other stromateoid genus. Three species occur in the Gulf of Mexico, although more nominal species were once thought to exist. The young of all are pelagic, although the adults generally occur at depths greater than one hundred fathoms. In all species the scales are highly deciduous, and lateral-line scale counts are very risky, if not untrustworthy, points of differentiation among the species. (Haedrich, 1967; Ginsburg, 1954; Haedrich and Horn, 1972; Horn, 1972)

1   Deep-bodied forms, with depth greater than 33 percent of standard length . . . . Spotted driftfish, *Ariomma regulus*.
 Slender-bodied forms, with depth less than 28 percent of standard length   2
2   Peritoneum dark, with many melanophores; scales small, 50–65 in lateral line . . . . Brown driftfish, *Ariomma melana*.
 Peritoneum light, without or with few melanophores; scales large, 30–45 in lateral line . . . . Silver rag, *Ariomma bondi*.

417. Spotted driftfish   *Ariomma regulus* (Poey)
 D. XI + I, 15–16; A. III, 15; P. 21–24; Gr. 7 + 16; teeth not cusped; body silvery, variously spotted; first dorsal and pelvic fins darkening with age. Even small fish are more common at depths greater than one hundred fathoms. New Jersey to Cuba and in the Gulf of Mexico. McKenny, 1961. (at least 8 inches; 20 cm)

418. Silver rag   *Ariomma bondi* Fowler
 D. XI–XII + 14–17; A. III, 12–16; P. 20–23; Gr. 8 + 15. The silver rag generally occurs in water shallower than one hundred fathoms and so is

ecologically somewhat different from the other species of *Ariomma*. *Ariomma* (or *Cubiceps*) *nigriargenteus* Ginsburg is a synonym. Gulf of Maine to Uruguay, including the Gulf of Mexico and Caribbean; also off West Africa. Horn, 1972. (at least 8 inches; 20 cm)

419. Brown driftfish *Ariomma melana* (Ginsburg)
    D. XI–XII + 15–18; A. III, 13–16; P. 21–23; Gr. 9–11 + 17–20; color uniformly dusky brown. This fish is a deep shelf species which generally occurs in one hundred to three hundred fathoms. The young, however, are pelagic and may occur over the shelf at times. New York to the Caribbean, including the Gulf of Mexico; also off West Africa. Horn, 1972. (at least 8 inches; 20 cm)

Centrolophidae

    The ruffs are pelagic, high-seas fishes found near the edge of the continental shelf. The adults of most species occur off the shelf in much greater depths. They are closely related to the butterfishes (Stromateidae). Their geographic ranges are uncertain. (Haedrich, 1967)

1   Spines of dorsal fin weakly developed . . . . Black ruff, *Centrolophus niger*.
    Spines of dorsal short and stout . . . . Black driftfish, *Hyperoglyphe bythites*.

420. Black ruff *Centrolophus niger* (Gmelin)
    D. 37–41; A. III, 20–23; P. 19–22; Gr. 5–6 + 13–16. This is apparently a single cosmopolitan species found in temperate waters. (3 feet; 91 cm)

421. Black driftfish *Hyperoglyphe bythites* (Ginsburg)
    D. VII–VIII, 22–25; A. III, 16–17; P. 20–21; Gr. 6–7 + 16–17. The young of this driftfish occur near flotsam but rarely associate with medusae. The adults form large schools near the bottom in one hundred to two hundred fathoms. It is perhaps a synonym of *H. macrophthalma* (Miranda-Ribeiro) from Brazil; otherwise, it is known only from the northern Gulf of Mexico. Dawson, 1971*d*. (30 inches; 76 cm)

Nomeidae

The nomeids also are closely related to the butterfishes (Stromateidae), but they remain pelagic as adults and are often associated with animals, such as jellyfish, or other objects. Only the man-of-war fish is normally found on the shelf.

1 Body elongate, depth less than 35 percent of standard length; origin of dorsal fin well behind (or in small fish, above) insertion of pectoral fins 2
    Body deep, maximum depth usually greater than 40 percent of standard length; origin of dorsal before (or in very large fish, directly above) insertion of pectoral fin 3
2 Anal count II–III, 20–23; pelvic fins inserted under or behind base of pectoral fins .... Longfin cigarfish, *Cubiceps gracilis.*
    Anal count I–II, 24–29; pelvic fins inserted before or under insertion of pectoral fins .... Man-of-war fish, *Nomeus gronovii.*
3 Dorsal IX–XI + 24–28; anal III, 24–28; small teeth in both jaws .... Freckled driftfish, *Psenes cyanophrys.*
    Dorsal X–XI + I–II, 27–32; anal III, 26–31; knifelike teeth in lower jaw .... Blackrag, *Psenes pellucidus.*

422. Longfin cigarfish   *Cubiceps gracilis* (Lowe)

D. IX–XI + I–II, 20–22; A. II–III, 20–23; P. 20–24; Gr. 8–9 + 15–18. This elongate, finely scaled fish reaches considerable size. It is of doubtful occurrence in the northwestern Gulf. Atlantic ocean and western Mediterranean. (30 inches; 76 cm)

423. Man-of-war fish   *Nomeus gronovii* (Gmelin)

D. IX–XII + 24–28; A. I–II, 24–29; P. 21–23; Gr. 8–9 + 16–19; bright blue above, blotched and spotted on sides; dark blotches on median and pelvic fins (blotches may cover nearly entire fin). This species commonly associates with *Physalia*, the Portuguese man-of-war, and has been observed feeding on the polyps. Apparently *Nomeus* is immune to the siphonophore's toxin. Numerous specimens have been collected from the Gulf, inshore waters, and occasionally more saline bays; these are probably juveniles of a deep-living fish. Circumtropical; in the western Atlantic from Bermuda and Massachusetts through the Caribbean to Brazil. (8 inches; 20 cm)

424. Freckled driftfish   *Psenes cyanophrys* Valenciennes

D. IX–XI + 24–28; A. III, 24–28; P. 17–20; Gr. 8–9 + 20 (Gulf of Mexico specimens having higher modal counts); numerous longitudinal streaks on body. Atlantic, Pacific, and Indian Oceans; Massachusetts to the Caribbean. (at least 8 inches; 20 cm)

425. Blackrag   *Psenes pellucidus* Lütken

D. X–XI + I–II, 27–32; A. III, 26–31; P. 18–20; Gr. 8–9 + 15–17; body plain. A mesopelagic and bathypelagic species found over shelf waters only rarely. Flabby musculature and knifelike teeth in the lower jaw characterize the species. Atlantic, Pacific, and Indian Oceans; New Jersey to the Gulf of Mexico. (at least 8 inches; 20 cm)

Scorpaenidae

Scorpionfishes are colorful fishes with large spines capable of inflicting painful wounds and injecting a poison. The large spiny bone under the eye (preorbital or suborbital stay) and the small maillike scales on the cheeks are characteristic of the group. Many species of *Sebastes*, commonly called redfish or rockfish, are of commercial importance in the northern Atlantic and Pacific Oceans, but these species do not occur in the Gulf of Mexico. In our area *S. plumieri*, the only species commonly encountered by anglers, is considered a dangerous nuisance. Deep-water scorpionfishes not included here but which occasionally venture upon the continental shelf are covered by Eschmeyer (1969).

1 Scales on body ctenoid 2
   Scales on body cycloid 3
2 All pectoral rays unbranched . . . . Longspine scorpionfish, *Pontinus longispinis*.
   Some pectoral rays branched . . . . Spinycheek scorpionfish, *Neomerinthe hemingwayi*.
3 Preorbital bone with three or four spines (except in small juveniles) 4
   Preorbital bone with two spines 5
4 Pectoral axil with whitish or yellowish spot; 19–21 pectoral fin rays; pale caudal peduncle . . . . Spotted scorpionfish, *Scorpaena plumieri*.
   Pectoral axil without spots; body mostly pale; 17–19 pectoral fin rays . . . . Hunchback scorpionfish, *Scorpaena dispar*.
5 Pectoral fin with brown spots in axil; 50–60 scale rows; 2–3 brown spots behind head; occipital pits present . . . . Barbfish, *Scorpaena brasiliensis*.
   Pectoral fin with dark pigment in patches; 42–49 scale rows; one spot on head; occipital pit absent . . . . Smoothhead scorpionfish, *Scorpaena calcarata*.

426. Longspine scorpionfish *Pontinus longispinis* Goode and Bean

D. XII, 8–10 (usually 9); A. III, 5; P. 16–18 (usually 17); Sc. 45–50; Gr. 6–8 + 8–10; upper parts of head and body, soft dorsal fin, and caudal fin with dusky blotches on pale background; third dorsal spine noticeably elongate. This scorpionfish seems to prefer soft bottoms and is virtually unknown off Caribbean islands. It is common in water over fifty fathoms off the mouth of the Mississippi, with scattered records in seventy-five to ninety-one fathoms off Texas but usually outside of one hundred fathoms. South Carolina to Brazil. (8 inches; 20 cm)

427. Spinycheek scorpionfish *Neomerinthe hemingwayi* Fowler

D. XII, 10 (rarely 9); A. III, 5; P. 16–17 (usually 17); third through seventh or eighth pectoral rays branched; Sc. 60–70; Gr. 6–7 + 9–12; no elongated dorsal spines; body reddish orange with numerous brown spots on body and fins; dark pigment on inside of pectoral fin. The coloration of this species resembles that of *Scorpaena brasiliensis*; however, the two species are otherwise quite distinct. Aside from possessing ctenoid scales (*Scorpaena* has cycloid scales), this species has a more pointed snout and a somewhat more terminal mouth. In the past it has been frequently misidentified as *Neomerinthe* (or *Pontinus*) *pollux* (Poey) or as *Pontinus castor* Poey. It usually occurs over the middle and outer shelf in thirty to one hundred fathoms. Maryland to Florida and the northern Gulf of Mexico. Eschmeyer, 1969. (1 foot; 30 cm)

428. Spotted scorpionfish *Scorpaena plumieri* Bloch

D. XII, 9; A. III, 5; P. 19–21; Sc. 42–49; Gr. 4–6 + 8–12; body and fins variously blotched, caudal peduncle somewhat pale; caudal fin with three vertical dark bars, white between; axil of pectoral fin dark with white or bright yellow spots on undersides which are supposed to warn off intruders. This is the most common scorpionfish in the inshore area, but it is not very poisonous. It is usually found near jetties, oil platforms, and reefs out to thirty fathoms. *S. ginsburgi* Gunter is a synonym. Massachusetts to Brazil, including the Gulf of Mexico and Caribbean. Eschmeyer, 1965. (1 foot; 30 cm)

429. Hunchback scorpionfish *Scorpaena dispar* Longley and Hildebrand

D. XII, 9; A. III, 5; P. 17–19; Sc. 42–47; Gr. 5 + 10–12. Apparently this is a deep-water species, replacing *S. calcarata* on the outer shelf (twenty to sixty-five fathoms). *S. similis* Gunter is a synonym. Florida to Brazil, including the northern Gulf of Mexico and Caribbean. Eschmeyer, 1965. (8 inches; 20 cm)

430. Barbfish *Scorpaena brasiliensis* Cuvier

D. XII, 9; A. III, 5; P. 18–20; Sc. 50–60; Gr. 4–5 + 8–10; colorful, usually redder than *S. plumieri*; caudal peduncle somewhat paler than rest of body, especially in juveniles, with dark brown spots in axil of pectoral fin (white spots in *plumieri*). Although it is more toxic than other species of *Scorpaena*, the barbfish is not common in our area but is common off the Florida panhandle. Elsewhere it prefers shallow bays and harbors, but it also occurs out to thirty fathoms. Virginia to Brazil, including the Gulf of Mexico and Caribbean. Eschmeyer, 1965. (8 inches; 20 cm)

431. Smoothhead scorpionfish *Scorpaena calcarata* Goode and Bean

D. XII, 9; A. III, 5; P. 19–21; Sc. 42–49; Gr. 4–5 + 7–11. This is the most common scorpionfish on the inshore shelf and is often taken by shrimp trawlers. It is rarely found in the bays. *S. russula atlantica* Nichols and Breder is a synonym. North Carolina to Brazil, including the Gulf of Mexico and Caribbean. Eschmeyer, 1965. (4 inches; 10 cm)

Triglidae

Sea robins are peculiar armored fishes with large pectoral fins which can be spread like wings. Despite this illusion of wings, sea robins are found close to the bottom, at least at night, and the lower pectoral rays are detached and are used as feelers or "legs" as the fish "walks" along the bottom. Sea robins also produce sounds, especially during spawning.

The heads of sea robins are armed with many spines, some of which change considerably with growth. Since these spines have been used to distinguish species, changes to or disappearance of the spines with growth has led to confusion. Most of the species which are likely to be encountered are not too difficult to identify if sufficient care is taken. Life colors and habitat can be used to separate many species.

This group of fishes has the unusual distinction of being revised independently by two researchers at the same museum at the same time, with their results (Ginsburg, 1950; Teague, 1951) being published within months of each other. Their results differed only slightly, but these differences will need to be clarified, and neither review is adequate. Several additional papers on triglids have noted the inadequacies of the previous works, but as yet no complete solution has been put forward. Since sea robins tend to be more variable than many fishes, some species may prove to be invalid. Species we consider as possibly doubtful are so noted. (Teague, 1952; Briggs, 1956; Miller and Kent, 1971)

1	Preorbital produced into spine extending beyond mouth .... Slender sea robin, *Peristedion gracile.*	
	Preorbital spine, if present, not extending beyond mouth	2
2	Dorsal spines usually XI, at least one filamentous	11
	Dorsal spines usually X, none filamentous	3
3	Posterior edge of pectoral fin emarginate, with middle rays shortest; chest largely scaled .... Mexican sea robin, *Prionotus paralatus.*	
	Posterior edge of pectoral straight or convex, with middle rays longest; chest largely naked	4
4	Nostril with large tentacle .... Bandtail sea robin, *Prionotus ophryas.*	
	Nostril without tentacle	5
5	Pectoral short, about same length as ventral fin .... Shortwing sea robin, *Prionotus stearnsi.*	
	Pectoral long, at least 1¼ times longer than ventral	6
6	Pectoral with many blue spots, usually persistent after preservation, although sometimes becoming dark .... Bluespotted sea robin, *Prionotus roseus.*	
	Pectoral without blue spots	7
7	Body depth 21 percent or less of standard length	10
	Body depth 22 percent or more of standard length	8
8	Lateral-line scales 68–90; interorbital at least as large as eye,	

7–11 percent of body length . . . . Bighead sea robin, *Prionotus tribulus*.

Lateral-line scales 88–115; interorbital width 75 percent or less of eye diameter, 4–6 percent of body length 9

9 Black spot between fourth and fifth dorsal spines persistent; preopercular and opercular spines extend well beyond operculum margin; lateral-line scales 88–106 . . . . Blackfin sea robin, *Prionotus rubio*.

Black spot on dorsal fin disappears with age; preopercular and opercular spines barely if at all extending beyond opercular margin; lateral-line scales 103–115 . . . . Blackwing sea robin, *Prionotus salmonicolor*.

10 Chest incompletely scaled; opercular flap scaled . . . . Leopard sea robin, *Prionotus scitulus*.

Chest completely scaled; opercular flap naked . . . . Northern sea robin, *Prionotus carolinus*.

11 Lachrymal plate with hornlike process projecting anteriorly; first two dorsal spines filamentous . . . . Horned sea robin, *Bellator militaris*.

Lachrymal plate without hornlike process; not more than one filamentous dorsal spine 12

12 Scales 95–112 . . . . Streamer sea robin, *Bellator egretta*.

Scales 62–70 . . . . Shortfin sea robin, *Bellator brachychir*.

432. Slender sea robin *Peristedion gracile* Goode and Bean

D. VIII + 20; A. I, 18; body slender, depth not more than 17 percent of standard length. The paired preorbital (rostral) spines extending anteriorly and the barbels on the maxilla are characteristic of this fish. A continental slope species, its juveniles are sometimes found on the outer shelf. It is sometimes placed in a separate family, the Peristediidae. New Jersey to the West Indies and at least Florida to Texas. (5 inches; 13 cm)

433. Mexican sea robin *Prionotus paralatus* Ginsburg

D. X + 12; A. 10–12; P. 12–13; Sc. 93–103; body uniformly brown or red without distinct bands or spots; pectoral fin uniformly dark, sometimes with darker cross-bands on upper part; dorsal spot on margin of fin in between fourth and fifth spines; caudal fin sometimes with blackish margin. This is a common species on the outer Texas shelf, but it is not so common off Louisiana. It is very closely related, and perhaps identical, to *P. alatus*, the spiny sea robin, which occurs from about the mouth of the Mississippi eastward to Florida and North Carolina. It is most easily distinguished from the other local species of *Prionotus* except *alatus* by the shape of its pectoral fin, and it is further distinguished from *P. alatus* by its longer pectoral fin (58–78 percent of standard length vs. 40–53 percent of standard length in *P. alatus*). Somewhere off Louisiana to the Gulf of Campeche. (6 inches; 15 cm)

434. Bandtail sea robin *Prionotus ophryas* Jordan and Swain

D. X + 11–13; A. 10–11; P. 14; Sc. 93–105; body variably shaded without definite pattern; pectoral variable in color, brown-spotted, often bicolorate; spinous dorsal without definite spot; second dorsal with two broad, clear bands alternating with dark; caudal fin cross-banded, typically with dark areas at base, center of fin, and margin, light between. Not a common species, but widely distributed across the shelf. The Bahamas and Georgia; Florida and throughout the Gulf. (7 inches; 18 cm)

435. Shortwing sea robin   *Prionotus stearnsi* Jordan and Swain
D. X + 12–13; A. 10–11; P. 12–13; Sc. 78–93; uniformly dusky in preservative; usually silvery in life, without distinctive markings on body or fins. The shape of this fish departs radically from that seen in most other sea robins and approaches that of a more typical fish. This more streamlined appearance makes the species unmistakable. A not uncommon species widely distributed across the shelf, it is usually not on the inner shelf. Georgia and Florida and throughout the Gulf. (5 inches; 13 cm)

436. Bluespotted sea robin   *Prionotus roseus* Jordan and Evermann
D. X + 11–13; A. 10–12; P. 12–14; Sc. 89–104; upper part of body lightly and irregularly marked; pectoral dusky to dark, cross-banded with darker areas, lower parts of fin with many bright blue spots standing out in live animals and usually persisting in preservative and with larger elongate spot between fifth and seventh rays (from top); dorsal spot not sharply marked, usually continuing diffusely forwards and backwards of fifth and sixth spines; soft dorsal dusky; anal fin clear. This is a middle shelf species, not common. North Carolina to Puerto Rico and throughout the Gulf. (9 inches; 23 cm)

437. Bighead sea robin   *Prionotus tribulus* Cuvier
D. X + 11–12; A. 10–12; P. 12–14; Sc. 69–85; upper parts of body with short oblique bands, one under soft dorsal fin being especially distinct; pectorals with dark cross-bands; dorsal spot at margin of fin. This is the common inshore shelf and bay sea robin and the only sea robin with young in very low salinities. North Carolina to Florida and throughout the Gulf. (14 inches; 36 cm)

438. Blackfin sea robin   *Prionotus rubio* Jordan
D. X + 12–13; A. 10–12; P. 12–13; Sc. 88–106; body darker dorsally, sometimes with a few faintly marked spots, often pinkish orange in life; pectoral fin with transverse rows of small light spots (orange) and with distinctive blue anterior edge and black spot posteriorly; first dorsal with irregular smoke-colored areas; smaller specimens with distinct ocellated dark spot between fourth and fifth dorsal spines; soft dorsal and anal dusky; inside of mouth orange red. This common species replaces the bighead robin in slightly deeper water out to near the shelf edge. It generally occurs further inshore off southern Texas than off Louisiana, and small fish are sometimes found in the saltier bays. Whole Gulf of Mexico to Cuba. (1 foot; 30 cm)

439. Blackwing sea robin   *Prionotus salmonicolor* Fowler
D. X + 12–13; A. 11–12; P. 12–13; Sc. 103–115; body uniformly shaded, sometimes with a few scattered spots; pectoral fins with lower parts uniformly dark but bright blue anterior edge without dark posterior spot, upper parts blotched or mottled; spinous dorsal without black spots; in small specimens, membranes between first, second, or third and fourth spines dusky.

This is a fairly common inshore shelf sea robin, previously known as *P. pectoralis*. North Carolina to Florida and throughout the Gulf. (9 inches; 23 cm)

440. Leopard sea robin *Prionotus scitulus* Jordan and Gilbert

D. X + 12–14; A. 11–13; P. 12–14; Sc. 123–132; chest incompletely scaled; upper part of body with many closely crowded spots, sometimes with diffuse oblique dark bands on sides; pectoral usually uniformly dark; distinct spot on spinous dorsal between fourth and fifth spines, with another smaller and often more diffuse spot behind first spine. Specimens of this fish from the western Gulf are generally less well marked than those from elsewhere. A common inshore and bay sea robin, it does not, however, occur in as low salinities as does *P. tribulus*. North Carolina to Venezuela. (8 inches; 20 cm)

441. Northern sea robin *Prionotus carolinus* (Linnaeus)

D. X + 12–13; A. 11–13; P. 14–15; Sc. 99–106; chest completely scaled; upper part of body with elongate reddish brown spots; second dorsal and caudal with many small, diffuse spots; small fish (less than 2⅓ inches—60 mm) with ill-defined cross-bands (usually four); dorsal spot placed near margin of fin and not extending past fifth spine and usually partly ocellated; small, elongate dark spot frequently found behind first dorsal spine; pectoral fin dusky to nearly black; branchiostegal membranes dusky or with scattered melanophores. This is a northern species, perhaps left as a relict in the northern Gulf. It is closely related to *P. scitulus*, with which it has often been confused. The Gulf population has been described as a separate species, *P. martis* Ginsburg. Nova Scotia to Venezuela. (16 inches; 41 cm)

442. Horned sea robin *Bellator militaris* (Goode and Bean)

D. XI + 11–12; A. 9–11; P. 12–13; Sc. 55–67. This peculiar robin with well-developed horns is primarily an outer shelf species. Two other species of this genus (see species key), which lack the hornlike process, are known from deep water in the northeastern Gulf. North Carolina to Florida and around the Gulf to Yucatán. (5 inches; 13 cm)

Dactylopteridae

The flying gurnards, which do not really fly, are armored fishes with large pectoral fins. They are superficially like sea robins, but they lack the free pectoral rays and have rectangular bodies.

443. Flying gurnard *Dactylopterus volitans* (Linnaeus)

D. II + IV, 8; A. 6; P. 28 + 6; first two dorsal spines free. The flying gurnard is a strangely armored tropical species rarely taken by shrimp trawlers. Tropical Atlantic, in the west from Massachusetts and Bermuda through the Caribbean to Brazil. (18 inches; 46 cm)

Bothidae

The Bothidae comprise the "left-handed" flatfishes—that is, flatfishes with their eyes and coloration on the left side. The tonguefishes of the family Cynoglossidae are also left-handed, but that family is further distinguished by a preopercle covered by skin; in the bothids the preopercle is not covered. All commercial flounders which occur south of Cape Hatteras through the Gulf are bothids, primarily of the genus *Paralichthys*. Most other species of bothids remain small even when fully grown. These small species occur frequently in shrimp catches and are often incorrectly thought of as "baby flounders."

Flatfishes, in general, begin life with normally arranged eyes, one on each side of the head. When the larvae are still less than one inch long, metamorphosis occurs and one eye migrates to the other side, the mouth usually shifts to one side, and a rearrangement of internal organs, gills, and so on completes the asymmetry of the fish. Occasionally "reversed" specimens occur in which the external features are on the wrong side, but internally these reversed fishes resemble their correctly arranged relatives. In some Pacific species of bothids reversal is as common as 30–40 percent of a population; however, it is quite rare in local species. Ambicoloration and partial or complete albinism are other abnormalities in flatfishes. Normally, the blind side is white or nearly so. Ambicolored fish, which are often reversed, exhibit varied amounts of color on the blind side.

As one would expect, bothids, like other flatfish, are primarily bottom fish. Most species lie buried in the bottom when they are at rest. They are famous for their ability to change the intensity of their skin coloration. Many species normally appear brown, but under the respective backgrounds they range from almost white to dark brown, with many various intermediate mottled phases. Dead fish are usually dark, whereas living ones are beautifully patterned.

In general, the life histories of most bothids are not well known. Accounts of collections in various localities contain information on different species, but there are few works which concentrate on specific species or bothids alone. Among the latter are recent papers by Fraser (1971) and Swingle (1971*b*). Recent systematic work by Gutherz (1967) has provided a good understanding of the taxonomy of the group. (Norman, 1934; Topp and Hoff, 1972).

1 Bases of pelvic fins symmetrical 2
   Bases of pelvic fins asymmetrical (subfamily Bothinae) ....
       Spottail flounder, *Bothus* sp.
2 Bases of both pelvic fins short, not extending forward onto
       urohyal; ocular pelvic fin may or may not be on median line
       of body (subfamily Paralichthinae) 3
   Bases of both pelvic fins long, extending forward onto urohyal

(subfamily Scophthalminae) .... Windowpane flounder, *Scophthalamus aquosus.**

3 Pectoral fin present on blind side 4

Pectoral fin absent from blind side .... Deepwater flounder, *Monolene sessilicauda.*

4 Lateral line with high arch over pectoral fin on ocular side 5

Lateral line without high arch over pectoral fin on ocular side 11

5 Three or four prominent ocellated spots on ocular side of body; additional spotting may be present 6

Body spotting may be present or absent; if present, not with three or four prominent ocellated spots 8

6 Three large, ocellated spots present 7

Four large, ocellated spots present .... Ocellated flounder, *Ancylopsetta quadrocellata.*

7 Anterior dorsal fin rays elongate; pelvic fin on ocular side longer than that on blind side .... Three-eye flounder, *Ancylopsetta dilecta.*

Anterior dorsal fin rays not elongate; pelvic fins equal in length .... Gulf flounder, *Paralichthys albigutta.*†

8 Pelvic fin on ocular side not inserted on median line; lateral line well developed on both sides 9

Pelvic fin on ocular side inserted on median line; lateral line poorly developed or lacking on blind side 10

9 Body depth greater than 47 percent (usually 50 percent) of standard length; blind side dusky in large individuals; lateral-line scales 104–117 .... Broad flounder, *Paralichthys squamilentus.*

Body depth less than 47 percent (usually 44 percent) of standard length; blind side immaculate or dusky; lateral-line scales 78–100 .... Southern flounder, *Paralichthys lethostigma.*

10 Upper jaw short, 20–25 percent of head length; spines present on interorbital ridge; tentacles on eyes .... Spiny flounder, *Engyophrys senta.*

Upper jaw moderate, 32–45 percent of head length; no interorbital spines or tentacles on eyes .... Sash flounder, *Trichopsetta ventralis.*

11 Large round spots on dorsal, anal, and caudal fin, or body with five or six broad bars 12

No large spots or bars on body or fins 13

12 Large black spot in center of caudal fin; three smaller spots on

* The windowpane flounder, *Scophthalamus aquosus* (Mitchill), is included here based on one doubtful record listed by Baughman (1950a) from Galveston. The species normally occurs on the Atlantic coast of the United States and is otherwise unknown from the Gulf of Mexico.

† *Paralichthys triocellatus*, with 67–69 anals rays and 8–9 gill rakers on the lower limb of the first arch, reported by Springer and Bullis (1956) from "Oregon Station 1086" eighteen fathoms off the South Texas coast, may refer to *P. albigutta. P. triocellatus* Ribero, according to Ginsburg (1952c), is probably a synonym of *Pseudorhombus isosceles*, which has not been reported north of the Brazilian coast, and all earlier reports of *P. triocellatus* are also from South American waters. Cervigon (1966) reports neither from Venezuela.

dorsal edges of caudal (may be absent); large black blotch on distal edge of pectoral fin on ocular side, with no blotch under this fin; distal edge of pectoral fin truncate; pectoral rays on ocular side 11 or 12 . . . . Spotfin flounder, *Cyclopsetta fimbriata.*

No large black spot in center of caudal fin, but three distinct spots along distal edge of caudal fin; no blotch on ocular pectoral fin, but with black blotch on body under this fin; distal edge of pectoral fin oblique (instead of spots and blotches on body and fins there may be five or six broad bars); 14–16 pectoral fin rays . . . . Mexican flounder, *Cyclopsetta chittendeni.*

13 Upper jaw very short, 25 percent of head length; maxillary extending only to anterior margin of lower eye 14

Upper jaw moderate to long; maxillary longer than 35 percent of head length, usually extending past middle of lower eye 16

14 Scales without secondary squamation . . . . Fringed flounder, *Etropus crossotus.*

Scales with secondary squamation 15

15 Primary body scales with only one row of secondary scales . . . . Gray flounder, *Etropus rimosus.*

Primary body scales densely covered with secondary scales . . . . Smallmouth flounder, *Etropus microstomus.*

16 Gill rakers short and stout with 6–9 on lower limb or long and stout with 6–7 on lower limb (total gill rakers 8 to 12) 17

Gill rakers long and slender with 9–13 on lower limb (total 13–22) 18

17 Body depth usually greater than 48 percent of standard length (45–53 percent); 46 to 55 scales in lateral line; gill rakers long and stout, 2–4 on upper limb and 6–8 on lower limb . . . . Shoal flounder, *Syacium gunteri.*

Body depth usually 45 percent of standard length or less (40–46 percent); 47–68 scales in lateral line; gill rakers short and stout, 2 + 8 . . . . Dusky flounder, *Syacium papillosum.*

18 Cephalic spines on snout and anterior orbital rim . . . . Male horned whiff, *Citharichthys cornutus.*

No cephalic spines on snout or orbitals 19

19 Body and fins profusely covered with regularly arranged spots and blotches . . . . Spotted whiff, *Citharichthys macrops.*

Body and fins not profusely covered with regularly arranged spots and blotches 20

20 Eye diameter usually 30 percent of head length or greater; pectoral fin on ocular side usually greater than 20 percent of standard length . . . . Female horned whiff, *Citharichthys cornutus.*

Eye diameter usually 25 percent of head length or less; pectoral fin on ocular side about 15 percent of standard length . . . . Bay whiff, *Citharichthys spilopterus.*

444. Spottail flounder   *Bothus* sp.

D. 78–90; A. 59–68; P. 8–11 (on ocular side); Gr. short, 2–7 + 5–9; Sc. 70–77; ocular side dark brown, generally with no spotting, but may be light tan with spotting or mottling; two large dark spots on median rays of caudal fin, one anterior to other; interorbital width greater in males than in females. In most areas it occurs together with the closely related species, *B. ocellatus*, in depths of less than twenty-five fathoms. *Bothus ocellatus* differs from the spottail flounder by having the two spots on the caudal fin in a vertical line instead of a horizontal line. *B. ocellatus* occurs in the northeastern and southern Gulf of Mexico (Gulf of Campeche), but we have been unable to verify its existence in the northwestern Gulf. Moore, 1975*b*. (6 inches; 15 cm)

445. Deepwater flounder *Monolene sessilicauda* Goode

D. 92–107; A. 76–84; P. 11–14 on ocular side, no pectoral fin on blind side; Gr. 8–10; Sc. 88–94; body elongate (for a flounder); light tan often with darker cross-bars; caudal fin usually with dark central spot; other dark spots along bases of dorsal and anal fins; lower distal portion of pectoral fin darkened; anterior lateral line arched over pectoral fin, with arch distinctly shaped, more square than curved. This last character is only found in species of *Monolene* and *Trichopsetta* in our area. This fish is known from relatively deep water (fifty to one hundred fathoms) off southern Texas. Elsewhere known only from Massachusetts to Florida. (6 inches; 15 cm)

446. Ocellated flounder *Ancylopsetta quadrocellata* Gill

D. 67–76; A. 54–61; P. 10–12 on ocular side; Gr. 2–3 + 6–7; Sc. 80–90; ocular side dark brown with four larger ocellated spots; anteriormost rays of dorsal fin somewhat elongated. This flounder is common in bays and the shallow Gulf from two to ninety fathoms, with the largest specimens in deeper water. North Carolina to Jupiter, Florida, and from Cape Sable, Florida, to Campeche, Mexico. Gutherz, 1966. (12 inches; 30 cm)

447. Three-eye flounder *Ancylopsetta dilecta* (Goode and Bean)

D. 68–79; A. 53–60; P. 10–12 on ocular side; Gr. 1–3 + 6–9; Sc. 73–82; ocular side tan or pale brown with numerous blotches and patches; three large ocellated spots on ocular side, arranged triangularly; ventral fin on ocular side and anteriormost dorsal rays noticeably elongate. Common in deeper water (thirty-two to two hundred fathoms) than *A. quadrocellata*. North Carolina to Yucatán. (7 inches; 18 cm)

448. Gulf flounder *Paralichthys albigutta* Jordan and Gilbert

D. 71–85; A. 53–63; P. on ocular side 10–12; Gr. 2–4 (usually 2–3) + 9–12 (usually 10–11); Sc. 78–83; body depth usually 39–47 percent of standard length; ocular side either dark or light brown with numerous blotches and spots; three conspicuous ocellated spots (sometimes faint) arranged in triangular pattern; other spots fainter and not ocellated. Like other Texas species of *Paralichthys*, the young of this species are found in the bays during the spring and summer and migrate to the Gulf with the onset of colder weather. Ginsburg called this flounder "sand flounder," since the adults appeared to be more common on hard, sandy bottoms. In the bays the young are found in grassflats. North Carolina at least to southern Texas and the Bahamas. Ginsburg, 1952*c*. (15 inches; 38 cm)

449. Broad flounder *Paralichthys squamilentus* Jordan and Gilbert

D. 76–85; A. 59–65; P. on ocular side 11–12; Gr. 3–5 (usually 3 or 5) + 9–12 (usually 10–12); Sc. 104–117; body depth usually 48–59 percent of standard length; eyed side brown, with numerous nonocellated spots; body tending to darken with age and increased size; broad area along dorsal and ventral edges of eyed side characteristically sprinkled with pigment, but center of ocular side virtually devoid of pigment; blind side frequently dusky. Like other *Paralichthys*, the young of this species occur inshore during the warmer months; however, the adults occur deeper than those of either *P. albigutta* or *P. lethostigma*, at depths of 60–120 fathoms. North Carolina at least to southern Texas. (16 inches; 41 cm)

450. Southern flounder   *Paralichthys lethostigma* Jordan and Gilbert

D. 80–95; A. 63–74; P. on ocular side 11–13; Gr. 2–3 (usually 2) + 8–11 (usually 9–10); Sc. 85–100. Body depth 39–47 percent of standard length; eyed side light or dark brown with diffuse nonocellated spots and blotches, which tend to disappear in the larger specimens; blind side immaculate or dusky. Young *P. lethostigma* are found in shallow bays, even in low salinities. The larger fish leave the bays for the open Gulf during the fall in order to spawn. A severe norther will cause a mass migration, resulting in excellent floundering or gigging, while a moderate or warm winter will cause the larger flounders to leave dispersed over a greater period of time and result in decreased sports and commercial catches. This fish has been called the "mud flounder." In the Gulf as well as in the bays this species is often more common over the softer mud bottoms. Large individuals of this species are often called "halibut." North Carolina to Florida, in the Gulf from Florida to northern Mexico. Ginsburg, 1952c; Fox and White, 1969. (3 feet; 91 cm)

451. Spiny flounder   *Engyophrys senta* Ginsburg

D. 74–83; A. 60–67; P. on ocular side 8–10 (usually 9); Gr. short, 0–3 + 4–7; Sc. 50; ocular side dark tan or brownish with darker blotches along lateral line and edges of body; usually three blotches on lateral line, with center one being largest; blind side of mature males with three to seven (usually five) vertical, diffuse bars on anterior portion of body; blind side of females and immature males immaculate. This is the smallest bothid occurring in these waters. The common name is derived from the interorbital spines. Both sexes also possess short tentacles extending from the posterior margin of the eyes, but these become reduced in males and may be absent in large males. This fish is common in twenty to one hundred fathoms of water. Gulf of Mexico and Caribbean south to Brazil. Anderson and Lindner, 1951. (3 inches; 8 cm)

452. Sash flounder   *Trichopsetta ventralis* (Goode and Bean)

D. 89–95; A. 69–75; P. on ocular side 12–13, on blind side 7–10; Gr. moderately long and slender, 0 + 9–11; Sc. 63–68; ocular side brownish with limited spotting on body and fins; three blotches along lateral line, with anteriormost being most distinct (these possibly indistinct or lacking); males having greatly elongate pelvic fin rays on blind side, with pectoral fin on blind side frequently longer than that on ocular side. Little is known of the life history of this fish, which is found between eighteen and sixty fathoms. Recent collections have revealed the presence of three new species of *Trichopsetta* from the tropical Caribbean. Throughout the Gulf of Mexico. Gutherz, 1967; Anderson and Gutherz, 1967. (6 inches; 15 cm)

453. Spotfin flounder   *Cyclopsetta fimbriata* (Goode and Bean)

D. 78–87; A. 59–67; P. on ocular side 11–12, on blind side 9–10; Gr.

3–4 + 9–10; Sc. 65–75; ocular side brown with several large black spots on dorsal, anal, and caudal fins; large black spot on distal portion of pectoral fin; caudal fin with large spot in center and sometimes with three smaller spots along posterior edge; pectoral fin on ocular side with truncate margin. While it occurs in 10–125 fathoms, in the northwestern Gulf of Mexico this species is not as common as *C. chittendeni*. North Carolina through the West Indies to British Guiana. (15 inches; 38 cm)

454. Mexican flounder *Cyclopsetta chittendeni* Bean

D. 82–90; A. 63–69; P. on ocular side 13–16, on blind side 11–13; Gr. 3–5 + 8–9; Sc. 74–80; ocular side brown with several large spots on dorsal, anal, and caudal fins and large black spot under pectoral fin; caudal fin with three large black spots on distal edge, none in center of fin; canine teeth large (larger than in *C. fimbriata*). *Cyclopsetta decussata* Gunter, based on one mounted specimen, is a color variant in which the black spots are merged into five or six broad bands which extend across the body and fins, a color pattern sometimes seen in live animals. *C. chittendeni* is a common fish. Gulf of Mexico and Caribbean Sea south to Columbia and Venezuela and on the Atlantic coast of South America to Brazil in ten to seventy-five fathoms. Dawson, 1968. (13 inches; 33 cm)

455. Fringed flounder *Etropus crossotus* Jordan and Gilbert

D. 75–85; A. 58–68; P. on ocular side 8–10, on blind side 7–9; Gr. 4–5 + 6–9 (usually 7–8); Sc. 41–47; ocular side brown; no spotting on body; dorsal, anal, and caudal fins with dusky blotches; caudal sometimes edged with black; body scales deciduous, with no secondary squamation. Two species with secondary squamation, *E. rimosus* Goode and Bean and *E. microstomus* (Gill), are known east but not west of the Mississippi Delta (see species key). This flounder is generally found in shallow water of five to thirty-five fathoms, entering the bay during the warmer months of the year. In the northwestern Gulf it occurs mostly in water shallower than seventeen fathoms. Chesapeake Bay through the Caribbean to French Guiana. (7 inches; 18 cm)

456. Shoal flounder *Syacium gunteri* Ginsburg

D. 74–85; A. 59–68; P. on ocular side 9–11 (usually 11); Gr. moderately long and thick, 2–4 (usually 3) + 6–8 (usually 7); Sc. 46–55; ocular side tan, sometimes with numerous circular or ocellated spots or blotches on body and median fins, generally with large, diffuse blotch on caudal peduncle; blind side immaculate. Found in five to fifty fathoms, but generally most abundant in water ten to forty fathoms deep, this is the most abundant flatfish, and indeed the most abundant fish caught on the brown shrimp grounds of Texas. For distinctions between *S. gunteri* and *S. papillosum*, see the discussion under the latter species. Florida and the Gulf through the Caribbean to French Guiana. (11 inches; 28 cm)

457. Dusky flounder *Syacium papillosum* (Linnaeus)

D. 82–94; A. 64–75; P. on ocular side 11–12 (usually 11); Gr. short and stout, 2 + 8–9 (usually 8); Sc. 47–60; ocular side brown with little if any spotting; large males with pigment lines from upper eye to snout, along dorsal, and on lips, mandible, and lower jaw; blind side dusky in large males, immaculate or slightly "dirty" in females and immature males. Found from seven to seventy-five fathoms, this species is less abundant in the northwestern Gulf than *S. gunteri*, but the situation is reversed east of the Mississippi. In general, large specimens (over three inches, or 80 mm, in standard length) of *Syacium* from the Gulf of Mexico can be readily separated by the greater interorbital width of S. *gunteri*. This difference is not apparent in smaller fish (less than three inches) but becomes more pronounced with increasing size. S. *micrurum* Ranzani, often reported from the Gulf, is a problem. It seems to have the coloration of *gunteri* but a body shape and meristics closer to those of *papillosum*. We have not been able to verify its presence here. North Carolina through the Caribbean to Brazil. Fraser, 1971. (11 inches; 28 cm)

458. Horned whiff   *Citharichthys cornutus* (Günther)

D. 74–83; A. 59–66; P. on ocular side 10–11; Gr. moderately long and slender 3–5 + 11–15; Sc. 40–45; ocular side brown; ocular pectoral with dark area in axil, sometimes with dark crossbars; adult males noted by pronounced cephalic spination, with single large spine projecting horizontally beyond margin of head as well as several smaller spines along anterior edge of upper eye. The horned whiff is found in relatively deeper water (15–200 fathoms, generally exceeding 75 fathoms). The only reports from the northwestern Gulf are from 103 fathoms. Georgia through the Caribbean to Brazil. (4 inches; 10 cm)

459. Spotted whiff   *Citharichthys macrops* Dresel

D. 80–85; A. 56–64; P. on ocular side 9–12; Gr. long and slender, 5–6 + 13–16; Sc. 37–44; ocular side brown with numerous spots and blotches on body and median fins, becoming indistinct when highly deciduous scales are lost. This flatfish is rare to uncommon off Texas and Louisiana but abundant on the shrimp grounds off Campeche and in the northeastern Gulf because it has a preference for hard, coarse, sand-shell bottoms, which are rare in the northwestern Gulf but common in those other areas. South Carolina to Florida and throughout the Gulf. (6 inches; 15 cm)

460. Bay whiff   *Citharichthys spilopterus* Günther

D. 75–84; A. 56–63; P. on ocular side 9–10; Gr. of moderate length and stoutness, 4–5 + 9–15; Sc. 41–49; ocular side brownish after death, varying from light to dark in life; two dark spots on caudal peduncle; light spot under pectoral. Found inshore to depths of forty fathoms, rarely exceeding twenty fathoms in the Gulf of Mexico, it moves into the bays and shallow Gulf during the warmer months of the year. It is one of the commonest small flatfish in this area. Atlantic Ocean, in the west from New Jersey to Brazil. (6 inches; 15 cm)

Soleidae

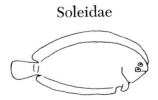

The soles are commonly represented by only three species in our area, although two others may also occur. Soles are short-bodied, often nearly round fishes with their eyes on the right side. They can use the blind side to adhere to hard objects such as aquarium walls.

1 Body covered with well-developed scales; upper eye in advance of lower eye; margin of ventral fin on blind side free   2
   Body not scaled; skin loose; upper eye vertically in line with lower eye; margins of both ventral fins attached to body . . . . Fringed sole, *Gymnachirus texae.*
2 Pectoral fins small, present on at least right (ocular) side . . . . Lined sole, *Achirus lineatus.*
   Pectoral fins wholly lacking on both sides . . . . Hogchoker, *Trinectes maculatus.*

461. Fringed sole (zebra sole) *Gymnachirus texae* Gunter

D. 57–66; A. 41–48; C. 14–17 (usually 16); P. on ocular side 1–3 (usually 2), sometimes not externally evident; right and left ventral fins enclosed in common fleshy envelope; body covered by scaleless, loose skin with distinct black and white stripes; blind side creamy, dusky, or with considerable pigment, especially about edges of median fins. There is a narrow zone of overlap between this species and the related *G. melas,* which is more common in the eastern Gulf of Mexico. The latter species could be expected to show up in Louisiana waters. Considerable confusion exists in the literature over the exact status of a third species, *Gymnachirus williamsoni* (Gunter), which has been reported from Texas and Louisiana.

Fairly common in the shallow Gulf, preferring mud bottoms, *G. texae* normally is collected in water thirty to fifty fathoms deep. The young are not uncommon in even shallower water during the summer and may go into saltier bays. Eastern Gulf of Mexico west and south to the Campeche Banks and the west coast of Yucatán. Caldwell and Briggs, 1957*b*; Dawson, 1964. (5 inches; 13 cm)

462. Lined sole (cover) *Achirus lineatus* (Linnaeus)

D. 50–58; A. 38–48; P. on ocular side 5–6; body with eight narrow bands becoming obsolete with age; median fins with small dark spots, especially distinct on caudal. Records of *Achirus achirus* (L.) refer to this species, a small, tan flatfish covered with spots and diffuse lines. It is fairly common in the shallow Gulf and bays, especially during the summer. South Carolina to Uruguay. (5 inches; 13 cm)

463. Hogchoker (cover) *Trinectes maculatus* (Bloch and Schneider)

D. 50–56; A. 36–42; P. lacking; ventral on right side 3, on left 1; Sc. 66–75; ocular side usually dark gray green to brown with seven or eight darker vertical bars. The hogchoker generally resembles *Achirus lineatus* but lacks the spotting. It is common in the bays and shallow Gulf (out to twenty-five fathoms). This species is apparently more tolerant of brackish waters than is *A. lineatus* and is correspondingly more common in the bays. Young run up rivers, which makes them practically catadromous. Young hogchokers are frequently sold in aquarium stores as "freshwater flounder." Early references to this species often refer to it as *Achirus fasciatus* Lacépède. Massachusetts to Panama. (6 inches; 15 cm)

Cynoglossidae

The tonguefishes are represented by only one genus (*Symphurus*) in the northwestern Gulf of Mexico. In this genus one of the key characters is the number of caudal rays. Since the caudal fin is continuous with both the dorsal and anal fins, some care must be taken to distinguish the caudal rays from those of the other fins. Generally the bases of the caudal rays lie on a more or less straight line and are more closely spaced than those of the dorsal or anal fins, and the outermost caudal rays (both top and bottom) have broadened bases, often with a projecting burr.

Species of *Symphurus* are markedly selective in their depth distributions, which also aids in identification. All are small-mouthed, bottom animals which feed on small invertebrates such as worms. (Ginsburg, 1951*b*)

1   Caudal rays 10 2
    Caudal rays 12 4
2   Teeth in upper jaw on eyed side extending no more than half
        length of jaw (or may be absent); teeth absent or few in lower
        jaw 3
    Teeth nearly completely filling both jaws on eyed side of head
        .... Pygmy tonguefish, *Symphurus parvus*.
3   Large black spots on posterior portions of dorsal and anal fins, or
        these regions quite dark; no spot on opercle; teeth absent from
        both jaws on eyed side of head .... Spottedfin tonguefish,
        Symphurus diomedianus.
    Large black spots lacking from fins, which are pale, sometimes with
        small, diffuse spots; distinct black patch on opercle; teeth ab-
        sent from lower jaw on eyed side of head, present only for about
        one-half length of upper jaw .... Blackcheek tonguefish, *Sym-
        phurus plagiusa*.
4   Teeth present in both jaws on eyed side of head, covering one-half
        to all of upper jaw 5
    Teeth absent from both jaws .... Offshore tonguefish, *Symphurus
        civitatus*.
5   Dorsal rays 85 or more; anal rays 72 or more; deepwater fish living
        in over 50 fathoms .... Deepwater tonguefish, *Symphurus
        piger*.
    Dorsal rays fewer than 82; anal rays fewer than 68; fish living in
        20–50 fathoms .... Longtail tonguefish, *Symphurus pelicanus*.

464. Pygmy tonguefish   *Symphurus parvus* Ginsburg
    D. 78–84; A. 64–68; C. 10 (rarely 11); Sc. 86–98; teeth in jaws on eyed side few or absent; body uniformly brown, with one to four dark spots on posterior portion of dorsal and anal fins, or these portions of fins uniformly dark. This fish is found from eight to fifty fathoms, and usually in water deeper than fifteen fathoms. North Carolina to Brazil. (3 inches; 8 cm)

465. Spottedfin tonguefish *Symphurus diomedianus* (Goode and Bean)
D. 89–93; A. 73–78; C. 10 (rarely 11); Sc. 86–98; teeth on eyed side usually absent, or with only a few at top of upper jaw and middle of lower jaws; uniformly brown with one to four distinct round spots on posterior dorsal and anal fins. North Carolina to Brazil, usually in fifteen to twenty-five fathoms. (8 inches; 20 cm)

466. Blackcheek tonguefish; patch *Symphurus plagiusa* (Linnaeus)
D. 85–92; A. 69–76; C. 9–11 (almost always 10); Sc. 71–86; teeth covering about half length of upper jaw on eyed side; teeth absent from lower jaw; color variable, with cross-bands present or not, but generally with dark spot on opercle (possibly faded in preserved specimens or absent entirely). The most common inshore species of *Symphurus*, rarely found deeper than twenty fathoms, this is the only species so far reported from brackish water. Long Island to Yucatán. (8 inches; 20 cm)

467. Offshore tonguefish; patch *Symphurus civitatus* Ginsburg
D. 87–92; A. 70–77; C. 12 (rarely 11); Sc. 69–80; teeth not extending over anterior one-half of upper jaw on eyed side; teeth absent from lower jaw; crossbands on body absent or faint; no black spots on fins or opercle. This fish is usually found inshore in four to thirty fathoms. North Carolina to Florida and the whole Gulf. (6 inches; 15 cm)

468. Deepwater tonguefish *Symphurus piger* (Goode and Bean)
D. 85–88; A. 72–73; C. 12; Sc. 69–74; teeth extending over anterior three-fourths of both jaws on eyed side; body pale, with contrasting narrow cross-bands. This tonguefish occurs in deep water from fifty to over one hundred fathoms. Gulf of Mexico and West Indies. (6 inches; 15 cm)

469. Longtail tonguefish *Symphurus pelicanus* Ginsburg
D. 80–81; A. 63–67; C. 12; Sc. 61–74; teeth small, extending entire length of jaws on eyed side; body uniformly brownish or irregularly shaded; black peritoneum often showing through skin behind head. This midshelf species occurs in twenty-five to fifty fathoms. Gulf of Mexico and West Indies. (3 inches; 8 cm)

Balistidae

These fishes, well armored with long dorsal spines, were formerly separated into two families, the triggerfishes (Balistidae) and the filefishes (Monacanthidae). Most live around hard substrates, to which they are well adapted with small mouths for browsing on small attached organisms. Young of many balistid species associate with *Sargassum* and other floating objects. Many species are observed by divers, but their hard mouths make them resistant to capture with hook and line. (Berry and Vogel, 1961; Moore, 1967; Böhlke and Chaplin, 1968)

1 Three dorsal spines; large, platelike scales 2
  Two dorsal spines; scales small 6
2 Two large canines in upper and lower jaws; dark but never
    black 3
  Teeth even, more incisorlike; almost entirely black .... Black
    durgon, *Melichthys niger.*
3 One or more bony plates behind gill openings 4
  Ordinary scales behind gill openings 5
4 Head with two blue stripes; 29–31 soft dorsal rays; 26–28 anal
    rays .... Queen triggerfish, *Balistes vetula.*
  Head without blue stripes; 27–29 soft dorsal rays; 23–26 anal
    rays .... Gray triggerfish, *Balistes capriscus.*
5 Cheek with narrow parallel grooves; chin projecting .... Sar-
    gassum triggerfish, *Xanthichthys ringens.*
  Cheek without grooves, closely scaled; chin not projecting ....
    Ocean triggerfish, *Canthidermis sufflamen.*
6 Pelvic bone with no evident external spine; gill openings at 45-
    degree angle 7
  Pelvic bone with large external spine; gill openings nearly verti-
    cal 9
7 Dorsal rays 43–50; anal rays 46–52 .... Scrawled filefish, *Alu-
    terus scriptus.*
  Dorsal rays 32–41; anal rays 33–44 8
8 Dorsal spine with small barbs only at base; live specimens with
    orange spots .... Orange filefish, *Aluterus schoepfi.*
  Dorsal spine with large barbs extending to tip; live specimens
    with purple lines .... Dotterel filefish, *Aluterus heudeloti.*
9 Deep groove behind dorsal spine where spine can be inserted 10
  No deep groove behind dorsal spine 11
10 Two pairs of strong spines on each side of caudal peduncle; pec-
    toral rays usually 14; gill rakers 29–35 .... Whitespotted file-
    fish, *Cantherhines macrocerus.*
  No strong spines on caudal peduncle; pectoral rays usually 13;
    gill rakers 34–46 .... Orangespotted filefish, *Cantherhines
    pullus.*
11 Caudal peduncle with two to four pairs of enlarged spines (re-
    curved in males); individual scales with unbranched spines; no
    elongated dorsal rays .... Fringed filefish, *Monacanthus
    ciliatus.*
  Caudal peduncle without spines; scales with branched spines in
    specimens greater than one-half inch (13 mm); dorsal rays
    elongated in adult males 12
12 Dorsal rays 31–34 (29–35); anal rays 31–34 (30–35) .... Plane-
    head filefish, *Monacanthus hispidus.*
  Dorsal rays 27–29 (27–30); anal rays 27–29 (26–30) .... Pygmy
    filefish, *Monacanthus setifer.*

470. Black durgon; black triggerfish *Melichthys niger* (Bloch)

   D. III + 32–34; A. 28–31; P. 16–17; Gr. 36–37; entirely black. This is a secretive but not uncommon fish on some offshore reefs. Probably circum-tropical; in the western Atlantic from Massachusetts and Bermuda through the Caribbean to Brazil. (15 inches; 38 cm)

471. Queen triggerfish *Balistes vetula* Linnaeus

D. III + 29–31; A. 26–28; P. 15–16; Gr. 35–38; dorsal, anal, and caudal fins with produced rays; two broad blue bands on face; broad blue band on caudal peduncle. This is an occasional fish on offshore reefs. Massachusetts to Brazil as well as the eastern Atlantic. (20 inches; 51 cm)

472. Gray triggerfish *Balistes capriscus* Gmelin

D. III + 27–29; A. 23–26; P. 15; Gr. 31–35; body grayish with irregular dark markings; small blue spots on upper sides and spinous dorsal membranes. This very common fish is found near reefs, oil rigs, and jetties; the young are found inshore. *B. carolinensis* is a synonym. Atlantic Ocean, in the west from Nova Scotia and Bermuda through the Caribbean to Argentina. (1 foot; 30 cm)

473. Sargassum triggerfish *Xanthichthys ringens* (Linnaeus)

D. III + 26–29; A. 24–26; P. 13; Gr. 36–37. The parallel grooves in the cheek and slightly protruding skin of this triggerfish are characteristic. The young associate with *Sargassum*, while the adults occur in deep water, usually over one hundred feet. Not definitely known from the western Gulf, but to be expected; otherwise circumtropical. (10 inches; 25 cm)

474. Ocean triggerfish *Canthidermis sufflamen* (Mitchill)

D. III + 26–27; A. 24; P. 16; Gr. 32–36; body gray with dark spot in axil of pectoral fin; outer caudal rays prolonged; dorsal and anal fins falcate, but not so extreme as those of *Balistes vetula*. The ocean triggerfish is fairly common on offshore reefs. Massachusetts and Bermuda through the Caribbean and Gulf to the Lesser Antilles. Moore, 1967; Bright and Cashman, 1974; Sonnier, Teerling, and Hoese, 1976. (2 feet; 61 cm)

475. Scrawled filefish *Aluterus scriptus* (Osbeck)

D. II + 43–49; A. 46–52; P. 13–15; Gr. 32–42; body elongate, depth 22–34 percent of standard length; snout long, upturned, projecting; body olive with dark scrawls. This is a rare fish on the offshore reefs, but the young are commonly taken inshore, especially in grass beds. Circumtropical; in the western Atlantic from Massachusetts and Bermuda through the Caribbean to Brazil. (16 inches; 41 cm)

476. Orange filefish *Aluterus schoepfi* (Walbaum)

D. II + 32–39; A. 35–41; P. 11–14; Gr. 21–27; depth 19–48 percent of standard length (smaller fish more elongate); profile of snout generally flattened; body plain, either orange or black or with orange spots in life which soon fade. The orange filefish is widespread on the offshore reefs; the young are common inshore. Nova Scotia and Bermuda through the Caribbean to Brazil. (16 inches; 41 cm)

477. Dotterel filefish *Aluterus heudeloti* Hollard

D. II + 36–41; A. 39–44; P. 13–15; depth 28–48 percent of standard length; body colored like *A. scripta*. This fish is only recently reported from the coast; its status is uncertain. Bermuda and Massachusetts to Brazil. Bullis and Thompson, 1965. (10 inches; 25 cm)

478. Whitespotted filefish   *Cantherhines macrocerus* (Hollard)

D. II + 34–36; A. 29–32; P. 13–14 (14); Gr. 29–35; sides of body with large white spots; 2–3 pairs of enlarged spines on caudal peduncle (not always apparent in juveniles); caudal fin dark. Northern Gulf of Mexico, Florida, and Bermuda through the Caribbean to Brazil. Sonnier, Teerling, and Hoese, 1976. (16 inches; 41 cm)

479. Orangespotted filefish   *Cantherhines pullus* (Ranzani)

D. II + 33–36; A. 29–32; P. 12–14; Gr. 34–46; body usually with indistinct light and dark stripes on sides and scattered orange spots; white spot on upper side of caudal peduncle. A rare fish from offshore reefs, this species is sometimes placed in the genus *Amanses*. Atlantic Ocean, in the west from Bermuda, Florida, and the northern Gulf of Mexico through the Caribbean to Brazil. (6 inches; 18 cm)

480. Fringed filefish   *Monacanthus ciliatus* (Mitchill)

D. II + 29–37; A. 28–36; P. 11; Gr. 15–23; depth 40–56 percent of standard length; color variable. This fish occurs irregularly west of the Mississippi River, but it is common in the grass beds of the Chandeleur Islands. Atlantic Ocean, in the west from Newfoundland and Bermuda through the Caribbean to Brazil. (5 inches; 13 cm)

481. Planehead filefish   *Monacanthus hispidus* (Linnaeus)

D. II + 29–35; A. 30–35; P. 12–14; body light tan or gray with irregular dark markings. This is the most common inshore filefish over most of the shelf, the young often entering bays. Atlantic Ocean, in the west from Nova Scotia and Bermuda to Brazil. (9 inches; 23 cm)

482. Pygmy filefish   *Monacanthus setifer* Bennett

D. II + 27–30; A. 26–30; P. 11–13; body tan or gray with distinct rows of dark spots on sides and two distinct bars on caudal fin, with these markings becoming more obscure with age. North Carolina, Bahamas, and Bermuda throughout the Gulf of Mexico and Caribbean. Bright and Cashman, 1974. (5 inches; 13 cm)

Ostraciidae

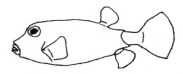

Trunkfishes are peculiarly shaped fishes whose bodies are protected by rigid, bony plates often supplied with protuberances. Because of the rigid shell, the fish can move only by use of the dorsal, anal, and pectoral fins, but they are still fairly fast swimmers. Two species are known to occur, but the possibility of four tropical species exists. The shell is sometimes sold as a curio. (Tyler, 1965)

1   Body with spines projecting in front of eyes; two spines projecting

in front of anal fin (unreported tropical species of *Lactophrys* also have these spines before anal fin but lack head spines. Very small cowfish lack all spines, but also lack body markings found in *Lactophrys*) . . . . Scrawled cowfish, *Acanthostracion quadricornis.*

Body without spines . . . . Smooth trunkfish, *Lactophrys triqueter.*

483. Scrawled cowfish *Acanthostracion quadricornis* (Linnaeus)

Dorsal, anal, and caudal fins all with 10 rays; P. usually 11; Gr. 13–17; spine in front of each eye as well as pair of posteriorly directed spines in front of anal fin; body yellowish with blue spots; irregular blue markings on body, caudal peduncle, and fins; two to four horizontal blue bands on cheek under eye. This is the common trunkfish over much of the shelf as well as in the saltier bays. *Lactophrys tricornis* is a synonym. Atlantic Ocean, in the west from Massachusetts and Bermuda through the Caribbean to Brazil. Tyler, 1965. (18 inches; 46 cm)

484. Smooth trunkfish *Lactophrys triqueter* (Linnaeus)

Dorsal, anal, and caudal fins each with 10 rays; P. 12; Gr. 8–9; no spines on head or before anal fin (although other species of *Lactophrys* have spines); carapace and caudal peduncle with dark hexagonal patterns; dark spot at base of dorsal and pectoral fins; margins of caudal and anal fins dark. Records of *L. trigonus* probably refer to this species, which is common on the offshore reefs. Two additional species of *Lactophrys* may eventually be found there also. Massachusetts and Bermuda through the Caribbean to Brazil. Reed, 1941; Tyler, 1965. (11 inches; 28 cm)

Tetraodontidae

The puffers differ from the porcupinefishes and burrfishes (family Diodontidae) by possessing a median division in each half of the beak (resulting in four "teeth" in the tetraodontids as opposed to two in the diodontids) and by having small prickles instead of large spines on the body. Both families are capable of inflating their stomachs with air or water. Inflation, together with the spines and prickles, protects the fish against predators.

Much confusion has existed in the past about the identity of the common puffer on the Texas and Louisiana coast. Recently the local form has been described as a new species, *Sphoeroides parvus*. References in the literature to *S. nephelus*, *S. marmoratus*, *S. maculatus*, and *S. spengleri* probably refer to this species, although *S. spengleri* is also known to occur here and near the Chandeleurs. The genus *Canthigaster* is sometimes placed in a separate family, the Canthigasteridae.

Most tetraodontids are known to be poisonous to some degree and so probably should not be eaten, but some of these species are commonly marketed. (Shipp and Yerger, 1969; Shipp, 1974)

1   Dorsal and anal each with 12–15 rays . . . . Smooth puffer, *Lago-cephalus laevigatus.*
    Dorsal and anal each with 6–8 or 9–10 rays   2
2   Dorsal rays 9–10; anal rays 8–9 . . . . Sharpnose puffer, *Canthi-gaster rostrata.*
    Dorsal and anal rays 6–8   3
3   Small fleshy tabs (lappets) present on dorsal surface, with either one pair behind eyes or many over posterior of body   4
    Small fleshy tabs absent   5
4   Single pair of black lappets behind eyes . . . . Marbled puffer, *Sphoeroides dorsalis.*
    Many tan lappets on posterior portion of body . . . . Bandtail puffer, *Sphoeroides spengleri.*
5   Body uniformly dark, except for a few scattered spots; skin smooth . . . . Blunthead puffer, *Sphoeroides pachygaster.*
    Body variously mottled; skin with prickles, at least on back   6
6   One or two distinct, white interorbital bars, often with white circular markings behind eyes . . . . Checkered puffer, *Sphoeroides testudineus.*
    One vague, black interorbital bar; body mottled but without white circular marks behind eye   7
7   Distinct dark spot in axil of pectoral fin . . . . Southern puffer, *Sphoeroides nephelus.*
    No distinct dark spot in axil of pectoral fin . . . . Least puffer, *Sphoeroides parvus.*

485. Smooth puffer   *Lagocephalus laevigatus* (Linnaeus)

D. 14; A. 12; skin smooth; silvery with black blotches. This large puffer is generally found on the inner and middle shelf, although it is known to enter the saltier bays. Cape Cod to Brazil. (1 foot; 30 cm)

486. Sharpnose puffer   *Canthigaster rostrata* (Bloch)

D. 10; A. 9; P. 16–18; body high, moderately compressed; brown on top; sides white, sometimes with faint blue spots; blue lines on head radiating from eye; upper and lower edges of caudal peduncle and caudal fin black. This puffer occurs commonly on offshore reefs. Atlantic Ocean, in the west from Bermuda, Bahamas, and Florida to Columbia. (4 inches; 10 cm)

487. Marbled puffer   *Sphoeroides dorsalis* Longley

D. 8; A. 7; P. 15; pair of small black lappets on either side of dorsal midline; pale irregular scrawls on face and lower sides of body. North Carolina to Surinam (Dutch Guiana), including the Gulf of Mexico and Bahamas. (7 inches; 18 cm)

488. Bandtail puffer   *Sphoeroides spengleri* (Bloch)

D. 8; A. 7; P. 14; sides usually with small lappets; body olive brown with numerous black spots as large as eye; spot in axil of pectoral most distinctive; caudal fin distinctly barred. In Texas waters it occurs on 7½-Fathom Reef and other offshore reefs, but it is more common in the northeastern Gulf. Atlantic Ocean, in the west from Bermuda and Massachusetts through the Caribbean to Brazil. (6 inches; 15 cm)

489. Blunthead puffer *Sphoeroides pachygaster* (Müller and Troschel)

D. 8; A. 8; P. 16; body uniformly colored black to tan, lighter shades usually with irregularly spaced dark spots; skin completely smooth; pectoral fin wing-shaped, with upper rays longest. The occurrence of this offshore puffer in the northwestern Gulf is based on three specimens originally identified as *Liosaccus cutaneus* collected at one hundred fathoms (27° 20′ N, 96° 20′ W). Bermuda and Massachusetts to Brazil. (5 inches; 13 cm)

490. Checkered puffer *Sphoeroides testudineus* (Linnaeus)

D. 8; A. 6; P. 14; body olivaceous with white curved lines running over body; large irregular dark spots on sides, creating a checkered pattern. There are rare records from Texas bays which we have not verified, but this puffer is to be expected more often about offshore reefs. Rhode Island through the Caribbean to Brazil. (3 inches; 8 cm)

491. Southern puffer *Sphoeroides nephelus* (Goode and Bean)

D. 7; A. 6; P. 14; body brown with numerous darker and lighter spots and blotches; interorbital with dark bar; distinct dark spot in axil of pectoral fin. This is the common puffer in the northeastern Gulf. East coast of Florida to the Chandeleur Islands and off Yucatán. (8 inches; 20 cm)

492. Least puffer *Sphoeroides parvus* Shipp and Yerger

D. 8–9; A. 6–8; P. 13–16; body small, usually less than 4 inches (100 mm) in standard length; body tan with irregular dark and light markings on sides and back, but no prominent dark spot in axil of pectoral fin. This is the common bay and inshore puffer off the Louisiana and Texas coasts. Apalachicola Bay, Florida, westward to Texas and south to Yucatán. (3 inches; 8 cm)

Diodontidae

Porcupinefishes and burrfishes are inflatable fishes, like the puffers, but they have longer spines and a strange beak for crushing armored prey. They are often dried and sold as curiosities. Several other tropical species may occur offshore, and one of these, the circumtropical porcupinefish, *Diodon hystrix*, was reported from Texas, but we have not verified it.

1   Spines fixed erect, most with three roots; body striped . . . .
    Striped burrfish, *Chilomycterus schoepfi.*
    Spines able to fold back, most with two roots; body spotted   2
2   Forehead spines shorter than those behind pectoral fin; spots about
    same diameter as spines . . . . Porcupinefish, *Diodon hystrix.*
    Forehead spines longer than those behind pectoral fin; most spots
    two or more times larger than spine diameter . . . . Balloonfish,
    Diodon holocanthus.

493. Striped burrfish *Chilomycterus schoepfi* (Walbaum)

D. 12; A. 10; large individuals light-colored with dark, wavy, roughly parallel lines and large dark spots on body and fins; young fish considerably different, having much darker (dark green) bodies, with lines and spots set much closer together. Burrfish are hardy animals and make excellent aquarium pets. Most will learn to accept food from the hand. Burrfish are common in the bays and shallow Gulf, especially in the summer. New England to Brazil, including the Gulf of Mexico and the Bahamas. (10 inches; 25 cm)

494. Porcupinefish *Diodon hystrix* Linnaeus

D. 15–17; A. 15–16; P. 25; spines on body shorter than those of balloonfish, about 20 in row between snout and origin of dorsal; light green on back, white underneath; numerous small spots on head, body, and fins. Circumtropical; in the western Atlantic from Massachusetts through the Caribbean to Brazil. Baughman, 1950*b*. (2 feet; 61 cm)

495. Balloonfish *Diodon holocanthus* Linnaeus

D. 13–14; A. 13–14; P. 22–23; spines on body long and moveable, about 15 in row between snout and origin of dorsal fin; light brown on back, white underneath; dark brown bar passing through eye; scattered brown spots, smaller than eye, on sides and back. Circumtropical; in the western Atlantic from the Bahamas, Florida, and the northern Gulf of Mexico to Brazil. (1 foot; 30 cm)

Molidae

The strange ocean sunfishes or headfishes are rarely seen, solitary surface fishes with a high, flattened body continuous with the head, giving them a chopped-off appearance. Specimens are occasionally harpooned or found dead on the beach. They reach great size, some exceeding seven feet (2 m) in length and height. Another worldwide genus, *Ranzania*, with a very long, slender body, may also occur in the area. (Dawson, 1965)

1 Eye nearer tip of snout than gill opening; caudal with rounded
    lobe in middle . . . . Sharptail mola, *Mola lanceolata.*
   Eye almost between tip of snout and gill openings; caudal without
    large central lobe . . . . Ocean sunfish, *Mola mola.*

496. Sharptail mola *Mola lanceolata* Lienard

The sharptail mola is rarely taken anywhere. A model of a specimen is on display at the Louisiana Wild Life and Fisheries Commission Office in New Orleans. Perhaps worldwide, but not known in the eastern Pacific. (7 feet; 2 m)

497. Ocean sunfish *Mola mola* (Linnaeus)

The ocean sunfish is a wide-ranging species which is apparently not rare far offshore. Occasional individuals come inshore. Worldwide in temperate and tropical waters; in the western Atlantic from Newfoundland to Argentina. Kemp, 1957. (10 feet; 3 m)

APPENDIXES

APPENDIX 1. Temperate and Subtropical Species Occurring in Either the Northeastern Gulf or the Southeastern U.S. Atlantic but Not Confirmed in the Northwestern Gulf.

	NE Gulf	SE U.S. Atlantic
Petromyzon marinus		X
Sphyrna tudes	X	X
Myliobatis freminvillei	X	X
Mobula hypostoma		X
Alosa pseudoharengus		X
Alosa sapidissima		X
Alosa aestivalis		X
Alosa mediocris		X
Brevoortia tyrannus		X
Brevoortia smithi	X	X
Anchoa lamprotaenia	X	
Saurida normani	X	
Muraena retifera	X	X
Ariosoma impressa	X	X
Callechelys muraena	X	
Letharchus velifer	X	X
Gordiichthys irretitus	X	
Bascanichthys scuticaris	X	X
Ophichthus ocellatus	X	X
Hemiramphus balao	X	X
Floridichthys carpio	X	
Fundulus heteroclitus		X
Fundulus confluentus	X	X
Fundulus majalis		X
Urophycis earlli		X
Amphelikturus dendriticus	X	
Syngnathus springeri	X	X
Corythoichthys albirostris	X	X
Oostethus lineatus	X	X
Holocentrus bullisi	X	
Corniger spinosus	X	
Rypticus saponaceus	?	X
Centropristis striata	X	X
Lutjanus buccanella	X	X
Lutjanus mahogoni		X
Pronotogrammus aureorubens	X	
Decapterus macarellus		X
Decapterus tabl	X	

	NE Gulf	SE U.S. Atlantic
Caulolatilus cyanops		X
Eucinostomus melanopterus	X	X
Haemulon chrysargyreum	X	
Cynoscion regalis		X
Calamus penna	X	
Calamus proridens	X	
Stenotomus chrysops		X
Tautoga onitis		X
Tautogolabrus adspersus		X
Gobionellus stigmaticus	X	X
Gobiosoma ginsburgi		X
Coryphopterus glaucofraenum		X
Prionotus evolans		X
Prionotus alatus	X	X
Bellator egretta	X	
Bellator brachychir	X	
Opistognathus macrognathus	X	
Dactyloscopus tridigitatus	X	X
Astroscopus guttatus		X
Paraclinus marmoratus	X	
Paraclinus fasciatus	X	
Otophidium omostigmum	X	X
Rissola marginata	?	X
Peprilus triacanthus		X
Menidia menidia		X
Bothus ocellatus	X	X
Paralichthys dentatus		X
Etropus rimosus	X	X
Etropus microstomus	X	X
Gymnachirus melas	X	X
Symphurus urospilus	X	X
Parahollardia lineata	X	X
Sphoeroides maculatus		X
Opsanus tau		X

APPENDIX 2. Rarely Caught Species of the Outer Shelf and Continental Slope Not Covered in the Keys or Species Accounts.

seven-gilled shark	*Heptranchias perlo*
longnose lanceletfish	*Alepisaurus ferox*
spaghetti eel	*Moringua edwardsi*
collared eel	*Kaupichthys nuchalis*
viper moray	*Enchelycore nigricans*
conger eel	*Conger oceanicus*
pike conger	*Hoplunnis tenuis*
pike conger	*Hoplunnis diomedianus*
longnose greeneye	*Parasudis truculenta*
shortnose greeneye	*Chlorophthalmus agassizi*
flyingfish	*Cypselurus melanurus*
American john dory	*Zenopsis ocellata*

deepbody boarfish	*Antigonia capros*
silk (yelloweye) snapper	*Lutjanus vivanus*
glasseye snapper	*Priacanthus cruentatus*
longspine snipefish	*Macrorhamphosus scolopax*
pomfret	*Brama brama*
bigscale pomfret	*Taractes longipinnis*
goldspot goby	*Gnatholepis thompsoni*
neon goby	*Gobiosoma oceanops*
island goby	*Lythrypnus nesiotes*
bluegold goby	*Lythrypnus spilus*
rusty goby	*Quisquilius hipoliti*
tusked goby	*Risor ruber*
longfin scorpionfish	*Scorpaena agassizi*
reef scorpionfish	*Scorpaenodes caribbaeus*
highfin scorpionfish	*Pontinus rathbuni*
goby flathead	*Bembrops gobioides*

APPENDIX 3. Freshwater Fishes Likely to be Found in Marine Waters.
This list is not at all complete since nearly any species might wash out to sea,
but these are the more regular strays. Freshwater species that normally tolerate salt water are included in the text.

paddlefish	*Polyodon spathula*
pallid sturgeon	*Scaphirhynchus albus*
shovelnose sturgeon	*Scaphirhynchus platorynchus*
shortnose gar	*Lepisosteus platostomus*
bowfin	*Amia calva*
chain pickerel	*Esox niger*
grass pickerel	*Esox americanus*
carp	*Cyprinus carpio*
golden shiner	*Notemigonus crysoleucas*
blacktail shiner	*Notropis venustus*
bullhead minnow	*Pimephales vigilax*
river carpsucker	*Carpiodes carpio*
smallmouth buffalo	*Ictiobus bubalus*
flathead catfish	*Pylodictis olivaris*
channel catfish	*Ictalurus punctatus*
black bullhead	*Ictalurus melas*
yellow bullhead	*Ictalurus natalis*
tadpole madtom	*Noturus gyrinus*
pirate perch	*Aphredoderus sayanus*
golden topminnow	*Fundulus chrysotus*
least killifish	*Heterandria formosa*
brook silverside	*Labidesthes sicculus*
yellow bass	*Morone mississippiensis*
largemouth bass	*Micropterus salmoides*
banded pygmy sunfish	*Elassoma zonatum*
bluegill and other	*Lepomis macrochirus* and
sunfishes	*Lepomis* spp.
white crappie	*Pomoxis annularis*
freshwater drum	*Aplodinotus grunniens*

APPENDIX 4. Marine Fishes That Regularly Invade Northern Gulf Coastal Fresh Water.

bull shark	*Carcharhinus leucas*
Atlantic stingray	*Dasyatis sabina*
Atlantic sturgeon°	*Acipenser oxyrhynchus*
ladyfish	*Elops saurus*
tarpon	*Megalops atlantica*
American eel†	*Anguilla rostrata*
Alabama shad°	*Alosa alabamae*
skipjack herring°	*Alosa chrysochloris*
Gulf menhaden	*Brevoortia patronus*
bay anchovy	*Anchoa mitchilli*
sea catfish	*Arius felis*
Atlantic needlefish†	*Strongylura marina*
sheepshead minnow	*Cyprinodon variegatus*
saltmarsh topminnow	*Fundulus jenkinsi*
bayou killifish	*Fundulus pulvereus*
Gulf killifish	*Fundulus grandis*
rainwater killifish	*Lucania parva*
tidewater silverside	*Menidia beryllina*
Gulf pipefish	*Syngnathus scovelli*
striped bass°	*Morone saxatilis*
sheepshead	*Archosargus probatocephalus*
pinfish	*Lagodon rhomboides*
spotted seatrout	*Cynoscion nebulosus*
sand seatrout	*Cynoscion arenarius*
spot	*Leiostomus xanthurus*
Atlantic croaker	*Micropogon undulatus*
red drum	*Sciaenops ocellata*
mountain mullet†	*Agonostomus monticola*
striped mullet†	*Mugil cephalus*
white mullet	*Mugil curema*
violet goby	*Gobioides broussonneti*
freshwater goby	*Gobionellus shufeldti*
naked goby	*Gobiosoma bosci*
clown goby	*Microgobius gulosus*
bay whiff	*Citharichthys spilopterus*
southern flounder	*Paralichthys lethostigma*
hogchoker†	*Trinectes maculatus*
lined sole	*Achirus lineatus*

° Anadromous.

† At least part of population catadromous.

APPENDIX 5. Common Fish Species with Protracted Spawning Seasons.

Year-round Spawners

bay anchovy	*Anchoa mitchilli*

Spring through Fall Spawners

finetooth shark	*Aprionodon isodon*
bonnethead	*Sphyrna tiburo*

striped anchovy	*Anchoa hepsetus*
Gulf killifish	*Fundulus grandis*
longnose killifish	*Fundulus similis*
sheepshead minnow	*Cyprinodon variegatus*
rough silverside	*Membras martinica*
naked goby	*Gobiosoma bosci*
harvestfish	*Peprilus paru*
least puffer	*Sphoeroides parvus*

Fall-Winter Spawners

red drum	*Sciaenops ocellata*
striped mullet	*Mugil cephalus*

Winter-Spring Spawners

pigfish	*Orthopristis chrysoptera*
black drum	*Pogonias cromis*

Spring Spawners

lesser electric ray	*Narcine brasiliensis*
ladyfish	*Elops saurus*
inshore lizardfish	*Synodus foetens*
skilletfish	*Gobiesox strumosus*
silver perch	*Bairdiella chrysura*
sheepshead	*Archosargus probatocephalus*
white mullet	*Mugil curema*
bighead sea robin	*Prionotus tribulus*

Summer Spawners

Atlantic sharpnose shark	*Rhizoprionodon terraenovae*
blacktip shark	*Carcharhinus limbatus*
scalloped hammerhead	*Sphyrna lewini*
roundel skate	*Raja texana*
Atlantic stingray	*Dasyatis sabina*
scaled sardine	*Harengula pensacolae*
sea catfish	*Arius felis*
gafftopsail catfish	*Bagre marinus*
Gulf toadfish	*Opsanus beta*
cobia	*Rachycentron canadum*
Florida pompano	*Trachinotus carolinus*
crevalle jack	*Caranx hippos*
dolphin	*Coryphaena hippurus*
red snapper	*Lutjanus campechanus*
sand seatrout	*Cynoscion arenarius*
spotted seatrout	*Cynoscion nebulosus*
spadefish	*Chaetodipterus faber*
great barracuda	*Sphyraena barracuda*
guaguanche	*Sphyraena guachancho*
Spanish mackerel	*Scomberomorus maculatus*
sailfish	*Istiophorus platypterus*
hogchoker	*Trinectes maculatus*

Fall Spawners

bluefish	*Pomatomus saltatrix*
silver seatrout	*Cynoscion nothus*
king mackerel (?)	*Scomberomorus cavalla*

Winter Spawners

speckled worm eel	*Myrophis punctatus*
Gulf menhaden	*Brevoortia patronus*
round herring	*Etrumeus teres*
southern hake	*Urophycis floridanus*
spot	*Leiostomus xanthurus*
croaker	*Micropogon undulatus*
pinfish	*Lagodon rhomboides*
butterfish	*Peprilus burti*
southern flounder	*Paralichthys lethostigma*

Spring and Fall Spawners

bull shark	*Carcharhinus leucas*
midshipman	*Porichthys porosissimus*
tidewater silverside	*Menidia beryllina*

APPENDIX 6. Some French (Cajun) Common Names for Marine Fish.

Cajun Name	Translation	AFS Common Name
requin	shark	shark
ange	angel	skate
terre	earth	stingray
poisson arme	armored fish	gar
sardine	sardine	menhaden
salop*	probably trash?	shad
grande écaille	big scale	tarpon
banane	banana	ladyfish
mashwadan*	?	sea catfish
tête dur	hardhead	sea catfish
mashwadan* passe	?	gafftopsail
anguille	eel	american eel
serpent mer	sea serpent	other eels
aiguille	needle	needlefish
poisson huître	oyster fish	toadfish
cochon	pig	cod
docteur	doctor	sea robin
patassa* l'eau salé	saltwater perch	striped bass
vielle	old lady	grouper
petit groupe	small grouper	grouper
poisson bleu	bluefish	bluefish
limon	lemon	cobia
dauphin	dolphin	dolphin
papino	pompano	pompano
cochon	pig	pigfish

* Phonetic spelling.

Cajun Name	Translation	AFS Common Name
poisson beurre	butterfish	pinfish
truite gris	gray trout	spotted seatrout
truite blanc	white trout	sand seatrout
sandigas*	?	spot
poisson rouge	redfish	red drum
tambour	drum	black drum
robal	robalo	kingfish
poisson blanche	whitefish	silver perch
mulle	mullet	mullet
poisson électricité	electric fish	stargazer
maquereau	mackerel	mackerel
plie	flounder	flounder
ferré au passe	file	filefish
cornard	horny	triggerfish
crapaud mer	sea toad	puffer

* Phonetic spelling.

APPENDIX 7. Some Spanish (Mexican) Common Names for Important Species of Marine Fish.

Spanish Name	Translation	AFS Common Name
carconetta	?	(small sharks, mostly *Carcharhinus*)
raya	ray	Atlantic stingray
machete	machete	ladyfish
matajuelo real	royal little killer	ladyfish
lisa francesca	French mullet	ladyfish
savanilla	little (grass) flat	tarpon
sábalo	shad	tarpon
chile	chili pepper	inshore lizardfish
bagre de mar	sea catfish	sea catfish
bandera	flag	gafftopsail catfish
signatido	?	pipefish
robalo	snook	snook
cabra mora	moorish goat	rock hind
mero	grouper	large grouper
aguají	gag	gag
bacalao	codfish	scamp
pampano	pompano	pompano
jurel	jack	jack crevalle
coronado	crowned one	amberjack
dorado	golden one	dolphin
pargo mulato	black porgy	gray snapper
guachinango	red porgy	red snapper
pargo colorado	red porgy	red or dog snapper
pargo criolla	creole porgy	mutton snapper
pargo prieto	dark porgy	gray snapper
manchego	spotted one	lane snapper
cagón de lo alto	?	vermilion snapper

Spanish Name	Translation	AFS Common Name
mojarra	mojarra	(any large mojarra, *Diapterus*)
chopa espina	spined bream	pinfish
pargo	porgy	sheepshead
tambor	drum	black drum
ronco amarillo	yellow grunt	silver perch
corvina	corvina	red drum or other member of drum family
pesca colorado	redfish	red drum
gurrubato	?	(*Micropogon furnieri*)
roncador	croaker	croaker
roncador	croaker	sand drum
trucha de mar	sea trout	spotted seatrout
trucha blanca	white trout	sand seatrout
chopa blanca	white bream	Bermuda chub
peto	?	wahoo
caballa	mare	king mackerel
sierra	mountain	Spanish mackerel
espandón	?	blue marlin and other billfish
volador	flier	sailfish
lenguado	flounder	flounder

APPENDIX 8. Deeper-dwelling Families Occasionally Found over the Continental Shelf.

These outline drawings may be used to identify families of fishes that normally dwell in deeper water but sometimes may occur over the shelf.

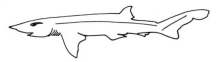

Hexanchidae

Lophiidae

Chlorophthalmidae

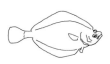

Pleuronectidae

Argentinidae

Macrouridae

Macrorhamphosidae   Polymyxiidae

Caproidae   Zeidae

Percophididae   Triacanthodidae

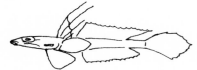 

Callionymidae   Merlucciidae

GLOSSARY

ACUMINATE. Somewhat pointed, but not as extreme as lanceolate.

ABDOMINAL. Referring to the belly region.

ADIPOSE. Referring to fatty tissue. For example, adipose eyelid—a transparent covering over the eye of some fishes—or adipose fin (see FIN).

ADNATE. Attached.

AIR BLADDER. Swim bladder; a gas-filled membranous organ responsible for buoyancy in many fishes. Some fish use their air bladder as a lung, and some others use it as a sound-producing organ.

AMBICOLORATE. In the flatfishes, part or all of the blind side having the same or similar pigment as the eyed side.

ANADROMOUS. Living in the sea but entering fresh water to spawn.

ANAL FIN. See FIN (Fig. 7).

ANGULATE. Having definite corners, forming an angle, with at least one point.

AXIL. The backside of the pectoral fin base; the "armpit."

AXILLARY SCALE (AXILLARY PROCESS). An elongate structure at the base of the pectoral or ventral fins in some fish (Fig. 7).

BARBEL. A threadlike structure on the head; usually sensory (Fig. 7).

BENTHONIC (BENTHIC). Referring to the sea bottom.

BIFURCATE. Branching into two lobes or sections.

BONY STAY. A prominent bony ridge running from a suborbital bone to the preopercle.

BRANCHIOSTEGAL MEMBRANE. A membrane connecting the gill cover or opercle with the throat (Figs. 8, 9).

BRANCHIOSTEGAL RAY. Slender bones in the branchiostegal membrane.

BUCKLER. Large, multispined structures in the skin of batfishes.

CANINE. A slender, rounded, pointed tooth for holding or tearing.

CATADROMOUS. Living in fresh water but entering the sea to spawn.

CAUDAL FIN. See FIN.

CAUDAL PEDUNCLE. The region between the last ray of the anal fin and the base of the caudal fin.

CHEST. The ventral area just behind the throat.

CIGUATERA. A disease of the nervous system caused by eating certain tropical fishes.

CIRCUMTROPICAL. Occurring around the world, in all oceans, in the warm areas extending approximately from twenty to thirty degrees north and south of the equator.

CIRRUS. A fleshy appendage, usually on the head or tips of the fins.

COMPRESSED. Laterally flattened.

CTENOID SCALE. See SCALE (Fig. 11).

CUSP. The base of a tooth; the region where it is attached.

CUTANEOUS FOLD. A low finlike fold on the tails of rays.

CYCLOID SCALES. See SCALE (Fig. 11).

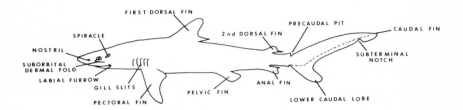

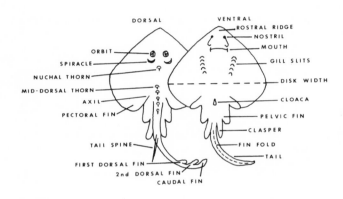

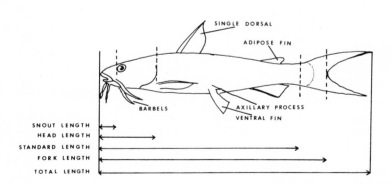

Fig. 7. Features important in fish identification

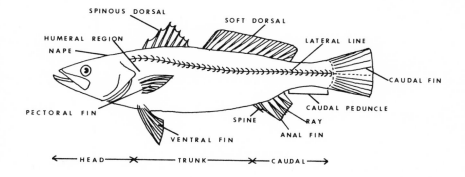

SPINOUS DORSAL

SOFT DORSAL

HUMERAL REGION

LATERAL LINE

NAPE

CAUDAL FIN

PECTORAL FIN

CAUDAL PEDUNCLE

SPINE

RAY

VENTRAL FIN

ANAL FIN

← HEAD → — TRUNK — → CAUDAL →

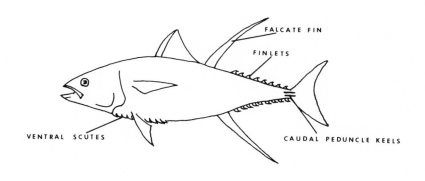

FALCATE FIN

FINLETS

VENTRAL SCUTES

CAUDAL PEDUNCLE KEELS

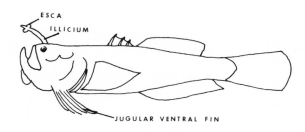

ESCA

ILLICIUM

JUGULAR VENTRAL FIN

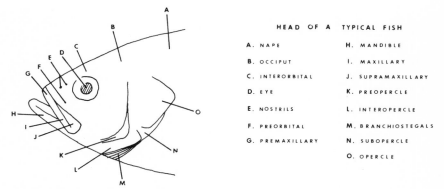

HEAD OF A TYPICAL FISH

A. NAPE	H. MANDIBLE
B. OCCIPUT	I. MAXILLARY
C. INTERORBITAL	J. SUPRAMAXILLARY
D. EYE	K. PREOPERCLE
E. NOSTRILS	L. INTEROPERCLE
F. PREORBITAL	M. BRANCHIOSTEGALS
G. PREMAXILLARY	N. SUBOPERCLE
	O. OPERCLE

Fig. 8. Head of a typical fish

DECIDUOUS. Tending to shed or break off.

DENTICLE. See SCALE (Fig. 11).

DISC LAMELLAE. In remoras, the flattened, overlapping folds in the sucker, actually modified dorsal rays.

DISTAL. Remote from the point of origin or attachment.

DORSAL. Referring to the back.

DORSAL FIN. See FIN (Fig. 7).

DORSUM. The upper (or dorsal) portion of the fish's body.

EMARGINATE. Having the margin indented, but not so deeply as to be forked (Fig. 12).

ENTIRE. Whole, complete, or smooth.

ESCA. The fleshy "bait" at the end of the illicium of frog-, goose-, and batfishes.

ESTUARY. An area where fresh water meets sea water.

EURYHALINE. Capable of withstanding large changes in salinity (salt concentration).

FALCATE. Sickle-shaped (Fig. 12).

FIN. Median or paired structure, usually membranous and supported by soft rays or spines. Fins may be variously modified into other structures such as sucking discs or "fishing poles." Different fins exist as follows (Fig. 7):

Adipose. A fleshy median dorsal fin without spines or rays.

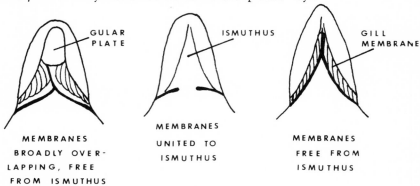

Fig. 9. Attachment of branchiostegal membranes

Anal. A median fin on the ventral surface between the anus and the base of the tail.

Caudal. The tail fin; the median fin at the base of the tail (Fig. 12).

Dorsal. A median fin on the dorsal surface; it may be single or divided into two or more fins.

Finlets. Detached median fins following the dorsal or anal.

Pectoral. Paired fins on either side of the body, usually near or just behind the gill opening; these correspond to the arm or foreleg of terrestrial vertebrates.

Pelvic or *Ventral.* Paired fins below or behind the pectorals, near the anus (abdominally inserted), under the pectorals (thoracically inserted), or in advance of the pectorals (jugular).

FORKED. Divided into two parts or branches.

GANOID SCALE. See SCALE (Fig. 11).

GILL ARCH. Unit of respiratory structures on either side of the pharynx (Fig. 10).

GILL FILAMENT. Slender respiratory structures which compose the posterior part of the gill arch where gas exchange occurs (Fig. 10).

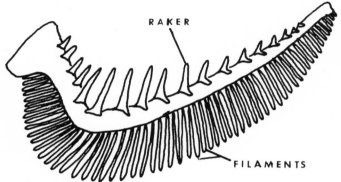

Fig. 10. Gill arch

GILL MEMBRANE. See BRANCHIOSTEGAL MEMBRANE.

GILL RAKERS. Usually stiff projections on the inner or anterior surfaces of the gill arch, used for straining food (Fig. 10).

GULAR PLATE. A bony median plate between the lower jaws of some fishes.

HEAD (HEAD LENGTH). The region from the tip of the snout to the posterior edge of the gill cover (Fig. 7).

HETEROCERCAL TAIL. See TAIL (Fig. 12).

HOMOCERCAL TAIL. See TAIL (Fig. 12).

HUMERAL. Pertaining to the shoulder region, just behind and above the pectoral fin in most marine fishes.

HYOID. Of or pertaining to the tongue.

HYPURAL PLATE. Posterior end of the vertebral column, noticeable as a vertical crease when the tail of the fish is bent forward.

ILLICIUM. Modified dorsal spines that serve as the "fishing rod" in angling fishes; see also ESCA.

INCISOR. A long but sharp-edged tooth for scraping or cutting.

INTERHAEMAL. Bones connecting the ventral vertebral arches.

INTERORBITAL. Region (or bone) on top of the head between the eyes (Fig. 8).

INTROMITTENT ORGAN. A modified structure (fin) in the male of fishes with internal fertilization that is used for transfer of sperm to the female.

ISOCERCAL TAIL. See TAIL (Fig. 12).

ISTHMUS. Fleshy region extending forward on the throat between the gills (Fig. 9).

JUGULAR. Of or pertaining to the throat.

KEEL. A raised ridge, often on a scale or on the caudal peduncle.

LACHRYMAL PLATE. In sea robins, a bone under the eye and above the maxilla.

LANCEOLATE. Tapering to a long, lancelike point (Fig. 12).

LATERAL LINE (LATERAL-LINE SCALES). A line of modified scales with pores in them connected by tubes usually running the length of the fish from behind the gill opening to the base of the caudal fin. The pressure-sensitive pores, but not the scales of the lateral line, usually extend onto the head of the fish and sometimes onto the caudal fin as well. The position, shape, and number of scales in the lateral line is of taxonomic importance in many fishes.

LATERAL SCALE ROWS (VERTICAL SCALE ROWS). The number of scales in a vertical row between the gill opening and the base of the caudal fin, used instead of the lateral-line scale count in fishes which lack a lateral line.

LENGTH. Measured in various ways (Fig. 7):
Fork length. From the tip of the snout to the fork of the caudal fin.
Standard length (SL). From the tip of the snout to the tip of the hypural plate.
Total length (TL). From the tip of the snout to the tip of the caudal fin.

LEPTOCEPHALUS. A laterally flattened, transparent larval stage of eels, bonefish, tarpon, and ladyfish. It has a small head and decreases considerably in size and body depth during metamorphosis.

LUNATE. Deeply forked, with curved branches (Fig. 12).

MANDIBLE. Lower jaw (Fig. 8).

MAXILLA. One of the bones which comprise the upper jaw (Fig. 8).

MEDIAL. Near the centerline of the body.

MELANOPHORE. A dark-colored pigment cell.

MERISTIC. Pertaining to the number of serial parts, for example, fin rays or lateral-line scales.

MOLAR. A short, blunt tooth for crushing.

NAPE. The posteriormost part of the head just before the dorsal fin.

NICTITATING MEMBRANE. A lid in the lower or back corner of the eye that can be used to cover the eye.

NUCHAL. Of or pertaining to the nape.

OCCIPUT. The posterior portion of the head behind the eyes but anterior to the nape.

OCELLUS. A round spot surrounded by a lighter region; the word *ocellus* means "eye."

OPERCLE (OPERCULUM). A gill cover, composed of the opercular bones (Fig. 8).

ORBIT. The socket of the eye.

PALATINE. One of a pair of bones often with teeth, on the anterior roof of the mouth posterior to and often fused to the vomer.

PECTORAL. Referring to the shoulder region; for example, pectoral fin.

PEDUNCLE. See CAUDAL PEDUNCLE.

PELVIC. Referring to the region of the pelvic girdle; for example, pelvic fins.

PERITONEUM. The membrane lining the body cavity, often visible through the outer layer of skin.

PHARYNGEAL. Referring to the throat or gill region; for example, pharyngeal arches.

PREDORSAL. Referring to the area immediately before the dorsal fin; for example, predorsal length, measured from the snout to the dorsal fin, or predorsal midline, a line on the predorsal region.

PREOPERCLE. One of the bones of the opercular series (Fig. 8).

PREORBITAL. A large bone just anterior to the eye (Fig. 8).

PREMAXILLARY (PREMAXILLA). The anteriormost bone of the upper jaw, often protrusible (Fig. 8).

PROXIMAL. Near to the origin or point of attachment.

PSEUDOBRANCHIUM. (pl., -IAE). Small gill-like structures on the inner surface of the gill cover; they may be covered by skin or absent in some species.

PYLORIC CAECA. Fingerlike projections or pockets of the intestine where it joins the stomach.

RAYS. Any support of fins whether spinous, segmented, or unsegmented; the term usually refers to a jointed, flexible support, usually branched unless rudimentary, which has a ladderlike appearance when viewed in transmitted light.

RELICT. A population left behind as conditions change and most of population moves; for example, as North America warmed in the Pleistocene, cold-adapted fish moved up the east coast, leaving small populations as relicts in deep, cool portions of the Gulf.

RETICULATE PATTERN. A network; a repeated intercrossing of lines on a background color.

ROSTRAL SPINES. Spines on the snout of sea robins and similar fishes.

ROSTRUM. A snout resembling a beak or bill.

SEGMENTED RAY. See RAY.

SCALE. A small, bony plate in the skin, occurring in various shapes and with various compositions (Fig. 11).

Scale counts often used in fish taxonomy are:

Lateral-line scales or *Lateral scale count*. The number of pored scales or scales where the lateral line should be.

Above lateral line. The number of scale rows from the base of the dorsal fin to the lateral line.

Below lateral line. The number of scale rows from the lateral line to the base of the anal fin. The scales of the lateral line are not included in these last two counts.

SCUTE. A modified scale, usually keeled, or in sturgeon an ossification imbedded in the skin.

SERRATE. Notched or with small saw teeth.

SCUTE   DENTICLE   GANOID   CTENOID   CYCLOID

Fig. 11. Scale types

SETIFORM. Comblike.

SNOUT. The region from the tip of the head to the front of the eye (Fig. 7).

SOFT RAY. See RAY.

SOFT FIN. A portion of a fin, especially the dorsal, supported by soft rays.

SPIRACLE. A small hole just behind the eye in some sharks and rays by which water may be passed out of the gill cavity.

SPINOUS FIN. A portion of a fin, especially the dorsal, supported by spines.

SQUAMATION. Development of scales. Primary squamation is development of the main body scales; secondary squamation is development of scales located on top of the primary row.

STENOHALINE. Inability to withstand large changes in salinity (salt concentration).

SUBEQUAL. Nearly or almost equal, but clearly not of identical size.

SUPRAMAXILLARY (SUPRAMAXILLA). A small bone lying along the upper posterior margin of the maxillary in some fishes.

SWIM BLADDER. See AIR BLADDER.

SYNONYM. An invalid scientific name of a species proposed later than the accepted name.

TAIL. Caudal region (Fig. 12).

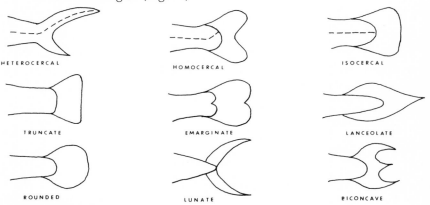

HETEROCERCAL   HOMOCERCAL   ISOCERCAL

TRUNCATE   EMARGINATE   LANCEOLATE

ROUNDED   LUNATE   BICONCAVE

Fig. 12. Tail types

THORACIC. Of or pertaining to the chest; the region below the pectoral fins in most fishes.

TRUNCATE. Squared off (Fig. 12).

TUBERCLE. A small prominence elevated above the surrounding area.

UNSEGMENTED RAY. Found in codlike and blennoid fishes; see RAY.

UROHYAL. A modified branchiostegal located posteriorly and ventrally in the hyoid apparatus under the throat.

VENTER. The ventral area.

VENTRAL. Pertaining to the lower side of the body.

VENTRAL FIN. See FIN.

VILLIFORM. Slender, closely packed projections like the teeth of a brush.

VOMER. A thin, flat bone anterior in the upper roof of the mouth (see PALATINE).

BIBLIOGRAPHY

Many of the important scientific publications covering the fishes of the area are mentioned with the family or species descriptions, but a few are general works of special importance that include long lists of fishes. These include:

For Texas: Gunter, 1945a, 1950; Baughman, 1950a, b; Baughman and Springer, 1950; Hildebrand, 1954, 1955; Reid, 1955a, b, 1957; Simmons, 1957; Breuer, 1957, 1962; Hoese, 1958a, 1965; Renfro, 1960; Parker, 1965; Miller, 1965; Causey, 1969; King, 1971.

For Louisiana: Gunter, 1938a, b; Gowanloch, 1933; Behre, 1950; Suttkus, Darnell, and Darnell, 1953–1954; Gunter and Shell, 1958; Darnell, 1958; Norden, 1966; Dawson, 1966a; Dugas, 1970; Fontenot and Rogillio, 1970; Perret et al., 1971; Herke, 1971; Dunham, 1972; Thomas, Wagner, and Loesch, 1971; Morton, 1973; Perret and Caillouet, 1974; Weaver and Holloway, 1974.

For Mississippi: Franks, 1970; Franks et al., 1972; Christmas, 1973; Cliburn, 1974.

For Alabama: Boschung, 1957; Swingle, 1971a; Swingle and Bland, 1974.

For the northwest coast of Florida: Bailey, Winn, and Smith, 1954; Kilby, 1955; Reid, 1954; Joseph and Yerger, 1956; Briggs, 1958; Springer and Woodburn, 1960; Moe and Martin, 1965; Hastings, 1972; Smith et al., 1975.

For the northeast coast of Mexico: Jordan and Dickerson, 1908; Alvarez, 1970; Hildebrand, 1954, 1955, 1958, 1969; Darnell, 1962.

Important general works including more than one state: Fowler, 1945; Christmas, Gunter, and Whatley, 1960; Springer and Bullis, 1956; Bullis and Thompson, 1965; Roithmayr, 1965; Moore, Brusher, and Trent, 1970; Topp and Ingle, 1972; Walls, 1975; Parker, Moore, and Galloway, 1975.

Offshore fishes are not usually treated, but LaMonte (1946, 1952) includes those important as game fishes. Some of them are also covered by Norman and Fraser (1949). The monumental work of Jordan and Evermann (1896–1900) is essential as a rich source of information. It led to two more popular works (Jordan and Evermann, 1923; Breder, 1948). Many of the continental slope fishes can be found in Goode and Bean (1895). Both nineteenth-century works are out of date, but until the completion of the progressing "Fishes of the Western North Atlantic" in the Sears Foundation Memoir no. 1, parts 1–6, which contains the work of various authors cited throughout this book, Jordan and Evermann's early work remains the most complete compendium of information on New World Atlantic marine fishes.

Extralimital works of use include Beebe and Tee-Van (1933); Bigelow and Schroeder (1953a); Smith (1907); Dahlberg (1975); Perlmutter (1961); Breder (1948); Cervigon (1966); Meek and Hildebrand (1923–1925); and Longley and Hildebrand (1941). The two recent western Atlantic tropical marine fish books (Böhlke and Chaplin, 1968; Randall, 1968) are essential for identifying tropical species not included here.

For freshwater fishes, some of which regularly enter estuaries with floods, the major works are Blair et al. (1968); Carr and Goin (1959); Eddy (1969); Knapp (1953); Douglas (1974); Cook (1959); and finally Hubbs and Lagler (1958), who present the most complete information on the way to study a fish taxonomically.

Journals of most importance to the study of fishes of the area are *Contributions in Marine Science* (formerly *Publications of the Institute of Marine Science of the University of Texas*), *Gulf Research Reports, Copeia, Transactions of the American Fisheries Society, Alabama Marine Resources Bulletin, Technical Bulletin of the Louisiana Wild Life and Fisheries Commission, Bulletin of Marine Science* (formerly *Bulletin of Marine Science of the Gulf and Caribbean*), *Journal of Marine Science, Texas Journal of Science, Transactions of the Louisiana Academy of Sciences, Florida Scientist* (formerly *Quarterly Journal of the Florida Academy of Science*), and bulletins and technical reports issued by the Texas Parks and Wildlife Commission and the Florida Board of Natural Resources.

The preceding lists are not complete, especially for older works, and do not include unpublished reports such as the annual reports of the various conservation agencies, but by using the literature cited in each paper the student of fishes should be able to find nearly all works on Gulf of Mexico temperate fishes.

General and Popular Works

Anderson, W. D., Jr. 1967. Field guide to the snappers (Lutjanidae) of the western Atlantic. *U.S. Fish Wildl. Serv. Circ.* no. 252, 14 pp.

Anderson, W. W., J. W. Gehringer, and F. H. Berry, 1966a. Field guide to the Synodontidae (lizardfishes) of the western Atlantic Ocean. *U.S. Fish Wildl. Serv. Circ.* no. 245. 12 pp.

Anonymous. 1917. The salt water fish of Louisiana. *Bull. La. Conserv. Comm.* 3.

Bailey, R. M., J. E. Fitch, E. S. Herald, E. A. Lachner, C. C. Lindsey, C. R. Robins, and W. B. Scott. 1970. *A list of common and scientific names of fishes from the United States and Canada.* Spec. Publ. no. 6. 3d ed. Washington, D.C.: Am. Fish. Soc. 150 pp.

Baughman, J. L., and S. Springer. 1950. Biological and economic notes on the sharks of the Gulf of Mexico, with especial reference to those of Texas, and with a key for their identification. *Am. Midl. Nat.* 44(1):96–152.

Beebe, W., and J. Tee-Van. 1933. *Field book of the shore fishes of Bermuda and the West Indies.* New York: G. P. Putman's Sons. Reprint New York: Dover Publ., 1970. 337 pp.

Bigelow, H. B., and W. C. Schroeder. 1953a. Fishes of the Gulf of Maine. *U.S. Fish Wildl. Serv. Fish. Bull.* 74:577 pp. 2d ed. rev. of Bigelow and Welsh 1925.

————, and W. W. Welsh. 1925. Fishes of the Gulf of Maine. *Bull. U.S. Bur. Fish.* 40:567 pp.

Blair, W. F., A. P. Blair, P. Brodkorb, F. R. Cagle, and G. A. Moore. 1968. *Vertebrates of the United States.* 2d ed. New York: McGraw-Hill. 819 pp.

Böhlke, J. E., and C. C. G. Chaplin. 1968. *Fishes of the Bahamas and adjacent tropical waters.* Wynnewood, Pa.: Livingston Publ. Co. 771 pp.

Breder, C. M., Jr., 1948. *Fieldbook of marine fishes of the Atlantic coast from Labrador to Texas.* 2d ed. New York: G. P. Putman's Sons. 332 pp.

Briggs, J. C. 1975. *Marine zoogeography.* New York: McGraw-Hill. 475 pp.

Burr, J. G. 1932. Fishes of Texas. *Bull. Texas Game, Fish, and Oyster Comm.* 5:41 pp.

Carr, A., and C. J. Goin. 1959. *Guide to the reptiles, amphibians and fresh-water fishes of Florida.* Gainesville: Univ. of Fla. Press. 341 pp.

Cervigon, M. F. 1966. *Los peces marinos de Venezuela.* Monografia no. 11. 2 vols. Caracas: Fundación LaSalle de Ciencias Naturales. 951 pp.

Cliburn, J. W. 1974. A key to the fishes of Mississippi Sound and adjacent waters. Mimeographed. Ocean Springs, Miss.: Gulf Coast Res. Lab. 36 pp.

Cook, F. A. 1959. *Freshwater fishes in Mississippi.* Jackson: Miss. Game and Fish. Comm. 239 pp.

Dahlberg, M. D. 1975. *Guide to coastal fishes of Georgia.* Athens: Univ. Georgia Press. 186 pp.

Douglas, N. H. 1974. *Freshwater fishes of Louisiana.* Baton Rouge, La.: Claitor's Bookstore. 443 pp.

Eddy, S. 1969. *How to know the freshwater fishes.* 2d ed. Dubuque, Iowa: Wm. C. Brown. 296 pp.

Feddern, H. A. 1972. Field guide to the angelfishes (Pomacanthidae) in the western Atlantic. *Natl. Mar. Fish. Serv. Circ.* no. 369. 10 pp.

Gowanloch, J. N. 1933. Fishes and fishing in Louisiana. *La. Dep. Conserv. Bull.* no. 23. 638 pp. Reprint Baton Rouge: Claitor's Bookstore, 1965.

Gutherz, E. J. 1967. Field guide to the flatfishes of the family Bothidae in the western North Atlantic. *U.S. Fish Wildl. Serv. Circ.* no. 263. 47 pp.

Heemstra, P. C. 1965. A field key to the Florida sharks. *Fla. State Board Conserv. Tech. Ser.* no. 45. 11 pp.

Hildebrand, S. F., and W. C. Schroeder. 1928. Fishes of Chesapeake Bay. *Bull. U.S. Bur. Fish.* 43(1):366 pp. Reprint Neptune City, N.J.: T.F.H. Publ., 1972.

Hubbs, C. 1969. Key to the fresh-water fishes of Texas. Mimeographed. Austin: Univ. Texas Dept. Zool.

Hubbs, C. L., and K. F. Lagler. 1958. *Fishes of the Great Lakes region.* 2d ed. Ann Arbor: Univ. Mich. Press. 213 pp.

Jordan, D. S., and W. B. Evermann. 1896–1900. The fishes of North and Middle America. *Bull. U.S. Natl. Mus.* 47 (1–4):3313 pp. Reprint Jersey City, N.J.: T.F.H. Publ., 1963.

———, and ———. 1903. *American food and game fishes.* New York: Doubleday, Page and Co. Reprint New York: Dover Publ. Co., 1969. 574 pp.

Knapp, F. T. 1953. *Fishes found in the freshwaters of Texas.* Brunswick, Ga.: Ragland. 166 pp.

Lagler, K. F., J. E. Bardach, and R. R. Miller. 1962. *Ichthyology.* 2d ed. New York: John Wiley and Sons. 545 pp.

LaMonte, F. 1946. *North American game fishes.* Garden City, N.Y.: Doubleday and Co. 202 pp.

———. 1952. *Marine game fishes of the world.* Garden City, N.Y.: Doubleday and Co. 190 pp.

Longley, W. H. 1941. *Systematic catalogue of the fishes of Tortugas, Florida,* ed. S. F. Hildebrand. Papers Tortugas Lab. no. 34. Carnegie Inst. Wash. Pub. 535. 331 pp.

Leim, A. H., and W. B. Scott. 1966. Fishes of the Atlantic coast of Canada. *Bull. Fish. Res. Board of Canada* no. 155. 485 pp.

Marshall, N. B. 1966. *The life of fishes*. Cleveland and New York: World Publ. Co. 402 pp.

———. 1971. *Explorations in the life of fishes*. Cambridge, Mass.: Harvard Univ. Press. 204 pp.

Meek, S. E., and S. F. Hildebrand. 1923–1925. *The marine fishes of Panama*. Publ. no. 215. Chicago: Field Mus. Nat. Hist. 1045 pp.

Nelson, J. S. 1976. *Fishes of the world*. New York: John Wiley & Sons. 416 pp.

Nikolskii, G. V. 1963. *The ecology of fishes*. London and N.Y.: Academic Press. 352 pp.

Norman, J. R., and F. C. Frazer. 1949. *Field book of giant fishes*. New York: G. P. Putman's Sons.

———, and P. H. Greenwood. 1975. *A history of fishes*. 3d ed. London: Ernest Bonn, Ltd. 467 pp.

Parker, J. C., D. R. Moore, and B. J. Galloway. 1975. *Key to the estuarine and marine fishes of Texas*. 2d ed. College Station: Texas A&M University Agricultural Extension Service.

Perlmutter, A. 1961. *Guide to marine fishes*. New York: New York Univ. Press. 431 pp.

Pew, P. 1954. Food and game fishes of the Texas coast. *Tex. Game and Fish Comm. Bull.* no. 33. 68 pp.

Randall, J. E. 1968. *Carribbean reef fishes*. Jersey City, N.J.: T.F.H. Publ. 318 pp.

Smith, H. M. 1907. *The fishes of North Carolina*, vol. 2. Raleigh: North Carolina Geol. Econ. Surv. 453 pp.

Springer, S., and H. T. Bullis. 1956. *Collections by the Oregon in the Gulf of Mexico*. U.S. Fish Wildl. Serv. Spec. Sci. Rept. Fish. no. 196. 134 pp.

Wahlquist, H. 1966. A field key to the batoid fishes (sawfishes, guitarfishes, skates, and rays) of Florida and adjacent waters. *Fla. State Board Conserv. Tech. Ser.* no. 50. 20 pp.

Walls, J. G. 1975. *Fishes of the northern Gulf of Mexico*. Neptune City, N.J.: T.F.H. Publ. 432 pp.

Zim, H. S., and H. H. Shoemaker. 1955. *Fishes, a guide to fresh- and salt-water species*. New York: Golden Press, Golden Nature Guide. 160 pp.

Specialized Works

Alvarez del Villar, J. 1970. *Peces Mexicanos (claves)*. Serie Investigaciones Pesqueras, Estudio no. 1. Mexico, D.F.: Com. Nac. Conservación de Pesca, Secretaría de Industrias y Comercio. 166 pp.

Anderson, W. D., Jr. 1966. A new species of *Pristipomoides* (Pisces: Lutjanidae) from the tropical western Atlantic. *Bull Mar. Sci.* 16(4):814–826.

Anderson, W. W., and E. J. Gutherz. 1967. Revision of the flatfish genus *Trichopsetta* (Bothidae) with descriptions of three new species. *Bull. Mar. Sci.* 17(4):892–913.

———, and M. J. Lindner. 1951. Notes on the flatfish, *Engyophrys sentus* Ginsburg. *Copeia*, no. 1, pp. 23–27.

———, J. W. Gehringer, and F. H. Berry. 1966b. Family Synodontidae. In *Fishes of the western North Atlantic*. Mem. no. 1, pt. 5, pp. 30–102. New Haven: Sears Found. Mar. Res.

Arata, G. F. 1954. A contribution to the life history of the swordfish, *Xiphias gladius Linnaeus*, from the South Atlantic coast of the United States and the Gulf of Mexico. *Bull. Mar. Sci. Gulf Caribb.* 4:183–243.

Avault, J. W., Jr., C. L. Birdsong, and W. G. Perry, Jr. 1969. Growth, survival, food habits, and sexual development of croaker, *Micropogon undulatus*, in brackish water ponds. *Proc. Ann. Conf. Southeastern Game and Fish Comm.* 23:251–255.

Backus, R. H., S. Springer, and E. L. Arnold. 1956. A contribution to the natural history of the white-tip shark, *Pterolamiops longimanus* (Poey). *Deep-Sea Res.* 3:178–188.

Bailey, R. M., H. E. Winn, and C. L. Smith. 1954. Fishes from the Escambia River, Alabama and Florida, with ecologic and taxonomic notes. *Proc. Acad. Nat. Sci. Philadelphia* 106:109–164.

Baird, R. C. 1965. Ecological implications of the behavior of the sexually dimorphic goby, *Microgobius gulosus* (Girard). *Publ. Inst. Mar. Sci. Univ. Tex.* 10:1–8.

Baird, S., and C. Girard. 1854. Descriptions of new species of fishes collected by John H. Clark on the U.S. and Mexican boundary survey, and in Texas, by Captain Stewart Vliet, U.S.A. *Proc. Acad. Nat. Sci. Philadelphia* 7:24–29.

Baughman, J. L. 1941a. On the occurrence in the Gulf Coast waters of the United States of the triple tail, *Lobotes surinamensis*, with notes on its natural history. *Am. Nat.* 75:569–579.

———. 1941b. Scombriformes, new, rare, or little known in Texas waters with notes on their natural history and distribution. *Trans. Tex. Acad. Sci.* 24:14–26.

———. 1943a. Some serranid fishes of Texas: the Centropomidae, Moronidae, and Epinephelidae. *Am. Midl. Nat.* 30(3):769–773.

———. 1943b. The lutjanid fishes of Texas. *Copeia*, no. 4, pp. 212–215.

———. 1943c. Additional notes on the occurrence and natural history of the triple tail *Lobotes surinamensis. Am. Midl. Nat.* 29(2):365–270.

———. 1947. Fishes not previously reported from Texas, with miscellaneous notes on the species. *Copeia*, no. 4, p. 280.

———. 1950a. Random notes on Texas fishes. Part I. *Tex. J. Sci.* 2(1):117–138.

———. 1950b. Random notes on Texas fishes. Part II. *Tex. J. Sci.* 2(2):242–263.

———. 1955. The oviparity of the whale shark, *Rhineodon typus*, with records of this and other fishes in Texas waters. *Copeia*, no. 1, pp. 54–55.

Behre, E. H. 1950. *Annotated list of the fauna of the Grand Isle region.* Occas. Pap. no. 6. Baton Rouge: Mar. Lab., La. State Univ. 66 pp.

Bellinger, J. W., and J. W. Avault, Jr. 1970. Seasonal occurrence, growth, and length-weight relationships of juvenile pompano, *Trachinotus carolinus*, in Louisiana. *Trans. Am. Fish. Soc.* 99(2):353–358.

———, and ———. 1971. Food habits of juvenile pompano. *Trachinotus carolinus*, in Louisiana. *Trans. Am. Fish. Soc.* 100(3):486–494.

Berry, F. H. 1959. Young jack crevalles (*Caranx* species) off the southeastern Atlantic coast of the United States. *U.S. Fish Wildl. Serv. Fish. Bull.* 59(152):417–535.

———. 1964. Review and emendation of family Clupeidae. *Copeia*, no. 4, pp. 720–730.

————. 1968. A new species of carangid fish (*Decapterus tabl*) from the western Atlantic. *Contrib. Mar. Sci.* 13:145–167.

————, and W. W. Anderson. 1961. Stargazer fishes from the western North Atlantic (family Uranoscopidae). *Proc. U.S. Natl. Mus.* 112(3448): 563–586.

————, and I. Barrett. 1963. Gillraker analysis and speciation in the thread herring, genus *Opisthonema*. *Inter-Am. Trop. Tuna Comm. Bull.* 7(2): 111–190.

————, and L. R. Rivas. 1962. Data on six species of needlefishes (Belonidae) from the western Atlantic. *Copeia*, no. 1, pp. 152–160.

————, and L. F. Vogele. 1961. Filefishes (Monacanthidae) of the western North Atlantic. *U.S. Fish Wildl. Serv. Fish. Bull.* 61(181):61–109.

Bigelow, H. B. 1963. Bony fishes: Superclass, class, subclass, and orders. In *Fishes of the western North Atlantic*. Mem. no. 1, pt. 3, pp. 1–19. New Haven: Sears Found. Mar. Res.

————, and W. C. Schroeder. 1948. Sharks. In *Fishes of the western North Atlantic*. Mem. no. 1, pt. 1, pp. 59–547. New Haven: Sears Found. Mar. Res.

————, and ————. 1953*b*. Sawfishes, guitarfishes, skates, and rays. In *Fishes of the western North Atlantic*. Mem. no. 1, pt. 2, pp. 1–514. New Haven: Sears Found. Mar. Res.

————, and ————. 1958. Four new rajids from the Gulf of Mexico. *Bull. Mus. Comp. Zool.* 119(2):201–233.

————, and ————. 1965. A further account of batoid fishes from the western Atlantic. *Bull. Mus. Comp. Zool.* 132(5):443–477.

Böhlke, J. E., and V. G. Springer. 1961. A review of the Atlantic species of the clinid fish genus *Starksia*. *Proc. Acad. Nat. Sci. Philadelphia* 113(3): 29–60.

Boothby, R. N., and J. W. Avault. 1971. Food habits, length-weight relationship, and condition factor of the red drum (*Sciaenops ocellata*) in southeastern Louisiana. *Trans. Am. Fish. Soc.* 100(2):290–295.

Boschung, H. T. 1957. The fishes of Mobile Bay and the Gulf coast of Alabama. Ph.D. thesis, Univ. Alabama, Montgomery. 626 pp.

Bradbury, M. G. 1967. The genera of batfishes (family Ogcocephalidae). *Copeia*, no. 2, pp. 399–422.

Breder, C. M. 1938. A contribution to the life histories of the Atlantic ocean flyingfishes. *Bull. Bingham Oceanogr. Collect.* 6(5):126 pp.

Breuer, J. P. 1954. The littlest biggest fish. *Tex. Game and Fish* 12(2):4–5, 29.

————. 1957. An ecological survey of Baffin and Alazan Bays, Texas. *Publ. Inst. Mar. Sci. Univ. Tex.* 4(2):134–155.

————. 1962. An ecological survey of the lower Laguna Madre of Texas 1953–1959. *Publ. Inst. Mar. Sci. Univ. Tex.* 8:153–183.

Briggs, J. C. 1955. A monograph of the clingfishes (order Xenopterygii). *Stanford Ichthyol. Bull.* no. 6. 224 pp.

————. 1956. Notes on the triglid fishes of the genus *Prionotus*. *Q. J. Fla. Acad. Sci.* 19(2–3):99–103.

————. 1958. A list of Florida fishes and their distribution. *Bull. Fla. State Mus. Biol. Sci.* 2(8):223–318.

————. 1964. The graysby, *Petrometopon cruentatum* (Lacépède), first occurrence in the northern Gulf of Mexico. *Tex. J. Sci.* 26(4):451–452.

————, and D. K. Caldwell. 1957. *Acanthurus randalli*, a new surgeon fish from the Gulf of Mexico. *Bull. Fla. State Mus. Biol. Sci.* 2(4):43–51.

————, H. D. Hoese, W. F. Hadley, and R. S. Jones. 1964. Twenty-two new marine fish records for the northwestern Gulf of Mexico. *Tex. J. Sci.* 16(1):113–116.

Bright, T. J., and C. W. Cashman. 1974. Fishes. In *Biota of the West Flower Garden Bank*, ed. T. J. Bright and L. H. Pequegnat, pp. 340–409. Houston: Gulf Publ. Co.

————, J. W. Tunnell, L. H. Pequegnat, T. E. Burke, C. W. Cashman, D. A. Cropper, J. P. Ray, R. C. Tresslar, J. Teerling, and J. B. Wills. 1974. Biotic zonation on the West Flower Garden Bank. In *Biota of the West Flower Garden Bank*, ed. T. J. Bright and L. H. Pequegnat, pp. 3–63. Houston: Gulf Publ. Co.

Brongersma-Sanders, M. 1957. *Mass mortality in the sea.* Vol. 1 Mem. Geol. Soc. Am. no. 67, pp. 94–1010.

Bruun, A. F. 1935. Flyingfishes (Exocoetidae) of the Atlantic, systematic and biological studies. *Dana-Rep. Carlsbergfondets*, no. 6. 106 pp.

Bullis, H. T., and J. R. Thompson. 1965. Collections by the exploratory fishing vessels *Oregon, Silver Bay, Combat,* and *Pelican* made during 1956 to 1960 in southwestern North Atlantic. *U.S. Fish Wildl. Serv. Spec. Sci. Rep. Fish.* no. 510, pp. 1–130.

Burgess, W. E. 1974. Evidence for the evaluation to family status of the angelfishes (Pomacanthidae) previously considered to be a subfamily of the butterflyfish family, Chaetodontidae. *Pac. Sci.* 28(1):57–71.

Caillouet, C. W., Jr., W. S. Perret, and B. J. Fontenot, 1969. Weight, length, and sex ratio of immature bull sharks, *Carcharhinus leucas,* from Vermilion Bay, Louisiana. *Copeia*, no. 1, pp. 196–197.

Caldwell, D. K. 1955a. Distribution of the longspined porgy *Stenotomus caprinus. Bull. Mar. Sci. Gulf Caribb.* 5(2):230–239.

————. 1955b. Notes on the distribution, spawning, and growth of the spottailed pinfish, *Diplodus holbrooki. Q. J. Fla. Acad. Sci.* 18(2):73–83.

————. 1957. The biology and systematics of the pinfish, *Lagodon rhomboides* (Linnaeus). *Bull. Fla. State Mus. Biol. Sci.* 2(6):77–173.

————. 1961. Populations of the butterfish, *Poronotus triacanthus* (Peck), with systematic comments. *Bull. South. Calif. Acad. Sci.* 60(1):19–31.

————. 1962a. Western Atlantic fishes of the family Priacanthidae. *Copeia*, no. 2, pp. 417–424.

————. 1962b. Development and distribution of the short bigeye *Pseudopriacanthus altus* (Gill) in the western North Atlantic. *U.S. Fish Wildl. Serv. Fish. Bull.* 62(203):103–150.

————. 1965. Systematics and variation in the sparid fish *Archosargus probatocephalus. Bull. South. Calif. Acad. Sci.* 64(2):89–100.

————, and J. C. Briggs. 1957b. Range extensions of western North Atlantic fishes with notes on some soles of the genus *Gymnachirus. Bull. Fla. State Mus. Biol. Sci.* 2(1):1–11.

Caldwell, M. C. 1962. Development and distribution of larval and juvenile fishes of the family Mullidae of the western North Atlantic. *U.S. Fish Wildl. Serv. Fish. Bull.* 62(213):403–457.

Camber, C. I. 1955. A survey of the red snapper fishery of the Gulf of Mexico, with special reference to the Campeche Banks. *Fla. State Board Conserv. Tech. Ser.* no. 12, pp. 1–64.

Carpenter, J. S. 1965. A review of the Gulf of Mexico red snapper fishery. *U.S. Fish Wildl. Serv. Circ.* no. 208. 35 pp.

Causey, B. D. 1969. The fishes of Seven-and-one-half Fathom Reef. M.S. thesis, Texas A&I Univ. Kingsville. 110 pp.

Christmas, J. Y., ed. 1973. *Cooperative Gulf of Mexico estuarine inventory and study, Mississippi*. Jackson: Miss. Mar. Conserv. Comm. 433 pp.

——, G. Gunter, and E. C. Whatley. 1960. Fishes taken in the menhaden fishery of Alabama, Mississippi, and eastern Louisiana. *U.S. Fish Wildl. Serv. Spec. Sci. Rep. Fish*, no. 339, pp. 1–10.

Clark, E., and K. von Schmidt. 1965. Sharks of the central Gulf coast of Florida. *Bull. Mar. Sci.* 15(1):13–83.

Colin, P. L, and J. B. Heiser. 1973. Associations of two species of cardinal-fishes (Apogonidae: Pisces) with sea anemones in the West Indies. *Bull. Mar. Sci.* 23(3):521–524.

Collette, B. B., and F. H. Berry. 1965. Recent studies on the needlefishes (Belonidae): An evaluation. *Copeia*, no. 3, pp. 386–392.

——, and L. N. Chao. 1975. Systematics and morphology of the bonitos (*Sarda*) and their relatives (Scombridae, Sardini). *Nat. Mar. Fish. Serv. Fish. Bull.* 73(3):516–625.

Connell, C. H., and J. B. Cross. 1950. Mass mortality of fish associated with the protozoan *Gonyaulax* in the Gulf of Mexico. *Science* 112(2909):359–363.

Copeland, B. J. 1957. Effects of decreased river flow on estuarine ecology. *J. Water Pollut. Control Fed.* 38(11):1831–1839.

Courtenay, W. R., Jr. 1961. Western Atlantic fishes of the genus *Haemulon* (Pomadasyidae): Systematic status and juvenile pigmentation. *Bull. Mar. Sci. Gulf Caribb.* 11(1):66–149.

——. 1967. Atlantic fishes of the genus *Rypticus* (Grammistidae). *Proc. Acad. Nat. Sci. Philadelphia* 119(6):241–293.

Cross, J. C., and H. B. Parks. 1937. Marine fauna and sea-side flora of the Nueces River basin and the adjacent islands. *Bull. Tex. Coll. A&I.* 8(3):36 pp.

Curran, H. W. 1942. A systematic revision of the gerrid fishes referred to the genus *Eucinostomus*, with a discussion of their distribution and speciation. Ph.D. diss., Univ. Mich., Ann Arbor. 183 pp.

Dahlberg, M. D. 1970. Atlantic and Gulf of Mexico menhadens, genus *Brevoortia* (Pisces: Clupeidae). *Bull. Fla. State Mus. Biol. Sci.* 15(3):91–162.

Daly, R. J. 1970. Systematics of southern Florida anchovies (Pisces: Engraulidae). *Bull. Mar. Sci.* 20(1):70–104.

Darnell, R. M. 1958. Food habits of fishes and larger invertebrates of Lake Pontchartrain, Louisiana, an estuarine community. *Pub. Inst. Mar. Sci. Univ. Tex.* 5:353–416.

——. 1962. Fishes of the Rio Tamesí and related coastal lagoons in east-central Mexico. *Publ. Inst. Mar. Sci. Univ. Tex.* 8:299–365.

——, and P. Abramoff. 1968. Distribution of the gynogenetic fish, *Poecilia formosa*, with remarks on the evolution of the species. *Copeia*, no. 2, pp. 354–361.

Dawson, C. E. 1962a. New records and notes on fishes from the north-central Gulf of Mexico. *Copeia*, no. 2, pp. 442–444.

——, 1962b. A new gobioid fish, *Microdesmus lanceolatus*, from the Gulf of Mexico with notes on *M. longipinnis* (Weymouth). *Copeia*, no. 2, pp. 330–336.

————. 1964. A revision of the western Atlantic flatfish genus *Gymnachirus* (the naked soles). *Copeia*, no. 4, pp. 646–665.

————. 1965. Records of two headfishes (family Molidae) from the north-central Gulf of Mexico. *Proc. La. Acad. Sci.* 28:86–89.

————. 1966a. Additions to the known marine fauna of Grand Isle, Louisiana. *Proc. La. Acad. Sci.* 21:175–180.

————. 1966b. Observations on the anacanthine fish *Bregmaceros atlanticus*, in the north-central Gulf of Mexico. *Copeia*, no. 3, pp. 604–605.

————. 1966c. *Gunterichthys longipenis*, a new genus and species of ophidioid fish from the northern Gulf of Mexico. *Proc. Biol. Soc. Wash.* 79:205–214.

————. 1966d. Studies on the gobies (Pisces: Gobiidae) of Mississippi Sound and adjacent waters: I. *Gobiosoma. Am. Midl. Nat.* 76(2):379–409.

————. 1967. Contributions to the biology of the cutlassfish (*Trichiurus lepturus*) in the northern Gulf of Mexico. *Trans. Am. Fish. Soc.* 96(2):117–121.

————. 1968. Contributions to the biology of the Mexican flounder, *Cyclopsetta chittendeni*, in the northern Gulf of Mexico. *Trans. Am. Fish. Soc.* 97(4):504–507.

————. 1969. *Studies on the gobies of Mississippi Sound and adjacent waters*, vol. 2, *An illustrated key to gobioid fishes.* Pub. no. 1. Ocean Springs, Miss.: Gulf Coast Res. Lab. Mus. 59 pp.

————. 1970. A Mississippi population of the opossum pipefish, *Oostethus lineatus* (Syngnathidae) *Copeia*, no. 4, pp. 772–773.

————. 1971a. Supplemental observations on *Gunterichthys longipenis*, a northern Gulf of Mexico brotulid fish. *Copeia*, no. 1, pp. 164–167.

————. 1971b. Records of the pearlfish, *Carapus bermudensis*, in the northern Gulf of Mexico and of a new host species. *Copeia*, no. 4, pp. 730–731.

————. 1971c. Occurrence and description of prejuvenile and early juvenile Gulf of Mexico cobia, *Rachycentron canadum*. *Copeia*, no. 1, pp. 65–71.

————. 1971d. Notes on juvenile black driftfish, *Hyperoglyphe bythites*, from the northern Gulf of Mexico. *Copeia*, no. 4, pp. 732–735.

————. 1972. Nektonic pipefishes (Syngnathidae) from the Gulf of Mexico off Mississippi. *Copeia*, no. 4, pp. 844–848.

de Sylva, D. P. 1955. The osteology and phylogenetic relationship of the blackfin tuna, *Thunnus atlanticus* (Lesson). *Bull. Mar. Sci. Gulf Caribb.* 5(1):1–41.

————. 1957. Studies on the age and growth of the Atlantic sailfish, *Istiophorus americanus* (Cuvier), using length-frequency curves. *Bull. Mar. Sci. Gulf Caribb.* 7(1):1–20.

————. 1963. Systematics and life history of the great barracuda, *Sphyraena barracuda* (Walbaum). *Stud. Trop. Oceanogr.* 1:1–179.

————. 1974. A review of the world sport fishery for billfishes (Istiophoridae and Xiphiidae). *Nat. Mar. Fish. Serv. Spec. Sci. Rep. Fish.* no. 675, pp. 12–33.

————, and W. P. Davis. 1963. White marlin, *Tetrapturus albidus*, in the Middle Atlantic Bight, with observations on the hydrography of the fishing grounds. *Copeia*, no. 1, pp. 81–99.

————, and W. F. Rathjen. 1961. Life history notes on the little tuna,

Euthynnus alletteratus, from the southeastern United States. *Bull. Mar. Sci. Gulf Caribb.* (112):161–190.

Dockart, G. 1973. A systematic revision of the genera *Diapterus* and *Eugerres*: With the description of a new genus, *Shizopterus* (Pisces: Gerreidae). M.S. thesis, Univ. of Northern Illinois, DeKalb. 74 pp.

Dooley, J. K. 1972. Fishes associated with the pelagic sargassum complex, with a discussion of the sargassum community. *Contrib. Mar. Sci.* 16: 1–32.

――――. 1974. Systematic revision and comparative biology of the tilefishes (Perciformes: Branchiostegidae and Malacanthidae). Ph.D. diss., Univ. North Carolina, Chapel Hill. 301 pp.

Dugas, R. J. 1970. An ecological study of Vermilion Bay, 1968–1969. M.S. thesis, Univ. Southwestern Louisiana, Lafayette. 105 pp.

Dunham, F. 1972. A study of commercially important estuarine-dependent industrial fishes. *La. Wild Life Fish. Comm. Tech. Bull.* no. 4. 63 pp.

Emery, A. R. 1968. A new species of *Chromis* (Pisces: Pomacentridae) from the western North Atlantic. *Copeia*, no. 1, pp. 49–55.

――――. 1973a. Comparative ecology and functional osteology of fourteen species of damselfish (Pisces: Pomacentridae) at Alligator Reef, Florida Keys. *Bull. Mar. Sci.* 23(3):649–770.

――――. 1973b. Atlantic bicolor damselfish (Pomacentridae): A taxonomic question. *Copeia*, no. 3, pp. 590–592.

――――, and W. E. Burgess. 1974. A new species of damselfish (*Eupomacentrus*) from the western Atlantic, with a key to known species of that area. *Copeia*, no. 4, pp. 879–886.

Eschmeyer, W. N. 1963. A deepwater-trawl capture of two swordfish (*Xiphias gladius*) in the Gulf of Mexico. *Copeia*, no. 3, p. 590.

――――. 1965. Western Atlantic scorpionfishes of the genus *Scorpaena*, including four new species. *Bull. Mar. Sci.* 15(1):84–164.

――――. 1969. *A systematic review of the scorpion fishes of the Atlantic Ocean (Pisces: Scorpaenidae).* Occas. Pap. no. 79. Calif. Acad. Sci. 143 pp.

Evermann, W. B., and W. C. Kendall. 1894. The fishes of Texas and the Rio Grande Basin, considered chiefly with reference to their geographic distribution. *Bull. U.S. Fish. Comm.* 12(1892):57–126.

Feddern, H. A. 1968. Hybridization between the western Atlantic angelfishes, *Holacanthus isabelita* and *H. ciliaris. Bull. Mar. Sci.* 18(2):351–382.

Fields, H. M. 1962. Pompanos (*Trachinotus* spp.) of South Atlantic coast of the United States. *U.S. Fish Wildl. Serv. Fish. Bull.* 62(207):189–222.

Fontenot, B. J., Jr., and H. E. Rogillio. 1970. *A study of estuarine sportfishes in the Biloxi Marsh Complex, Louisiana.* Baton Rouge: La. Wild Life and Fish. Comm. 172 pp.

Fore, P. L. 1971. The distribution of the eggs and larvae of the round herring *Etrumeus teres* in the northern Gulf of Mexico. *Assoc. Southeast. Biol. Bull.* 18(2):34.

Forman, W. W. 1968a. The ecology of the Cyprinodontidae (Pisces) of Grand Terre Island, Louisiana. M.S. thesis., La. State Univ., Baton Rouge. 116 pp.

――――. 1968b. Notes on the ecology of six species of cyprinodontid fishes from Grand Terre, Louisiana. *Proc. La. Acad. Sci.* 31:39–40.

Fowler, H. W. 1945. *A study of the fishes of the Southern Piedmont and*

Coastal Plain. Monograph No. 7. Philadelphia: Acad. Nat. Sci. Philadelphia. 408 pp.

Fox, L. S., and C. J. White. 1969. Feeding habits of the southern flounder, *Paralichthys lethostigma*, in Barataria Bay, Louisiana. *Proc. La. Acad. Sci.* 32:31–38.

Franks, J. S. 1970. An investigation of the fish population within the inland waters of Horn Island, Mississippi, a barrier island in the northern Gulf of Mexico. *Gulf Res. Rept.* 3(1):3–104.

————, J. S. Christmas, W. L. Siler, R. Coombs, R. Waller, and C. Burns. 1972. A study of nektonic and benthic faunas of the shallow Gulf of Mexico off the State of Mississippi. *Gulf Res. Rept.* 4(1):1–148.

Fraser, T. H. 1971. Notes on the biology and systematics of the flatfish genus *Syacium* (Bothidae) in the straits of Florida. *Bull. Mar. Sci.* 21(2):491–509.

————, and C. R. Robins. 1970. A new Atlantic genus of cardinalfishes with comments on some species from the Gulf of Guinea. *Stud. Trop. Oceanogr.* 4(2):302–315.

Garrick, J. A. F. 1964. Additional information on the morphology of an embryo whale shark. *Proc. U.S. Natl. Mus.* 115(3476):1–8.

————. 1967a. Revision of sharks of genus Isurus with description of a new species (Galeoidea, Lamnidae). *Proc. U.S. Natl. Mus.* 118(3537):663–690.

————. 1967b. A taxonomic synopsis of the hammerhead sharks (family Sphyrnidae). In *Sharks, skates, rays,* pp. 69–77. Baltimore: Johns Hopkins Univ. Press.

————, T. H. Backus, and R. H. Gibbs, Jr. 1964. *Carcharhinus floridanus,* the silky shark, a synonym of *C. falciformis. Copeia,* no. 2, pp. 369–375.

Garwood, G. P. 1968. Notes on the life histories of the silversides, *Menidia beryllina* (Cope) and *Membras martinica* (Valenciennes) in Mississippi Sound and adjacent water. *Proc. Ann. Conf. Southeastern Game and Fish Comm.* 22:314–323.

Gibbs, R. H., Jr. 1957. Preliminary analysis of the distribution of white marlin, *Makaira albida* (Poey), in the Gulf of Mexico. *Bull. Mar. Sci. Gulf Caribb.* 7(4):360–369.

————, and B. B. Collette. 1959. On the identification, distribution, and biology of the dolphins, *Coryphaena hippurus* and *C. equiselis. Bull. Mar. Sci. Gulf Caribb.* 9(2):117–152.

————, and ————. 1967. Comparative anatomy and systematics of the tunas, genus *Thunnus. U.S. Fish Wildl. Serv. Fish. Bull.* 66:65–130.

Gilbert, C. R. 1961. First record for the hammerhead shark, *Sphyrna tudes,* in United States waters. *Copeia,* no. 4, p. 480.

————. 1966. Western Atlantic sciaenid fishes of the genus *Umbrina. Bull. Mar. Sci.* 16(2):230–258.

————. 1967. A revision of the hammerhead sharks (family: Sphyrnidae). *Proc. U.S. Natl. Mus.* 119(3539):1–88.

————. 1971. Two new Atlantic clinid fishes of the genus *Starksia. Q. J. Fla. Acad. Sci.* 33(3):193–206.

Ginsburg, I. 1931. On the differences in the habitat and size of *Cynoscion arenarius* and *Cynoscion nothus. Copeia,* no. 3, p. 144.

————. 1932. A revision of the genus *Gobionellus* (family Gobiidae). *Bull. Bingham Oceanogr. Collect.* 4(2):3–51.

————. 1933. A revision of the genus *Gobiosoma* (family Gobiidae) with an account of the genus *Garmannia*. *Bull. Bingham Oceanogr. Collect.* 4(5):1–59.

————. 1937. A review of the seahorses (*Hippocampus*) found on the coasts of the American continents and of Europe. *Proc. U.S. Natl. Mus.* 83 (2997):497–594.

————. 1942. Seven new American fishes. *J. Wash. Acad. Sci.* 32(12):364–370.

————. 1948. Some Atlantic populations related to *Diplectrum radiale* (Serranidae) with description of a new subspecies from the Gulf coast of the United States. *Copeia*, no. 4, pp. 266–270.

————. 1950. Review of the western Atlantic Triglidae (fishes). *Tex. J. Sci.* 2(4):489–527.

————. 1951a. The eels of the northern Gulf coast of the United States and some related species. *Tex. J. Sci.* 3(3):431–485.

————. 1951b. Western Atlantic tonguefishes with descriptions of six new species. *Zoologica* (N.Y.) 36(3):185–201.

————. 1952a. Eight new fishes from the Gulf coast of the United States, with two new genera and notes on geographic distribution. *J. Wash. Acad. Sci.* 42(3):84–101.

————. 1952b. Fishes of the family Carangidae of the northern Gulf of Mexico and three related species. *Publ. Inst. Mar. Sci. Univ. Tex.* 2(2): 43–117.

————. 1952c. Flounders of the genus *Paralichthys* and related genera in American waters. *U.S. Fish Wildl. Serv. Fish. Bull.* 52(71):267–351.

————. 1954. Four new fishes and one little known species from the east coast of the United States including the Gulf of Mexico. *J. Wash. Acad. Sci.* 44(8):256–264.

Girard, C. 1858. Notes upon various new genera and new species of fishes in the Museum of the Smithsonian Institution, and collected in connection with the United States and Mexican Boundary Survey, Major William Emory, Commissioner. *Proc. Acad. Nat. Sci. Philadelphia* 10:167–171.

————. 1859. United States and Mexican Boundary Survey under order of Lt. Col. W. H. Emory, Major First Cavalry, and the United States Commissioner. Ichthyology of the Boundary. In *Report of the U.S. and Mexican Boundary Survey*, vol. 2:1–77.

Goode, G. B. 1879. A revision of the American species of the genus *Brevoortia*, with a description of a new species from the Gulf of Mexico. *Proc. U.S. Natl. Mus.* 1:30–42.

————, and T. H. Bean. 1895. *Oceanic ichthyology.* Smithson. Contrib. Knowl. no. 981. Washington, D.C.: Smithsonian Inst. 553 pp.

Greenfield, D. W. 1975. *Centropomus poeyi* from Belize, with a key to the western Atlantic species of *Centropomus*. *Copeia*, no. 3, pp. 582–583.

Greenwood, P. H., D. E. Rosen, S. H. Weitzman, and G. Myers. 1966. Phyletic studies of teleostean fishes, with a provisional classification of living forms. *Bull. Am. Mus. Nat. Hist.* 131(4):339–456.

Guest, W. C., and G. Gunter. 1958. The seatrout or weakfishes (genus *Cynoscion*) of the Gulf of Mexico. *Gulf States Mar. Fish. Comm. Tech. Summ.* no. 1. 40 pp.

Gunter, G. 1935. Records of fishes rarely caught in shrimp trawls in Louisiana. *Copeia*, no. 1, pp. 39–45.

————. 1938a. Seasonal variations in abundance of certain estuarine and marine fishes in Louisiana, with particular references to life histories. *Ecol. Monogr.* 8(3):313–346.

————. 1938b. The relative numbers of marine fishes on the Louisiana coast. *Am. Nat.* 72:77–83.

————. 1938c. Notes on invasion of fresh waters by fishes of the Gulf of Mexico with special reference to the Mississippi-Atchafalaya river system. *Copeia*, no. 2, pp. 69–72.

————. 1941. Relative numbers of shallow water fishes of the northern Gulf of Mexico, with some records of rare fishes from the Texas coast. *Am. Midl. Nat.* 26(1):194–200.

————. 1944. A perpetuated error concerning the capitaine, *Lachnolaimus maximus* (Walbaum) in Texas waters. *Copeia*, no. 1, pp. 55–56.

————. 1945a. Studies on marine fishes of Texas. *Publ. Inst. Mar. Sci. Univ. Tex.* 1(1):1–190.

————. 1945b. Some characteristics of ocean waters and the Laguna Madre. *Tex. Game and Fish* 3(11):7, 19, 21–22.

————. 1950. Distributions and abundance of fishes on the Aransas National Wildlife Refuge with life history notes. *Publ. Inst. Mar. Sci. Univ. Tex.* 1(2):89–102.

————. 1951. Mass mortality and dinoflagellate blooms in the Gulf of Mexico. *Science* 113(2931):250–251.

————. 1952a. The import of catastrophic mortalities for marine fisheries along the Texas coast. *J. Wildl. Manag.* 16(1):63–69.

————. 1952b. Historical changes in the Mississippi River and the adjacent marine environment. *Publ. Inst. Mar. Sci. Univ. Tex.* 2(2):118–139.

————. 1953. Observations on fish turning flips over a line. *Copeia*, no. 3, pp. 188–190.

————, and H. H. Hildebrand. 1951. Destruction of fishes and other organisms on the south Texas coast by the coldwave of January 28–February 3, 1951. *Ecology* 32(4):731–736.

————, and L. Knapp. 1951. Fishes, new, rare or seldom recorded from the Texas coast. *Tex. J. Sci.* 3(1):134–138.

————, and W. E. Shell, Jr. 1958. A study of an estuarine area with water level control in the Louisiana marsh. *Proc. La. Acad. Sci.* 21:5–34.

————, R. H. Williams, C. C. Davis, and F. G. Walton Smith. 1948. Catastrophic mass mortality of marine animals and coincident phytoplankton bloom on the west coast of Florida, November 1946–August 1947. *Ecol. Monogr.* 18(3):309–324.

Gutherz, E. J. 1966. Revision of the flounder genus *Ancylopsetta* (Heterosomata: Bothidae) with descriptions of two new species from the Antilles and the Caribbean Sea. *Bull. Mar. Sci.* 16(3):445–479.

Haburay, K., R. W. Hastings, D. DeVries, and J. Massey. 1974. Tropical marine fishes from Pensacola, Florida. *Fla. Scientist* 37(2):105–109.

Haedrich, R. L. 1967. The stromateoid fishes: systematics and a classification. *Bull. Mus. Comp. Zool.* 135(2):31–139.

————, and M. H. Horn. 1972. A key to the stromateoid fishes. *Woods Hole Oceanogr. Inst. Tech. Rept.* WHO 1-72-15. 46 pp.

Hastings, R. W. 1972. The origin and seasonality of the fish fauna on a new jetty in the northeastern Gulf of Mexico. Ph.D. diss., Florida State Univ. Tallahassee. 555 pp.

————. 1973. Biology of the pygmy sea bass, *Serraniculus pumilio* (Pisces: Serranidae). *U.S. Fish. Wildl. Serv. Fish. Bull.* 71(1):235–242.

Herald, E. S. 1942. Three new pipefishes from the Atlantic coast of North and South America, with a key to the Atlantic American species. *Stanford Ichthyol. Bull.* 2(4):125–134.

———. 1965. Studies on the Atlantic American pipefishes with descriptions of new species. *Proc. Calif. Acad. Sci.*, 4th ser., 32:363–375.

Herke, W. H. 1968. Weirs, potholes, and fishery management. In *Proc. Marsh and Estuary Management Symposium*, ed. J. D. Newsom, pp. 193–211. Baton Rouge: Div. Cont. Educ., La. State Univ.

———. 1969. An unusual inland collection of larval ladyfish, *Elops saurus*, in Louisiana. *Proc. La. Acad. Sci.* 32:29–30.

———. 1971. Use of natural, and semi-impounded, Louisiana tidal marshes as nurseries for fishes and crustaceans. Ph.D. diss., La. State Univ., Baton Rouge.

Hildebrand, H. H. 1954. A study of the fauna of the brown shrimp (*Penaeus aztecus* Ives) grounds in the western Gulf of Mexico. *Publ. Inst. Mar. Sci. Univ. Tex.* 3(2):233–366.

———. 1955. A study of the fauna of the pink shrimp (*Penaeus duorarum* Burkenroad) grounds in the Gulf of Campeche. *Publ. Inst. Mar. Sci. Univ. Tex.* 4(1):169–232.

———. 1958. Estudios biologicos preliminares sobre la Laguna Madre de Tamaulipas. *Ciencia* (Mexico City) 17(7–9):151–173.

———. 1969. Laguna Madre, Tamaulipas: Observations on its hydrography and fisheries. In *Lagunas Costeras, un Simposio Mem. Simp. Intern. Lagunas Costeras UNAM-UNESCO*, Nov. 28–30, México, D.F., pp. 679–686.

———, H. Chavez, and H. Compton. 1964. Aporte al conocimiento de los peces del Arrecife Alacranes, Yucatán (México). *Ciencia* (Mexico City) 23(3):107–134.

Hildebrand, S. F. 1963. Families Elopidae and Albulidae. In *Fishes of the western North Atlantic*. Mem. no. 1, pt. 3, pp. 111–147. New Haven: Sears Found. Mar. Res.

———. 1964. Family Engraulidae. In *Fishes of the western North Atlantic*. Mem. no. 1, pt. 3, pp. 152–249. New Haven: Sears Found. Mar. Res.

———, and L. E. Cable. 1934. Reproduction and development of whitings or kingfishes, drum, spot, croaker, and weakfishes or sea trouts, family Sciaenidae, of the Atlantic coast of the United States. *Bull. U.S. Bur. Fish.* 48:41–117.

———, L. R. Rivas, and R. R. Miller. 1963. Family Clupeidae. In *Fishes of the western North Atlantic*. Mem. no. 1, pt. 3, pp. 259–454. New Haven: Sears Found. Mar. Res.

Hoese, H. D. 1958a. A partially annotated checklist of the marine fishes of Texas. *Publ. Inst. Mar. Sci. Univ. Tex.* 5:312–352.

———. 1958b. The case of the pass. *Tex. Game and Fish* 16(6):16–18, 30–31.

———. 1960. Biotic changes in a bay associated with the end of a drought. *Limnol. Oceanogr.* 5(3):326–336.

———. 1965. Spawning of marine fishes in the Port Aransas, Texas, area as determined by the distribution of young and larvae. Ph.D. diss., Univ. Texas, Austin. 144 pp.

———. 1966a. Ectoparasitism by juvenile sea catfish, *Galeichthys felis*. *Copeia*, no. 4, pp. 880–881.

————. 1966b. Habitat segregation in aquaria between two sympatric species of *Gobiosoma. Publ. Inst. Mar. Sci. Univ. Tex.* 11:7–11.

————, and R. B. Moore. 1958. Notes on the life history of the bonnetnose shark, *Sphyrna tiburo. Tex. J. Sci.* 10(1):69–72.

Horn, M. H. 1970. Systematics and biology of the stromateid fishes of the genus *Peprilus. Bull. Mus. Comp. Zool.* 140(5):165–261.

————. 1972. Systematic status and aspects of the ecology of the elongate ariommid fishes (suborder Stromateoidei) in the Atlantic. *Bull. Mar. Sci.* 22(3):537–558.

Hubbs, C. 1964. Interactions between a bisexual fish species and its gyno-genetic sexual parasite. *Bull. Tex. Memorial Mus.* no. 8. 72 pp.

Hubbs, C. L. 1939. The characters and distribution of the Atlantic coast fishes referred to the genus *Hypsoblennius. Pap. Mich. Acad. Sci. Arts Lett.* 24(2):153–157.

————. 1963. *Chaetodon aya* and related deep-dwelling butterflyfishes: their variations, distribution and synonymy. *Bull. Mar. Sci. Gulf Caribb.* 13(1):133–192.

Irwin, R. J. 1970. Geographical variation, systematics, and general biology of shore fishes of the genus *Menticirrhus*, family Sciaenidae. Ph.D., diss., Tulane Univ., New Orleans. 295 pp.

Johnson, M. S. 1975. Biochemical systematics of the atherinid genus *Menidia. Copeia*, no. 4, pp. 662–691.

Jolley, J. W., Jr. 1974. On the biology of Florida east coast Atlantic sailfish (*Istiophorus platypterus*). *Nat. Mar. Fish. Serv. Spec. Sci. Rep. Fish.* no. 675, pp. 81–88.

Jordan, D. S., and M. C. Dickerson. 1908. Notes on a collection of fishes from the Gulf of Mexico at Vera Cruz and Tampico. *Proc. U.S. Natl. Mus.* 34:11–22.

————, and C. H. Gilbert. 1883. Notes on fishes observed about Pensacola, Florida, and Galveston, Texas, with description of new species. *Proc. U.S. Natl. Mus.* 5:241–307.

Joseph, E. B., and R. W. Yerger. 1956. The fishes of Alligator Harbor, Florida, with notes on their natural history. *Fla. State Univ. Stud.* no. 22. *Pap. Oceanogr. Inst.* no. 2, pp. 111–156.

Joutel, H. 1714. *A journal of the last voyage performed by Monsr. de la Sale, to the Gulph of Mexico.* Reprint London: Corinth, 1962. 187 pp.

Kanazawa, R. H. 1958. A revision of the eels of the genus *Conger* with descriptions of four new species. *Proc. U.S. Natl. Mus.* 108:219–267.

————. 1961. *Paraconger*, a new genus with three new species of eels (family Congridae). *Proc. U.S. Natl. Mus.* 113:1–14.

Kemp, R. J., Jr. 1957. Occurrences of the ocean sunfish, *Mola mola* (Linnaeus), in Texas. *Copeia*, no. 3, pp. 250–251.

Kilby, J. D. 1955. The fishes of two Gulf coastal marsh areas of Florida. *Tulane Stud. Zool.* 2(8):176–247.

King, B. D., III. 1971. Study of migratory patterns of fish and shellfish through a natural pass. *Tech. Ser. Tex. Parks and Wildl. Dept.* no. 9. 54 pp.

Klawe, W. L., and B. M. Shimada. 1959. Young scombroid fishes from the Gulf of Mexico. *Bull. Mar. Sci. Gulf Caribb.* 9(1):100–115.

Kramer, D. 1950. A record of the swordfish, *Xiphias gladius* Linnaeus, from the Texas coast. *Copeia*, no. 1, p. 65.

Lane, E. D. 1967. A study of the Atlantic midshipmen, *Porichthys porosissimus*, in the vicinity of Port Aransas, Texas. *Contrib. Mar. Sci.* 12:1–53.

———, and K. W. Stewart. 1968. A revision of the genus *Hoplunnis* Kaup (Apodes, Muraenesocidae) with a description of a new species. *Contrib. Mar. Sci.* 13:51–64.

Laska, A. L. 1973. Fishes of the Chandeleur Islands, Louisiana. Ph.D. diss., Tulane Univ., New Orleans. 260 pp.

Leary, T. R. 1956. The occurrence of the parrotfish, *Sparisoma radians*, in a Texas Bay. *Copeia*, no. 4, pp. 249–250.

———. 1957. The bonefish, *Albula vulpes*, in Texas. *Copeia*, no. 3, pp. 248–249.

Livingston, R. J. 1971. Circadian rhythms in the respiration of eight species of cardinal fishes (Pisces: Apogonidae): Comparative analysis and adaptive significance. *Mar. Biol.* 9(3):253–266.

McCosker, J. E. 1973. The osteology, classification, and relationships of the eel family Ophichthidae (Pisces: Anguilliformes). Ph.D. thesis, Univ. of Calif., San Diego. 289 pp.

McEachran, J. D., and J. A. Musick. 1975. Distribution and relative abundance of seven species of skates (Pisces: Rajidae) which occur between Nova Scotia and Cape Hatteras. *Nat. Mar. Fish. Ser. Fish. Bull.* 73(1): 110–136.

McKenny, T. W. 1961. Larval and adult stages of the stromateoid fish *Psenes regulus* with comments on its classification. *Bull. Mar. Sci. Gulf Caribb.* 11:210–236.

Mansueti, A. J., and J. P. Hardy. 1967. *Development of fishes of the Chesapeake Bay region.* College Park: Nat. Res. Inst., Univ. Md. 202 pp.

Mansueti, R. 1963. Symbiotic behavior between small fishes and jellyfishes, with new data on that between the stromateoid, *Peprilus alepidotus*, and the scyphomedusa, *Chrysaora quinquecirrha. Copeia*, no. 1, pp. 40–80.

Marshall, A. R. 1958. A survey of the snook fishery of Florida, with studies on the biology of the principal species, *Centropomus undecimalis* (Bloch). *Fla. State Board of Conserv. Tech. Ser.* no. 22. 37 pp.

Marshall, N. B., and D. M. Cohen. 1973. Anacanthini (Gadiformes). In *Fishes of the western North Atlantic.* Mem. no. 1, pt. 6, pp. 479–665. New Haven: Sears Found. Mar. Res.

Matsui, T. 1967. Review of the mackerel genera *Scomber* and *Rastrelliger* with descriptions of a new species of *Rastrelliger. Copeia*, no. 1, pp. 71–83.

Mead, G. W. 1957. On the bramid fishes of the Gulf of Mexico. *Zoologica* (N.Y.) 42(4):51–62.

———, and G. E. Maul. 1958. *Taractes asper* and the systematic relationships of the Steinegeriidae and Trachyberycidae. *Bull. Mus. Comp. Zool.* 119(6):391–418.

Miller, A. C., and D. M. Kent. 1972. Redescription of *Prionotus beani* (Pisces: Triglidae). *J. Fla. Acad. Sci.* 34(3):223–242.

Miller, J. M. 1965. A trawl survey of the shallow Gulf fishes near Port Aransas, Texas. *Publ. Inst. Mar. Sci. Univ. Tex.* 10:80–107.

Miller, R. J. 1959. A review of the seabasses of the genus *Centropristes* (Serranidae). *Tulane Stud. Zool.* 7(2):35–68.

Miller, R. R. 1945. *Hyporhamphus partis*, a new species of hemiramphid fish from Sinaloa, Mexico, with an analysis of the generic characters of

Hyporhamphus and *Hemiramphus. Proc. U.S. Natl. Mus.* 96(3195): 185–193.

————. 1960. Systematics and biology of the gizzard shad (*Dorosoma cepedianum*) and related fishes. *U.S. Fish Wildl. Serv. Fish. Bull.* 60(173): 371–392.

Moe, M. A. 1968. First Gulf of Mexico record for *Lutjanus cyanopterus. Q. J. Fla. Acad. Sci.* 29(4):285–286.

————. 1969. *Biology of the red grouper* Epinephelus morio *(Valenciennes) from the eastern Gulf of Mexico.* Prof. Pap. Ser. no. 10. St. Petersburg: Fla. Dept. Nat. Resour. Mar. Res. Lab. 95 pp.

————, and G. T. Martin. 1965. Fishes taken in monthly trawl samples offshore of Pinellas county Florida, with new additions to the fish fauna of the Tampa Bay area. *Tulane Stud. Zool.* 12(4):129–151.

Moore, D. 1962. Development, distribution, and comparison of rudder fishes, *Kyphosus sectatrix* (Linnaeus) and *K. incisor* (Cuvier) in the western North Atlantic. *U.S. Fish. Wildl. Serv. Fish. Bull.* 61(196):451–480.

————. 1967. Triggerfishes (Balistidae) of the western Atlantic. *Bull. Mar. Sci.* 17(3):689–722.

————, H. A. Brusher, and L. Trent. 1970. Relative abundance, seasonal distribution, and species composition of demersal fishes off Louisiana and Texas, 1962–1964. *Contrib. Mar. Sci.* 15:45–70.

Moore, R. H. 1974. General ecology, distribution, and relative abundance of *Mugil cephalus* and *Mugil curema* on the South Texas coast. *Contrib. Mar. Sci.* 18:241–255.

————. 1975*a.* Occurrence of tropical marine fishes at Pt. Aransas, Texas, 1967–1973, related to sea temperatures. *Copeia*, no. 1, pp. 170–172.

————. 1975*b.* New records of three marine fish from Texas waters with notes on some additional species. *Tex. J. Sci.* 26(1, 2):155–163.

Morrow, J. E., and S. J. Harbo. 1969. A revision of the sailfish genus *Istiophorus. Copeia*, no. 1, pp. 34–44.

Morton, T. 1973. The ecological effects of water-control structures on an estuarine area, White Lake, Louisiana. M.S. thesis, University of Southwestern Louisiana, Lafayette. 43 pp.

Moseley, F. N. 1966*a.* Notes on fishes from the snapper banks off Port Aransas, Texas. *Tex. J. Sci.* 18(1):75–79.

————. 1966*b.* Biology of the red snapper, *Lutjanus aya* Bloch, of the northwestern Gulf of Mexico. *Publ. Inst. Mar. Sci. Univ. Tex.* 11:90–101.

Nichols, J. T., and C. M. Breeder, Jr. 1922. *Otophidium welshi*, a new cusk eel, with notes on two others from the Gulf of Mexico. *Proc. Biol. Soc. Wash.* 35:13–15.

————, and ————. 1924. New Gulf races of a Pacific *Scorpaena* and *Prionotus*, with notes on other Gulf of Mexico fishes. *Proc. Biol. Soc. Wash.* 37:21–23.

Norden, C. R. 1966. The seasonal distribution of fishes in Vermilion Bay, Louisiana. *Wis. Acad. Sci. Arts Lett.* 55:119–137.

Norman, J. R. 1934. *A systematic monograph of the flatfishes (Heterosomata)*, vol. 1, *Psettodidae, Bothidae, Pleuronectidae.* London: British Mus. Nat. Hist. 459 pp.

Overstreet, R. M., and C. H. Lyles. 1974. A rubber band around an Atlantic croaker. *Gulf Res. Rept.* 4(3):476–478.

Parker, J. C. 1965. An annotated checklist of the fishes of the Galveston Bay system, Texas. *Publ. Inst. Mar. Sci. Univ. Tex.* 10:201–220.

Pearson, J. C. 1929. Natural history and conservation of redfish and other commercial sciaenids on the Texas coast. *Bull. U.S. Bur. of Fish.* 44: 129–214.

Perret, W. S. 1971. *Cooperative Gulf of Mexico estuarine inventory and study, Louisiana; phase I, area description; phase IV, biology.* Baton Rouge: La. Wild Life and Fish. Comm. 175 pp.

————, and C. W. Caillouet, Jr. 1974. Abundance and size of fishes taken by trawling in Vermilion Bay, Louisiana. *Bull. Mar. Sci.* 24(1):52–75.

Perry, W. G., Jr. 1969. Food habits of blue and channel catfish collected from a brackish water habitat. *Prog. Fish Cult.* 31(1):47–50.

Pew, P. 1957. Occurrence of young dolphin, *Coryphaena hippurus,* in a Texas bay. *Copeia,* no. 4, p. 300.

Powell, C. R., and K. Strawn. 1963. Notes on the fringed pipefish, *Micrognathus crinigerus,* from the west coast of Florida. *Publ. Inst. Mar. Sci. Univ. Tex.* 9:112–116.

Price, W. A. 1952. Reduction of maintenance by proper orientation of ship channels through tidal inlets. *Proc. Second Conf. Coastal Eng. L.S.U.,* Baton Rouge, La., 1951, pp. 243–255.

Randall, J. E. 1956. A revision of the surgeon fish genus *Acanthurus. Pac. Sci.* 10(2):159–235.

————. 1963. Review of the hawkfishes (family Cirrhitidae). *Proc. U.S. Natl. Mus.* 114(3472):389–451.

————, and J. E. Böhlke. 1965. Review of the Atlantic labrid fishes of the genus *Halichoeres. Proc. Acad. Nat. Sci. Philadelphia* 117(7):235–259.

————, and D. K. Caldwell. 1966. A review of the sparid fish genus *Calamus,* with descriptions of four new species. *Bull. Los Angeles County Mus. Nat. Hist. Sci.* no. 2. 47 pp.

Raymond, R. I. 1905. The fishes of Louisiana. M.S. thesis, Tulane Univ., New Orleans. 318 pp.

Reed, C. T. 1941. *Marine life in Texas waters.* San Angelo: Tex. Acad. Sci. 88 pp.

Reid, G. K. 1954. An ecological study of the Gulf of Mexico fishes in the vicinity of Cedar Key, Florida. *Bull. Mar. Sci. Gulf Caribb.* 4(1):1–94.

————. 1955a. A summer study of the biology and ecology of East Bay, Texas, part I. *Tex. J. Sci.* 7(3):316–343.

————. 1955b. A summer study of the biology and ecology of East Bay, Texas, part II. *Tex. J. Sci.* 7(4):430–453.

————. 1957. Biologic and hydrographic adjustment in a disturbed Gulf coast estuary. *Limnol. Oceanogr.* 2(3):198–212.

Renfro, W. C. 1959. Survival and migration of freshwater fishes in salt water. *Tex. J. Sci.* 11(2):172–180.

————. 1960. Salinity relations of some fishes in the Aransas River, Texas. *Tulane Stud. Zool.* 8(3):83–91.

————. 1963. Gas-bubble mortality of fishes in Galveston Bay, Texas. *Trans. Am. Fish. Soc.* 92(3):320–322.

Rivas, L. R. 1950. A revision of the American clupeid fishes of the genus *Harengula,* with descriptions of four new subspecies. *Proc. U.S. Natl. Mus.* 100:275–309.

————. 1951. A preliminary review of the western North Atlantic fishes of the family Scombridae. *Bull. Mar. Sci. Gulf Caribb.* 1(3):209–230.

————. 1960. The fishes of the genus *Pomacentrus* in Florida and the western Bahamas. *Q. J. Fla. Acad. Sci.* 23(2):130–162.

————. 1962. The Florida fishes of the genus *Centropomus*, commonly known as snook. *Q. J. Fla. Acad. Sci.* 25:53–64.

————. 1964. Key to the Atlantic Ocean tuna fishes of the genus *Thunnus*. *Proc. Symp. Scombroid fishes, Mar. Biol. Assoc. India*, pt. 1, pp. 427–428.

————. 1966. Review of the *Lutjanus campechanus* complex of red snappers. *Q. J. Fla. Acad. Sci.* 29(2):117–136.

————. 1970. Snappers of the western North Atlantic. *Commer. Fish. Rev.* 32(1):41–44.

Robins, C. H., and C. R. Robins. 1970. The eel family Dysommidae (including the Dysomminidae and Nettodaridae), its osteology and composition, including a new genus and species. *Proc. Acad. Nat. Sci. Philadelphia* 122(6):293–335.

Robins, C. R. 1957. Effects of storms on the shallow water fish fauna of southern Florida with new records of fishes from Florida. *Bull. Mar. Sci. Gulf Caribb.* 7(3):266–275.

————. 1974. The validity and status of the round-scale spearfish, *Tetrapterus georgei*. *Nat. Mar. Fish. Ser. Spec. Sci. Rep. Fish.* no. 675, pp. 54–61.

————, and W. A. Starck II. 1961. Materials for a revision of *Serranus* and related fish genera. *Proc. Acad. Nat. Sci. Philadelphia* 113(11):259–314.

Robinson, M. C. 1969. Elasmobranch records and range extensions for the Texas Gulf coast. *Tex. J. Sci.* 21(2):235–236.

Roithmayr, C. M. 1965. Industrial bottomfish fishery of the northern Gulf of Mexico, 1959–1963. *U.S. Fish. Wildl. Serv. Spec. Sci. Rep. Fish.* no. 518, pp. 1–23.

Rosen, D. E. 1973. Suborder Cyprinodontoidei. In *Fishes of the western North Atlantic*. Mem. no. 1, pt. 6, pp. 229–262. New Haven: Sears Found. Mar. Res.

Sage, M., R. G. Jackson, W. L. Klesch, and V. L. deVlaming. 1972. Growth and seasonal distribution of the elasmobranch *Dasyatis sabina*. *Contrib. Mar. Sci.* 16:71–74.

Schlicht, F. G. 1959. First records of the mountain mullet, *Agonostomus monticola* (Bancroft), in Texas. *Tex. J. Sci.* 11(2):181–182.

Schultz, L. P. 1957. The frogfishes of the family Antennariidae. *Proc. U.S. Natl. Mus.* 107(3383):47–105.

————. 1958. Three new serranid fishes, genus *Pikea*, from the western Atlantic. *Proc. U.S. Natl. Mus.* 108(3405):321–329.

————, L. P. Woods, and E. A. Lachner. 1966. Fishes of the Marshall and Marianas Islands: Families Kraemeriidae through Antennariidae. *Bull. U.S. Natl. Mus.* 202(3):1–176.

Shipp, R. L. 1974. The pufferfishes (Tetraodontidae) of the Atlantic Ocean. *Publ. Gulf Coast Res. Lab. Mus.* no. 4, pp. 1–162.

————. 1975. Pirates in the northern Gulf of Mexico. *Mar. Aquar.* 6(7):16–20.

————, and R. W. Yerger. 1969. A new pufferfish, *Sphoeroides parvus*, from the western Gulf of Mexico, with a key to species of *Sphoeroides* from the Atlantic and Gulf coasts of the United States. *Proc. Biol. Soc. Wash.* 82:477–488.

Simmons, E. G. 1957. An ecological survey of the upper Laguna Madre of Texas. *Publ. Inst. Mar. Sci. Univ. Tex.* 4(2):156–200.

————, and J. P. Breuer. 1962. A study of redfish, *Sciaenops ocellata* Linnaeus, and black drum, *Pogonias cromis* Linnaeus. *Publ. Inst. Mar. Sci. Univ. Tex.* 8:184–211.

Simpson, D. G., and G. Gunter. 1956. Notes on habits, systematic characters and life histories of Texas saltwater Cyprinodontes. *Tulane Stud. Zool.* 4(4):115–134.

Smith, C. L. 1964. Hermaphroditism in Bahama groupers. *Nat. Hist.* 73(6): 42–47.

————. 1965. The patterns of sexuality and the classification of serranid fishes. *Am. Mus. Novit.* no. 2207, pp. 1–20.

————. 1971. A revision of the American groupers: *Epinephelus* and allied genera. *Bull. Am. Mus. Nat. Hist.* 146(2):67–241.

Smith, D. G., and P. H. J. Castle. 1972. The eel genus *Neoconger* Girard: Systematics, osteology, and life history. *Bull. Mar. Sci.* 22(1):196–249.

Smith, G. B., H. M. Austin, S. A. Bortone, R. W. Hastings, and L. H. Ogren. 1975. Fishes of the Florida middle ground with comments on ecology and zoogeography. *Fla. Mar. Res. Publ.* 9:1–14.

Sonnier, F., J. Teerling, and H. D. Hoese. 1976. Observations on the offshore reef and platform fish fauna of Louisiana. *Copeia*, no. 1, pp. 105–111.

Springer, S. 1950a. Notes on the sharks of Florida. *Proc. Fla. Acad. Sci.* 3: 19–41.

————. 1950b. Natural history notes on the lemon shark, *Negaprion brevirostris. Tex. J. Sci.* 2(3):349–359.

————. 1960. Natural history of the sandbar shark, *Eulamia milberti. U.S. Fish Wildl. Serv. Fish. Bull.* 61(178):1–38.

————, and R. H. Lowe. 1963. A new smooth dogfish, *Mustelus higmani*, from the equatorial Atlantic coast of South America. *Copeia*, no. 2, pp. 245–251.

Springer, V. G. 1958. Systematics and zoogeography of the clinid fishes of the subtribe Labrisomini Hubbs. *Publ. Inst. Mar. Sci. Univ. Tex.* 5: 417–492.

————. 1959. Blenniid fishes of the genus *Chasmodes. Tex. J. Sci.* 11(3): 321–334.

————. 1960. A new gobiid fish from the eastern Gulf of Mexico. *Bull. Mar. Sci. Gulf Caribb.* 10(2):237–240.

————. 1964. A revision of the carcharhinid shark genera *Scoliodon*, *Loxodon*, and *Rhizoprionodon. Proc. U.S. Natl. Mus.* 115(3493):559–632.

————, and H. D. Hoese. 1958. Notes and records of marine fishes from the Texas coast. *Tex. J. Sci.* 10(3):343–348.

————, and K. D. Woodburn. 1960. An ecological study of the fishes of the Tampa Bay area. *Fla. State Board Conserv. Mar. Res. Lab. Prof. Pap. Ser* no. 1. 104 pp.

Staiger, J. C. 1965. Atlantic flyingfishes of the genus *Cypselurus*, with descriptions of juveniles. *Bull. Mar. Sci.* 15(3):672–725.

Starck, W. A., II, and W. R. Courtenay, Jr. 1962. *Chlorististium eukrines*, a new serranid fish from Florida, with notes on related species. *Proc. Biol. Soc. Wash.* 75:159–167.

Stephens, J. S. 1963. *A revised classification of the blennioid fishes of the American family Chaenopsidae.* Univ. Calif. Publ. Zool. no. 68. 165 pp.

————. 1970. Seven new chaenopsid blennies from the western Atlantic. *Copeia*, no. 2, pp. 280–309.

Strawn, K. 1958. Life history of the pigmy seahorse, *Hippocampus zosterae* Jordan and Gilbert, at Cedar Key Florida. *Copeia*, no. 1, pp. 16–22.

Sundararaj, B. I., and R. D. Suttkus. 1962. Fecundity of the spotted seatrout, *Cynoscion nebulosus* (Cuvier), from Lake Borgne area, Louisiana. *Trans. Amer. Fish. Soc.* 9(1):84–88.

Suttkus, R. D. 1954. Seasonal movements and growth of the Atlantic croaker (*Micropogon undulatus*) along the east Louisiana coast. *Proc. Gulf and Carribb. Fish. Inst., 7th Ann. Sess.*, pp. 1–7.

————. 1956. First record of the mountain mullet, *Agonostomus monticola* (Bancroft) in Louisiana. *Proc. La. Acad. Sci.* 19:43–46.

————. 1963. Order Lepisostei. In *Fishes of the western North Atlantic.* Mem. no. 1, pt. 3, pp. 61–88. New Haven: Sears Found. Mar. Res.

————, R. M. Darnell, and J. H. Darnell. 1953–1954. *Biological study of Lake Pontchartrain.* Ann. Rept. New Orleans: Zool. Dept., Tulane Univ.

Svetovidov, A. N. 1948. Fauna of the U.S.S.R.: Pisces, Gadiformes. *Zool. Ins. Acad. Sci. U.S.S.R.* 9(4):1–304. Trans. Washington, D.C.: U.S. Dept. of Commerce, 1962.

Swann, R. 1957. A stranger takes the bait. *Tex. Game and Fish* 15(12):15, 28.

Swingle, H. A. 1971a. Biology of Alabama estuarine areas—cooperative Gulf of Mexico estuarine inventory. *Ala. Mar. Res. Bull.* 5:1–123.

————. 1971b. A color variation of the Mexican flounder, *Cyclopsetta chittendeni* Bean, 1895, and a revision of the taxonomic status of *Cyclopsetta decussata* Gunter. *Copeia*, no. 2, pp. 335–336.

————, and D. G. Bland. 1974. A study of fishes of the coastal watercourses of Alabama. *Ala. Mar. Res. Bull.* 10:17–102.

Tavolga, W. N. 1971. Acoustic orientation in the sea catfish, *Galeichthys felis. Ann. N.Y. Acad. Sci.* 188:80–97.

Teague, G. W. 1951. The sea robins of America. A revision of the triglid fishes of the genus *Prionotus. Comm. Zool. Museo Hist. Nat. de Montevideo* 3(61):1–53.

————. 1952. The "Mercator" sea robins. A revision of the triglid fishes of the genus *Prionotus* collected off the east coast of America, during the ninth cruise (1936) of the Belgian ship "Mercator," together with a review of those taken on a subsequent voyage (1939). *Bull. Inst. R. Sci. Nat. Belg.* 28(59):1–18.

Thomas, J., P. Wagner, and H. Loesch. 1971. Studies on the fishes of Barataria Bay, an estuarine community. *Coastal Stud. Bull. La. State Univ.* 61:56–66.

Thresher, R. 1975. Atlantic *Chromis. Mar. Aquar.* 6(8):23–32.

Topp, R. W., and F. H. Hoff, Jr. 1972. Flatfishes (Pleuronectiformes). *Mem. Hourglass Cruise* 4(2):1–135.

————, and R. M. Ingle. 1972. Annotated list of post 1950 literature pertaining to distribution of Gulf of Mexico fishes. *Fla. Dept. Nat. Res. Spec. Sci. Rep.* no. 33. 17 pp.

Tyler, J. C. 1965. The trunkfish genus *Acanthostracion* (Ostraciontidae: Plectognathi) in the western Atlantic: Two species rather than one. *Proc. Acad. Nat. Sci. Philadelphia* 117:1–18.

Vladykov, V. D. 1955. A comparison of Atlantic sea sturgeon with a new subspecies from the Gulf of Mexico (*Acipenser oxyrhynchus desotoi*). *J. Fish. Res. Board. Can.* 12(5):754–761.

————, and J. R. Greeley. 1963. Order Acipenseroidei. In *Fishes of the western North Atlantic.* Mem. no. 1, pt. 3, pp. 24–60. New Haven: Sears Found. Mar. Res.

von Schmidt, K. 1969. *Remorina albescens* in the Gulf of Mexico, with a note on pigmentation. *Copeia,* no. 1, pp. 194–195.

Voss, G. L. 1953. A contribution to the life history and biology of the sailfish *Istiophorus americanus* Cuv. and Val. in Florida waters. *Bull. Mar. Sci. Gulf Caribb.* 3:206–240.

Wagner, P. R. 1973. Seasonal biomass, abundance, and distribution of estuarine dependent fishes in the Caminada Bay system of Louisiana. Ph.D. diss., Louisiana State Univ., Baton Rouge.

Walls, J. G. 1973. Noteworthy marine fishes from eastern Louisiana. *Q. J. Fla. Acad. Sci.* 35(2):109–112.

Walters, V., and C. R. Robins. 1961. A new toadfish (Batrachoididae) considered to be relict in the West Indies. *Am. Mus. Novit.* no. 2047, pp. 1–24.

Ward, J. W. 1957. The reproduction and early development of the sea catfish, *Galeichthys felis,* in the Biloxi (Mississippi) Bay. *Copeia,* no. 4, pp. 295–298.

Weaver, J. E., and L. F. Holloway. 1974. Community structure of fishes and macrocrustaceans in ponds of a Louisiana tidal marsh influenced by weirs. *Contrib. Mar. Sci.* 18:57–69.

Welsh, W. W., and C. M. Breeder, Jr. 1923. Contributions to the life histories of the Sciaenidae of the eastern United States coast. *Bull. U.S. Bur. Fish.* 39:141–201.

Whatley, E. C. 1962. Occurrence of breeding Gulf pipefish, *Syngnathus scovelli,* in the inland freshwaters of Louisiana. *Copeia,* no. 1, p. 220.

———. 1969. A study of *Syngnathus scovelli* in freshwaters of Louisiana and salt waters of Mississippi. *Gulf Res. Rep.* 2(4):437–474.

Whitehead, P. J. P. 1963. A revision of the recent round herrings (Pisces: Dussumieriidae). *Bull. Br. Mus. (Nat. Hist.) Zool.* 10(6):305–380.

———. 1973. The clupeoid fishes of the Guianas. *Bull. Br. Mus. (Nat. Hist.) Zool., Suppl.* 5:1–227.

Woods, L. P. 1942. Rare fishes from the coast of Texas. *Copeia,* no. 3, pp. 191–192.

———. 1955. Western Atlantic species of the genus *Holocentrus. Fieldiana Zool.* 37:91–119.

———. 1965. A new squirrelfish, *Adioryx poco,* of the family Holocentridae from the Bahama Islands. *Notulae Naturae Acad. Nat. Sci. Philadelphia,* no. 377, pp. 1–5.

———, and P. M. Sonoda. 1973. Order Berycomorphi (Beryciformes). In *Fishes of the western North Atlantic.* Mem. no. 1, pt. 6, pp. 263–396. New Haven: Sears Found. Mar. Res.

Yerger, R. E. 1961. Additional records of marine fishes from Alligator Harbor, Florida, and vicinity. *Q. J. Fla. Acad. Sci.* 24(2):111–116.

INDEX

312   *Index*

Index 315

Index 317

Index   327